OLDER SCOTS

A LINGUISTIC READER

SCOTTISH
TEXT
SOCIETY

The Scottish Text Society
Fifth Series
no. 9

OLDER SCOTS

A LINGUISTIC READER

Jeremy J. Smith

The Scottish Text Society

2012

First published 2012 by The Scottish Text Society, Edinburgh

ISBN 978-1-89797-634-0

A Scottish Text Society publication

Published by The Boydell Press
an imprint of Boydell & Brewer Ltd
PO Box 9, Woodbridge, Suffolk IP12 3DF, UK
and of Boydell & Brewer Inc.
668 Mt Hope Avenue, Rochester, NY 14620, USA

website: www.boydellandbrewer.com

The publisher has no responsibility for the continued existence or accuracy of URLs for external or
third-party internet websites referred to in this book, and does not guarantee that any content on such
websites is, or will remain, accurate or appropriate.

A CIP catalogue record for this book is available
from the British Library

Papers used by Boydell & Brewer Ltd are natural, recyclable products
made from wood grown in sustainable forests

Typeset in Minion by Word and Page, Chester, UK

Printed and bound by
CPI Group (UK) Ltd, Croydon, CR0 4YY

Contents

In memoriam Michael Samuels

Preface

This book has had a long gestation, and has changed radically in the process. Some twenty years ago I became involved in the teaching of the history of the Scots language at Glasgow University, and rapidly found that, although there were numerous excellent studies available, there was no concise textbook which I could use for the particular courses I was asked to teach. I therefore produced a short synthesis of current scholarship, accompanied by a selection of photocopies and rough transcriptions, and this work in various updatings has served Glasgow students ever since. This privately printed booklet drew upon a number of sources, most notably the excellent materials put together in the late 1980s by Glasgow's Department of Scottish Literature for a new and at that time ground-breaking distance-taught postgraduate degree.

At a fairly early stage, it was suggested to me that this little booklet could be more widely circulated, accompanied by a reader of diplomatic texts reflecting the 'raw' state of Older Scots. The new book was envisaged primarily for the philological training of undergraduates and postgraduates working on the history of Scots, though certain trends in textual scholarship and book history (later reflected in e.g. Marcus 1996) suggested a renewal of interest in diplomatic editing which had implications for literary students as well. The so-called 'crisis of the critical edition' was another driver (see e.g. Brewer 1996).

The prime mover in this enterprise was my then senior colleague at Glasgow, Rod Lyall, who, with another colleague Caroline Macafee (who moved to Aberdeen in the late 1980s), had been largely responsible for encouraging the development of the Older Scots linguistic and literary components of Glasgow's undergraduate and postgraduate programmes. Rod, at that time a highly successful – and quite extraordinarily dynamic – head of the only autonomous Department of Scottish Literature in the world, suggested, with his characteristic intellectual generosity, that we work together on the book, but the demands on his as well as my time, especially when he moved to a chair at the Free University of Amsterdam in the mid-1990s, were such that little progress could be made. Subsequently his role in the project was taken up by another colleague, Graham Caie, who had been appointed to the chair in English Language at Glasgow in the early 1990s. But once more various pressures – Graham was rapidly identified as an outstanding 'safe pair of hands' to undertake numerous national and international leadership roles in academic administration – meant that it was again hard to find time to devote to this task. And I myself, attempting to develop my own research and teaching over a range of subjects, was unable to engage with the project in any consistent way. However, the Council of the Scottish Text Society has demonstrated exemplary patience, and when I finally determined, largely out of frustration with myself, to produce this book, the Council has supported me with (rightly tempered) enthusiasm.

There are some advantages in this delay, since there have been, and continue to be, many exciting developments in the historical study of Scots, and English in Scotland, since the early 1990s. I have, for instance, been able in this book to draw upon important new resources.

The first of these resources is the *Dictionary of the Older Scottish Tongue* (*DOST*), which was completed in 2002; perhaps even more useful has been the subsequent online version, with massively enhanced functionality, which also includes the *Scottish National Dictionary* (*SND*): the *Dictionary of the Scots Language/Dictionar o the Scots Leid* (*DSL*). *DSL* also makes easily accessible the authoritative 'History of Scots before 1700', edited by Caroline Macafee from materials put together by the late Jack Aitken: an invaluable reference-point (Macafee 2002).

Major new surveys have also appeared, e.g. the *Edinburgh History of the Scots Language* (edited by Charles Jones, 1997) and the *Edinburgh Companion to Scots* (edited by John Corbett, Derrick McClure and Jane Stuart-Smith, 2003). I have also been able to use the equally ground-breaking online beta-version of Keith Williamson's *Linguistic Atlas of Older Scots* (version 1.1 = *LAOS*), and to refer to Anneli Meurman-Solin's *Corpus of Scottish Correspondence*. The appearance of *Early English Books Online* (*EEBO*) has revolutionised the study of early printed books; although *EEBO* should of course be seen as a prompt to further research on the originals (as with manuscripts, photographs of early printed books often miss key features, and necessarily omit the peculiarities of particular copies of texts), it is nevertheless an absolutely invaluable resource. And, although this book covers a period largely before the Glasgow *Corpus of Modern Scottish Writing 1700–1945*, it is a necessary element in the programme of research of which that project forms a part. Other key resources which have appeared in the 1990s and 2000s are described in ch. 1.

The outcome is a much more ambitious – and larger – volume than was originally intended, designed to offer something not only to students but also to fellow-researchers. The book is now envisaged as a resource on which scholars can draw as a starting-point for further work. I have conceived of it as a component in a longer-term programme of research: it may be seen within the frame of what might be called the '"new" new philology', looking at the linguistic detail (in the broadest sense) of the reception and afterlife of medieval and early modern Scottish texts at the time of composition and in subsequent generations. It is hoped that those interested in literary form in Older Scottish literature will be provided in this book with a 'kit' for stylistic analysis; that book historians will appreciate the detailed studies offered here of processes of production and reception, and be reminded of the importance of integrating disciplines such as codicology, paleography and philology which are sometimes seen as discrete; and that philologists and linguists will be encouraged by the material presented here to shift their focus – in line with modern theoretical trends – in the direction of *parole-* (as opposed to *langue-*) based studies.

I should like to thank the Council of the Scottish Text Society, most notably Sally Mapstone and Nicola Royan as my editors, for their outstanding support and encouragement in this somewhat speculative project. Sally and Nicola have been hugely helpful throughout, always engaged and interested and ready with helpful, detailed and practical advice and comment, even though I am well aware of the many other demands on their time.

I owe a very special debt of friendship and gratitude to Caroline Macafee, who welcomed me so warmly to Glasgow in 1979 and made me, a southern Englishman, realise why Scots matters; it will be clear that I have depended on her formidable published scholarship throughout this book. I am grateful to Graham Caie for encouraging discussions about the project, and especially to Rod Lyall, an inspirational colleague.

I should also like to thank other colleagues and students, at Glasgow and else-where, for support, comments, conversation and practical help. I am conscious of debts to Juulia Ahvensalmi, Priscilla Bawcutt, Rhona Brown, Alan Bryson, Ardis Butterfield, Gerry Carruthers, John Corbett, Ian Cunningham, Jane Dawson, Tony Edwards, Liz Elliott, Douglas Gifford, Lionel Glassey, Crawford Gribben, Dorian Grieve, Ralph Hanna, George Head, Jonathan Hope, Simon Horobin, Carole Hough, Elspeth Jajdelska, Ian Johnson, Joshua Katz, Christian Kay, Colin Kidd, John Kirk, Meg Laing, Nigel Leask, Katie Lowe, Kate McClune, Derrick McClure, Kirsteen McCue, Kirsty Macdonald, Francesca Mackay, Margaret Mackay, Imo-gen Marcus, Joanna Martin, Rob Maslen, Felicity Maxwell, Robert McColl Mil-lar, Janneke Mol, Rosemary Morris, Roibeard ÓMaolaolaigh, Malcolm Parkes, Derek Pearsall, Murray Pittock, Andrew Prescott, Jane Roberts, Beth Robertson, Diane Scott, Maggie Scott, Merja Stenroos, Kirsten Stirling, John Thompson, Theo van Heijnsbergen, Sebastiaan Verweij, Gillian Weir, David Weston, Alison Wig-gins and Keith Williamson, to the late Jack Aitken, Angus McIntosh and Michael Samuels, and to the staff and students of Sanquhar Academy. I should like to thank Clive Tolley for his outstanding skill in setting a complex book. I am especially grateful to Dauvit Broun, who cast a critical yet friendly historian's eye over parts of the book. And, as ever, I am grateful to my wife Elaine Higgleton and our daughter Amy Smith.

Several generations of undergraduate and postgraduate students in Glasgow's departments of English Language and Scottish Literature have also contributed to the creation of this book, and I should like to acknowledge their help here.

I am deeply grateful to the Warden and Fellows of All Souls College, Oxford, who most generously elected me to a Visiting Fellowship in 2010, allowing me to complete this book and develop further the programme of scholarship of which it forms a part. I am grateful to the Arts and Humanities Research Council, whose award for the Corpus of Modern Scottish Writing Project enabled me to undertake work related to that presented here. I am grateful to the College of Arts, Univer-sity of Glasgow, and to John Corbett and Beth Robertson as successive Heads of Glasgow's English Language programme, for awarding me research leave to pursue this and other projects. I am also indebted to the staff of the following institutions: the Beinecke Library, Yale University; the Bodleian Library, Oxford; the British Library, London; Edinburgh University Library (both for its own holdings of manuscripts and for its invaluable collection of microfilms); Glasgow University Library; the National Archives (*olim* the Public Record Office), Kew; the National Archives of Scotland, Edinburgh; the National Library of Scotland, Edinburgh; St Andrews University Library.

This book is dedicated to the memory of Michael Samuels, who died just before I could discuss it with him properly, as I had wished to do.

I am of course responsible for any errors or infelicities that remain.

Jeremy Smith
Glasgow 2011

Abbreviations

BL	British Library, London
CSC	*Corpus of Scottish Correspondence*
CSD	*Concise Scots Dictionary*
DOST	*Dictionary of the Older Scottish Tongue*
DSL	*Dictionary of the Scots Language/Dictionar o the Scots Leid*
ECCO	*Eighteenth-Century Collections Online*
EEBO	*Early English Books Online*
EETS	Early English Text Society
IPA	International Phonetic Alphabet
LALME	*Linguistic Atlas of Late Mediaeval English*
LAOS	*Linguistic Atlas of Older Scots*
MED	*Middle English Dictionary*
MS	manuscript
NAS	National Archives of Scotland, Edinburgh
NLS	National Library of Scotland, Edinburgh
ODNB	*Oxford Dictionary of National Biography*
OED	*Oxford English Dictionary*
RP	Received Pronunciation
SND	*Scottish National Dictionary*
SSE	Scottish Standard English
STC	Short Title Catalogue
STS	Scottish Text Society
TNA	The National Archives (*olim* Public Record Office), Kew

The International Phonetic Alphabet

For discussion, see ch. 2, section 1. The key words given are those used in ch. 2, i.e. for the most part as pronounced by a modern speaker of Scottish English.

Vowels

i	*see*	close unrounded front vowel
e	*say*	mid-close unrounded front vowel
ɪ	*pin*	mid-close unrounded centralised vowel
ɛ	*pen*	mid-open unrounded front vowel
a	*sat*	open unrounded front vowel
u	*fool*	close rounded back vowel
o	*coat*	mid-close rounded back vowel
ʌ	*pun*	mid-open unrounded back vowel
ə	*about*	mid-open central vowel ('schwa')*
y	*tu*†	close rounded front vowel
ɔ	*cot*	mid-open rounded back vowel
ø	*work*	mid-close rounded front vowel
*		= as pronounced by a Southern British English speaker
†		= French 'you' (sg.)

Consonants

b	*bat*	voiced bilabial plosive
p	*pat*	voiceless bilabial plosive
v	*vat*	voiced labio-dental fricative
f	*fat*	voiceless labio-dental fricative
θ	*thin*	voiceless dental fricative
ð	*that*	voiced dental fricative
t	*tip*	voiceless alveolar plosive
d	*dip*	voiced alveolar plosive
s	*sip*	voiceless alveolar fricative
z	*zip*	voiced alveolar fricative
ʃ	*ship*	voiceless palato-alveolar fricative
ʒ	*treasure*	voiced palato-alveolar fricative
r	*rip*	voiced alveolar trill
l	*lip*	voiced lateral approximant
x	*loch*	voiceless velar fricative
ʧ	*child*	voiceless palato-alveolar affricate
ʤ	*jam*	voiced palato-alveolar affricate
m	*mat*	voiced bilabial nasal
n	*nip*	voiced alveolar nasal
ŋ	*sing*	voiced velar nasal
w	*web*	voiced labial-velar approximant
ʍ	*whisky*	voiceless labial-velar fricative
j	*yard*	voiced palatal approximant

PART I. INTRODUCTION

CHAPTER 1

About Older Scots

1. *How to use this book*

1.0 This book is intended for students and more advanced scholars who are working on the history of Scots, of English, or of other related varieties, or on early Scottish literature or history, and who wish to develop a comprehensive understanding of Older Scots, the form of Scots which survives in records from the period up to around 1700. Readers who have worked through this book will have acquired not only an understanding of the essential characteristics of Older Scots but will also be able to engage with some of the fascinating textual and linguistic problems with which this variety presents us. The book also contains a substantial set of freshly edited and extensively annotated texts, many of them comparatively difficult of access, which will allow readers to see a range of Older Scots forms in context.

   1.1 This book is organised as follows. The remainder of this chapter offers a short external history of Scots from its origins to the present day, and engages with questions of evidence for Older Scots. Chapters 2 and 3 are concerned with the internal history of Older Scots, dealing with the levels of language which are traditionally distinguished, i.e. *meaning (semantics), lexicon, grammar* and *transmission*. These levels of language are related as follows: *meaning* is expressed through the *lexicon* and *grammar* of a language; the lexicon (*vocabulary*) of a language is made up of the words it uses; the grammar of a language is to do with how words are put together (its *morphology*) or relate to one another (its *syntax*). In turn, the lexicon and grammar of a language are *transmitted* through *speech* or *writing*. Chapter 2 deals with transmission, including a special section on standardisation and anglicisation. Chapter 3 deals with the lexicon, including *word-formation*, sometimes known as *lexical morphology*, and with grammar, i.e. with syntax, and with the special endings that relate words to each other (*inflexional morphology*). Chapter 4 engages with the evolution and use of verse and prose *styles* in Older Scots texts. Chapters 1 to 4 constitute Part I of the book.

   1.2 Part II consists of a series of short texts, chosen and edited in such a way as to illustrate the range of linguistic features to be found in representative genres of Older Scots writing, both literary (poetry, prose) and non-literary (documents, letters, works on language and literature, Bible translation). Each text is preceded by a contextualising introduction, which identifies key linguistic features but also offers

1

a biographical/historical contextualisation for the text which follows; it is held as axiomatic that the language of a text can only be understood if placed within its socio-cultural context.

1.3 The texts in Part II are edited *diplomatically*, in order to make accessible the spellings, punctuation and layout found in the *witnesses* for the text in question, i.e. the source-materials (manuscripts, early printed books) from which they derive. Some of these usages reflect those of the author of the text in question; others reflect those of scribes, printers and contemporary editors. Thus users of this book are placed in the position of encountering Older Scots more directly than in those modern critical editions where editors have introduced present-day conventions of layout and punctuation, have made corrections of perceived errors, have changed the spelling (sometimes very radically), and have expanded contractions silently.

1.4 Such a presentation is, it must be admitted, controversial. It is of course in principle impossible to re-create a truly medieval or early modern 'reading experience': to do so, we would need to re-create a medieval or early modern readership. Yet just as with the 'original-instruments' movement in early music studies, so there has recently been a flurry of interest in the study of older texts in an early form, e.g. in the editing of Shakespeare. Jonathan Bate and Eric Rasmussen's edition of the plays of Shakespeare, for instance, is at least partially a response to such impulses, being modelled on the First Folio (Bate and Rasmussen 2007), albeit with modern spelling and punctuation 'to ensure that Shakespeare remains a living dramatist' (2007: 56), while the standard edition of Shakespeare is, probably and more formidably, the 'old-spelling' Clarendon edition (Wells and Taylor 1986). Such editions challenge modern readers in many ways, not least by reminding them of the alterity of texts from the past.

1.5 It is very important to emphasise at the outset that reproducing texts in this way is not in any way intended to negate the value of traditional critical editing: rather, it is a reminder that traditional textual criticism is precisely that, textual *criticism*, an act of literary interpretation in which the editor intervenes consciously in the presentation of the text. Readers of this book are invited constantly to reflect on editorial practice, for example through comparing the diplomatic texts presented here with modern critical editions.

1.6 Diplomatic editions of course also raise questions of authenticity, whether or not the spellings and punctuation of the source-text are modified to fit with present-day conventions. What is the status of the resulting edition where the source-text adopted is not an authorial holograph? Authorial? Scribal? Compositorial? As Vivian Salmon has pointed out, with reference to Shakespeare's works, 'it is clear from the discrepancies between manuscripts and printed texts, or between first edition and reprints, that printers did not follow copy in punctuation any more than in spelling, so that it is dangerous to place too much reliance on punctuation (as some scholars have done) as an indication of the author's directions for dramatic pauses at – sometimes – unexpected places in the text' (Salmon 1986: liii).

1.7 Researchers in the developing area of book history, however, have emphasised recently how texts are produced by a series of 'actors': authors, scribes or compositors, editors, printers, publishers, readers (the last of which betray their presence through, e.g., annotation; see Sherman 2007), and have shown that all these actors are of interest in their own right. For instance, punctuation may be scribal rather than authorial, but if so it is of course evidence for the *scribe's* behaviour, which is itself of interest. It seemed therefore a useful exercise to offer texts, several of which are well-known to modern readers in excellent critical editions, in a form which allows easy comparison with modern usage. Again, the goal is to invite readers to make comparisons and reflect on changes in usage.

1.8 Part III, the shortest section of the book, contains a glossary of the most common words used in Scots, and a set of references. Many other words are discussed in the introductions to the texts. Readers are also recommended to use the online *Dictionary of the Scots Language* (*DSL*) at http://www.dsl.ac.uk (see further below).

2. Present-day Scotland: language and dialects

2.0 Present-Day Scotland, with a population of some 5.2 million people, is a multi-lingual as well as a multi-ethnic society. At one end of the chronological scale, and brought to what is present-day Scotland from Ireland gradually during the course of the so-called 'Dark Ages', lies Gaelic, a Celtic language which existed in Scotland before Scots. At the other end are languages new to Scotland, such as Urdu and Cantonese, which are spoken by substantial communities throughout the country, especially in the 'central belt' of settlement stretching from Edinburgh in the east to Glasgow in the west.

For the population of modern Scotland, see ⟨http://www.gro-scotland.gov.uk/press/index.html⟩ (last accessed 1 June 2011).

2.1 In the Scottish section of the UK-wide census held in 2001, questions about ethnicity and language ability were largely not distinguished: a rather frustrating elision which has been remedied in part for the 2011 census, though only for those citizens of the UK living in Scotland; persons of Scottish ethnicity living elsewhere in the UK – a very considerable number – were not questioned. The results of the 2011 exercise are not yet available.

2.2 In 2001, 1.09% of the population were recorded as from South Asian backgrounds (of which 0.63% were described as of Pakistani origin, and thus potentially with an Urdu-speaking background), while 0.32% were described as Chinese (who would have, most probably, a Cantonese-speaking background). The only language-specific question asked in 2001, relevant to the Scottish situation was to do with Gaelic; the 'percentage of people aged 3 and over understanding, speaking, reading or writing Gaelic' was recorded as 1.89%. See ⟨http://www.scrol.gov.uk/scrol/warehouse/NewWards_ER_N.jsp⟩ (last accessed 27 July 2010).

2.3 The population of Scotland has of course grown considerably since the medieval period. During the eighteenth century, the population seems to have been of the order of 1.3 million, while during the Middle Ages and the early modern period the usual estimate is of between 500,000 and 800,000 (see Flinn 1977): roughly the population of the modern city of Glasgow, though of course much more thinly spread across the country.

2.4 Most inhabitants of present-day Scotland may be presumed to speak varieties of language that ultimately derive from Old English, a Germanic language that was brought to Britain in the fifth century AD (see 3.1 below). Three such speech-communities may be roughly distinguished. It should be noted that these communities overlap.

3

(a) First, there are speakers of non-Scottish varieties of English, notably *English spoken in England*. Of these the most socially salient variety is *Southern Standard British English*, consisting of the grammar and vocabulary of Standard English transmitted in so-called Received Pronunciation, the prestigious accent of England. This variety is spoken by two groups of speakers living in Scotland: many English immigrants, and (much less significantly) certain members of the vestigial Scottish aristocracy. Scottish people most regularly encounter Southern Standard British English, along with other varieties of English, through radio and TV. The impact of radio and TV on Scottish speech has until recently been considered somewhat slight, though recent research suggests it may be more important than hitherto thought (see Stuart-Smith forthcoming).

(b) Secondly, there are speakers of *Scots*, a variety derived from Old English but with a distinctive history since at least the late Middle Ages. Spoken Scots is used throughout the Lowlands, and it has spread from there into the north-east of Scotland, Caithness and the Northern Isles. It can be divided into sub-varieties, all with distinctive characteristics, e.g. North-East Scots (often referred to as *Doric*) around the city of Aberdeen and including the areas of Nairn, Moray, Banff and Buchan, or South Mid-Scots, stretching from mid-Ayrshire into Dumfries and Galloway (for a map of the traditional dialects of Scots, see ⟨http://www.dsl.ac.uk/INTRO/map.php?num=2⟩). A derived variety, Ulster Scots, was taken to Northern Ireland in the sixteenth century, and has developed its own distinctive characteristics, and there are even Scots usages which have spread elsewhere in the world through Scottish participation in imperial projection from the eighteenth century onwards (e.g. in the Appalachian Mountains of the United States, where it has been argued – somewhat controversially – that certain features characteristic of Scots still survive, or in Jamaica, where expressions such as **crabbit** 'bad-tempered' entered local usage through interaction with Scottish plantation-overseers). Scots today is in general the preserve of working-class speakers, both rural and urban, and is still subject to stigmatisation (Macaulay 1977) – although this situation may change in the light of political developments. Especially in towns and cities, it is losing much of its distinctive character, notably in the lexicon. This 'bleaching' of Scots features is partially, it seems, the result of exposure to UK-wide radio and television, but is probably mainly to do with the greater range of social interaction possible in conurbations; weaker social ties, characteristic of towns and cities, seem to correlate with more rapid linguistic change (see Milroy 1992). Nevertheless, as will be seen, there have been and are developments favourable to the development of Scots for more than a restricted register of spoken, 'non-standard' use.

(c) Finally, there are speakers of what is usually called *Scottish Standard English* (see most importantly the classic account in Abercrombie 1979). This variety, which was first described by scholarly observers in the eighteenth century (Jones 1993, 1995), is frequently defined as Standard English with a Scottish accent. It has a grammar and vocabulary almost (although not quite) the same as that used by high-prestige speakers of Standard English in England, but it combines these characteristics with a distinctively Scottish pronunciation. It thus lies between English and Scots on the same linguistic continuum, and many middle-class speakers tend to use more Scots forms in informal situations. Evidently, middle-class people feel the pull of two different linguistic centres of gravity, and it is therefore unsurprising that Scottish Standard English is a somewhat fluid phenomenon.

2.5 This present-day configuration derives from historical developments. English (both Southern British Standard and, more commonly, Scottish Standard) has *overt* prestige in present-day Scotland because, since the Act of Union in 1707, Scotland has been governed as part of the United Kingdom, and speakers of Standard English within the UK have, traditionally, occupied positions of power. Indeed, many eighteenth-century Scots went out of their way to speak the ancestor of present-day Standard English as part of their association with the new British state. But Scots has *covert* prestige in Scotland, in part because some social groups have resisted perceived oppression by English-speakers more strongly than others who have prospered under the Union, and in part because antiquarian impulses since at least the time of Robert Burns and Walter Scott have assigned to the Scots language a degree of what might be called 'cultural capital'.

For the overt/covert distinction, see famously Labov 1972, and for its application to Scots see Millar (with Horsbroch) 2000, Millar 2004; for an account of the politics involved in the Union, see famously Colley 1992, and also Lynch 1991. On questions of British national identity during the seventeenth and eighteenth centuries, see most importantly Kidd 1999, 2008.

2.6 Whether Scots is a distinct language from English, or simply a markedly differentiated variety of English, is hard to decide. Indeed, any question about the precise status of Scots in relation to English used in England is probably unanswerable in clear-cut terms; recent trends in linguistic categorisation have tended to emphasise fuzziness between usages rather than distinct differentiation. It is often claimed that a language is a 'dialect with a flag', and there is much truth in this statement. The difficulty is that, although Scotland has a flag – indeed, two flags – of her own, her flag is also included, at least at present, in that of a larger entity, the United Kingdom.

2.7 The heart of the problem, of course, is that languages are dynamic, evolving phenomena. English, after all, was originally a dialect of West Germanic, only gradually becoming distinguished from the other dialects which eventually became Dutch, German and so on. The precise moment when English ceased to be a dialect and became a language is impossible to determine; the distinction is one of the 'more/less' rather than of the 'either/or' kind. The Scots/English distinction seems similarly fuzzy. An extra problem is that languages evolve through interaction with their geographical neighbours, and Scots and English have (rather obviously) always been neighbours. Moreover, like all living languages, both English and Scots have evolved very considerably over time, and continue to do so; the urge to 'fix' a language is simply not capable of being achieved, even though societies, by means of such institutions as Academies, have fairly regularly attempted to do so. We might recall for instance Samuel Johnson's famous preface to his *Dictionary* of 1755, in which he commented ruefully on his failure to 'fix' the language, 'enchain[ing] syllables, and . . . lash[ing] the wind' of language change (conveniently cited in Bolton 1966: 152).

2.8 The twenty-first century border between Scotland and England certainly corresponds with a frequent correspondence or 'bundling', in non-standard usage, of *isoglosses*: an isogloss is a line on a map indicating roughly where one linguistic feature gives way to another. This correspondence of political and linguistic boundaries has been steadily developing since the Middle Ages, as non-standard usage in England was affected by a process of standardisation which for some time did not spread north of the border. Especially on the level of lexis (Glauser 1974, Smith 1994, 1996a: 177–86), a dialectal distinction is probably more marked here than anywhere else in Britain.

2.9 It is probably fairest to state that the relationship between Scots and English is in linguistic terms much the same as that between Dutch and certain varieties of German, or that between some of the Scandinavian languages. That is, they are part of the same dialect continuum and are to a fair extent mutually comprehensible. Thus whether you count Scots as a language or a dialect depends, it could be argued, on your political viewpoint.

2.10 It is during the Older Scots period, though, that the 'separateness' of Scots and English became most marked. Scots became *elaborated* during the fifteenth century, i.e. available for use in a range of high– as well as low-prestige situations. Apart from the developing London Standard in England, Scots was the first variety descended from Old English to develop in this way, and it is for this reason that Scots has even now retained a cultural identity – and cultural capital – distinct from the varieties of English found in England.

3. *External history of Scots*

3.0 In what follows, the following comparative chronology, taken with slight modifications from the *Concise Scots Dictionary* (*CSD* 1985: xiii), is a helpful point of reference. All dates are approximate.

Old English (Old Anglian):	to 1100
Older Scots:	1100 to 1700

Older Scots is generally sub-divided into the following periods:

Pre-literary:	to 1375
Early:	to 1450
Middle:	1450–1700
Early Middle:	1450–1550
Late Middle:	1550–1700
Modern Scots:	1700 onwards

A corresponding list of the periods for English is as follows:

Old English (all varieties):	to 1100
Middle English:	1100–1475
Early Middle:	1100–1350
Late Middle:	1350–1475
Modern English:	1475 onwards
Early Modern:	1475–1700
Later Modern:	1700 onwards

3.1 Varieties of present-day Scots derive ultimately from the Old Anglian dialect of Anglo-Saxon/Old English, brought to Britain by Germanic invaders in the fifth century AD. The speakers of Old Anglian, the Angles, spread north and northwest, whereas the Saxons spread south and southwest. Old Anglian was almost certainly distinct from the Saxon dialects even before the Anglo-Saxons arrived in

Britain, although subsequent interaction between Anglian and Saxon is important for the later history of English.

3.2 By the early seventh century the Angles had reached what is now Scotland, and began to interact and compete with the Celtic peoples – mostly Gaelic-speaking – who had occupied the country hitherto. In 638 they captured the strongpoint called **Din Eidyn** 'sloping-ridge fortress'. They changed the name, replacing Celtic **din** 'fortress' with its Anglian equivalent **burh**, and reversing the place-name's Celtic-style element-order (generic + qualifier = **Din** + **Eidyn**) to conform to Germanic patterns of word-formation (qualifier + generic = **Eidyn** + **burh**): the form **Edinburgh** resulted. The possession of Edinburgh made the Angles an important grouping. A new hegemony spread over the Lowlands of what is now Scotland into northern England, forming the Anglian kingdom of Northumbria. The sub-variety of Old Anglian spoken in this area is known as Old Northumbrian, contrasted with the sub-variety known as Old Mercian, the Old Anglian variety spoken in the English Midlands.

3.3 Northumbrian kings of the period, of whom the most famous is probably St Oswald (reigned 633–51), were active Christian proselytisers, and left symbols of their power throughout their kingdom. They had a particular veneration for the cult of the True Cross; it is therefore not surprising that the best-known of their monuments are the great stone crosses such as that at Ruthwell in Dumfriesshire. Cross-images also appear on their coinage; acceptance of a coinage correlates even now with acceptance of the political hegemony associated with that coinage. Such objects were not simply religious statements; they were a public attestation of the power of Christianised Germanic kings. On the Ruthwell Cross appears part of an Old English poem on Christ's crucifixion carved in the ancient Germanic alphabet known as *runes*. This text, related to a much fuller poem, *The Dream of the Rood*, which has survived in a West-Saxon manuscript from the tenth century, is occasionally claimed as the earliest piece of Scottish literature. The claim is of course somewhat anachronistic (although see McClure 1988: 8, Murison 1978: 1).

3.4 However, Gaelic continued to be spoken and written throughout what is now Scotland, even in the South-East Lowlands. Gaelic even seems to have become resurgent in the tenth century with the emergence of the Celtic kingdom of *Alba*, a precursor of present-day Scotland which was focused on the area between the rivers Forth and Spey.

3.5 The Anglo-Saxon area as a whole was considerably affected by a later wave of invasions: the arrival of Norse peoples in the British Isles from the ninth century onwards. The primary Norse settlement was focused on the so-called 'Great Scandinavian Belt' across Northern England (especially Lancashire and Yorkshire where interaction between Anglian and Norse brought about significant linguistic change) and in eastern Ireland. Norsemen also settled in the Northern and Western Isles and Caithness; their Norse is generally referred to as *Norn* (cf. Norse **Norrœn**).

3.6 Norse had little effect on the evolution of Scots until the Norman Conquest of England in 1066. In Scotland, a major effect of the Norman Conquest, albeit somewhat delayed, was the expansion of Anglian usage at the expense of Gaelic. The accession in Alba of Normanised kings – especially David I (1124–53) and his successors – meant that Gaelic was no longer so widely used. The king and his immediate circle seem to have spoken Anglo-Norman, a variety of French. As the

English author Walter of Coventry wrote (in Latin) in the thirteenth century: 'the more recent kings of Scots profess themselves to be rather Frenchmen, both in race and in manners, language and culture; and, after reducing the Scots [i.e. Gaels] to utter servitude, they admit only Frenchmen to their friendship and service' (cited Dickinson and Duncan 1977: 83; see also Macafee 1988: 4). Many of the great families of medieval Scotland had Norman roots, indicated by their French-derived names, e.g. **Bruce, Comyn**. Noble Anglo-Norman families invited from England brought with them English-speaking servants and retainers; many of these retainers spoke varieties of English that had been strongly influenced by Norse.

3.7 Another important group were so-called 'pioneer burgesses' (*CSD* 1985: ix) from Northern England who settled in the new royal and baronial burghs that were established during the period. These burgesses from the 'Great Scandinavian Belt' spoke a heavily Scandinavianised English, which blended with the Anglian speech of South-East Scotland. By the twelfth century the resulting variety of English, heavily influenced by Norse, was strongly established in the eastern Lowlands. And by the mid-fourteenth century it had replaced Gaelic in much of eastern Scotland as far north as the Moray Firth, and also in much of the south-west of the country. Scots also spread into Caithness and the Northern Isles to replace Norn.

3.8 Written records in something we can call Scots begin to appear from the late fourteenth century onwards; before that date, the period of *pre-literary Scots*, the only evidence of any significance is to be found in place-names and in occasional glosses on Latin material. However, in the *Early Scots* period (*c.* 1375–1450) it seems that the Anglian-derived variety spoken in Scotland was not viewed by contemporaries as distinct from English. The term **Inglis**, used to describe the non-Celtic language of the Lowlands of Scotland, was only joined (and not replaced) by **Scottis** in the late fifteenth century; until that date, the term **Scottis** was used to refer to Gaelic (Templeton 1973: 6).

The study of names (*onomastics*), especially place-names, has become increasingly important for historians of the languages of Scotland in recent years. Place-names, among other things, record the ebb and flow of cultures across the landscape. Thus, for instance, in Nithsdale in Dumfries and Galloway, Celtic, Norse and Anglo-Saxon place-names are blended, e.g. **Sanquhar**, from Celtic **sean** 'old' + Celtic **cathair** 'fort', first recorded as **Sanchar** *c.* 1150, beside **Kirkconnel** (originally **Cille Chonaill**) with Norse **kirk–** 'church' (replacing Celtic **cille** 'monastic cell') blended with the Celtic personal name **Chonaill**. Nearby **Kelloholm** blends Celtic-derived **Kello** (cf. **kel–** 'loud') with Germanic **holm** 'field'; the name emerged in the eighteenth century, based on **Kello Burn** (cf. Germanic **burn**). **Nithsdale** itself blends **Nith** (an element with an obscure etymology, possibly pre-Celtic) with the Norse-derived element **–dale**. This complex blend represents the complex culture of the border country; Nithsdale in medieval and early-modern times was one of several bases for the notorious Border Reivers. For further information about Scottish place-names, see the website of the Scottish Place-Name Society, ⟨www.spns.org.uk⟩. An important introduction is Nicolaisen (1976 and subsequent editions).

3.9 Whatever its precise relationship to English, *Early* and *Early Middle Scots* developed as an *elaborated* language, i.e. a variety which could be used in more than one register, including writing as well as speech. In 1398, the Scottish Parliament began to record proceedings in Scots rather than in Latin, and the Early and Early Middle Scots periods saw an efflorescence of literary activity. Barbour's national epic-romance, *The Bruce*, was composed in 1375, although the manuscripts in which it has survived date from a century later. James I of Scotland composed *The Kingis Quair* in the vernacular while in exile in England, and major poets, such as Robert Henryson, William Dunbar, Gavin Douglas and David Lyndsay followed after him. A flourishing prose-tradition also emerged from the end of the fifteenth century onwards.

3.10 As in England, the elaboration of the vernacular meant that contemporaries embellished their Scots with vocabulary derived from the high-status languages of the late-medieval period, French and Latin; French – like the other *Romance* languages, viz. Spanish, Catalan, Italian, Romanian – is descended from Latin. This practice was encouraged by close contacts with France under the 'Auld Alliance' against England, and by the evolution of a distinctive Scots law-code. (Even present-day Scottish law-texts contain Latin-derived terminology not used in England, e.g. **homologation** 'ratification in a legal sense of a document hitherto not legally binding', **nimious** 'vexatiously burdensome in a legal sense'.) As Scots became elaborated, it underwent some of the formal changes also found in Middle English. Dialectal diversity, which seems to have been a feature of Early Scots, seems to have become muted for communicative reasons in the later Middle Scots period. This muting may be termed *standardisation*, even though a fixed form of Middle Scots was never fully achieved (Agutter 1989, Aitken 1971, Devitt 1989, and especially Meurman-Solin 1997 and references there cited).

3.11 For, whereas standardised written English eventually became in England the educationally enforced (and fixed) written norm, political and cultural events supervened in Scotland to prevent Scots following the same path. England was always the big neighbour, and there was a continuing cultural gravity-effect that could not be ignored. The most significant cultural event of the sixteenth century was the Reformation, which took place in Scotland in 1560, and this event fed a demand for translations of the Bible. Murdoch Nisbet produced a New Testament in Scots in *c.* 1520, but his text was not printed until the twentieth century. Nisbet's translation was based on a version of the English Wycliffite Bible from the late fourteenth century, which was itself a translation from the Latin Vulgate of St Jerome, and contemporary biblical scholarship demanded a return to the original New Testament Greek or Old Testament Hebrew (as in William Tyndale's English Bible of 1525–6). Nisbet's anglocentric cultural connexion is significant, however. Throughout the sixteenth century, Protestant religious writers looked to England for their cultural models; indeed, the use of written Scots became in certain registers identified with Catholicism. It was the Catholic Ninian Winzet who attacked the great reformer John Knox thus: **Gif ze, throw curiositie of nouationis, hes forzet our auld plane Scottis quhilk zour mother lerit zou[,] in tymes cuming, I sall wryte to zou my mynd in Latin, for I am nocht acquyntit with zour Southeron** (cited Tulloch 1989: 14).

Winzet's claim is, it seems, an exaggeration for polemical effect; the evidence of Knox's letters is that he wrote in both Scots and English, choosing his language in relation to his intended audience. For an interesting discussion, see Aitken 1997; see also Dawson and Glassey 2004, Smith 2010.

3.12 This anglicising tendency was reinforced by major political events of the seventeenth and eighteenth century: the Union of the Crowns in 1603 (when James VI of Scots succeeded Elizabeth I as James I of England), and the Union of Parliaments in 1707. James VI had patronised Scots poets but they, like himself, began to write in English when they moved to London; and recent research has drawn attention to the evolution of Scottish Standard English (not Scots) as a prestigious variety in the Scottish Enlightenment of the eighteenth century (Jones 1995; see also Smith 2007).

3.13 *Late Middle Scots* was therefore under cultural pressure, and both Amy Devitt (1989) and more recently Anneli Meurman-Solin (1997) have charted the increasingly restricted use of written Scots during the sixteenth and seventeenth centuries. By 1700, written Scots was largely confined to material with a local or private currency, such as letters between family-members, and even there was under pressure as the Bible provided a written model for all literate persons. However, it was retained in some literary contexts, e.g. in repeated printings of texts such as Barbour's *Bruce* and Hary's *Wallace*, and in the repackaging of old ballads for contemporary readership. During the eighteenth century written Scots became essentially a curiosity, albeit sometimes a fashionable one, in (for instance) the poetry of Robert Burns, or one with a surreptitious political connotation, as in the verse of Robert Fergusson, or complex social statement, as in the verse of Janet Little. Burns himself, in poems like *Tam O'Shanter* or *The Cotter's Saturday Night* notoriously used Scots for conversation and narrative but his own version of written Augustan English for more elevated discourse. However, recent work has shown that the Scots/English relationship in Burns's writing was much more carefully nuanced than he is sometimes given credit for (see for instance Smith 2007a).

For a more developed discussion of issues to do with standardisation and anglicisation, see ch. 2 below, section 3.

3.14 In the nineteenth century a Scots prose tradition flourished in the developing 'popular' press (Donaldson 1986, 1989), and in fiction generally (as in so-called *Kailyard* writing). Scots appeared in verse, of course, but often (as in, for instance, the poetry of Allan Cunninghame) as a trigger for sentimentality. In the twentieth century Scots was widely used in fiction, and there was even an attempt to create a prestigious written Scots, in the shape of *Lallans*, a 'synthetic' mixture of Scots varieties, invented by the poet Hugh MacDiarmid and others. However, despite persistent enthusiasm for Lallans on the part of cultural activists, the use of this so-called 'plastic' variety of 'Standard Scots' has never become common.

3.15 A comparison is sometimes made between Lallans and Norwegian *Nynorsk*, which similarly emerged in the nineteenth century; interestingly, both varieties developed strong political associations, especially (though not exclusively) radical nationalist ones. Unlike Lallans, Nynorsk received some state support, and developed as an everyday language, spoken as well as written by socially prestigious persons. However, both Lallans and Nynorsk are marked by artificiality and, especially in the case of the former, restriction to a particular kind of literary usage, and their long-term prospects outside this register do not look good (despite McClure 1981). Even in poetic use, Lallans seems now to be declining, to be replaced by an attempt to reflect more 'authentic' working-class urban speech in writing, e.g. in the poetry of Tom Leonard, or in the novels of James Kelman and Irvine Welsh. However, even in the work of some of these writers Scots, as opposed to English, is sustained only fitfully. Thus Welsh's novel *Trainspotting*, which had a considerable vogue in the 1990s, arguably distinguishes Scots and English in a way which parallels, rather well, Burns's fluctuating, complex usage.

4. Futures for Scots

4.0 Until quite recently, the future prospects for Scots were considered to be rather bleak. In the eighteenth and nineteenth centuries antiquaries attempted to record all aspects of Scottish culture which were perceived to be under threat; James Johnson's *Scots Musical Museum*, Sir Walter Scott's fiction – novels, verse and indeed his own house at Abbotsford – and John Jamieson's great *Etymological Dictionary of the Scottish Language* of 1808 are all manifestations of this impulse. Major projects of linguistic record began to be published from the middle of the twentieth century: the *Dictionary of the Older Scottish Tongue* (Craigie *et al.* 1937–2002, dealing with Older Scots), the *Scottish National Dictionary* (Grant and Murison 1931–76, designed to record Modern Scots) and the continuing *Linguistic Survey of Scotland* (see McIntosh 1952). Again, however, one driver behind this substantial programme of research was to record a variety that was perceived to be dying out. Some authorities (e.g. McClure 1988) have continued to argue that Scots is a threatened usage, and have called for vigorous programmes of language-planning to sustain Scots as a national treasure, a significant component of Scotland's cultural capital.

4.1 More recently, it has been suggested that this view of Scots as a vulnerable usage is over-pessimistic. Scots is a living language, still spoken by a substantial body of people, and, like all living languages, Scots continues to change. Indeed, it could be argued that, if it did not change, it would be truly dead, like Latin. Some have suggested that it is losing a good deal of its character as a result of exposure to UK-wide radio and television, but there is evidence that Scots is continuing to be a creative language, and that the interaction between Scots and the English of the broadcast media is complex and subtle. The urban vernaculars of the great cities of Scotland, for instance, may have lost many traditional usages but continually develop their own new and distinctive linguistic patterns. For instance, Michael Munro's fascinating study of Glasgow vocabulary, *The Patter* (1985 and subsequent editions), is marketed as a humorous book, but it contains numerous examples of the productiveness of Glaswegian vernacular and has serious implications (see further, for instance, Macafee 1983). Literary use of varieties of Scots in the closing years of the twentieth century – especially urban varieties – is an important by-product of this vernacular confidence, even though the impact of literary usage on broader culture tends to be overstated.

4.2 Such 'bottom-up' developments are currently being complemented by 'top-down' initiatives, part of that political reassertion of Scottish national identity which was also expressed in the reconvening of the Scottish Parliament in 1999. Recent initiatives in Scottish schools and universities, such as the development of the children's Scots language resource *The Kist* and the establishment of Scottish Language courses in university curricula, have reaffirmed the value of Scots in Scottish culture.

4.3 Of course, it remains to be seen how effective any such official, 'top-down' initiatives in language-planning will be; it is an observable fact that politicians tend to tie themselves in knots over questions of language. It is perhaps worth pondering on the truism that the socio-cultural status granted any linguistic variety cannot be divorced from the socio-cultural status allotted to those who use it. Languages are human tools; it can be argued that Scots is valued when the human users of Scots are valued.

For an interesting discussion of issues to do with language, national identity and language-planning, including some discussion of Scots, see Millar 2005. For an important survey of the standing of Scots, still resonant, see Aitken 1981a.

4.4 From a European perspective, there are other varieties in comparable situations with Scots within the traditional nation-states: Occitan in France, Catalan in Spain. (It is perhaps of interest that in the fifteenth century the parallel was drawn between English and Scots on the one hand and, on the other, varieties of Spanish, such as Castilian and Aragonese.) The interest in Scots in universities beyond Britain, notably in Germany, Scandinavia and Italy, is indicative of its recognition as an internationally salient variety.

5. *Evidence for Older Scots*

5.0 Older Scots, like all natural languages, was not a monolithic entity. Scots in the fifteenth century, like contemporary emerging written 'standard' English, allowed a degree of formal variation which would be unacceptable in present-day written English. Although, as we have seen, an incipient, 'proto-standard' Scots was emerging in the early sixteenth century, much variation remained even in material associated with this emerging proto-standard, and markedly dialectal usages also survive into present-day usage.

5.1 It is important for students to be aware of the partial nature of this written evidence. Modern linguistic surveys are conducted on rigorous principles of selection: informants are chosen on the basis of social class and geographical location in quite precise ways. Writing from the Middle Ages – there is of course no direct recording of speech – survives almost accidentally. Pretty well all Older Scots poetry, for instance, comes down to us in a handful of key manuscripts and a few surviving copies of early printed books.

5.2 Thus Barbour's *Bruce*, though composed in the late fourteenth century, only survives in two late-fifteenth-century manuscripts, both generally held to be copied by the same scribe, John Ramsay; one is in the National Library of Scotland in Edinburgh (MS Advocates' 19.2.2), and the other in the library of St John's College, Cambridge (MS G.23). The Edinburgh manuscript also contains a copy of Blind Hary's *Wallace* (see Cunningham 1973). *The Kingis Quair*, the other major Early Scots poem, is traditionally ascribed to King James I of Scotland (1394–1437). It survives in one manuscript only: MS Oxford, Bodleian Library, Arch. Selden.B.24 (see Boffey, Edwards and Barker-Benfield 1997).

5.3 Verse by Middle Scots poets, or *makars* as they are often called (e.g. Henryson, Dunbar, Douglas etc.), is found in a number of manuscripts from the late fifteenth and early sixteenth centuries, the most important of which are the following:
• The Makculloch Manuscript, now Edinburgh, University Library Laing III.49, was begun in 1477. Most of this manuscript consists of lecture notes in Latin taken by Magnus Makculloch from lectures delivered at Louvain in that year. But there is also a collection of short religious and instructional verse, including texts of parts of Henryson's *Moral Fabillis* and *Prais of Age*.
• The Asloan Manuscript is now MS Edinburgh, National Library of Scotland 16500. It is named after John Asloan (Asloane/Sloan) who wrote it early in the sixteenth century. Asloan provided a table of contents at the beginning of the

manuscript; of the sixty items mentioned in the contents only thirty-four survive. The material that survives includes poetry by Dunbar and Henryson, and much anonymous verse and prose. The manuscript also includes a Scotticised version of the 'English Chaucerian' John Lydgate's *Complaint of the Black Knight*; this text is also found in MS Arch. Selden. B.24, and was printed by Chepman and Myllar, thus illustrating the cultural transactions which transcended the Scottish/English border. (For a discussion, see van Buuren 1982, Houwen 1990; for a full description of the manuscript, with extra material, see Cunningham 1994.)

• The Bannatyne Manuscript (MS Edinburgh, National Library of Scotland, Advocates' 1.1.6) was written by George Bannatyne in 1568, and is one of the most significant manuscripts of Older Scots verse. It is an important authority for much of Dunbar's poetry and a key witness for Henryson's verse; it also contains an interesting (if modified) text of Sir David Lyndsay's *Ane Satyre of the Thrie Estaitis*. See further Fox and Ringler 1980; see also van Heijnsbergen 2010.

• The Maitland Folio Manuscript, now MS Cambridge, Magdalene College, Pepys Library 2553, is a miscellany compiled *c.* 1570 for Sir Richard Maitland (1496–1586), Keeper of the Great Seal of Scotland in 1562 and a lord of session. This manuscript, unfortunately comparatively neglected (see Bawcutt 1998: 8), is the only authority for much of Dunbar's court poetry; it also contains copies of anonymous verse such as *King Hart*, once ascribed to Gavin Douglas, alongside some of Maitland's own work.

• The Cambridge Manuscript (MS Cambridge, Trinity College o.3.12), which dates from *c.* 1515, is the main witness for Gavin Douglas's translation of *The Aeneid*. The manuscript was copied by Douglas's secretary, and contains annotations that were possibly made by the poet himself.

5.4 The earliest printing of Older Scots verse was undertaken in Edinburgh by Walter Chepman and Andrew Myllar in 1508, who produced editions of Dunbar, Henryson and Hary, and possibly of other texts which have not survived; however, their enterprise was somewhat short-lived, and Scottish printing really gets under way only in the second half of the sixteenth century, as evidenced by the wills of booksellers which have survived. Robert Gourlaw, a bookseller whose will appeared in 1586, had in his stock the following: **Item, Testament of Cresside, blak, thrie, at iiijd. the piece – summa, xijd** (the term **blak** refers to the font, i.e. black-letter); but Gourlaw seems to have lived at the low end of the market. Henry Charteris' inventory of 1606 records **in his Buith** (i.e. shop) numerous copies of major poets, e.g. **fyve scoir tua Wallaces . . . sevin hundreth lxxxviij Dauid Lyndesayis . . . iijmlxxij . . . vcxlv Testamentis of Cresseid** (Dickson and Edmond 1890: 353). Such editions link the Older Scots poets with the so-called Vernacular Revival of the eighteenth century, represented by (e.g.) Allan Ramsay the elder, Robert Fergusson and (most famously) Robert Burns.

5.5 The printing of Barbour's *Bruce* and Hary's *Wallace* began in the sixteenth century and continued throughout the seventeenth (see Geddie 1912; see also the discussions in Part II, section 4 below). Thus we have copies of Barbour's *Bruce* by significant printers such as the Edinburgh printer Andro Hart (1620 – **newly corrected and conferred with the best and most ancient Manuscripts**), Gedeon Lithgow (1648 – **Printer to the Universitie of Edinburgh**, 1648), Andrew Anderson (**EDINBURGH, . . . and are to be sold at his House, on the north side of the Cross, Anno Dom. 1670**), and Robert Sanders (**GLASGOW, . . . Printer to the**

City and University, and are to be sold in his Shop, 1672). Hary's *Wallace* was even more commonly printed. In addition to the Chepman and Myllar print (of which only a few leaves survive, shared between the Mitchell Library in Glasgow and Cambridge University Library), there are numerous editions of the poem appearing throughout the sixteenth, seventeenth and eighteenth centuries; the Sanders firm (father and son) alone printed the work no fewer than six times over a period running from 1665 to 1713, and the poem is the first book of verse to be printed in Belfast, in 1728. Another much-printed author was Sir David Lyndsay, whose works survive in a series of prints beginning in the late sixteenth century. Henry Charteris's edition of Lyndsay's *Squyer Meldrum* was printed in Edinburgh in 1594, and is the earliest version of this work to survive; it is now in the National Library of Scotland. Henry's son Robert produced an edition of *Ane Satyre* in Edinburgh in 1602; seven copies of this edition survive.

5.6 Some Older Scots poetry survived in a more underground fashion. As recorded by the National Library of Scotland's *The Word on the Street* project (⟨http://www.nls.uk/broadsides/⟩), *Christ's Kirk on the Green*, traditionally (if erroneously) ascribed to James I of Scotland, survives as a broadside ballad, printed in the eighteenth century, and influential on both Robert Fergusson (*Leith Races*) and Robert Burns (*The Holy Fair*).

5.7 Prose texts survive in a range of early manuscripts and early printed books now in various collections; some examples follow. Sir Gilbert Hay's works survive in a fifteenth-century manuscript from Sir Walter Scott's collection at Abbotsford; it is currently accessioned at the National Library of Scotland in Edinburgh (MS Acc. 9253). John of Ireland's work of moral instruction for the young James IV survives in a manuscript in the National Library in Edinburgh (MS Advocates' 18.2.8), where John Bellenden's translation of Livy is also preserved in a mid-sixteenth-century manuscript (MS Advocates' 18.3.12; several other manuscripts of this work survive). The anonymous *Complaynt of Scotlande* was printed in Paris in the middle of the sixteenth century; a copy is in the National Library of Scotland. John Knox's *History of the Reformation* survives not only in print but also in a (non-autograph) manuscript now in Edinburgh University Library (MS Laing 210), where one of the manuscripts of Robert Lindsay of Pitscottie's *Historie and Cronikles of Scotland* is also preserved (MS Laing 218; an extract appears in Part II); George Buchanan's *Chamaeleon* survives in a manuscript in the British Library in London (MS Cotton Caligula C.iii; an extract also appears in Part II). 'Catholic Scots' survives in numerous anti-Reformation pamphlets printed abroad and circulated in Scotland in the late sixteenth century, e.g. Nicol Burne's *Disputation* (Paris, 1581), and Ninian Winzet's *Buke of Fourscoir-thre Questionis* (Antwerp, 1563), extracts from which appear in Part II, or John Hamilton's *Certane Orthodox and Catholik Conclusions* (Paris, 1581). James VI of Scotland published *Ane Schort Treatise conteining some Revlis and Cautelis to be observit and eschewit in Scottis Poesie* in 1584, printed by Thomas Vautroullier in Edinburgh; the *Revlis and Cautelis* are presented in Part II. Important sources for early Scots prose are burgh records and the Register of the Privy Council; the original copy of the latter is preserved in the National Archives of Scotland in Edinburgh.

5.8 But the tendency from now on was to shift from Scots to English. Andro/ Andrew Hart (d.1621/2), who was the most successful publisher in Scotland in the early seventeenth century, for instance, had already in 1603 printed *A True*

Description of the Nobill Race of the Stewards, mainly in Scots, but subsequently shifted, in general, to English; there is a clear parallel here with the linguistic behaviour of James VI and I, who changed the Scots of his manuscript version of his *Basilikon Doron* to the English of the printed version (1599; see Part II). It may be significant that Hart's bestseller was the Geneva Bible of 1610.

On the history of the book in Scotland, see in the first place Bevan 2002, Mann 2000 and the very useful pamphlets issued by the Scottish Printing Archival Trust (1990–2000). The ongoing *Edinburgh History of the Book in Scotland* has yet (2010) to reach the periods covered here, but judging by the standard of the volumes completed so far it will offer an authoritative account. Still extremely useful is Dickson and Edmond 1890.

5.9 Scots continued to be used in documents throughout the seventeenth century. For instance, many burgh records sustain the use of Scots, as in the documents pertaining to witch-craft in Dumfries, for which see ⟨http://www.scan.org. uk/exhibitions/witchhunt_contents.htm⟩ (last accessed 2 June 2011).

5.10 It is important to realise that all this material comes down to us not as the result of a process of careful selection but as the vagaries of time and chance have allowed. Unlike modern sociolinguists and dialectologists, researchers in Older Scots have to make do with what has survived. This fact means that all students of Older Scots have to spend some time analysing the peculiar circumstances of individual texts before their evidential value for linguistic discussion can be assessed.

6. A note on linguistic terminology

6.0 *Linguistics*, the academic discipline which seeks to understand language, has developed its own descriptive and technical terminology. This terminology can seem somewhat daunting to students whose interests are not primarily linguistic. However, the ability to describe language is a skill which users of this book will need. Both ch. 2 and 3 below therefore begin with a short section on terminology, which is then applied later in the chapter. The terminology used is that which is in very common agreed use amongst linguists, and readers may skip these sections if they feel confident of their knowledge in this area.

The discussions in ch. 2 and 3 relate closely to outlines provided in Horobin and Smith 2004 and in Smith 2009, and this relationship is intentional; the purpose of using the same terminology in distinct books is to allow for easy comparisons between distinct language-states.

7. Key resources

7.0 It should be noted that the study of the Older Scots language has a very respectable academic pedigree. Bibliographical references appear in Part III. However, it may be appropriate to identify certain key resources at the outset, all of which have been absolutely essential in the preparation of this book. The first two resources in particular have been used throughout, and are the source of much of the information presented in chapters 2 through 4, and in the head-notes to the Texts in Part II.

• The *Dictionary of the Older Scottish Tongue* (*DOST*) is essential for serious students of Older Scots. The beginnings of *DOST* are traditionally ascribed to 1919, when William Craigie set out proposals for a series of 'New Dictionary Schemes', including a Scots dictionary, in an address to the Philological Society of London. Craigie began to work intensively on Older Scots in 1921, and the first fascicule of *DOST* was published in 1931, as was the first part of the *Scottish National Dictionary (SND)*, which covered the post-1700 period and was completed in 1976. Work continued on *DOST* for many years under a series of editors, notably A. J. (Jack) Aitken and Margaret C. Dareau. The final volume, which included an important and authoritative *History of Scots to 1700* by Caroline Macafee (with some materials by Jack Aitken), was finally completed in 2002; Macafee's account replaces earlier descriptions such as the introduction to G. Gregory Smith's *Specimens of Middle Scots* (1902) (Smith's work, however, also contains a useful set of texts, still of considerable value for serious students). Subsequently, *DOST* has been linked online with *SND* to form the *Dictionary of the Scots Language/Dictionar o the Scots Leid (DSL)*. *DSL* is currently freely available at:

⟨http://www.dsl.ac.uk⟩

See also Christian J. Kay and Margaret A. Mackay (eds), *Perspectives on the Older Scottish Tongue. A Celebration of DOST* (2005); a description of the working methods used in *DOST*'s creation appears in Dareau 2004. A convenient abridged version of *DOST* and *SND* is *The Concise Scots Dictionary* (= *CSD*, 1985); a useful accompaniment to *CSD* is *The Scots Thesaurus* (Macleod *et al.* 1990). For a discussion of the Scottish lexicographical tradition, see Murison 1987.

• In addition to *DOST* and *SND*, it is often useful to consult the *Oxford English Dictionary* (= *OED*), especially for up-to-date etymological information but also for additional citations. The most famous editor of *OED* was Sir James Murray, himself a Scot whose other academic work included a pioneering dialectal survey of Lowland Scots. The *OED* online appears (subscription required) at:

⟨http://www.oed.com⟩

• The online *Edinburgh Linguistic Atlas of Scots 1380–1500* (*LAOS*) appeared in a beta-version in 2007, and is being continuously updated. It includes useful links to other resources, notably the manual to Helsinki's *Corpus of Scottish Correspondence* (*CSC*, 2007), which covers the period 1500–1730. The following URLs may be consulted:

LAOS – ⟨http://www.lel.ed.ac.uk/ihd/laos1/laos1.html⟩
CSC – ⟨http://www.helsinki.fi/varieng/csc/manual/⟩

LAOS is a successor project to *A Linguistic Atlas of Late Mediaeval English* (*LALME*), published in 1986, an electronic version of which (e-*LALME*) is in preparation. Although the primary focus of *LALME* is on Middle English, a fair amount of Early Scots material, dating from before around 1450, is also included in that publication, and has been used on occasion in this book.

LAOS, version 1.1, was last consulted for items referred to in this book on 3 December 2010. *LAOS* asks for the following citation reference to be given: *A Linguistic Atlas of Older Scots, Phase 1: 1380–1500*, ⟨http://www.lel.ed.ac.uk/ihd/laos1/laos1.html⟩ (Edinburgh: © 2008– The University of Edinburgh).

• An important online corpus of sixteenth-century Scottish documents is the *Breadalbane Collection*, edited by Jane Dawson: see

⟨http://www.ed.ac.uk/schools-departments/divinity/research/
resources/breadalbane⟩

This corpus consists of some 324 letters, now housed in the National Archives of Scotland.

• The online *Corpus of Modern Scottish Writing* (CMSW) is of course strictly speaking outside the ambit of this book, since it covers the period 1700–1945. However, those wishing to compare the materials provided here with the later period will undoubtedly find it a valuable resource, and the materials in this book are envisaged as part of the same programme of research. It is freely available at:

⟨http://www.cmsw.gla.ac.uk⟩

• The *Edinburgh History of the Scots Language* (1997), edited by Charles Jones, contains a series of important essays on aspects of the history of Scots. The discussion of Older Scots sounds presented there should be supplemented by Jack Aitken's monograph (originally designed for the *Edinburgh History*) *The Older Scots Vowels* (2002), which is a comprehensive survey bringing together a lifetime of research on Older Scots phonology. Also important is Derrick McClure's chapter, 'Scotland', in the *Cambridge History of the English Language* (1994). Useful introductory accounts, from various perspectives, include Jones 2002, McClure 1988, Murison 1978 and 1979. The *Edinburgh Companion to Scots* (2003), edited by John Corbett, Derrick McClure and Jane Stuart-Smith, includes both historical and modern material.

• Manfred Görlach's *A Textual History of Scots* (2002) is a valuable resource for students working at an advanced level on the history of Scots throughout its history, with a handy appendix of texts. Useful anthologies include Jack and Rozendaal 1997.

• It is important to place Older Scots within a comparative context, most notably in relation to the contemporary development of English. A useful introductory survey of Middle English is Horobin and Smith 2004; for Early Modern English, see Nevalainen 2006. Also highly recommended are Barber 1976, Görlach 1991.

• The standard survey of Scottish handwriting is Simpson 1998. The National Archives of Scotland give a useful link for the study of handwriting in Scottish documents:

⟨http://www.scottishhandwriting.com/⟩

• Many insights into particular linguistic choices are to be found in works on Scottish literature. A full bibliography is not possible here, but Gifford *et al.* (2002) and Brown *et al.* (2006) may be recommended as authoritative; both offer comprehensive references for further study.

CHAPTER 2

Transmission

0.0 This chapter falls into three sections. The first section deals with linguistic terminology; if readers are comfortable with such terminology they may find they are able to skip this section, although there are certain usages (e.g. derived from the ancient and medieval doctrine of *littera*) which they may find unfamiliar. Section 2 offers an overview of Older Scots spelling-and speech-systems, while section 3 deals with questions of variation (dialectal and diatopic), standardisation and anglicisation.

1. Linguistic terminology

1.1 Languages have been transmitted for the last four millennia in two ways: by speech, which – until mechanical and electronic recording was invented – was not recorded directly and was thus transient, and through writing, which is comparatively permanent. Speech and writing are both modes of what is sometimes known as *transmission*, and in that sense both modes map onto the 'same' grammatical and lexical structures. However, the distinction between transience and permanence means that the two modes of transmission are likely to diverge in important ways. The mapping of sound onto symbol is not after all a natural one: for instance, ⟨w⟩ maps onto the sound [w] for an English speaker, but onto the sound [v] for a German. There is in short nothing intrinsically sound-symbolic about a letter; communities have simply agreed collectively, as they do when assigning values to money (coins, paper), to assign sound-values to particular symbols.

1.2 In classical times, writers such as Donatus (fourth century AD) and Priscian (sixth century AD) developed the 'doctrine of *littera*' to express the relationship between spellings and sounds, and this doctrine still underpins traditional ways of teaching children to read. According to this doctrine, distinctions were made between *figura* ('figure', i.e. written symbol), *potestas* ('power', i.e. sound-equivalent) and *nomen* ('name' of the letter), with *littera* (letter) as the superordinate term to describe the combination of the three. In the Middle Ages and renaissance, children were 'taught their letters' by means of *abecedaries*, primers aligning letters with particular sounds. In recent years this terminology has been recuperated by some scholars interested in the sound-spelling relationship (e.g. Benskin 1982). The doctrine of *littera* underpins modern practices of editorial transliteration, and thus the editions in Part II of this book. Written examples within the discussions are expressed here in figurae, appearing in **bold**.

1.3 More recently, linguists have developed more sophisticated notions and approaches. First, a special alphabet for representing sounds with greater delicacy than the standard English alphabet has been devised: the International Phonetic

Alphabet (IPA). A list of IPA symbols appears at the beginning of this book, and some are repeated below. Secondly, linguists have developed a four-fold system of definition which allows for distinctions between underlying form and contextual realisation: *phonemes* and *allophones*, *graphemes* and *allographs*. These terms may be defined as follows:

• *phoneme*: either the smallest speech-unit that distinguishes one word from another in terms of meaning, or the prototypical sound being aimed at by speakers within a speech community. Replacement of one phoneme by another changes the meaning of the word in which it occurs; thus /a/ and /ɔ/ are distinct phonemes, illustrated by the pair /pat, pɔt/ 'pat', 'pot'. It is conventional to place phonemes in slash brackets, thus: /. . ./.

• *allophone*: the realisation of the phoneme in speech. Replacement of one allophone with another realisation of the same phoneme does not change the meaning of the word in which it occurs; thus [l] and [ɫ] are allophones of the phoneme /l/. It is conventional to place allophones in square brackets, thus [. . .].

• *grapheme*: the written language equivalent of the phoneme, i.e. the symbolic unit being aimed at by the scribe. Replacement of one grapheme by another changes the meaning of the word in which it occurs; thus ⟨a⟩ and ⟨o⟩ are distinct graphemes, illustrated by the pair ⟨pat⟩, ⟨pot⟩. It is conventional to place graphemes in angle brackets, thus: ⟨. . .⟩.

• *allograph*: the realisation of the grapheme in writing. Replacement of one allograph by another realisation of the same grapheme does not change the meaning of the word; thus ⟪a, a, *a*, ɑ, ᵃ⟫ and ⟪*a*⟫ are all allographs. There seems to be no accepted notation, distinct from that used for the grapheme, for signalling allographs; I have used ⟪. . .⟫ here, but will otherwise not use a distinctive practice.

1.4 In addition to the distinctions between phoneme and allophone, grapheme and allograph just outlined, there are also of course additional realisational issues. Thus allophonic realisations will vary from speaker to speaker, and indeed within a speaker's repertoire of usage, in ways which are idiosyncratic and may well vary depending on the particular circumstances of an utterance, e.g. the formality of a situation. And personal idiosyncrasies in forming graphemes are also relevant, especially when the writing-system is produced by scribes rather than printers; paleographers, scholars who are interested in the history and classification of ancient scripts, have sometimes distinguished between *script* (i.e. the set of allographs used in handwriting equating to a particular font in printing) and *hand*, the idiosyncratic set of forms used by an individual in aiming at a particular script. The way in which I write ⟨a⟩ will differ from the way in which you write ⟨a⟩, even if we have been taught by the same teacher and model our handwriting on the same script. Those persons interested in the detection of the same handwriting in different documents, e.g. some forensic scientists, seek a 'scribal fingerprint', whereby the precise way in which a script is written may be described. The problem is of course much less acute in printing, though the appearance of the same fonts may differ in printed form depending on the quality of the reproductive process.

1.5 Letters and letter-clusters in the written mode map onto sounds in speech, though obviously there is not necessarily a one-to-one mapping between writing and speech, cf. the sound-equivalent of ⟨y⟩ in Present-Day English **yacht** and **many**. Broadly speaking, written languages are either *phonographic*, where there is a mapping (however conventional) between grapheme and phoneme, or *logographic*, where there is a mapping between a conventional symbol and a word or morpheme (for *word, morpheme* see ch. 3).

1.6 The boundary between these different systems is of course not clear-cut. A truly logographic system is that used for representing mathematics; symbols such as ⟨8⟩ or ⟨=⟩ map onto a set of notions whose spoken expression varies widely from language to language (thus ⟨8⟩ is **eight** in English, **otto** in Italian, **kahdeksan** in Finnish). The logographic-phonographic cline is, with natural languages, more nuanced. Towards the logographic end of the scale is Chinese, whose convention-alised characters derive ultimately from pictorial representations of certain key concrete concepts, though this practice was rapidly modified to deal with more abstract notions. Present-Day English, despite its various conventionalisations, is by comparison broadly phonographic; Older Scots writing systems were even more so.

1.7 In an ideal phonographic system, phonemes map onto graphemes; allophonic representation in a writing-system would be uneconomical and communicatively inefficient. Of course, as in all human institutions, ideal phonographic systems do not exist; since they are designed to give permanence to something as dynamic and ever-changing as human language, historical residualisms and conventionalisations are to be expected.

1.8 Languages have *inventories* of phonemes; distinctions between phonemic inventories are matters of *accent*. It is usual, in discussing phonemic inventories, to identify (a) *vowels* and (b) *consonants*. Vowels may be defined as those segments of sound where the airstream from the lungs does not give rise to audible friction, or is not prevented from escaping through the mouth; all other sound-segments are consonants. Groups of sound-segments may be formed into (c) *syllables*.

1.9 *Vowels* may be defined as either *monophthongs* or *diphthongs*. Diphthongs are vowel-clusters with a glide from one vowel to another, as in most Present-Day English pronunciations of **doubt**; monophthongs are so-called 'pure' vowels without any change in that vowel's quality in its duration, as in most Present-Day English pronunciations of **soup**. Different vowels are made by a combination of the following procedures: raising and lowering the tongue; pushing the tongue forward or dragging it back; opening the mouth or making it less open; rounding or unrounding the lips. It is usual to define a vowel with reference to the positioning of the highest point of the tongue combined with the presence or absence of lip-rounding. Vowels can thus be classified as follows:

• as *close, mid* (*mid-close* and *mid-open*), *open* (with reference to the height of the tongue and the degree of openness of the mouth);

• as *front, centre* or *back* (with reference to the positioning of the highest point of the tongue in relation to the front, centre or back of the mouth);

• as *rounded* or *unrounded* (with reference to whether or not the lips are rounded). Thus, in most Present-Day English and Scots accents, the vowel in **feel** is close front unrounded, symbolised in the IPA by [i]; the vowel in **fat** is open front unrounded, symbolised by [a]; and the vowel in **more** is back mid-open rounded, symbolised by [ɔ].

1.10 The following are the common monophthongs relevant for the study of Older Scots. Each IPA symbol is accompanied by a Present-Day English *keyword*; the underlined letter in the keyword corresponds to the sound symbolised. The pronunciation symbolised is for the most part that of many modern Scottish speakers.

i	see	e	say
ɪ	pin	ɛ	pen
a	sat	u	fool
o	coat	ʌ	pun
ə	about*	y	tu†
ɔ	cot	ø	work*

* = as pronounced by a Southern British English speaker who is 'non-rhotic' (i.e. does not pronounce ⟨r⟩ in **clerk, bar, farm** etc.)

† = French 'you' (sg.)

1.11 Diphthongs might be conveniently thought of as clusters of two monophthongs, e.g. in **why** /ʍʌɪ/. If the first element in the diphthong is more prominent, as in **pride**, then it usual to refer to the diphthong as *falling*; when the second element is more prominent, as in the Scandinavian name **Bjorn**, then the diphthong is referred to as *rising*.

1.12 *Consonants* are made by a combination of the following procedures: bringing one of the organs of the vocal tract (e.g. teeth, lips, tongue) into contact or very near proximity with another; varying the nature of the contact between the organs of the vocal tract, such as allowing a small explosion of air to escape as the organs part (*plosive*, e.g. **b** in **bat**) or allowing a small quantity of air to pass between them, producing a hissing sound (*fricative*, e.g. **s** in **sat**); vibrating or opening the *vocal folds* or (an older term) *vocal cords*, a pair of membranes housed in the *larynx*, an organ in the windpipe (*trachea*) through which air passes on its way from the lungs to the mouth. Consonants can thus be classified with reference to the following:

• the *place of articulation*, with reference to the lips, teeth, *alveolar ridge* (the ridge of cartilage behind the top teeth), the hard *palate* ('roof of the mouth'), and the soft palate or *velum*;

• the *manner of articulation*, such as fricative or plosive, but also including *nasals*, where the airstream is diverted to emerge through the nostrils, e.g. **m** in **mat**), *laterals*, where a partial closure is made in the mouth but air allowed to escape around it (e.g. **l** in **lap**), and *approximants*, *trills* and *taps*. *Affricates* may be defined as units that begin with plosives and end as fricatives, e.g. **ch** in **chat**.

• the *state of the vocal folds*; if the vocal folds are vibrating then a sound is referred to as *voiced* (e.g. **z** in **zoo**), but if the vocal folds are relaxed a sound is *voiceless* (e.g. **s** in **sue**).

1.13 The following list of consonantal phonetic symbols especially relevant for the study of Older Scots consonants also employs IPA notation. As with the discussion of vowels above, each symbol is accompanied by a keyword; the underlined letter in the keyword corresponds to the sound symbolised. The pronunciation symbolised is again that of many modern Scottish speakers, although in most cases these pronunciations are also common to speakers of many varieties of English.

b	bat	p	pat
v	vat	f	fat
θ	thin	ð	that
t	tip	d	dip
s	sip	z	zip
ʃ	ship	ʒ	treasure

r	*r*ip	l	*l*ip
x	lo*ch*	ʧ	*ch*ild
ʤ	*j*am	m	*m*at
n	*n*ip	ŋ	si*ng*
w	*w*eb	ʍ	*wh*isky
j	*y*ard		

1.14 In addition, Older Scots had two additional consonants not found in Present-Day use, viz. *n-mouillé* /ɲ/ and *l-mouillé* /ʎ/ in words of French and Gaelic origin, e.g. **cunʒe** 'coin' (vb.) (Old French **cungner**), **ganʒe** 'arrow' (Gaelic **gainne**), **bailʒie** 'baillie' (Old French **baillie**), **spuilʒie** 'spoil' (Old French **espoillier**), **assoilʒe** 'assail' (Old French **asaillir**). *N*-mouillé is still found in French, e.g. the French pronunciation of ⟨gn⟩ in si**gn**e 'sign'; *l*-mouillé is still heard in the Italian pronunciation of –**gl**–, as in ta**gl**iatelle '(kind of) pasta'. As these words were assimilated into Scots they lost their French/Gaelic pronunciations and more common, if phonetically similar, usages were adopted; thus these two sounds were later replaced by /nj, ŋj, ŋ/ and /lj/ respectively (see 2.10 below).

1.15 Groups of vowels and consonants make up *syllables*. A syllable in English prototypically consists of a vowel, sometimes referred to as the *peak* of the syllable, which may be preceded and/or followed by consonants; a consonant which precedes the vowel is known as the *onset*, while a following consonant is the *coda*. Thus, in a Present-Day English word such as **meat**, **m** /m/ is the onset, **ea** /i/ is the peak, and **t** /t/ is the coda; the combination of peak and coda is known as the *rhyme*. Syllables may be *light* (with rhymes consisting of V, VV or VC, where V = any vowel and C = any consonant), or *heavy* (with rhymes consisting of VVC, VCC), or *superheavy* (with rhymes consisting of VVCC). Many handbooks refer to light syllables as *short* syllables and heavy syllables as *long* syllables. The issue of syllable-*boundaries* is sometimes a controversial one, in that where one syllable ends and another begins can be difficult to determine if a precise boundary is sought; but distinguishing such boundaries is fairly easy in perceptual terms (for a convenient illustration of syllable-boundaries using sound-spectrograms, see Ladefoged 2001: 170).

1.16 Scholars commonly discuss the short/long distinction in terms of *morae* 'beats' (singular *mora*). A short consonant consists of a single mora, C; a long consonant consists of two morae, CC. A short vowel consists of a single mora, V, while diphthongs and long vowels consist of two morae, VV, as do sequences such as VC, CV etc. In some varieties, short/long distinctions are meaningful. Thus, in Present-Day spoken Scots and Scottish Standard English, the distinction in meaning between **brood** (with /u/, i.e. V) and **brewed** (with /uː/, i.e. VV) is indicated by length (see further 2.9 below).

1.17 Syllables may be *stressed* or *unstressed*. Stress is to do with the assignment of prominence to a particular syllable. A prominent, or stressed, syllable, may be louder, or longer, or distinct in pitch, or may manifest any combination of these features; thus, in many varieties of English, where a stressed syllable is louder, longer and higher in pitch than an unstressed syllable. Thus, in the word **booklet**, the syllable represented in writing as **book** is more prominent than the syllable represented by **let**: **book**– is stressed, –**let** is unstressed. Syllables and stress are phenomena at a 'higher' analytic level than segments; the standard handbooks therefore refer to them as *suprasegmental* features.

1.18 As well as speech-systems, languages have writing-systems. In phonographic languages (see 1.5 above), these writing-systems are generally known as *alphabets*, after the first two letters of the Greek alphabet; other terms for such systems include *futhark*, after the first six letters of the Germanic system of runic writing. The theorising of alphabets has received less attention than that applied to speech-systems, but a set of categories parallel to those for speech can be fairly easily established (see further Sampson 1985).

1.19 An alphabet represents the graphological inventory of a language, i.e. the set of graphemes used. As pointed out in 1.3 above, realisations of graphemes, i.e. allographs, can be related in printing to particular *fonts*, e.g. Arial, Times New Roman, Verdana etc.; in some fonts, choice of allograph depends on the positioning of the allograph in relation to others. Thus, for instance, capital letters are generally employed at the beginning of sentences, while in certain eighteenth-century fonts so-called 'long-s' occurs in initial position or as the first element in ⟨ss⟩; cf. Present-Day German ß in **fuß** 'foot' = **fuss**. The equivalent to the font in handwriting is the *script*, i.e. the set of letters which is aimed at by a scribe, e.g. *textura, court-hand, secretary, italic, round-hand*. The last of these scripts, the 'clerks' script' of the eighteenth and nineteenth centuries, is the basis for most modern handwriting in English. Court-hand, secretary and round-hand are cursive (i.e. 'joined-up') scripts; textura and italic are non-cursive display scripts. A scribe's individual realisation of a script is known as a *hand*.

The script/hand distinction made here is in accordance with the useful discussion in Parkes 1979: xxvi. It should be noted that not all *palaeographers* – students of older handwriting – make this distinction.

1.20 The equivalent in writing-systems to the suprasegmentals of speech is punctuation, in which may be included word-division and issues to do with the distribution of upper-case (sometimes known as *litterae notabiliores* 'more noticeable letters') and lower-case letters. Present-Day English punctuation is essentially grammatical, based on the analysis of grammatical structure and designed to help readers, but throughout its history punctuation has also had a 'rhetorical' function, correlating with the elocutionary needs of those reading aloud.

The terms *upper-* and *lower-case* relate to the frame or cupboard in which compositors traditionally keep their type; the upper case contains capitals etc.

1.21 The role of punctuation has thus changed over time, these changes relating to changing patterns of literacy. In antiquity, writing functioned as secondary to speech, i.e. as a record of what had been spoken and as an *aide-memoire* for subsequent performance. The transition from this state of affairs to the present day, when the written mode is a primary means of communication, means a change in what might be termed the pragmatics of writing, i.e. how writing functioned, and this change had an implication for practices of punctuation.

1.22 The primary purpose of punctuation 'is to resolve structural uncertainties in a text, and to signal nuances of semantic significance which might otherwise not be conveyed at all, or would at best be much more difficult for a reader to figure out' (Parkes 1992: 1). During periods of *intensive literacy* when the primary role of the written text was to support speech and when readers would encounter a few texts a great deal, the need for comprehensive punctuation was less urgent; readers would know their way round the text, and would remember how the text was to be performed. During periods of *extensive literacy*, however, when readers regularly encounter texts which are new to them and which they encounter for the first time with eye rather than ear, the role of punctuation to resolve uncertainties becomes much more important.

1.23 Conditions of literacy during the Older Scots period were at a transitional stage. The Reformation made literacy – for study of the vernacular Bible – a duty, and the use of written texts for the purposes of religious controversy encouraged extensive reading, which was itself facilitated through the transition from script to print; as has often been pointed out, printing succeeded because of demand for its products rather than because of supply-side technological innovation. Thus it may be noted that, in the texts supplied in this book, a wide range of practices of punctuation are used. These practices reflect the potential tension between grammatical and rhetorical approaches to punctuation: is the primary role of punctuation to identify the grammatical boundaries of large meaning-units, i.e. *sententiae* (later 'sentences'), and the sub-units of which sententiae were composed, or is it to reflect the rhetorical *periodus* ('period'), i.e. the unit of oral delivery, flagging a closer relationship between writing and speech during the Older Scots period than obtains in present-day conditions?

1.24 In the transition from script to print – which should be seen as a gradual rather than sudden process – more standardised practices of punctuation emerged in Scottish texts as they were disseminated along with fonts. These practices remain even now culture-specific; a book published in Present-Day French or German or Spanish 'looks' very different in terms of its handling of punctuation and litterae notabiliores than one published in English, even though in historical terms these languages are comparatively close in comparison with, say, English and Chinese, or English and Arabic. Obvious changes, visible in the texts in Part II, include the replacement of the *virgule* (/) with the comma and the introduction of the semi-colon to flag a balance between two units of equal position in grammatical hierarchy (the colon developed a new, more limited function, though even now some older present-day writers occasionally use it in place of the semi-colon). Later on, inverted commas, used to mark the reproduction of direct speech, replaced the old *diple* (⟩) which had become used on occasion during the Middle Ages to mark citations from the scriptures, while apostrophes were introduced to indicate a sound which was perceived to have been omitted, however erroneously in historical terms (thus the use of the apostrophe in, e.g. **John's**, where the inflexion in –s was perceived to be an abbreviation for **his**).

1.25 However, continuities in practices of punctuation are as noticeable as the innovations, and even now children are taught to use punctuation in school with reference to speech as well as writing: thus the old saying that a comma may be used to mark when one pauses for breath. Such practices were encouraged by the emergence of *elocutionist* teaching during the so-called 'reading revolution' of the eighteenth century, which saw punctuation as an aid to formal declamation, valued by the Augustans of the eighteenth century as a reflection of their admired classical models (see further Parkes 1992; see also Jajdelska 2007).

2. Older Scots sounds and spellings: an overview

2.0 The evidence for writing in Older Scots is direct: the manuscript and printed materials which survive, and which were described in ch. 1. Most Older Scots manuscripts are written in varieties of court-hand and secretary script, also regularly used for documents; since many Scottish scribes copying literary manuscripts had training in copying documents this correlation is not surprising.

For further details with a full history, see Simpson 1998 and references there cited; see also Parkes 1979. For links to illustrations of various handwritings, with references, see Part III, Bibliography.

2.1 The earliest printed texts in Older Scots, those produced by Walter Chepman and Andrew Myllar in the Cowgate in Edinburgh in 1508–9, are printed in a so-called 'Gothic' or *black-letter* font, based on the textura script found in manuscripts; this font had already been used by other early printers such as Johannes Gutenberg and William Caxton. Black-letter continued to be used in some German books (until banned for general printing by the Nazis in 1941); however, it died out in the rest of Europe from the late fifteenth century onwards, where it was replaced by the simpler (and less fragile) 'roman' type, so-called because it was believed to have been an ancient Roman usage. Black-letter was retained, interestingly, in some Scottish books where it had an antiquarian function; thus, for instance, seventeenth-century editions of Barbour's *Bruce* were regularly printed in black-letter, although the accompanying elements of apparatus (introductions, glossaries, running-heads) were generally printed in roman fonts.

2.2 For speech, however, the evidence is indirect. Students of present-day languages have of course a major advantage: they have direct access to informants, and can choose their informants to map onto a variety of social/cultural groupings. Until the invention of mechanical and electronic means of recording, however, it was not possible to capture the transient nature of speech in a permanent or semi-permanent form, and as a result we have no direct access to speech from the period before the end of the nineteenth century.

2.3 Instead, we have to make do with the partial information which reaches us indirectly. For Older Scots pronunciation, the following resources are available, all of which may be regarded as of complementary value:

• The evidence supplied by *residualisms* in Present-Day Scots accents. Some varieties of Present-Day Scots are more conservative in pronunciation than others. For instance, there are characteristics of North-Eastern Scots accents which seem to reflect a more archaic usage than, say, that of the modern Central Belt.

• The evidence supplied by *older commentators* on Scots and Scottish English. A very great deal of evidence survives for the period from 1700 (see Jones 1991); before that date there is comparatively little evidence for Scottish usage. Some hints are to be found about Scottish pronunciation by writers whose main focus is on 'correct' English (see further Dobson 1968). Of these pre-1700 witnesses, perhaps the most valuable is Alexander Hume, a Scotsman who moved as a schoolmaster to Bath in England in 1592 (not to be confused with the poet Alexander Hume, who died in 1609). Hume subsequently returned to Scotland, first as Rector of Edinburgh High School in succession to the splendidly named Hercules Rollock (now best-known as the composer of verses prefixed to James VI's *Essays of a Prentise in the Divine Art of Poesie*), and subsequently as headmaster of the new grammar school at Prestonpans. He ended his academic career as Master of Dunbar Grammar School. Hume composed *Of the Orthographie and Congruitie of the Britan Tongue*, probably in or just after 1617, dedicating the work to James VI and I; it possibly dates from the time when Hume delivered a Latin address to James when the king visited Scotland in that year. The work survives in a single manuscript (MS London, British Library, Royal 17.A.xi); it was only printed in the middle of the nineteenth century (Wheatley 1865).

• The evidence supplied through *the analysis of verse*, viz. practices of rhyme, alliteration and metre, based on the assumption – which is occasionally challenged by scholars – that Older Scots poets attempted to reflect accurately the patterns of contemporary speech in their verse. Very occasionally, imaginative authors represent particular accents in literary works; these representations can have some value.

• The evidence supplied through *the analysis of spellings* in manuscripts and early printed books, based on the assumption that Older Scots was in essentials a phonographic language.

• The evidence supplied through *reconstruction*, whereby comparison with other closely related (*cognate*, from Latin **co** + **gnātus** 'born together') varieties of language, or of varieties within the one language, can result in the reconstruction of the accent of some common ancestor.

2.4 None of these resources may be used without qualification, but taken in combination they allow us to have a pretty good understanding of how Older Scots was pronounced, and how these pronunciations related to Older Scots spelling. Present-Day English, even with its various conventionalisations, is broadly phonographic in comparison with languages such as modern Chinese, and it is generally accepted by scholars that Older Scots was even more phonographic.

For an outline of Older Scots pronunciation, see in the first place Macafee 2002 and references there cited, supplemented by Aitken 2002. For a history of Scots spelling, see again Macafee 2002; see also Agutter 1987, for a discussion of the taxonomy of Older Scots spelling, and Kniezsa 1997 for a thorough historical account.

2.5 The inventories of Older Scots phonemes and graphemes were essentially the same as Present-Day Scots. Most Older Scots *consonants* have identical values of pronunciation to those of Present-Day English, although they are distributed rather differently in the lexicon and there are some usages which no longer survive in Present-Day English, e.g. /x/, which disappeared in England gradually during the Middle Ages and Early Modern periods, but is retained in Scots (although even there the sound is under pressure; many younger speakers of Scots have /k/ in place of /x/). The most important difference from Present-Day Scots is that there are almost no 'silent' consonants. As evidenced by alliterative practice in verse, the initial consonants in ⟨kn, gn, wl, wr⟩ were all pronounced, e.g. **knicht** 'knight' was pronounced /knɪxt/. An exception to this rule is final ⟨-t⟩ in **witht** 'with' etc., which is not pronounced (see Smith 1902: xxvii); forms ending in ⟨-tht⟩ are common in the Acts of Parliament before 1500, and then diffuse into other genres (see Macafee 2002: cxxiv and references there cited).

2.6 Older Scots used two letters we no longer use, viz. *thorn* and *yogh*, which mapped onto the sounds /θ, ð/ and [j] respectively. These letters derive from the Anglo-Saxon period.

2.7 Yogh originated in the written realisations of [g] and [j] used in manuscripts written in the British Isles between roughly 600 and 1100; when scribes wrote Old English, they reflected these 'powers' in writing through the 'figure' ⟨ȝ⟩. During the transition from Old English to Middle English and Older Scots, ⟨ȝ⟩ was replaced by ⟨g⟩ (for [g]) and by ⟨ʒ⟩ (for [j, x]). The figure ⟨g⟩ was known in Anglo-Saxon times, but used only in copying Latin; ⟨ʒ⟩, used in copying French as an alternative figure for ⟨z⟩, was adopted to replace ⟨ȝ⟩. ⟨ʒ⟩ was also used for /z/, as it still is in many varieties of modern handwriting.

2.8 Thorn was an ancient runic letter, derived from the ancient Germanic alphabetic system used for inscriptions. In Old English scripts, it was written thus ⟨þ⟩, and it was retained in this form in southern varieties of written Middle English. In northern Middle English, and in almost all varieties of Older Scots, thorn was written indistinguishably from the letter 'y', as ⟨y⟩. In many varieties of English and Scots it was used interchangeably with ⟨th⟩. The only varieties of Scots in which 'thorn' and 'y' are distinguished as figurae are, according to Benskin (1977: 507), 'in texts from the Scots periphery, Dumbarton and Glasgow'. An exception is the early Scone Glosses (see Text 1(a)), where an attempt is made to distinguish thorn and 'y' by using a superposed dot to mark the latter; however, misplacement of the dot in the Scone Glosses is fairly frequent and suggests that the distinction was breaking down. A distinction is also found in the Arch. Selden. manuscript of *The Kingis Quair*, although there thorn and ⟨y⟩ alternate in a very restricted set of words (see Text 4(b)). Benskin notes that ⟨y⟩ for thorn 'is restricted to word-initial voiced contexts' (i.e. as in Present-Day English, high-frequency members of the closed-class parts of speech, e.g. **they**, **then**, **there**) except for 'medial contexts which are immediately followed by a suspension [i.e. a kind of mark of abbreviation]'; else-where ⟨th⟩ was used. Eventually, ⟨th⟩ was adopted in all positions. There are one or two oddities, e.g. John Knox's habit of using ⟨ht⟩ in place of ⟨th⟩ in **pleaseht** 'pleases' (see Text 2(g)), or Marion Home's use of ⟨tht⟩ in **batht** 'both' (see Text 2(f)).

2.9 The early printers of the late fifteenth century, who imported their fonts from abroad, replaced thorn and yogh with ⟨y⟩ and ⟨z⟩ respectively, e.g. in **ye** 'the' and the personal name **Menzies** (traditionally pronounced [mɪŋɪz], but see 2.10 below). Both ⟨y⟩ (for thorn) and yogh are sometimes followed by ⟨h⟩, e.g. **yhow** 'thou', **ʒheris** 'years'.

2.10 Other consonantal features to note are as follows:

• ⟨quh⟩ for Present-Day English ⟨wh⟩, e.g. **quhen** 'when'; other spellings include ⟨qw(h), qh, qhu, qhw⟩. There is some evidence, provided by Alexander Hume in the seventeenth century, that ⟨quh⟩ was pronounced as /xʍ/ rather than, as in Present-Day Scots, /ʍ/.

• ⟨g⟩ can be used for /dʒ/ as well as /g/, e.g. **hege** 'hedge'. In words borrowed from French, ⟨g⟩ could signify /dʒ/, e.g. words ending in ⟨-age⟩.

• ⟨c⟩ and ⟨k⟩ are used in **callit** 'called', **knokyt** 'knocked'. ⟨c⟩ can also be used for /s/ in **certane, Bruce**.

• ⟨ch⟩ can be used for /tʃ/, as in **wich** 'witch', as well as /x/, as in **loch**. This usage seems to derive from traditions established in late Old Northumbrian (see Kniezsa 1997). ⟨ch⟩ is also used where Present-Day English uses ⟨gh⟩, e.g. **knicht** 'knight', **taucht** 'taught'

• Older Scots tends to use ⟨k⟩ (= /k/) where English has ⟨ch⟩ (= /tʃ/), e.g. **kirk, sic** cf. English **church, such**. The reason for this difference is that forms such as **kirk,**

though cognate with **church**, have a distinct etymology, being derived from Norse.
- Older Scots generally (although not invariably) uses ⟨sch⟩ instead of ⟨sh⟩ for /ʃ/ in words like **scho** 'she', **flesch** 'meat, flesh'. ⟨sch⟩ was also common in Middle English, especially in northern varieties, but it was retained in Older Scots after it was replaced by ⟨sh⟩ in English.

sall, suld (with initial /s/) correspond to English **shall, should**; see further ch. 3 below.

- ⟨f⟩ is often (though not always) used where Present-Day English has ⟨v⟩, e.g. **luf(e)** 'love', **gif** 'give', **gaf** 'gave', **haf** 'have', beside **gaue** etc. Sometimes the final consonant is doubled, e.g. **giff** 'give', **luff** 'love', **affter** 'after'. It seems that such spellings reflect a final voiceless sound, /f/ rather than /v/, contrasting with the common voiced fricative sound /v/ found in southern English from the medieval period onwards.
- It seems likely from the rhyming evidence that final –s in (e.g.) **stanis** 'stones' was pronounced voiceless. Initial /z/ is very rare in Older Scots, and is found only in loanwords, e.g. **zele** 'zeal' (from Old French **zel**), **zodiak(e)** 'zodiac' (from Old French **zodiaque**). The phonological distinction /s, z/ was therefore marginal in Older Scots.
- ⟨u, v, w⟩ were often interchangeable (see also 2.11 below), with ⟨v⟩ and ⟨w⟩ (less commonly ⟨u⟩) used in initial position in a word and ⟨u⟩ (less commonly ⟨v, w⟩) medially, thus **vpon, wpon, uppon** 'upon', **deuill, dewyll, devyl** 'devil', **heuie** 'heavy', **awys** 'advice' (from French **avis** rather than, as in Present-Day English, with the Latin prefix ad-) . An Older Scots sound-change meant that medial ⟨u, v, w⟩ representing /v/ was becoming rare; see 2.14 below. The interchangeability of ⟨u, v, w⟩ can also be derived from Old Northumbrian practices (see Kniezsa 1997). The form ⟨vv⟩ is occasionally used instead of ⟨w⟩.
- ⟨nȝ, ngȝ, ng, nyh⟩ seems to have developed the power /ɲ/ (*n-mouillé*), later /nj, ŋj/ and even /ŋ/ in Older Scots in certain words derived from French or Gaelic, e.g. **fenȝeit** 'pretended, feigned'. The figures ⟨nz⟩ in **Menzies** (see 2.9 above) were originally pronounced as n-*mouillé*.
- ⟨lȝ, lȝh, hlȝ, ly⟩ were pronounced /ʎ/ (*l-mouillé*), later /lj/, in Older Scots, again in words derived from French or Gaelic, e.g. **bailȝe** 'bailiff, baillie'.

2.11 Older Scots distinguished between *long* and *short* vowels, though the distinction was beginning to break down at the phonological level. Phonological distinctions of length are no longer made in many varieties of English, but some length-distinctions remain in varieties of Scots, including Ulster Scots, e.g. the distinctions between the vowels in **brewed** and **brood**, or between the stressed vowels in **agreed** and **greed**. The –**d** in **brewed** and **agreed** represents an inflexional ending, and Present-Day Scots has a rule whereby the stressed vowel is lengthened in such environments: the Scottish Vowel-Length Rule (see further Aitken 1981b). The Scottish Vowel-Length Rule is found throughout the Scots-speaking area of Scotland, and also in parts of Northern Ireland; it seems to date from the sixteenth century.

The Scottish Vowel Length Rule (SVLR), sometimes called after the scholar who first formulated it as 'Aitken's Law', is a process whereby length was sustained as a phonological distinction although it originated as an 'essentially allophonic' rule (Aitken 2002: 124–5). The minimal pair **brewed: brood** suggests that length remains phonemic in Scots and Scottish English, but it has been argued that the length-distinction remains 'essentially allophonic', caused by particular environments. Indeed, Aitken (2002: 125) argues that SVLR is essentially a *shortening* rule, whereby vowels shorten in the environment of following /l, m, n, b, d, g, dʒ/, while in other environments length is sustained. It will be noted that in Scots Present-Day English –ed is reflected prototypically as –it, and this fact may be part of the conditioning process. See also Collinge 1985: 3–6 and references there cited, and for further discussion of the theoretical implications see McMahon 2000.

2.12 The study of Older Scots vowels has been massively enhanced by the publication of Aitken 2002, which may be regarded as authoritative. The following account is based on Aitken's survey, with one or two modifications.

I have given references in footnotes to Aitken's special vowel-numbering system, useful for those who wish to follow the development of particular vowels throughout the history of Scots. Aitken numbered historic long vowels 1 through 7, diphthongs 8 through 14, and short vowels 15 through 19. See Aitken 2002: 3 and *passim*.

2.13 The historic *short vowels* of Older Scots have barely changed to this day. They were /ɪ, ɛ, a, ɔ/ and /u/, usually reflected by the figures ⟨i, e, a, o, u⟩ respectively. (The sound [ʌ] as in Present-Day southern English **bud** was not used in Older Scots.)

These vowels were numbered by Aitken as follows:

> Vowel 15: /ɪ/
> Vowel 16: /ɛ/
> Vowel 17: /a/
> Vowel 18: /ɔ/
> Vowel 19: /u/

2.14 Occasionally, however, different spellings were used. Thus ⟨y⟩ is used for ⟨i⟩, especially in the neighbourhood of ⟨m, n, u⟩. The reason is to do with medieval handwriting. ⟨i, m, n, u⟩ could appear as ⟨ɪ, ɪɪɪ, ɪɪ, ɪɪ⟩ respectively, and a word like 'minimum' could therefore in theory be written ⟨ɪɪɪɪɪɪɪɪɪɪɪɪɪ⟩. The stroke ɪ is known, appropriately, as a *minim*. This usage was obviously confusing in a number of environments, and a number of graphic strategies were adopted to avoid the use of minims. ⟨y⟩ was used as a substitute graph for ⟨i⟩ in some positions, notably when it is the last letter in a word. ⟨o⟩ is occasionally used for ⟨u⟩ in similar circumstances, e.g. **come** 'come' (alongside more commonly attested **cum(e)**, **cwm**, **cumpany** etc.). ⟨u, v, w⟩ were also interchangeable; see 2.10 above. Short vowels are often followed by double consonants, e.g. **sitt**, **legg**.

2.15 The *long vowels* of Older Scots present a few more problems. Old Anglian, the variety of Old English from which Older Scots primarily descended, seems to have had what linguists call a 'three-height' long-vowel system, with two close vowels, (front ī /iː/ and back ū /uː/), two mid-vowels (front ē /eː/ and back ō /oː/) and two open vowels (front ǣ /æː/ and back ā /ɑː/). For reasons much debated by philologists, but perhaps to do with interaction with Norse (see 2.26 below), the mid- and open back vowels underwent, it seems in the twelfth century, a sound-change known as 'fronting', whereby these vowels were shifted to the front series, i.e. /oː/ became /øː/ (a rounded front vowel) and /ɑː/ became /aː/. This change left a system consisting of the long front vowels /iː, eː, øː, æː, aː/ and a single long close rounded back vowel /uː/; /æː/ seems to have developed into /ɛː/, which eventually merged with /eː/. A few forms with a mid-rounded vowel, probably /ɔː/, emerged subsequently as the result of an unconnected lengthening of the short vowel /ɔ/. In Early Scots, therefore, there was a long-vowel system as follows: /iː, eː, øː, ɛː, aː, uː, ɔː/.

Aitken's numbering for these vowels is as follows:

    Vowel 1: /iː/
    Vowel 2: /eː/
    Vowel 3: /ɛː/
    Vowel 4: /aː/
    Vowel 5: /ɔː/
    Vowel 6: /uː/
    Vowel 7: /øː/

Students of Aitken 2002 will observe two modifications to his system, which deserve explanation, given Aitken's authoritative status. First, I use /ɔː/ for vowel 5, and not /oː/ with supposed /·/, which seems to me overly narrow a notational choice. More serious is my use of /øː/ for Vowel 7 rather than /yː/. My view is that /øː/ is likely to have been the early Scots form, which subsequently moved to /yː/; the distribution of /øː/ in Present-Day Scots accents suggests to me that /øː/ is a residualism of an older usage rather than a subsequent lowering. However, those readers not convinced by this view may wish to replace /øː/ with /yː/ throughout.

2.16 It will be noted that some of these long vowels were distinguished from their short equivalents only by length, viz. /iː, ɛː, aː, uː, ɔː/, corresponding, very roughly, to the short vowel system. Thus in the Early Scots pronunciations of **fire** (with /iː/), **ship** (with /ɪ/), the sounds spelt ⟨i⟩ were very similar in *quality* but differed in *quantity*. This simple pattern was disrupted at the end of the Middle Ages by a major sound-change known as the *Great Vowel Shift*, whereby long vowels were redistributed within the lexicon in an ordered way: thus, Early Scots [aː] > Middle Scots [eː], [eː] > [iː], [øː] > [yː], [iː] > [əɪ]. The Great Vowel Shift did not, in Scots and Northern England, affect the long back vowel /uː/; thus the modern Scots pronunciation of **house** /huːs/ retains the undiphthongised vowel of the pre-Great Vowel Shift period (cf. Southern English /haʌs/).

2.17 The Great Vowel Shift affected all varieties of English and Scots, but in different ways. The processes and effects of the Shift have often been described, but generally with reference to its development in Southern England where, it has been argued, it was the result of sociolinguistic interaction between varieties of London English.

2.18 The development of the Shift in Scots and in Northern English is different from that in Southern English. Whereas in the South all Middle English long vowels were affected, in the North, as we have seen, only front vowels underwent raising or diphthongisation. As a result, where Present-Day English has a diphthong in (e.g.) 'now', Present-Day Scots retains a monophthong in 'noo'; cf. Old English **nū** /nuː/. It seems probable that the Northern and Southern Shifts, though sharing some characteristics, may have been distinct processes whose outcomes were coincidentally similar. The distinction seems to derive from different inputs to the Shift in northern and southern varieties. In the North, mid- and low back vowels were fronted from the thirteenth century onwards, possibly as a result of interaction between more and less 'Norsified' English, and as a result the 'upward' pressure exerted by mid- and low back vowels in southern English could not be exerted in Scots and northern dialects. This Northern Fronting is a crucial input to the Great Vowel Shift in northern England and lowland Scotland; see also 2.22 below.

2.19 Paragraphs 2.15–2.18 offer, of course, a much abbreviated summary of some quite complicated developments. See further Aitken 1977 and 2002, Macafee 2002, and Smith 1996a, especially ch. 5; see also Kohler 1967. For some suggested explanations of the processes involved, see Smith 2007b: ch. 6 and references there cited.

2.20 In summary, the Middle Scots (i.e. post-Great Vowel Shift) long-vowel system, with corresponding figures, was as follows:

/iː/	⟨ei, ey⟩	e.g. **deid** 'deed'
/eː/	⟨a, ai/y⟩	e.g. **stane** 'stone', **haill** 'whole', **day** 'day'
/oː/	⟨o, oi/y⟩	e.g. **befoir** 'before'
/uː/	⟨ou, ow/v⟩	e.g. **toune** 'town'
/yː/	⟨ui, uy⟩	e.g. **guid** 'good'

2.21 Older Scots developed two ways of marking long vowels in orthography. One corresponds to that used in Present-Day English: the addition of 'silent e' in words like **stane** /steːn/ 'stone', **gude** 'good'. The other is found only in Scots and Northern Middle English: the addition of ⟨i⟩ after the vowel in question, e.g. **deid** /diːd/ 'deed', **guid** /gyːd/ 'good' (see Kniezsa 1989 and references there cited, also Kniezsa 1997), and seems to have spread into Older Scots from northern England. In the environment of a following ⟨ld⟩ Old English ā is, in later texts, reflected as ⟨au⟩, cf. **auld** 'old' (Kniezsa 1997: 37).

2.22 Two minor features of Older Scots should be mentioned here: *l-vocalisation* and *v-deletion*. L-vocalisation is a source of long vowels in Middle Scots, e.g. for Early Scots /ul/, Middle Scots has /uː/, cf. Early Scots **ful**, Middle Scots **fow** /fuː/. It will be observed that the /l/ has disappeared and that the /u/ has lengthened to compensate for this loss. So-called 'back-spellings' with 'silent l' added also appear, e.g. **chalmer** 'chamber' (from French **chambre**). V-deletion (i.e. the dropping of /v/ with compensatory lengthening of the vowel) is exemplified by spellings such as **deill** /diːl/ 'devil'. Both features are common in Scots after *c.* 1450.

2.23 Unstressed vowels (i.e. vowels in unstressed syllables) are often, especially in Middle Scots, spelt ⟨i, y⟩, pronounced /ɪ/, e.g. **stanis** /steːnɪs/ 'stones', **matteris** 'matters' etc., though ⟨e⟩ is fairly common in Early Scots, e.g. **lettres** 'letters'. It may be noted that, in contrast with Middle English, final e in Middle Scots is often a silent diacritic indicating length of the preceding vowel (see 2.21 above). In words of French origin it retains the pronunciation of the parent language, viz. /eː/, e.g. **pite** 'pity' /pɪteː/; however, final e is also commonly simply a flourish with no sound-equivalent, as in **flesche** 'flesh'.

2.24 The Middle Scots (i.e. post-Great Vowel Shift) *diphthongs* were as follows:

/əɪ/ ⟨i, y⟩ e.g. **ch*i*ld** 'child' (derived from Early Scots /iː/ through the Great Vowel Shift)

/ɔɪ, uɪ/ ⟨oy, oi⟩ e.g. **io*y*e** 'joy', **po*y*nt** 'point'.

The distribution of these last two sounds in the lexicon is hard to determine; both diphthongs are found in loanwords from French, as in the case of **ioye, poynt**. That the diphthongs eventually merged is obvious from their modern pronunciation, viz. /ɔɪ/, and it seems likely that there was fairly free variation between the two pronunciations throughout the Middle Scots period.

/ɔu/ ⟨ou⟩ e.g. *four* 'four'.

/ɛu/ ⟨ew, eu⟩ e.g. **newe** 'new', **yneuch** 'enough'

Aitken's numberings for the Early Scots diphthongs are as follows:

Vowel 8: /aɪ/
Vowel 9: /ɔɪ/
Vowel 10: /uɪ/
Vowel 11: /eɪ/
Vowel 12: /au/
Vowel 13: /ɔu/
Vowel 14a: /iu/
Vowel 14b: /ɛu, ɛɔu/

I have again replaced Aitken's /o/ with subposed /·/ by /ɔ/; I have also replaced Aitken's /i/ as the second element in Vowels 8 through 11 with what seems to me as likely to be the more accurate /ɪ/. Vowels 9 and 10 seem to have merged on /ɔɪ/, and have in this form been retained to the present day. Vowel 11 merged with the long Vowel 2 and thus disappeared. Vowel 8 seems to have disappeared as a distinct phoneme, having merged with long Vowel 4, as does Vowel 12. Vowel 13 was retained, while Vowels 14a and 14b merged on /ɛu/.

2.25 Finally, and as may be noted from discussion so far, the distribution of vowels in Middle Scots differs in a few instances from that in Middle English, especially in the long vowels. Notable are:

• Where southern Middle English had ⟨o(o)⟩ /ɔ:/, Older Scots and Northern Middle English had ⟨aCe⟩, ⟨a(i)⟩, ⟨au⟩ /a:/, e.g. **stane** 'stone', **nane** 'none', **swa** 'so', **baith** 'both', **lang** 'long', **haill** 'whole, healthy', **maist** 'most', **auld** 'old', cf. Middle English **stoon, lord, so, bo(o)th, long(e), hole, mo(o)st**. Such words contain the reflex of Old English/Old Norse ā/á, which was fronted to /a:/ in Pre-Scots and Northern English but was raised and rounded in Southern Middle English to /ɔ:/. Forms such as **laird** 'lord' are also found, though it is noticeable that in many texts it is replaced by the English form **lord**, even when the ⟨a⟩-form is retained in other 'Old English ā-words', possibly because this item was frequently used as a term of formal address (see, e.g., **ye Lord of Fournevalle** in text 2(a)).

In accordance with usual practice, long vowels in Norse are marked with an acute accent (e.g. á) rather than a macron (e.g. ā).

• Where southern Middle English had ⟨o(o)⟩ /o:/, Older Scots and Northern Middle English had /ø:/, subsequently /y:/, spelt ⟨uCe, ui⟩, e.g. **fute** 'foot', **guid** 'good' cf. Middle English **fote**. Such forms represent the reflex of Old English ō, fronted in Pre-Scots and Northern Middle English but retained as a close rounded mid-vowel in Southern Middle English.

2.26 Fronted reflexes of Old English ā and ō seem to correspond originally in dialectal distribution to the area settled most heavily by Norsemen, the so-called Great Scandinavian Belt, and it has therefore been argued that interaction between Norse and English produced this development.

See further Samuels 1989; see also Horobin and Smith 2002: 57; see also Britton 2002 and references there cited. However, recent research has suggested that this process of fronting may be related to Celtic/Old English interaction, see Laker 2010 and references there cited.

2.27 As the discussion offered in James VI's *Reulis and Cautelis* (Text 3(a)) shows, in general stressing patterns in Older Scots seem to have been similar to those found in contemporary Early Modern English, i.e. much as in Present-Day English. However, it seems likely that some polysyllabic words were differently stressed. The Yorkshireman Peter Levins's *Manipulus Vocabulorum* of 1570 records – using the acute accent to mark the vowels in stressed syllables – pronunciations such as **bárbarity** (cf. Present-Day English **barbárity**), **éxcusable** (cf. Present-Day English **excúsable**), **préferment** (cf. Present-Day English **preférment**), and it seems probable that similar pronunciations were found in nearly related varieties such as Scots. Alexander Hume (see Wheatley 1865: 22, see also Text 3(b) below) gives examples for the most part as in Present-Day English, e.g. **preténce**, **súbject**, **insátiable**, but does give **difficultie** (cf. Present-Day English **dífficulty**) (see Cercignani 1981: 31–44 and references there cited).

2.28 James VI's discussion of stress shows that he was well aware of the dominance of the monosyllable in core vocabulary, a feature of English and Scots since large-scale inflexional loss during the Middle English and pre-literary Scots periods: **Ze aucht lykewise to be war with oft composing zour haill lynis of monosyllabis only, (albeit our language haue sa many, as we can nocht weill eschewe it)** . . . (Text 3(a), cap. 1).

2.29 Practices of punctuation in Older Scots texts vary widely, but in general they tend to reflect rhetorical structures rather than grammatical ones, i.e. they distinguish rhetorical periods. Two symbols are commonly used in manuscripts: the *punctus* ('point', i.e. ⟨.⟩), and the *virgula* ('virgule', 'slash', i.e. ⟨/⟩); variants of the punctus include the *punctus elevatus* ⟨:⟩ and the *punctus interrogativus* ⟨?⟩. These symbols were replaced in print by the full-stop, comma, colon and question-mark respectively. Typically, the punctus marked the end of a rhetorical period, the virgula a pause relating to a shift in phrase-structure within the period, and the punctus elevatus indicating typically a semantic/syntactic relationship between the two elements linked by it. There were also combinations of units, which were developed often idiosyncratically to reflect gradations of pause in oral delivery; and many scribes used litterae notabiliores in combination with these usages, or indeed instead of them. However, it should be noted that there was a good deal of variation in practices of punctuation, and many texts, e.g. verse, frequently had no punctuation at all as we would understand it.

2.30 The reason for this tension between rhetorical and grammatical approaches to punctuation clearly lies in contemporary conditions of literacy. Speech still had what might be termed 'performative primacy' during the medieval period, with the written mode having a secondary role of record; documents, letters and (broadly conceived) literary works seem to have been conceived of as recording utterances whose first instantiation was conceived of as being spoken. By contrast, in present-day conditions, written record offers the performative act: a signature on (e.g.) a cheque validates the transaction being undertaken. Texts in Older Scots represent an intermediate stage between medieval and modern conditions of literacy, and it is therefore unsurprising that many features of the written mode are more 'speech-like' than a modern reader might expect.

2.31 Some of the practices adopted are illustrated in the texts in Part II of this book. Thus it will be observed, for instance, that Text 4(a)(1), the extract from the Edinburgh manuscript of Barbour's *Bruce*, has no punctuation as we understand it at all; clearly, punctuation was deemed unnecessary by the scribe since the use of discourse-markers (e.g. **and, yat**) was considered adequate for the task. By contrast, the complex syntax of Henryson's *Morall Fabillis* (Text 4(c)), in rhyme royal, seems to have encouraged the printer Bassandyne to impose an extensive repertoire of punctuation along essentially modern lines (as a comparison with modern critical editions demonstrates). The change may well have paralleled changes in conditions of literacy; comparison of Text 4(a)(1) with text 4(a)(2), the 1616 print of Barbour's *Bruce* by Andro Hart, shows the imposition of a comprehensive set of punctuation-marks – albeit almost always at the end of lines, in an arguably random way – even though an attempt has been made to sustain the appearance of antiquity by the use of black-letter fonts. A similar contrast might be drawn between the handling of punctuation in the prose *Spektakle of Luf* (Text 5(a)) and the usage of the print of Knox's *First Blast* (Text 5(c)). The *Spektakle* uses a combination of litterae notabiliores and discourse markers to assist the reader, while the punctuation of the *First Blast* – whether authorial or imposed by the printer – uses commas to mark rhetorical periods (see further ch. 4 below). Finally, we might observe that the usages of some of the letters in Texts 2 – which has been considered likely to be the most 'speech-like' of genres (see Culpeper and Kyto 2010) – deploy practices of punctuation which seem especially to reflect the rhythms of speech.

3. *Standardisation and anglicisation*

3.0 Whereas the Present-Day English writing-system is standardised and thus fixed, the writing-system of Older Scots was not yet fixed. The degree of variation in Older Scots writing was therefore, in comparison with that of Present-Day English, fairly large, and many words are recorded in Older Scots with a variety of spellings. Thus the headword **bailȝe** 'bailiff, baillie' cited in 2.10 above is recorded in *DSL* with the following Older Scots variants: **bailȝe, balȝe, bailȝee, bailȝie, bailȝhe, baileȝe, baillȝe, bailliȝe, baillȝie, bayle, baylȝea, baylȝhe, bayhlȝe, bayllȝie, balȝee, balȝei, balȝie, baylȝee, balȝhe, balȝae, baleȝe, baliȝee, ballȝe, ballȝie, ballȝhe, ballieȝe, belȝe, belȝie, bealȝe, bealȝie**; *DSL* also notes that ⟨y⟩ was 'freq[uently]' used in place of ⟨ȝ⟩ in these forms, especially in printed texts but also occasionally in manuscripts.

3.1 Wide variation in written form correlates with the functional status of the language in question; variant spellings were acceptable as long as the vernacular was seen as a comparatively ephemeral, local/personal stepping-stone to higher-level literacy in another, more prestigious language, i.e. Latin. However, once it was possible to use the vernacular in prestigious functions, and as a language of long-term/long-distance record, variation became inconvenient, and began to be suppressed. Middle English variation, therefore, was replaced by the comparatively fixed spellings of Modern English during the course of the early-modern period. However Scots spelling never became fixed according to educational norms. The reason for this contrast is fairly obvious, and to do with political developments (see ch. 1 above).

3.2 Variation in Older Scots spelling can be categorised in three ways: *personal* variation, *diachronic* variation and *diatopic* variation. There is some evidence that many writers developed their own spelling-systems, and *DSL* cites a legal case from 1609 when a writer's practices of spelling were used to ascribe a series of unsigned, treasonable letters to his authorship (cited Macafee 2002: lxxi):

> ffirst, that he newer vseit to wrytt ane '3' in the begynnyng of ony word, sik as '3ow', '3ouris', '3eild' '3ea', and siclyk; bot ewir wrait 'y' in steid of the said '3'; that he wrait all wordis begynnyng with 'w' with ane singill 'v'; and quhan that leter 'v' fell to be in the myddis or end of ane word, he wrait ane doubill 'w' . . .

3.3 A few usages seem to have disappeared *diachronically* (i.e. 'through time'); *DSL*, for instance, records a range of Older Scots forms for the item 'year', viz. **3er, 3ere, 3eir, 3eire, yeir, yeire, 3her, 3here, yher, yhere, iere, 3heir, yheir, yheire, 3eyr, 3eyre, yeyr, yeyre, 3ier, 3iere, yier, yiere, 3eer, 3eere, yeer, yheere, 3ear, 3eare, year, yeare, yir, 3air, yar, heir.** However, it is noticeable from entries in *DSL* that forms with initial ⟨3h, yh⟩ tend to be earlier, and are gradually phased out in favour of ⟨3, y⟩. The letter ⟨y⟩ = ⟨þ⟩ becomes rare after the mid-sixteenth century, while the use of ⟨i⟩ as a diacritic 'length-mark' in e.g. **guid** 'good' (cf. earlier **gude**) is rare before the beginning of the sixteenth century. For ⟨-tht⟩, see 2.8 above. In general, variation seems to have become greater over time as spelling-repertoires extended to include English-type spellings in addition to those common in Scots, e.g. ⟨sh, gh, ea/ee, –ed⟩ in addition to what had become characteristically Scots ⟨sch, ch, ei/ ey, –it/–yt⟩. Some of these usages had disappeared between Early and Middle Scots times, but then reappeared, e.g. ⟨-ed⟩.

3.4 Some anglicisations in spelling have, it is often claimed, resulted in 'mixed' forms, e.g. **quho(me)** 'who(m)' (cf. English **who(m)**, more common Older Scots **quha(m)**), found in some poetry (particularly 'high-style' – see ch. 4) produced by some Older Scots poets; *DSL* cites (e.g.) *The Kingis Quair*, Gavin Douglas's translation of the *Aeneid*, and poems by Dunbar, Lyndsay and Scott, and they appear in several other texts in Part II, e.g. James VI's *Reulis and Cautelis*. The status of these spellings is somewhat uncertain; *DSL* states that 'the phonological history has perh[aps] been complicated by the presence of labial consonants before and after the vowel' (sv. **Quhom**). So it is possible that these forms are not anglicisations at all, but simply a distinct Older Scots development. Anglicisation of spelling is indeed an area of considerable controversy, which perhaps is more complicated than is sometimes claimed.

For further discussion in addition to that in *DSL*, see Bald 1926, Agutter 1988, Devitt 1989.

3.5 Older Scots spellings varied not only diachronically; they also varied *diatopically* ('through space'). Recent work in this field, notably in the creation of the *Linguistic Atlas of Older Scots* (*LAOS*), has added – and will continue to add – hugely to our understanding of this tricky area. Two items in *LAOS* may be taken to illustrate such variation in spelling: THAT (demonstrative) and SIX (numeral). Maps in *LAOS* show that, for THAT, forms with initial ⟨th⟩ are restricted to the east coast of Scotland during the period 1450–1500, whereas forms with initial ⟨y⟩ for ⟨þ⟩ are much more widespread during the same period. For SIX, two forms are currently mapped in *LAOS*, viz. **sax** and **sex**. During the same period 1450–1500, the form **sax** is clustered in the East Mid-Scots areas, stretching from Angus through the Fife coast to Edinburgh, while **sex** is much more widespread in the Scots-speaking area. The form **sex** was much more common in the period 1380–1449 than **sax**, which is at that time much more sporadic; **sax** would therefore seem to be an innovation. Interestingly, *SND* records that **sax** is much more common and widespread in Scots in the period post-1700 than **sex**. It may also be noted that ⟨th⟩-⟨y⟩ variation in THAT is unlikely to signal a pronunciation-difference, whereas the difference in vowel-spelling between **sax** and **sex** probably does, demonstrating the ways in which diatopic variation is relevant for both written and spoken modes (see further McIntosh 1994).

CHAPTER 3

Grammar and Lexicon

0.0 This chapter falls into three sections. As in chapter 2, section 1 deals with linguistic terminology relevant to the study of lexicon and grammar. Section 2 gives an overview of Older Scots vocabulary and section 3 deals with Older Scots grammar.

1. Linguistic terminology

1.0 For some scholars, the term *grammar* is used to refer to all linguistic categories other than the lexicon, but in this book a more restricted definition has been adopted: grammar is taken to refer to *syntax* and *morphology*. Syntax is concerned with the ways in which words combine to form phrases, clauses and sentences, i.e. *constructions*. For example the relationship between words in such constructions as **Amy loves horses** and **We love horses**, where the choice of **loves** or **love** is determined by the relationship between this word and other words in the construction. Morphology is concerned with word-form, such as the kinds of ending which the form **love** can adopt, for example **loves** as opposed to **loved**; it is also concerned with how words can be put together from other words, such as **blackbird** (from **black + bird**) or **undo** (from **un + do**). Morphology dealing with alternations of the **love-loves** kind is known as *inflexional morphology*. Morphology dealing with such forms as **blackbird** or **undo** is known as *lexical morphology* or *word-formation*.

1.1 Syntactic categories can be formed into a *hierarchy of grammatical units*. *Sentences* are composed of one or more *clauses*; *clauses* are composed of one or more *phrases*; *phrases* are composed of one or more *words*; *words* are made up of one or more *morphemes*.

1.2 The morpheme is often defined as the minimal unit of grammatical analysis. It is probably easiest to demonstrate what a morpheme is by example. Thus, in the sentence

(1) The kind girls have given presents to all their relatives

there are ten words but fourteen morphemes. This can be demonstrated if we separate each morpheme with a hyphen (-):

(1a) The-kind-girl-s-have-give-n-present-s-to-all-their-relative-s

These morphemes cannot be placed in any order to produce acceptable English sentences. Some permutations are acceptable (*well-formed*) in Present-Day English, for example

(1b) The presents were being given by the kind girls to all their relatives but other combinations are not, e.g.

(1c) *Present-the-s-were-be-give-ing-n-by-the-kind-s-girl-to-their-all-s-relative

Thus **present**, **girl**, **relative** and so on are potentially mobile or *free*, and can be employed in many positions within a construction, whereas s and **ing** are immobile or *bound* morphemes, that is they must be attached to some other element to produce a 'block' in a construction. Moreover, this ordering of elements within the block is *stable*, in the sense that s and **ing** have to follow, not precede, the element to which they are attached: thus **girl-s** and **giv(e)-ing** are acceptable, but not *s-girl or *ing-giv(e). These stable, uninterruptible blocks, made up from a free morpheme and (optional) bound morphemes, may be termed *words*.

1.3 Bound morphemes are sometimes used to express syntactic relationships; thus, in the sentence

(2) The girl loves her horse

the bound morpheme –s in **loves** indicates that the verb **loves** is 'governed' by the subject-noun phrase **The girl**. Such bound morphemes are often referred to as *inflexions*.

Linguists sometimes use the term *allomorph* to refer to the alternate phonetic forms morphemes can take in particular contexts, e.g. variation between [z], [s] as plural markers in **logs**, **books**, where s is pronounced differently depending on the quality of the preceding consonant. However, the term is comparatively rarely employed, and not used elsewhere in this book.

1.4 Students will also encounter another term in word-studies: the *lexeme*. A lexeme is the overall term for words which are related in *paradigmatic* terms, that is, which vary inflexionally; thus **love**, **loves**, **loved** are members of one lexeme, **horse**, **horses** are members of another, and so on.

1.5 The definition of the notion *word* offered above is a formal one, in that it relates to the grammatical role of the category in question and its structural characteristics. However, another older definition is that words map onto *concepts*. There are several theoretical problems with this definition, but it has its uses. The practice of *lexicography* (i.e. dictionary-making) would be very difficult without the ability to map a lexeme and the words which constitute it onto a definition, and children's language-learning would be impossible, since children build up their lexicons by isolating individual words and attaching them to individual concepts. Most readers are able to recognise words in Present-Day English since they are clearly marked in our writing system. The set of words found in a particular language makes up its *vocabulary* or *lexicon*. The study of words – both their structure and their meaning – is called *lexicology*.

1.6 Words are traditionally classified into *parts of speech*. Parts of speech fall into two classes: *open* and *closed*. Open-class words are:

- *Nouns* (for example **table, thing, idea, James**)
- *Lexical Verbs* (for example **sing, drive, go, love, dance**)
- *Adjectives* (for example **good, bad, friendly, sociable**)
- *Adverbs* (for example **now, then, calmly, actually, today**)
- *Interjections* (for example **oh!, argh!**)

Open-class words can be joined readily by new coinages, e.g. **scooter** (noun), **jive** (verb), **hip** (adjective), **groovily** (adverb), or by *borrowings* from other languages.

1.7 Closed-class words are:

- *Determiners* (for example **the, a, this, that, some, any, all**)
- *Pronouns* (for example I, **me, she, you, they**)
- *Prepositions* (for example **in, by, with, from, to, for**)
- *Conjunctions* (for example **and, but, if, when, because, although**)
- *Auxiliary verbs* (for example **can, may, will, shall, be, have**)
- *Numerals* (for example **one, two, first, second**).

Closed-class words cannot be joined readily by new coinages; they form a restricted set of forms which play important *cohesive* roles in discourse. They are therefore sometimes known as *grammar words*, a rather confusing description which will be generally avoided here.

1.8 The basic lexical element in open-class words is the *root*, which carries the primary semantic content of the word. The root may be followed by an *ending*, often referred to as an *inflexion*, which offers some grammatical information about the word, e.g. whether the word is singular or plural. Thus in Present-Day English the word **book** consists of a root without an ending, while the word **books** consists of the root **book** followed by the ending or inflexion –s.

Historical linguists working on the ancient Indo-European languages often make further distinctions. In many Indo-European languages, the root may be followed by a *theme*. Together, the root and theme make up the *stem* of a word, to which an *ending* may, or may not, be added. Roots and themes were carefully distinguished in the ancestor-language of all Indo-European languages, Proto-Indo-European; they were also distinguished in the common ancestor of the Germanic languages, i.e. Proto-Germanic. For understanding word-formation in some later varieties (e.g. Old English) it is still important to distinguish the two; however, in later dialects (such as Older Scots) many themes have disappeared or have become obscured. Distinct themes are better preserved in older varieties of Indo-European, such as Latin and Greek; thus in Latin, for instance **manus** 'hand', **man**– is the root, –**u**– is the theme and –**s** is the ending. There were also consonantal themes in Proto-Indo-European, e.g. –**in**– in Latin **hominis**, an inflected form of **homo** 'man' (= **hom**– + –**in**– + –**is**). However, themes are not really relevant to the study of Older Scots; thus in this discussion of Older Scots word-formation only the terms *root* (referring to the lexical element) and *ending* (referring to the inflexion) will be used. See further Smith 2009.

1.9 Open- and closed-class words both function within the next element in the grammatical hierarchy, viz. the phrase. Prototypically, nouns function as the *headwords* (principal elements) of *noun phrases* (for example *girl*, **good** *girls*, **the good** *girl*) and lexical verbs function as the headwords of *verb phrases* (e.g. *sings*, **was** *singing*). Adjectives prototypically function as *modifiers* of nouns within noun phrases (e.g. **the** *good* **girl**), although they can also function as the headword of an adjective phrase (e.g. *good*, **very** *good* in **The girls were very** *good*). Adverbs can function as the headwords or modifiers of adverb phrases (for example, *carefully*, *very* **carefully**), or as modifiers of adjectives within adjective phrases (for example, *very* **good**).

1.10 Determiners always act as modifiers to nouns within a noun phrase, for example *the* **girl**. Auxiliary verbs act as modifiers to lexical verbs, e.g. *was* **singing**. Prepositions can be linked to noun phrases to produce *prepositional phrases*, in (e.g.) *in* **the room**. Conjunctions prototypically link phrases or clauses together, e.g. **the girl *and* the boy** (linked phrases), *If you eat that, you will be sick* and **The girl was singing a song, *and* the boy was eating a banana** linked clauses). Pronouns function in place of nouns within noun phrases, e.g. *She* **was singing a song**. Numerals prototypically act as modifiers within noun phrases, e.g. *two* **bananas**.

1.11 Phrases may be classified as follows: *noun phrases* (including *genitive* and *prepositional phrases*), *verb phrases*, *adjective phrases* and *adverb phrases*. In Present-Day English, the noun phrase prototypically consists of a headword with optional modifiers, the latter being determiners, adjectives and numerals; thus the phrases **girls**, **good girls**, **the good girls**, **two girls** are all noun phrases. In prepositional and genitive phrases, nouns are prototypically headwords accompanied by prepositions and marked by special possessive endings respectively. Thus, **with the girls** is a prepositional phrase, while, within the phrase **the girl's book**, the phrase modifying **book**, viz. **the girl's**, is a genitive phrase. Noun phrases prototypically function as *subjects* and *objects*; thus, in a clause such as **The girl reads the book**, the noun phrase **The girl** is the subject whereas **the book** is the object. Noun phrases can also be *complements*, e.g. the phrase **a good boy** in the clause **John is a good boy**. Adjective phrases also function as complements, e.g. **The girl was *very good***. Adverb phrases function as *adverbials*, e.g. **The girl rode the pony *very carefully***. Verb phrases function prototypically as *predicators* within a clause, e.g. **The girl *was reading* the book**.

1.12 Finally, clauses can be classified as *main* or *subordinate*; main clauses can stand as sentences on their own, while subordinate clauses function within a main clause. Thus, in the sentence **If you eat that, you will be sick**, **If you eat that** is a subordinate clause while **you will be sick** is a main clause. Subordinate clauses often have *non-finite verb phrases*, e.g. ***Having crossed* the Rubicon, Caesar marched on Rome**.

2. *Older Scots lexicon: an overview*

2.0 Much of the Older Scots *lexicon* derives from *Old Anglian*, the variety of *Old English* used from the Midlands of England to the south-east Lowlands of Scotland, and this percentage (some 34.6% of Scots vocabulary, according to Macafee 2002: lxvii) includes some of the most commonly used words in Older Scots. Some Scots words of Old English origin no longer survive south of the border, e.g. **bannock** 'meal-cake', **haugh** 'level ground', both of which are cited in *SND*; the latest English citation for **bannock** in *OED* dates from 1674, and almost all citations in *OED* for **haugh** are from Scottish sources (the one exception refers to the Newcastle area and dates from 1827; its author, Eneas Mackenzie, was according to his *ODNB* entry a Scotsman from Aberdeen). The form **thole** 'undergo, be afflicted with' is now wholly Scots, even though it may derive from Old English þolian (see, however, 2.4 below). The Old Anglian element in the Scots lexicon may derive from the early settlement in South-East Scotland, or it may date from the twelfth-century influx of Northern English-speakers; it is not possible to distinguish the two sources.

2.1 There are comparatively few loanwords from varieties of *Celtic* in Older Scots, some 0.8% of Older Scots vocabulary according to Macafee (2002: lxvii). *Cumbric*, the language of the Britons closely related to modern Welsh, may have contributed **lum** 'smoke-hole, chimney', and possibly **cobill** 'flat-bottomed rowing-boat', cf. Welsh **ceubal**; **brok** 'badger', which also occurs in English as a traditional name for the animal, is cited in *DOST* as from Gaelic **broc**, but may be from Cumbric. *Scottish Gaelic*, a language brought to the island of Britain from Ireland, has contributed rather more lexemes to Older Scots vocabulary, but the examples are still few. Gaelic loans tend to be topographical features, e.g. **glen** 'valley between hills' (cf. Older Gaelic **glenn** > Present-Day Gaelic **gleann**), **loch** 'expanse of standing water' (Gaelic **loch**), and **cairn** (Gaelic **carn**), or culture-specific objects or customs, e.g. **quaich** 'drinking cup' (Gaelic **cuach**), **tocher** 'dowry' (Gaelic **tochar**), **ganʒe** 'arrow' (Gaelic **gainne**). Some Gaelic words are not recorded in Older Scots but appear in post-1700 Scots, e.g. **sonse** 'good fortune' (and its derived adjective **sonsie** 'attractive'), from Gaelic **sonas**. The lack of Celtic vocabulary in Older Scots may at first sight seem puzzling. It may correlate with the traditional opinion of scholars that Celtic was a despised language amongst speakers of an Anglian-derived variety; alternatively – and this view has recently become more widespread among scholars – it may reflect a common tendency observed in language-contact situations where two languages are of equal social status, whereby grammatical/phonological structures are transferred rather than lexical ones (see further 3.6 below).

Celtic is traditionally split into two broad varieties: *p-Celtic* and *q-Celtic*, so-called because of the different forms these varieties have for the words 'head' and 'son'. P-Celtic languages include Cumbric (spoken in ancient Cumbria, which used to span northern England and lowland Scotland), Welsh, Cornish and Breton, and also Gaulish, the language of ancient Gaul (i.e. modern France). Q-Celtic languages include Irish and Scottish Gaelic and the ancient Celtiberian languages spoken in what is now modern Spain. Thus in p-Celtic languages the forms **pen** 'head' and **mab** (earlier **map**) 'son' appear; in the q-Celtic language Gaelic cognate forms are **ceann**, **mac**. However, it has been argued (e.g. by Schrijver 1995) that this distinction is a trivial one brought about through language-contact, and that there are more significant connexions between the 'insular' Celtic languages such as Welsh and Gaelic on the one hand and the 'continental Celtic' languages such as Gaulish and Celtiberian on the other.

2.2 *Norse* impacted more strongly than Celtic on the lexicon of Older Scots: some 8.4% of the total Scots vocabulary, according to Macafee (2002: lxvii), including some very common words, e.g. forms such as **war** 'were' (Norse **váru**, cf. Old English **wæron** > **were**), the auxiliary verb **gar** 'cause' (Norse **gera**), or third-person pronouns (see 3.15–3.19 below). Norse vocabulary was introduced as part of the twelfth-century influx of 'pioneer burgesses' into Scotland (see ch. 1, 3.7 above); the Norn spoken in the far north of Scotland seems by contrast to have had little impact on the evolution of Scots. Examples of Norse words in Scots include **gate** 'road' (Norse **gata**), **ba(i)rn** (Norse **barn**), **flit** '(re)move' (Norse **flytja**), **lass** (according to *OED*, ?Norse *lasqa**), **kirk** (Norse **kirkja**), **dreich** 'dreary' (Norse **drjúga**), **brig** 'bridge' (Norse **bryggja** 'landing-stage'), and also common words such as **eftyr** 'after' (Norse **eptir**) and possibly **til** 'to' (though the latter form is also recorded in pre-Viking Old Northumbrian). The Norse-derived **hundreth** 'hundred' seems to have been the most commonly used variant for this number; already dominant in comparison with the second most-common variant **hunder** etc., in the period 1380–1449, it became if anything even more widespread in the period 1450–1500, with **hunder** becoming more diatopically restricted to the south-east of the Scots-speaking area (for which see the relevant map in *LAOS*).

2.3 A number of Norse-derived words, though originally used in both Northern England and Lowland Scotland, have survived in Present-Day Scots but not in Present-Day Northern English; their disappearance in the latter variety is the result of standardising pressures that have not extended into Scotland. A good example of such a form is **starn** 'star', which is recorded in Middle English dialects as far south as the north Midlands of England but which has since receded; it is now almost entirely restricted to Scots (see McIntosh 1973, Smith 1996a: 181–2). Sometimes the Norse word remains in Northern place-names but has disappeared in other contexts, e.g. the element **kirk**, found in Northern English place-names such as **Ormskirk, Kirby, Kirk Ella** etc. but not found otherwise in present-day local usage. During the Middle English period, expressions such as **kirk** had a much wider currency (see Smith 1996a: 183–4 and references there cited).

2.4 Many Norse words have cognates in Old English, to be expected given the close relationship between the two languages. Interestingly, in some varieties reflexes of both Norse and English cognates have survived, but with different meanings, cf. in Present-Day English the forms **skirt** (Norse **skyrta**) and **shirt** (Old English **sceort**). Something similar happens in Older Scots; the word **gate**, from Old Norse **gata** meaning 'road', survives alongside **yett** 'gate' from Old English **geat** (recorded in *SND*; *DOST* has the form only in the compound **watter yett** etc. 'water-gate'). A more subtle example is provided by Scots **thol(e)** 'suffer, endure'; the retention of the word in modern Scots but not in English is probably due to a coincidence of form between Old English **þolian** and Old Norse **þola**. It will be noted that many Norse words have **k**, **g** where English has **ch**, **dg**, e.g. **kirk/church**, **brig/bridge**; see also **mikil** 'much'. The English forms are in such instances derived from Old English cognates rather than from Norse, e.g. Old English **cirice, brycg, micel**. The form **sic** 'such' (cf. Old English **swilc**, pronounced with a final affricate), according to *OED*, 'may have arisen [in Older Scots] under the influence of **slike**' (from Norse **slíkr**).

2.5 Other Germanic-derived languages also came into contact with Scots through trade etc., i.e. *Low German* (the ancestor of Present-Day *Dutch* and *Flemish*), yielding words such as **golf** 'the game of golf' (cf. Dutch **kolf** 'the club used in the game of golf', though *OED* is sceptical of this etymology), **scone** (cf., perhaps, Middle Dutch **schoonbrot** 'fine bread'). However, for the most part the influence of Low German varieties on the Scots lexicon was comparatively small, supplying some 2.2% of Older Scots vocabulary (Macafee 2002: lxvii).

2.6 *Latin* was the language of learning and the church. Loanwords into Scots tend to be rather restricted until the 'aureate' poets of the fifteenth century, such as William Dunbar, borrowed many Latin words into Scots for decorative effect, e.g. **sempitern** 'everlasting' (cf. Latin **sempiternus**), **matern** 'maternal' (cf. Latin **maternus**) (see further ch. 4 below). The form **superne** 'dwelling in the heavens' is, according to *DOST* and *OED*, derived from Old French **superne**, but Macafee considers the word to derive from Latin 'since French does not show forms without –al' (Macafee 2002: lxiv). Some forms which in English were borrowed from French were borrowed in Older Scots from Latin e.g. **dispone** (cf. Present-Day English **dispose**, cf. Latin infinitive **disponere**, Old French **disposer**). A special set of Latin borrowings are to do with Scots law, and are first recorded with legal meanings during the Older Scots period, e.g. **narrative** 'statement of alleged facts as the basis of a legal action', **dative** 'legally appointed' (e.g. **curator dative,**

executour dative), **homologate** 'to confirm a deed already executed by the addition of another expressing formal approval (because the original deed was legally defective in some way)'; the word **nimious** 'excessive, unreasonable' (Latin **nimius**) seems to have been in Older Scots derived from Early Modern English, but has since become a term restricted to Scots law. Macafee considers some 8.4% of words in the Older Scots lexicon to be definitely from Latin (2002: lxvii).

2.7 *French* has had a major influence on the Older Scots lexicon (some 27.6% of the Older Scots lexicon, according to Macafee 2002: lxvii). As with Middle English, French words enter Scots in two overlapping phases: an earlier Anglo-Norman phase and a later Central French phase. It is often hard to determine which variety of French is the source of Older Scots forms, but the following examples seem likely to be Anglo-Norman in origin: **rial** (Anglo-Norman **rial, riel**), **warrand** 'guardian' (cf. Present-Day French **garant**), **wer** 'war' (Anglo-Norman **were**, Present-Day French **guerre**), **carpentar** 'carpenter' (cf. Present-Day French **charpentier**, though see Latin **carpentarius**), **caldron** 'cauldron' (cf. Present-Day French **chaudron**). The traditional Scottish term for New Year's Eve, **Hogmanay**, may derive from Anglo-Norman **hoguinané** (see *OED* for etymological discussion). Other French forms in Older Scots include **cummer** 'trouble' (cf. Old French **combre** 'heap of stones', according to *OED*), **corby** 'raven, carrion crow' (cf. Old French **corb**), **lel** 'loyal' (cf. Old French **leel**), **haknay** 'horse used for ordinary riding' (Old French **haquenée**). Some cognate words that entered English from Latin enter Older Scots from French, e.g. **spreit** 'spirit' (from French **esprit**); although **sprit** etc. 'spirit' appears in some Middle English texts, Present-Day English distinguishes semantically between **spirit** (from Latin **spiritus**) and **sprite** 'demon' (from French **esprit**). Some French words are characteristic of Scots and not shared with English, e.g. **fas(c)h** (verb) 'anger, trouble', and derived forms such as **faschious** 'angry' (*OED* has only two non-Scottish citations for **fash**, from 1556 and 1874; all other citations are from Scottish sources). French vocabulary in Older Scots, as in Middle English, seems to have been regarded as 'high-style', e.g. **possessioun** 'possession', **reuerence** 'reverence', and some forms were associated with aureate diction (see ch. 4, 2.0), possibly because both French and Latin etymologies were possible, e.g. **angelicall** 'angelic', **femynyne** 'female'. Macafee notes that 10.7% of words in Older Scots may be derived from either French or Latin (2002: lxvii); since French is descended from Latin, this difficulty in distinguishing etymologies is not surprising.

2.8 Words containing ⟨oi, oy⟩ are almost all from French, e.g. **point** 'point', **join** (cf. Old French **joign-**); words with ⟨c⟩ for /s/ are almost all from French, e.g. **cite, citie** 'city' (Old French **cité**), although there are some analogous spellings, e.g. **myce** 'mice' alongside **mise, mys(e), mysse, myis** (Old English **mȳs**, singular **mūs** 'mouse').

2.9 In addition to borrowing, Older Scots could extend its wordstock through word-formation (lexical morphology), i.e. through *affixation* and *compounding*. Affixation at its simplest made it possible to produce derived forms in other word classes through the addition of affixes (bound morphemes). According to Macafee and Anderson (1997: 270–4), most prefixes are French or Latin in origin, e.g. **re–**, **in–, dis–, per–, pro–** etc. (from Latin), **contre–, demi–, en–** (from French), beside **mis–** (from Old English). Most words beginning with these prefixes are themselves borrowings from French or Latin, but some of these prefixes could be on occasion added to roots of Germanic origin, e.g. **rebring** 'bring back'. The most productive suffixes are Germanic in origin, e.g. –ing, –it. Many Older Scots words derived from French have characteristic endings, including, e.g., –abill, –age, –ance/y, –ence/y, –ate, –ess, –ory, –ant, –ent, –ician, –ize, –ise, –tion, -(i)o(u)n. Only rarely (Macafee and Anderson 1997: 272) are such suffixes attached to Germanic roots.

The study of affixation, whereby the meaning or syntactic category of a word is changed, is sometimes referred to as *derivational morphology*; thus **boyish** (adjective) is said to be *derived* from **boy** (noun) with the addition of the suffix –ish.

2.10 It is worth noting that the adoption of loanwords often has a structural effect on the semantic organisation of the lexicon, i.e. the set of words contained in a language. To use a Present-Day English example, words such as **regard** and **commence** are borrowed from French, but they occupy distinct slots in the two languages; in English, **regard** (in contrast with more colloquial native **look at**) has a connotation of formality which it does not have in French.

2.11 To illustrate this last point, we might examine the lexemes in *The Scots Thesaurus* (Macleod *et al.* 1990) for the category 'tiredness, exhaustion' (category 9.13). *The Scots Thesaurus*, based on *CSD* rather than *DSL*, is restricted to words exclusive to Scots, but still helps to illuminate the relative roles of Germanic- and Romance-derived vocabulary in Scots. Many words in this category (according to *OED* and *DSL*) are either of Germanic or obscure etymology, e.g. **bauch** (perhaps Old Norse **bagr** 'awkward' or **bágr** 'uneasy, in straits'), **disjaskit** (cf. Norwegian dialect **daska** 'go slowly', with intensifying prefix **dis-**), **ergh** (cf. Old English **earg**, Old Norse **argr**), **forfauchlet** (probably from Old English **fealuwian** 'wither', with an intensifying prefix **for–** and a frequentative suffix in –le), **lowsed** (probably relating to Old Norse **lauss**), **pingled** (perhaps relating to e.g. Norwegian/Swedish **pyngla** 'to work with small things, to struggle with trifling but difficult work'), **puggled** (possibly army slang derived from Hindustani **pagal** 'mad', but perhaps from Dutch non-standard **puggen** 'to hit hard' with frequentative –le), **wabbit** (just possibly, according to *DSL*, derived from **wobat/wolbet** 'a hairy caterpillar, applied pejoratively to a person'). Comparatively few forms, and these formal, are Romance-derived, e.g. **forjidget** (apparently derived from Older Scots **forjuge** 'exclude by judgement, condemn, sentence', though that form is found in Older Scots texts in legal contexts), **exowst** (cf. English **exhausted**; the earliest record in Scots is from 1739), **fus(h)ionless** (cf. Older Scots **foysoune** 'plenty' with suffixed –less, from Old French **fusion**). (There are numerous other words recorded for this notion in *The Scots Thesaurus*, but the forms cited here have a general rather than local currency.)

2.12 Changes in meaning are an important part of the evolution of the lexicon, and many words in Older Scots have distinct meanings from those of their present-day descendants. Older Scots **selie**, for instance means 'innocent', cf. Present-Day English **silly**; Older Scots **meit** can mean any kind of food (the form is fossilised in present-day 'sweetmeat'), cf. Present-Day English **meat**. Other words can have a more complex series of connotations than their present-day descendants; thus **kynd** (cf. Present-Day English **kind**) has in Older Scots associations with theological notions of naturalness implanted by God in his creation.

3. Older Scots grammar: an overview

3.0 This section is divided into two parts: (1) *morphology*, and (2) *syntax*. Morphology (sometimes more carefully specified as *inflexional morphology*, to distinguish it from lexical morphology, or word-formation) relates to grammatical form, and can best be demonstrated by listing *paradigms*, or model patterns, for the various classes of lexemes. Syntax relates to the sequential relationship of lexemes in accordance with the grammatical rules of the language.

3.1 *Morphology.* This section is concerned with the following categories in the following order: Nouns, Adjectives, Verbs, Adverbs, Pronouns, Determiners, other minor word-classes.

3.2 Most Older Scots *nouns* follow the following paradigm:

singular **king**   singular possessive **kingis**   plural **kingis**

The inflexion –**is**, characteristic of Scots, is sometimes replaced by –**es**. As in Present-Day English, e.g. **sheep, mice, children**, there are some irregular plurals. These irregular forms are fossils left over from Old English paradigms that were once more productive than they are in Present-Day English (see Smith 2009: ch. 7). Older Scots has rather more of these irregular forms than does Present-Day English, although there is a fair degree of variation. Examples include: **thing** 'things' (beside **tynkgis** etc.), **deir** 'wild animals' (cf. Present-Day English plural **deer**), **fete** 'feet' and **mise** 'mice' (cf. singular **fute, mous**), **oxin** 'oxen', **eine** 'eyes' (beside **eis**), and **childer** 'children' (beside **childrin** etc.). Also notable is the possessive **sister** etc. in **sister son** 'nephew on the sister's side' (an Old English expression), although it is perhaps notable that, in the citations of **sister son** in *DOST*, the usage is glossed by the doublet **neuoy** 'nephew'; the expression **sister son** may therefore have been regarded as archaic. As in Present-Day English, prepositions are commonly used with nouns to flag possession, agency etc., e.g. **of** 'of, from', **be** 'by' etc.

3.3 In Old English, *adjectives* had what seems to the present-day Scots- or English-speaker a complex system of inflexion and agreement, reflecting singular/plural and definite/indefinite distinctions in the manner of Present-Day German (see Smith 2009: 105–7). By recorded Older Scots times this system had died out, though *DOST* records traces of inflexional –**e** in place-names in pre-literary Scots, e.g. **Blakepol** (circa 1190) (see Aitken 2002: 69). Inflected plural forms of adjectives are sometimes found, but this may be the result of French or Latin influence on Scots phrasing, e.g. **the saidis lordis** (in Text 1(g)), or **otherris** in **Send a boy . . . witht ane letter of mainteinance and otherris letteris**; see the entry for **other** in *DSL*.

3.4 Two adjectives in Scots had different forms according to whether the noun modified was either a *countable* or a *mass* noun; a countable noun can have plural forms, e.g. Present-Day English **book – books**, as opposed to mass nouns, which do not have plural forms, e.g. Present-Day English **butter – *butters**. The adjectives involved are the reflexes of Present-Day English **more** and **enough**. More appears as **ma** before countable nouns, **mair** elsewhere; **enough** appears as **enow** before countable nouns, **eneuch** elsewhere, e.g. **ma wormis** 'more worms', **mair space** 'more room' (as in the expression 'no more room'), **wa eneuch** 'sufficient woe', **enow bukis** 'sufficient books'.

3.5 *Verbs.* There are two formal tenses in Older Scots: *present* and *preterite* (or *past*). The formal distinction between *indicative* and *subjunctive moods*, i.e. between verb-forms flagging real (**Tom *kicked* Dick**) as opposed to hypothetical (**Tom *might have kicked* Dick**) events was dying out in Older Scots. Mood-distinctions were flagged generally, as in Present-Day English, through *modal auxiliaries*.

3.6 *Present tense.* In Older Scots, as in Northern Middle English, there were two paradigms for the present tense; this system is sometimes referred to as the Northern Personal Pronoun Rule. Relics of this system still remain in certain rural varieties of Present-Day Scots, and indeed elsewhere; its origin is much debated, but the current scholarly consensus is that its occurrence is the result of interaction with Celtic (see further Benskin 2011 and references there cited). The system works as follows: if the subject of the clause is a personal pronoun (i.e. 'I', 'thou', 'he' etc.), *and comes immediately before or after the verb*, the paradigm is as follows:

Singular   1 **I keip**   2 **thou keipis**   3 **he/scho/it keipis**
Plural   **we/ʒe/thai keip**

Otherwise the –**is** form is used throughout the paradigm. Cf. Barbour, *Bruce* I: 487–8, **Yai sla our folk but enchesoune,** | **And haldis yis land agayne resoune;** *Excommunication of Border Reivers* (36–7) **I denunce, proclamis, and declares.** When a formal subjunctive was used it was indicated simply by the omission of inflexional endings found in the formal indicative mood, e.g. **I/thou/he** etc. **keip.**

3.7 *Preterite tense.* In Old English, as in Present-Day English, most verbs fell into two large classes: verbs which add a suffix to form their preterite (e.g. **love/loved**) and those which change their stressed vowel (e.g. **sing/sang/sung**). These classes are traditionally termed *weak* and *strong* respectively. This distinction also existed in Older Scots. Weak preterite verbs were marked by the ending –**it**, e.g. **lufit** 'loved'. The following forms exemplify the kind of variation which could take place in strong verbs:

	infinitive	*preterite*	*past participle*
DRIVE	drive	drafe, drave	drivin
CLEAVE	cleve	cleve	clovin
CLIMB	clime	clam	clumbyn
BEAR	bair	bare	born
EAT	ete	ete	etin
FARE	fare	fure	faryn
HOLD	hauld	held	hauldin

Some verbs lay half-way between strong and weak conjugations. Thus, for instance, HELP, a strong verb in Old English and a weak verb in Present-Day English, has a preterite **helpit** and a past participle **helpin** (cf. the Old English preterite **healp/hulpon**, past participle **geholpen**). CREEP, a strong verb in Old English, had two forms of the preterite available in Older Scots: **crap(e)** (strong) and **crepit** (weak). COME (Old English **cuman**) is generally treated as a strong verb, as in Present-Day English, but weak forms occasionally appear, e.g. **cumit** 'come' (past participle).

The examples given above exemplify respectively the seven classes of strong verb traditionally distinguished in Germanic languages. See further Smith 2009: 109 ff., and references there cited.

3.8 There is also, as in Present-Day English, a group of *irregular verbs*: have, be, do, gar, gan, can, couth, may, micht, will, wald, dow, docht, man, tharf, thurst, sal, suld. A number of these verbs were used in Older Scots in combination with the infinitive or participial forms of other verbs to express such verbal categories as *mood, aspect* or *futurity*, e.g. **3our grace sall wnderstand we haif nocht tane wp ane penny of orknay or 3etland** (Text 2(d), 11-12), where **sall** could be glossed 'must', i.e. with a sense of obligation. The verbs **do** and **gar** can be used *causatively*, e.g. **to gar the cullour and ryme be in the penult syllabe** 'to cause the colour and rhyme to be in the penultimate syllable' (Text 3(a), 395).

3.9 A difference from Present-Day English practice is that forms of **be** are sometimes used with the past participle where Present-Day English would use **have**. The distinction in Older Scots is to do with transitivity; if the verb is transitive (i.e. it governs an object), then **have** is used; if the verb is intransitive, then **be** is used. Cf. **I have come** in Present-Day English with **I am come** in the (Early Modern English) Authorised Version of the Bible. An Older Scots example of this usage is **Quhen Merche wes with variand windis past** (Dunbar, cited *DSL*).

3.10 The paradigms for 'have' and 'be' in Older Scots are as follows:

HAVE	*Present*		*Preterite*	
	Adjacent Pronoun	*Other*		
sing.1	I haf	hafis, hes	had	
sing.2	thou haist	hafis, hes	had	
sing.3	he etc. hafis, hes	hafis, hes	had	
plural	thai etc. hafe	hafis, hes	had	

BE	*Present*		*Preterite*	
	Adjacent Pronoun	*Other*	*Adj. Pr.*	*Other*
sing.1	I am	is, be	wes	wes
sing.2	thou art, ar	is, be, beis	wes	wes
sing.3	he etc. is	is, be, beis	wes	wes
plural	thai etc. are	is, be, beis	wer	wes

Subjunctive forms were **be, beis** and **hafe**. Forms such as **havys** were fairly common in Early Scots, replaced by **hafis, hes** etc. in Middle Scots.

3.11 Do, gan (later can) and couth are all used in Middle Scots verse as simple past tense markers, apparently for metrical reasons. Do (beside gar) can be used causatively; e.g. **And grene levis doing of dew down fleit** (Dunbar, cited *DSL*).

3.12 The remaining irregular verbs do not present any special difficulties of form. However, some present difficulties of meaning for a present-day student; thus **may, micht** are best translated as 'can', 'could', and **wil/wald, sal/ suld** have, in comparison with Present-Day English, strong connotations of *volition* and *obligation* respectively. Inflexional loss, leading to the loss of a distinctive formal (i.e. inflexional) subjunctive, seems to have encouraged the meaning-change of **may** and **might** which overlapped semantically with the old formal subjunctive; the ancestors of present-day **can** and **could** extended their meaning to take over the slots in the system vacated by **may** and **might**. The forms **sal/suld**, which appear in northern Middle English as well as Older Scots, may also be noted. In terms of modern standard British varieties of English they look deviant (cf. **shall/should**), but in the wider context of the Germanic languages the sh-type forms are the oddities; cf. such forms as Present-Day German **soll**–, Present-Day Dutch **zoll**–.

3.13 In Present-Day English there are two *participles*: present and past. All present participles end in –ing; past participles end in -(e)n (strong verbs) and in -(e)d/–t (weak verbs). There are similarly two participles in Older Scots, ending in –and (present) and –in/–it (past). Examples are: **The Lark lauchand the Swallow thus couth scorne** (Henryson, Text 4(c), 140), **howbeit w***ith* **bost yair breistis wer als bendit** (Dunbar and Kennedy, Text 4(d), 6), **Lyke as ane man wer bundin in presoun** (Henryson, Text 4(c), 14). Apparently anglicised forms of the present participle with –ing are occasionally found in 'high-style' verse (see ch. 4), e.g. **Glading the mery foulis in thair nest** (Dunbar, Text 4(f), 6); the forms –and (frequently written –an, and presumably pronounced without the final plosive) and –ing later become confused (see Macafee 2002: cxvi).

3.14 Older Scots *adverbs* usually take the suffix –ly/–like/–lie etc., but this suffix is occasionally omitted in Older Scots where it would appear in Present-Day English, e.g. **with trumpe and talburn playit lowde** (*Seuyne Sagis*, cited *DSL*).

3.15 *Pronouns.* The Older Scots personal pronouns were as follows:

1st person:	**I, me, my, we, us, our**
2nd person:	**thou, thee, thy, ȝe, ȝou, ȝour**
3rd person:	masculine: **he, him, his**;
	feminine: **scho, hir**;
	*neuter: **it, his**;
	plural: **thai, thaim, thair.**

(*its does not appear as a genitive pronoun in Older Scots; **of it** and **tharof** are frequent periphrases used instead)

3.16 Changes in the third person pronoun system reveal many aspects of how change happens in language. In Old English, third-person pronouns were fairly indistinct in pronunciation. All began with ⟨h-⟩, e.g. **hē** 'he', **hēo** 'she', **hīe** 'they', and the 'tracking' device which is a major part of Present-Day English discourse grammar was carried out not only by pronouns – which in certain circumstances were optional – but also by what seems to modern speakers of English to have been a complex system of inflexional endings applied to nouns, verbs etc.

3.17 Some of these inflexions remain in Present-Day English, as do some of the ⟨h-⟩ forms of the pronoun, e.g. **he, his, her**. But many inflexions have disappeared and, as a result, pronouns have a more important tracking function than they had in Old English; their increased importance means that there are communicative advantages in their being more distinctive. The Present-Day English forms **she, they, their, them**, and their Scots equivalents **scho, thay, thair, thaim** etc., are in fact innovations in the history of English and Scots. The establishment of the system of contrast between **he, she** and **they** provided these varieties with a set of much more phonetically salient forms than the equivalent system in Old English, viz. **hē, hēo, hīe** – the latter two of which were sometimes used interchangeably.

3.18 Innovations can only be adopted from a pool of available variants, and the variants which have become Present-Day English **she, they** etc. seem first to have become available in northern Middle English and Scots. It seems most probable that they derive from Old Norse (or Norse-influenced) forms which were earliest available in northern varieties; their adoption would have been encouraged by inflexional loss, which was also earliest in these areas. It is interesting that a fully developed set of forms – **scho, thay, thaim, thair** – appears in Scots by the late fourteenth century when a less developed set was still in use in most varieties of southern English. A comparison may be made with the usage of the well-known Ellesmere manuscript of Chaucer's *Canterbury Tales*, a text copied in London in the early fifteenth century; in the Ellesmere text, the equivalent forms are **sche, they, hem, here.** The earlier adoption of innovative nominative (i.e. 'subject') rather than other forms is probably to do with the greater importance of the subject-case as a discourse tracking-device.

3.19 The forms **thay, thaim, thair** all seem to derive from Norse; cf. Old Icelandic þeir, þeim, þeira. The form **scho** most probably derived from a slightly more complex process, whereby the Old English form hēo /heːə/'she' developed a variant pronunciation, /hjoː/; in other words, the stress on the diphthong shifted. Such 'rising' diphthongs were common in Norse; the variant pronunciation seems to have arisen in areas where English was pronounced with a Norse accent (cf. the 'Gaelicised' pronunciation of English in the Highlands of Scotland, or the 'Welsh' pronunciation of English in South Wales). Since [hjoː] was a more distinctive pronunciation, it began to be adopted in varieties of English and Scots; the form **ȝho**, found in *The Ormulum*, a Lincolnshire text dated to around 1200, seems to represent the use of figure ⟨ȝh-⟩ for power [hj-].

3.20 The form with figure ⟨s(c)h-⟩, power [ʃ], seems to have emerged because the cluster [hj-] is a rarity in varieties of English and Scots, and has a tendency to shift to [ʃ]; cf. present-day 'Shetland', derived from Old Norse **Hjaltland**, or 'Shug', the Scots pet-form of the personal-name 'Hugh'. Thus **scho** seems to have arisen in Scots through a series of quite well-attested steps, ultimately deriving from interaction between English and Norse.

[ʃ]-forms may have arisen differently in southern England, where the Middle English form **sche** etc. has a distinct vowel.

3.21 There was a stylistic/sociolinguistic distinction between **thou**-forms and **ȝe**-forms of the second person pronoun, comparable with that found in Modern French (**tu** vs. **vous**) and Modern German (**du** vs. **Sie**). Whereas **ȝe** etc. was used for plurality, and to indicate respect for the person addressed, **thou** etc. marks intimacy, or address to one lower in social position, or, in certain circumstances, contempt.

3.22 Three types of *relative pronoun*, equivalent to Present-Day English 'who', 'which' etc., were used in Middle Scots. They seem to have been employed according to the stylistic register the writer wished to adopt (the usage is discussed exhaustively in Romaine 1982; see also Macafee 2002: cxx–cxxi):

- **that** was the usual, neutral form.
- **at** was, in Middle Scots, a reduced form, used in low-style contexts.
- **quh**–type (e.g. **quhilk** (sg.), **quhilkis** (pl.), **quhaim, quhais**) was frequent in high-style poetry, sometimes in quasi-anglicised spellings (e.g. **quhois**). **Quha** replaced **quhilk** after *c.* 1520 when referring to human antecedents.
- occasionally, a relative pronoun could simply be omitted, e.g. **ye french men yat wes heyr cald not agre with ye capeden wes sent to tham** 'The Frenchmen who were here could not agree with the captain [who] was sent to them' (Text 2(f), 8).

3.23 *Determiners.* The definite article was **the** (**ye**), the indefinite article **ane** (even before consonants). In comparison with the two-way Present-Day English system ('this'/'these' = proximal, 'that'/'those' = distal), the Older Scots system allowed for a three-way distinction: **this, thir** 'these' = proximal, **that, tha(e)** 'those' = distal, and **yon/ȝon** (no exact single-word Southern Standard English equivalent, 'yon, that/those over there' = more distal).

3.24 *Other minor word-classes.* The cardinal numbers were **ane, twa, thre** etc., and do not present any difficulties. The ordinals began as follows: **first, second, thrid**, but Older Scots used ⟨t⟩ for Present-Day English '-th', e.g. **fourt, fift, saxt** etc. 'Dummy' **that** was frequently added to subordinating conjunctions, often for metrical reasons, e.g. **eftir that** 'after'. Common conjunctions with possibly confusing forms include: **thocht** 'though', **gif** 'if', **forquhy** 'because', **nor** 'than' and **quhen/quhair/quhy** 'when/where/why'.

3.25 *Syntax* is closely connected with style, and will thus be discussed further in ch. 4. However, the following features are worth commenting on, since they were usual constructions in Older Scots and not – as they would be in Present-Day English – stylistically foregrounded. They all derive from Old English (see further Smith 2009: 85–93).

3.26 The usual *element-order* in Older Scots is Subject – Predicator (i.e. Verb) – Object/Complement. However, the positions of Subject and Predicator are reversed in the following situations:

• when the clause begins with an Adverbial (i.e. an Adverb or Adverb Phrase, or a Subordinate Clause adding extra circumstantial information), the usual element-order is: Adverbial – Predicator – Subject, e.g. **Here spekis the auctour** . . . (Hay, cited *DSL*).

• in questions: Predicator – Subject, e.g. **Quhat alis lufe** . . . (Henryson, cited *DSL*).

• sometimes, in subordinate clauses: Subject – Object – Predicator (the Predicator can be 'split', as in **Quhen Merche *wes* with variand windis *past*** . . . (Dunbar, cited *DSL*).

3.27 *Parataxis* (i.e. a grammatical structure involving coordination rather than subordination), associated with less ornate styles, is useful in verse for reducing unstressed syllables (viz. conjunctions) which may disturb metre. In prose, there is an interesting contrast between writers who use a paratactic style, which derives from native traditions, and those who employ complex *hypotaxis* (i.e. involving the widespread use of subordinate clauses) which reflects the influence of French and Latin practices on Older Scots phrasing (see further ch. 4 below, 3.1 ff.).

3.28 *Negation.* The negative particle **not/nocht** generally follows the verb in Older Scots, e.g. **. . . and comptit *not*, . . .** (Henryson), **Seis coud he *nocht*** . . . (Henryson). However, pre-verbal **ne** is recorded in early texts, e.g. **Yat he *ne* suld lyff and lymmys tyne** (Barbour).

CHAPTER 4

Style in Older Scottish Texts

0.0 This chapter goes beyond the strictly philological concerns of the previous two chapters and deals with matters which are of more interest to literary scholars: the study of *style*. It shows how linguistic notions can be harnessed to the stylistic study of Older Scots texts, allowing for a non-impressionistic analysis of literary works and a deeper appreciation of how the forms of these texts relate to their cultural functions. Such concerns have recently come once again to the fore in literary criticism, as part of what is sometimes referred to as *new formalism* (see Levinson 2007). The focus of this chapter will be on texts which are traditionally studied as part of the 'canon' of older Scottish literature (i.e. literature in Older Scots, including works by Scots where Older Scots elides with Early Modern English). However, it is important to realise that canonicity is a shifting phenomenon, and that the approaches offered here can be applied to all texts, not simply those which modern literary critics have reified as of particular importance.

0.1 The chapter falls into three sections. In section 1, a definition of 'style' is offered, followed by some discussion of the terminology adopted by both medieval and modern writers. The remaining two sections deal with verse- and prose- style respectively. For further discussion, see Macafee 2002: cxxix–cxlv; see also Agutter 1988, Corbett 1997, Jack 1997.

1. What is style?

1.0 A good starting-point for the study of style might be the following statement: 'In literature, the resources of the language . . . are used not only for efficient communication of ideas, but for effective communication in a broader sense: communicating and interpreting people's experience of life, individual and collective. This means using language in special ways.' (Leech *et al.* 1984: 13)

1.1 'Using language in special ways' might seem a good definition of style. However, even this definition attempts to distinguish between the literary and the non-literary, and the dividing-line between these two kinds of discourse is a tricky one; fuzziness about the definition of literature has implications for the study of style.

1.2 We might, for instance, take the notion of *metaphor*, which might seem to be an obvious literary 'figure'. But, as has often been pointed out by linguists, metaphor is endemic to our usual language. The following metaphorical expressions based on the linking of ideas with food, for instance, are usages which are familiar to many if not all of us from everyday discourse (cited from Lakoff and Johnston 1980: 46–7):

> What he said left a bad taste in my mouth. All this paper has in it are raw facts, half-baked ideas, and warmed-over theories. There are too many facts here for me to

digest them all. I just can't swallow that claim. That argument smells fishy. Let me stew over that for a while. Now there's a theory you can really sink your teeth into. That's food for thought. He's a voracious reader. We don't need to spoon-feed our students.

1.3 So it seems that *figurative* language is not necessarily a defining characteristic of literature, even if literature tends to use such figurative language in highly imaginative ways. Rather, the raw materials – another metaphor! – for literature, as taught on 'literature' courses in schools, colleges and universities, lies in everyday language. This fact was known to the classical and medieval *rhetoricians*, who referred to the concept of *inventio*, or 'invention', in its old meaning, viz. 'finding'; when his disciple Thomas Hoccleve referred to Geoffrey Chaucer as the **fyrst fynder** of our language he was drawing upon a terminology of invention established by Roman texts such as the pseudo-Ciceronian *Rhetorica ad Herennium*, and transmitted to the medieval and renaissance periods by writers such as John of Garland or Geoffrey of Vinsauf.

1.4 The notion of invention is valuable in defining 'style', a notoriously slippery term in criticism. If invention is about finding, then, it might be argued, style is about choice from what is available to the person exercising invention (i.e. 'finding') in relation to the required *register* of the discourse in question. Register has a number of aspects, usually known as *mode, tenor* and *domain*. Speakers or writers – linguists refer to speech and writing as distinct modes – can choose expressions appropriate to particular situations, e.g. to do with degrees of formality (tenor), or with a particular genre, e.g. medical writing, political speech, conversation between friends, public ceremonial etc. (domain).

1.5 Notions such as register, mode, tenor and domain are part of the terminology of modern linguistics; classical and medieval literary theoreticians had, of course, their own terminology. They distinguished three styles – *high, middle* and *low* – and these three styles were widely recognised by medieval writers as having distinct functions; Chaucer's Host in *The Canterbury Tales* speaks of **Heigh style, as whan that men to kinges write** (*Clerk's Prologue*, E.16). The Host may not use the terminology of mode, tenor and domain but he is very clearly aware of the social situation that underpins them. William Caxton, England's first printer, in the prologue to his translation of the *Aeneid*, distinguished between *curious* (high/ornate), *plain* (middle) and *rude* (low/**vplondyssh**) styles, recommending the use of **a meane bytwene bothe**, appropriate **for a clerke & a noble gentylman that feleth and vnderstondeth in faytes of armes in loue & noble chyualrye** (cited Bolton 1966: 3). And, although James VI, in his *Reulis and Cautelis* (Text 3(b), 200–1), does not explicitly refer to the high/low distinction, he is very clear on the necessity of aligning content with appropriate expression: **Ze man also take heid to frame zour wordis and sentencis according to the mater**. James's phraseology is of course not at all new; it draws upon a well-established tradition stretching back to antiquity.

1.6 However, the distinction between the three styles is, as David Burnley memorably emphasised, 'complicated by shifting moral, social, and artistic values' (1982: 199); high style is variously described by medieval authorities as ornate, as the language appropriate for addressing kings and thus of social display, and as the language of elevated moral fervour, while low style is the undecorated language of villainous churls. Middle style is notoriously difficult to define; it is sometimes described as the plain language appropriate to moral discussion.

1.7 It is perhaps better, using some more modern stylistic terminology, to refer to *norm* and *foregrounding*; speakers and writers can vary against a stylistically neutral norm by using 'lower' or 'higher' language, as appropriate. High and low styles can therefore be seen not as separate categories, but as poles on a stylistic cline.

2. *Older Scots verse*

2.0 Older Scots poets developed some quite specific devices to reflect gradations of style; and if the style of verse is seen as a cline rather than a set of discrete categories, it is possible to see a range of intermediate usages. The 'highest' style of all is represented by poems such as William Dunbar's *The Goldyn Targe*, a dream allegory that reflects the court culture of James IV (see Part II, Text 4(f)). A dominant feature of the poem is its use of expressions such as **goldyn candill matutyne** 'golden morning candle' (i.e. the sun), or **in purpur cape revest** 'dressed in purple cape'. Later in *The Goldyn Targe* Dunbar refers to **Your tongis aureate**, which flags the origin of this usage: he is employing *aureate diction*, vocabulary drawn primarily from the sonorous, polysyllabic Latin of the Catholic liturgy. Aureate diction was first, it seems, developed in the first half of the fifteenth century by the monk-poet John Lydgate, who used it to add dignity to English by extending its range, i.e. making it more *copious*, to use a contemporary term in order to reflect the growing elaboration of the language (see ch. 1, 2.10; see also Text 3(c)); Lydgate's verse was described by a contemporary, John Metham, as **half-chongyd Latyn**, which is a rather good summation of Lydgate's technique. (Important discussions of Dunbar's aureate diction appear in Mapstone 2001, notably the essays by Corbett and by Lyall.) Dunbar was a master of stylistic variation, and it is therefore not surprising that his verse also includes numerous examples illustrating the 'lowest' end of the stylistic cline, e.g. *The Flyting of Dunbar and Kennedy* (see Part II, Text 4(d)); expressions such as **beschittin** 'defiled with excrement' or (notoriously) **cuntbittin** 'bitten by female genitalia = ?diseased with pox, ?impotent', used insultingly, are clearly part of the lowest register of expression, even allowing for changes in semantic connotation since the Older Scots period.

2.1 *The Goldyn Targe* and *The Flyting*, as just flagged, represent extremes of style; much Older Scots verse lies between these two poles. The opening of Henryson's *The Preiching of the Swallow*, for instance, although not strictly aureate in diction, nevertheless represents a heightened language appropriate to the discussion of profound philosophical notions to do with the difference between the spiritual plane of God and the corporal level of humanity (see Text 4(c)), while Barbour's *Bruce* (Text 4(a)) draws upon a lexicon of traditional romance, comparable with that found in thirteenth-/fourteenth-century Middle English texts such as *Sir Orfeo*, *Havelok the Dane* or *Floris and Blancheflower*.

2.2 The lexicon, of course, was only one means whereby Older Scots poets achieved their effects. The highest styles were distinguished from lower ones not only by using a higher lexicon, but also by the use of more complex syntax. Here, for instance, is an edited version of the opening stanza of Henryson's *The Preiching of the Swallow*, which engages with how God's wisdom, being independent of time, exceeds that of humans; God can therefore foresee human actions without predetermining them. The punctuation is that provided in Thomas Bassandyne's print of 1571 (see further the discussion in Part II, Text 4(c)).

> The hie prudence, and wirking meruelous,
> The profound wit off God omnipotent,
> Is sa perfyte, and sa Ingenious
> Excellent ffar all mannis Jugement.
> for quhy to him all thing is ay present,
> Rycht as it is, or ony tyme sall be,
> Befoir the sicht off his Diuinitie.

A fairly close prose translation of this stanza might be: 'The high wisdom and wondrous creation, the deep knowledge of almighty God, are [for 'is'] so perfect and so subtle, excelling by far all human judgement, because to Him everything is always present, exactly as it is or shall be at any time, from the perspective of His divinity'.

2.3 It will at once be observed that Henryson's syntax is highly complex, mirroring the complexity of his thought. Such skilled handling of subordination (**Excelland . . . Jugement, For quhy . . . Diuinitie**) and parentheses (**The profound wit . . . omnipotent**), and including postposed adjectives (**wirking meruelous, God omnipotent**) in the French manner, would have flagged to a contemporary, quite apart from the content, that Henryson was engaging with some highly sophisticated theological/philosophical notions – potentially ironic, of course, given that Aesop's *Fables* seem to have been commonly used in the late-medieval and early-modern schoolroom for the teaching of early literacy, both in the vernacular and Latin. Henryson has adopted for the *Fabillis* – as for his *Testament of Cresseid* – the stanza form used by Chaucer in *Troilus and Criseyde*, and which was described by James VI as appropriate **For tragicall materis, complaintis, or testamentis**; James described the stanza as ***Troilus*** **verse**. It is better known now as *rhyme royal*.

The term 'rhyme royal', first attested in *OED* from 1827, is a modification of the earlier usage, *rhythm royal*, for which the earliest citation is from George Gascoigne's *The posies of George Gascoigne Esquire* (1575): **Rythme royall is a verse of tene syllables, and seuen such verses make a staffe [etc.] . . . This hath bene called Rithme royall, & surely it is a royall kinde of verse, seruing best for graue discourses** (*OED*). The next citations in *OED* for both 'rhyme royal' and 'rhythm royal' are from the nineteenth century.

2.4 By contrast, here is a short passage from Barbour's *Bruce*. I have added my own punctuation; there is little or none in the original (cf. Text 1(a)):

> Thusgat levyt thai and in sic thrillage,
> Bath pur and thai off hey parage,
> For off the lordis sum thai slew
> And sum thai hangyt and sum thai drew,
> And sum thai put in presoune
> Forowten caus of enchesoun.
> And, amang other of Dowglas,
> Put in presoun Schir Wilyam was,
> That off Douglas was lord and syr;
> Off him thai makyt a martyr.

A prose translation of this passage might be: 'In this way they lived, and in such servitude, both poor and those of high lineage, for they slew some of the lords, and some they hanged, and some they disembowelled, and some they put in prison without cause or reason. And, among others of [the] Douglas [family], Sir William was put in prison, who was lord and sire of [clan] Douglas; they made a martyr of him'.

2.5 The syntactic structure of the passage from the *Bruce* is, in comparison with that of the *Preiching*, much looser, with clauses linked by coordinating conjunctions such as **and**, and parenthetical statements (**Bath pur and thai off hey parage**) only loosely attached to a main clause. Such structures, which are closer to the usages found in the spoken mode, are characteristic of medieval verse romances and of other texts modelled on them (e.g. the Middle English cyclical history *Cursor Mundi*), and a contemporary reader would therefore have seen the *Bruce*, arguably appropriately, as part of that genre.

It is noticeable that syntactic complexity is a feature in particular of the rhyme-royal stanza, as seen in (e.g.) *The Kingis Quair* or Henryson's *Fabillis*. It could be argued that such complexity is a particular characteristic of texts which were primarily intended for reading rather than hearing, and that there is therefore an implication for the literacy-conditions under which such stanzaic – as opposed to couplet-based – texts were produced. I owe this insight to discussion with Derek Pearsall. For a general discussion of Middle Scots as a literary language, see Agutter 1988.

2.6 In addition to lexical and syntactic effects, of course, verse is characterised by the use of sound-effects: *rhythm* and *metre*, and also sound-patterning such as *rhyme* and *alliteration*. It seems likely that such effects were even more salient for the original audiences of Older Scots poetry, who were more likely than are modern readers to have encountered verse in oral, public performance rather than in private. It may be observed that James VI saw poetry as closely tied to performance, linking it to music (Text 3(a), 114–19):

Bot specially tak heid, quhen zour lyne is of fourtene, that your Sectioun in aucht be a lang monosyllabe, or ellis the hinmest syllabe of a word alwais being lang, as I said before. The cause quhy it ma[n] be ane of thir twa, is, for the Musique, because that quhen zour lyne is ather of xiiij or xij fete, it wilbe drawin sa lang in the singing, as ze man rest in the middes of it, quhilk is the Sectioun: . . .

2.7 Derek Attridge (1995) has identified a series of effects achieved through the rhythm/metre interplay:
- *emphasis*: 'Organized rhythm sets up expectations, and any departure from the expected norm is potentially a matter of emphasis.' (1995: 15)
- *articulation*: 'A departure from a norm that has been set up can also mark a shift of subject or tonality, as when a poem moves into a different meter and thereby alters the focus and feeling of a poem.' (1995:16)
- *mimetic effects*: 'A common type of commentary on poetic rhythm involves relating a particular rhythmic sequence in a poem to a quality or event referred to by the words.' (1995:16)
- *emotional effects*: 'More important than imitations of the world referred to by the words are the ways in which changes in the mental and emotional state of the imagined speaker of the words are suggested by the rhythm.' (1995: 17)

- *meaning in process*: 'Because verse heightens the reader's sense of language moving through time, the poet can suggest meanings that are then modified or contradicted a moment later (and once a meaning in poetry has been suggested, even contradicting it doesn't expunge the fact that for a time it existed).' (1995: 17–18)
- *connection and contrast*: '[We may note] the general unifying power of organized rhythm; it is also possible for particular parts of a poem to be connected by rhythmic similarities' (1995: 18)

Of course, as Attridge points out, 'an exhaustive commentary on the rhythmic dimension of any poem would be an enormous project' (1995: 19), and it is usual to be selective in identifying such effects and how they function in a given piece of verse.

2.8 Such a commentary might begin through the analysis of a traditional defining feature of poetry: metre. The terminology of metrical analysis is long-established. It derives from classical Greek writers, who operated on a system of *length* (sometimes referred to as *weight*) of syllables. These conventions were transferred to English verse, which operates using *stress* (*accent*, thus *accentual metre*), whereby a stressed syllable (usually marked /) alternates with an unstressed syllable (x) to form a *foot* (cf. the *bar* in music); a sequence of feet forms a verse *line*. The most common feet in English are two-syllable forms, viz. the *iamb* (e.g. **imbibe** x /), the *trochee* (e.g. **trousers** / x), the *pyrrhic* (e.g. **of the** x x) and the *spondee* (e.g. **sports day** / /). A sequence of four feet forms a *tetrameter* line; a sequence of five feet forms a *pentameter* line.

Three-syllable feet in English may also be distinguished: the *dactyl* (e.g. **daffodil**, / x x), the *anapaest* (e.g. **acquiesce**, x x /) and the *amphibrach* (e.g. **abrasive** x / x). It is traditional in the English and Scottish critical tradition to refer to long and short syllables – as does James VI – rather than refer, more accurately, to stress; see ch. 2, 1.17.

2.9 In the natural rhythm of speech, it is an observed fact that stress is assigned according to the grammatical category of the word in question. Closed-class (sometimes *grammatical*) words are prototypically less-stressed than open-class (*lexical*) words, since the information-content of the latter is largely predictable from context. Thus, in a phrase such as **the book, the** will be unstressed and **book** will be stressed, yielding an iamb x /. With open-class words of more than one syllable, one syllable will prototypically be more prominent, and thus receives stress: **booking** is therefore a trochee, / x.

2.10 It is important in metrical analysis to be aware of the difference between metre and rhythm. To quote Attridge again (1995: 15):

> Organized rhythm sets up expectations, and any departure from the expected norm is potentially a matter of emphasis.

Metre (James VI's **fete**) is, in Attridge's terms, the 'expected norm'; rhythm (James VI's **flowyng**), which is the actual realisation of the words according to the stressing they would naturally receive in normal speech, may coincide with the metre but may deviate from the metre for the purposes of emphasis.

2.11 Applying such notions to Older Scots verse can be highly illuminating. Here, for instance, is a sonnet by William Fowler (1560–1612), one of many poets favoured by James VI (see Text 4(l)). The lack of punctuation is that found in the original; sense units are flagged by discourse-markers such as **quhen, Euen so, whils, and** and **so**.

> Schip brokken men whome stormye seas sore toss
> protests with oaths not to adventur more
> yet all there perrells promeses and loss
> they quyte forgett quhen they come to the schore
> Euen so ffair dame whils sadlye I deplore   5
> the schipwrak of my witts proceurd by yow
> your lookes rekendleth love as of before
> and dois reviue which I did disavowe
> so all my former voues I disallowe
> and buryeis in oblivions grave my grones   10
> yea I forgiue herefter euen as now
> my feares my teares my cares my sobbs and mones
> in hope gif I agane \on/ roks be dreven
> ȝe will me thole to ancer in your heaven.

James VI defined the sonnet in the following terms (Text 3(a), 361–4):

> For compendious praysing of any bukes, or the authouris thairof, or ony argu-
> mentis of vther historeis, quhair sindrie sentences, and change of purposis are
> re- *[folio M iij v]* quyrit, vse Sonet verse, of fourtene lynis, and ten fete in euery lyne.

Although James's discussion of the distinction between metre (**fete**) and rhythm (**flowing**) is arguably rather unclear, he nevertheless sees a distinction between the two; and this distinction is important in the interpretation of Fowler's poem.

James VI, unlike most contemporaries, seems to deem sonnets inappropriate for the discussion of love-relations. See the important discussion in Jack and Rozendaal 1997: 460–73.

2.12 In a tightly controlled formal poem such as a sonnet, the metre is pre-scribed: lines should be composed in the metre known as iambic pentameter, a sequence of five iambs. But analysis of the opening line of Fowler's poem, placing the stresses on open-class elements as is required by the grammatical categories of the various words deployed, demonstrates a marked rhythmical deviation from the metre to be expected in a sonnet:

/   /   x   /   x   /   x   /   /   /

Schip brokken men whome stormye seas sore toss

There are no fewer than seven stressed syllables in this line, the line beginning and ending with spondees where iambs are to be expected. The effect is clearly, in Attridge's terms, mimetic; the image of the storm, reflecting both image and the love-torment which the image is designed to mirror, is paralleled by the **brokken** rhythm.

2.13 The notion of deviation from the norm is also relevant to the analysis of another tradition of Older Scots verse with an older Germanic pedigree: *alliterative verse*, represented in this book by Dunbar's *Tretis of the Twa Mariit Wemen and the Wedo* and referred to by James VI as **Tumbling verse** (Text 3(a), 230–6):

Ze man obserue that thir *Tumbling* verse flowis not on that fassoun, as vtheris dois. For al vtheris keipis the reule quhilk I gaue before, To wit, the first fute short the secound lang, and sa furth. Quhair as thir hes twa short, and ane lang throuch all the lyne, quhen they keip ordour: albeit the maist pairt of thame be out of ordour, & keipis na kynde nor reule of *Flovving*, & for that cause are callit *Tumbling* verse: except the short lynis of aucht in the hinder end of the verse, the quhilk flowis as vther verses dois . . .

2.14 Alliterative verse in both Scots and Middle English derives from the characteristic verse-form found in Old English, viz. pure-stress poetry; the dominance of pure-stress poetry in Old English related to the grammatical structure of the language at the time. Whereas a prototypical grammatical unit in Present-Day English consists of an unstressed determiner or auxiliary verb followed by a monosyllabic stressed noun or lexical verb, e.g. **the book, has gone** – both iambs – in Old English determiners were to a much greater degree optional, the status of 'auxiliary' verbs was uncertain, and inflexional endings (with reduced stress) were used to link units together. Thus the dominant metrical unit in Old English was a trochee, in which the beginning of the word was stressed, and it is therefore unsurprising that linking between metrical units operated through alliteration (at the beginning of a word) rather than through rhyme (at the end).

2.15 This tradition continued into Middle English and Older Scots, though necessarily changed given developments in the language. Whereas in Old English alliteration was a cohesive device in addition to the stress-pattern, in Middle English and Older Scots alliterative verse the primary poetic signifier was alliteration, whereby alliterative lines consisted of the pattern *aa//ax* as the norm, with deviation, especially but not always in the first half-line (the 'A-stave'), offering the opportunity for variation (see most recently the essays in Jefferson and Putter 2009 and references there cited).

2.16 Recent work on alliterative ('pure-stress') verse has demonstrated that it operates according to rules of quite considerable sophistication, but the essential notion, deviation from norm, is the same as for the 'stress-syllabic' metres which have dominated English poetry since the end of the Middle Ages. Ann Matonis has developed a powerful argument as to how pure-stress verse functioned, enquiring 'into the authority of the normative pattern [of alliteration] and into some of *the narrative and rhetorical contexts* [my emphasis] where we might expect to find departures from it' (1986: 135). Matonis argues in line with common ideas about poetics that, as in other kinds of verse, deviations from the alliterative norm have expressive functions. Extra alliterations, including those on 'grammatical' words, correlate with special effects that poets are trying to achieve in order to put across the message they wish to communicate, and, *mutatis mutandis*, the same goes for lexical words (which would naturally attract stress) that do not alliterate (see further Kane 1981).

2.17 Analysis of the opening lines of Dunbar's *Ane Tretis of the Twa Mariit Wemen and the Wedo* (Text 4(e)) demonstrates the ways in which alliteration can be harnessed for expressive effect by a skilled poet:

> Apon the Midsummer evin mirriest of nichtis
> I muvit fur*th* allane [in] meid as midnicht wes past
> Besyd ane gudlie grein garth full of gay flouris
> Hegeit of ane huge hicht *with* hawthorne treis

> Quhairon ane bird on ane bransche so birst out hir notis   5
> That neuer ane bly*th*fullar bird was on the beuche harde
> Quhat throw the sugarat sound of hir sang glaid
> And throw the savour sanative of the sueit flouris
> I drew in derne to the dyk to dirkin efter mirthis
> The dew donkit the daill and dynnit the feulis   10
> I hard under ane holyn hevinlie grein hewit
> Ane hie speiche at my hand *with* hautand wourdis
> With yat in haist to the hege so hard I inthrang
> That I was heildit *with* hawthorne and *with* heynd leveis
> Throw pykis of the plet thorne I presandlie luikit   15
> Gif ony persoun wald approche within yat plesand garding

2.18 The metrical norm in this passage may be illustrated by

> Quhairon ane **bird** on ane **bransche** so **birst** out hir **notis**

in which the first three stressed words, viz. **bird**, **bransche** and **birst**, all alliterate and the last stressed word does not, viz. **notis**; such patterns, traditionally schematised as aa//ax (where a = the alliterating stressed word, x = the non-alliterating stressed word, and // = a medial caesura), are common to all Middle English and Older Scots alliterative verse.

2.19 However, it will be clear that Dunbar deviates from this norm in almost all the remaining lines in the passage, from the first line (where the unexpectedly non-alliterating stressed word **evin** appears for a word alliterating with m-) onwards. Additional alliterating stressed words, alliteration on a particular sound carrying on to subsequent lines – all such deviations from the norm demonstrate Dunbar's ability to exploit the expressive possibilities of tumbling verse. We might, for instance, examine line 3:

> Besyd ane gudlie grein garth full of gay flouris

Here, an extra alliteration in the first half of the line (**garth**) is followed by a secondary alliterative pattern (**full . . . flouris**), which is itself emphasised by interposing a word linked to the first alliterative pattern (**gay**). Various interpretative possibilities present themselves here: the words **full** and **gay** are clearly emphasised, linking beauty and fecundity in a way that is interrogated later in the poem.

2.20 In addition to structural alliteration, as found in tumbling verse, there is decorative alliteration that also has an expressive function. One such function is *onomatopoeia*, whereby a word is formed in imitation of the sound made. It could be argued that the sonority of much aureate diction (i.e. characterised by the use of especially sonorous consonants, such as the nasals /n, m/) imitates the sonority of musical instruments; but onomatopoeia is a comparatively marginal characteristic within the English and Scots lexicons.

2.21 A more subtle handling of sound with an expressive function is illustrated by the following lines, again from Henryson's *The Preiching of the Swallow*:

> Thir small birdis ffor hunger famischit neir,   245
> Full besie scraipand ffor to seik thair fude.
> The counsall off the Swallow wald not heir.

Suppois thair laubour dyd thame lytill gude.
Quhen scho thair fulische hartis vnderstude
Sa Indurate, vp in ane tre scho flew.   250
With that this Churll ouer thame his Nettis drew,
Allace it wes grit hart sair for to se
That bludie Bowcheour beit thay birdis doun.
And ffor till heir, quhen thay wist weill to de,
Thair cairfull sang and lamentatioun.   255
Sum with ane staf he straik to eirth on swoun:
Off sum the heid he straik: off sum he brak the crag:
Sum half on lyfe, he stoppit in his bag.

The passage is rightly famous: the foolish birds are beaten to death by the brutal bird-catcher. Most readers agree that there is something brutal about the repetition of voiced bilabial plosives in line 258, correlating with the brutal actions described. But what is intrinsically brutal about the sound /b/? Why should words beginning with /b/ have such associations? The answer is to do with *phonaesthesia*.

2.22 Phonaesthesia was first distinguished explicitly (although not by this name) in 1653, in John Wallis's *Grammatica Linguae Anglicanae*; Wallis noted the semantic connexions between words beginning with **gl–**, e.g. **glance, glare, glow, gleam, glimmer** etc. The modern linguist David Crystal sees the process as one of extension, whereby 'associations [which] may have been accidental at first . . . [were] extended to other words of similar meaning' (1995a: 250); thus the principle, basic to modern linguistics, of the arbitrary nature of signs is retained (see Saussure 1915 [2005]). As J. R. Firth famously put it (1930 [1964: 187]; see further Crystal 1995), the notion of phonaesthesia is

> not to be interpreted as a theory of inherent sound symbolism. [. . .] with the doubtful exception of certain sibilant consonants, there would appear to be no inherent phonaesthetic value in any speech sound. It is all a matter of habit.

2.23 Phonaesthetic notions allow us to give a name to the expressive functions of /b/ in the Henryson passage; Henryson is harnessing the violent phonaesthetic associations of initial /b/, mimetically, to enhance the pathos of his narrative. Although, of course, many /b/-words do not have phonaesthetic associations to do with violent activity – **bed, boring, bless**, for instance – it is however undeniable that many do, both in Present-Day English and Older Scots.

2.24 This characteristic of /b/-words is demonstrated nicely in *CSD*, where the following lexemes – a substantial proportion of those cited with initial /b/ – all signify violent or sudden action or temper, argument or insult, or weaponry of some kind or another:

> **bang, bank** 'drum-beat', **bargle, barrat, bash, bastion, bat, batailȝe, bate, batoun, battard, batter, bauch, bauchle** (vb), **bauld, beal, beff, bicker, birkie, birr, birst, bite, bittle, blaff, blast, blaud, blaw, blowder, bluiter** etc.

(See further Macafee 2002: cxxxiii–cxxxiv.)

3. Older Scots prose

3.0 When present-day readers first encounter prose from the Older Scots period, they are often struck by its oddness from a modern perspective; this oddness derives from its being composed using criteria of taste that are no longer current. As with verse, there was 'high' and 'low' prose, with the latter based upon vernacular models and the former based on more Latinate usage. As with verse, lexical and grammatical phenomena are both involved; however, sound-patterns (a defining characteristic of verse) are of course less salient. As has been pointed out (e.g. Häcker 1999: 239, see also Macafee 2002: cxxii), the distinction between subordination and coordination in Older Scots (as in older forms of English) was not as clear-cut as it is in Present-Day English formal written prose, and this characteristic can be disconcerting to a modern reader.

3.1 In the analysis of Older Scots prose, some further descriptive terminology is helpful: *parataxis* and *hypotaxis*. Paratactic prose is characterised by loosely connected clauses not placed in an explicitly causal relationship; it uses coordinating conjunctions (*syndetic* parataxis) or simple parallelism without coordinating conjunctions (*asyndetic* parataxis). Hypotactic prose is characterised by the extensive use of subordination, allowing for explicit relationships of meaning between clauses. A useful illustration of the two kinds of prose is as follows (after Mitchell and Robinson 2002: 99–100):

• *Parataxis*:

> I came, I saw, I conquered (*asyndetic parataxis*)

> I came and I saw and I conquered (*syndetic parataxis*)

• *Hypotaxis*:

> Because I came, I saw. Because I saw, I conquered.

3.2 Paratactic usage was dominant in Old English prose, and continued to be practised by many writers throughout the Middle Ages and afterwards; it is common in Malory's great Arthurian cycle, the *Morte Darthur*, for instance (see further Smith 1996b). It should not be regarded as in any sense 'primitive'; rather, parataxis is an audience-centred rather than author-centred mode. The use of parataxis pushes responsibility for the interpretation of what is presented onto audiences or readers, who have to make connexions which are only implicit in the text; hypotactic prose vests authority in the author, who has made the connexions explicit through syntax. Hypotactic prose did, however, become more common in the vernacular during the Middle Ages, based on French and Latin models, and by Older Scots times complex hypotaxis reflecting Latin models seems to have been regarded as the 'highest' kind of prose, however inappropriate it might have been for a language, like English or Scots, which did not have the same inflexional system as Latin.

3.3 Many varieties of prose in Older Scots – like poetry – require from modern readers a reassessment of the notion of the sentence. The word *sentence* is not in origin a grammatical term but rather semantic; the Latin word *sententia* referred to a meaning-unit. Perhaps a more useful notion is the *period*, or rhetorical unit, which may, but need not, correspond to the sentence. Rhetoric is, of course, primarily to do with the spoken mode; the punctuation-practices to be described below, based on periods, may seem clumsy to modern readers, but make more sense if seen as a prompt for speech. It is worth comparing, say, a modern essay or article written in prose with a transcript, say, of a television interview. The latter may seem completely coherent when listened to, but will generally look much looser than (say) a formal piece of written prose in terms of grammatical structure when seen transcribed into written form. Many of the prose texts in this book (perhaps especially the letters, which have been considered the most 'speech-like' of written genres) make more sense when listened to rather than when read (see Culpeper and Kyto 2010).

3.4 It is for this reason that an attempt has been made in this book to reproduce older punctuation; even if – as is almost certain – that punctuation is very probably not authorial but scribal, or introduced by an early-modern printer, it represents a practice which relates more closely to rhetorical notions than do present-day models. Modern critical editions generally introduce modern punctuation, for excellent reasons to do with making older texts accessible to modern readers whose primary encounter with text will be through reading rather than listening. However, it is worth noting that attempting to impose modern grammar-based punctuation onto texts that were designed for rhetorical presentation, in an oral setting, can obscure interesting aspects of the linguistic structure of the text in question.

3.5 Broadly speaking, there are five styles of prose commonly employed in Older Scots: the *native*, the *trailing*, the *Ciceronian*, the *Senecan* and the *baroque*. The first two styles derive from medieval practice, while the remaining three are characteristic of the early-modern period. Some examples of each style follow. Since there is sometimes a correlation between the selection of a particular prose style and the particular circumstances of a text's composition, some biographical information about each author is given here as well as in Part II.

For a typology along these lines with still valuable discussion, see Jack 1971. See also Gordon 1966, Mueller 1984.

3.6 The native style derives, ultimately, from the practice of Old English prose, e.g. that found in the *Anglo-Saxon Chronicle*. In this style of prose, parataxis (both syndetic and asyndetic) is dominant, with main clauses often placed in parallel. In Older Scots prose, the native style is well illustrated in the Bible translation by Murdoch Nisbet (*c.* 1520), although of course in this case the parataxis of the Nisbet translation reflects the parataxis of the biblical source (see further Mueller 1974 for a useful and sensitive discussion of 'scriptural' prose).

3.7 Very little is known of Murdoch Nisbet. He was possibly one of the 'Lollards of Kyle' in south-west Scotland, one of the late-fifteenth century proto-Protestant followers of the English reformer, John Wycliffe, whose writings were condemned in England almost a century before. Around 1520, Nisbet produced a translation of the New Testament, based on Wycliffe's; it was never published in his lifetime. The following passage comes from Nisbet's version of St John's Gospel. The text below reproduces the punctuation – or lack of it – in the original manuscript, but the use of **And**, **&**, **Tharfor** etc. – often marked by *litterae notabiliores*, i.e. capital letters – flags the use of syndetic parataxis:

Ande in aan day of die wolk Marie Magda-|lene com airlie to ye graue quhen it was|ȝit mirk And scho saw ye staan mouet away|fra ye graue Tharfor scho ran and com to Symon petir|and to ane vther discipile quham Jesus luvit and sais to|yame: yai haue takin ye Lord fra ye graue And we|wate nocht quhare yai haue laid him Tharfore petir went|out & yat ilk vyir discipile: & yai com to ye graue:

3.8 The trailing style, by contrast, seems to derive from medieval French traditions. Between 1168 and 1175, Maurice of Sully, bishop of Paris and chancellor of the university in that city, composed a cycle of French homilies on the Gospel lessons for the year. These homilies – they were translated into English – represented a new departure in style; they are hypotactic, consisting of trailing subordinate clauses marked by link-words. Such trailing structures were commonly adopted by English prose-writers such as Chaucer and Caxton, though (interestingly) Malory did not adopt them; although the trailing style was a feature of Malory's French sources, an important feature of Malory's technique was to replace it in his translation with the native paratactic style (see Smith 1996a).

3.9 The trailing style is common to many Older Scots writers, even when writing privately, and might be exemplified by Gavin Douglas in his letters to Adam Williamson (see Bawcutt 1994: 60, and also Text 2(c) in Part II). It may be illustrated here from *The Historie and Cronikles of Scotland* by Robert Lindsay of Pitscottie (*c.* 1532 – *c.* 1592), which may be dated from before 1577-9 (see Text 5(g)). Little is known of Lindsay of Pitscottie. Pitscottie is situated in Fife, on the road from Cupar to St Andrews, and the author seems to have spent most of his life there as a tenant of local gentry; the *Historie* is his only known work. *The Historie and Cronikles* was never published in the author's lifetime – he was waiting (he tells us in a preliminary dedication to the bishop of Caithness) for more favourable times, since his work **mellis with authoritie**. It was first printed in 1728. The work was one of Sir Walter Scott's principal sources for the period it covers, viz. 1435 to 1565; it was intended in part as a continuation of Hector Boece's *Scotorum Historiae*. In the text below, describing the birth of a pair of Siamese twins, the lack of the punctuation of the original has been adopted, but we night note the deployment of words such as **quhilk, quhairby, quho** etc., and of intransitive verbs acting as the predicators of subordinate clauses, e.g. **perteinand**. Litterae notabiliores are used fairly frequently, sometimes for discourse markers, e.g. **Bot, To.**

[folio 78v] in this meane tyme thair was|ane great marvell sene in scottland ane bairne was|borne raknit to be ane man chyld Bot frome the|waist wpe was tuo fair persouns witht all memberis and|protratouris perteinand to tua bodyis to wit tua heidis|weill eyit weill erit & weill handit be tua bodyis [The *catchword*] |*[folio 79r]* The on bak was to ye wyeris Bot frome ye|waist done they war bot on personage & could|not weill knaw be ye ingyne of man quhilk 'of' ye tua|bodyis ye legis & previe memberis proceidit not witht|standing ye kingis majestie gart tak great cure|& deliegence upoun ye wpbringing of thir tuo|bodyis in ane per-sonage gart nurische them & leir them|To pley & singe wpoun ye Instrumentis of musick|quho war become in schort tyme werie Ingeneous|& cunning in ye art of musick quhairby they could pleay|and singe tuo pertis ye on ye tribill ye wyer the|tennour quhilk was werie dulse & melodious to|heir ye Common pepill, quho treatit yame wondrous|weill

3.10 The native and trailing styles were clumsy to humanist tastes, however, and in the sixteenth century they were replaced in high-style Scots (and English) prose by the Ciceronian style. The renaissance of classical learning led to attempts to imitate classical style in the vernacular, even when this imitation meant the transference of markedly Latinate syntax to a language with a very different grammatical structure. As Janel Mueller states, 'The basic source of tension between native and Latinate sentence forms lies in the differential requirements of the two languages regarding (1) the sequential arrangement of major constituents within clausal units and (2) the overall intactness of those units in surface sentential structure' (Mueller 1984: 203). The Ciceronian sentence, based on the complex usage associated with the Roman writer Cicero (106–43 bc), was hypotactic, but – unlike the trailing style – highly controlled; an attempt was made to delay the verb to the end of the *sententia*, and 'its sense not completed till the last word had been written' (Gordon 1966: 77).

3.11 Perhaps the best-known practitioner of Ciceronian prose in Scottish literature is – unsurprisingly – one of Scotland's greatest Latinists. George Buchanan (1506–82), born at Killearn in Stirlingshire, was one of the foremost classical scholars of his age, well-known as one of Europe's leading humanists. With degrees from Paris and St Andrews, he became at various times tutor to the son of the Marshal of France, teacher of Montaigne at Bordeaux, professor at a college of the University of Coimbra in Portugal, principal of St Leonard's College in St Andrews, and tutor to James VI of Scotland. In this last role he seems to have been a somewhat demanding teacher; James himself, until the end of his life, recollected with some horror Buchanan's harshness to him. Buchanan is buried in Greyfriars Churchyard in Edinburgh, and he is commemorated by a large obelisk at Killearn. He is best known as author of a string of Latin works: four plays, viz. *Medea* and *Alcestis* (translations from the Greek of Euripides), *Jephthes* and *Baptistes* (original works); various satirical and legal works; and a twenty-book history of Scotland (see further McFarlane 1981, Ford 1982). Buchanan was a fierce enemy of Mary Queen of Scots; he made out the Latin statement of the charges against her and went with other commissioners to place it before Elizabeth I of England. *The Chamaeleon* is a vernacular attack on Mary's secretary, William Maitland of Lethington; we might note the complex syntactic structure, and the deployment of transitive and intransitive verbs. The punctuation of the manuscript is comparatively sophisticated, with deployment of virgules (/) and even parentheses; these features are used alongside discourse markers such as **And**, **but**, **quha**, **so**, **forsaid** etc.

From *The Chamaeleon*

[folio 280r] And seeing that his nature could | not ⸌bow⸍ to imitat in veritie/ but one-lie to contrafat fenȝeitlie the gudnes | of yir two parsonis nor ȝit change yame to his nature/ thocht expedient | [folio 280v] to leane to yame for ⸌a⸍ [tym *deleted*] tyme and clym vp be yair branches to hiear degre | as ye wod bind clymeth on ye oik and syne with tyme distroyis ye tre yat it wes supportit be/ So he havyng cum to sum estimatioun throw | hanting [of *deleted*] ⸌of⸍ yir nobill lordis/ (quha wer yan estemit of euery man as yair | vertuus meritit)/ wes sone be gud report of yame and ane fenȝeit | gudnes in him self put in credit with ye quene regent verelie ane | nobill lady and of greit prudence bot ȝit could not espy ye gilt vyces | vnder cullour of vertew hid in ye said monster/ specialie being clokit | be favour of ye two forsaid lordis in quhais company ʾgraceʾ [ye said qwenis *deleted*] | wald neuir haue belauit yat sic ane pestilent venum could have bene | hyd.

3.12 The Ciceronian style was, as might be expected, hard to sustain in languages (like English and Scots) without a comprehensive inflexional system. More commonly adopted was the Senecan style, which blended the authority of a Latin model with native, speech-based traditions. Senecan style, as its name suggests, was modelled on the looser Latin prose of the Roman author and playwright Seneca (3 BC – AD 65). Senecan prose balanced longer and shorter periods on the model of the classical writer, but allowed a larger role for parataxis; it was thus closer to the native style. John Aubrey, the seventeenth-century English biographer and antiquarian, in his *Brief Lives* (1669–96) famously quoted Dr Kettle of Oxford's claim that **Seneca writes, as a boar doth pisse: scilicet, by jirkes**; this description aptly sums up the Senecan style as transferred to English and Scots. The style which emerged was 'loose and free': not slapdash, but non-Ciceronian and accretive in terms of meaning. The earlier Senecan writers avoided ornateness of expression; plainness was their recommended mode, and it was thus attractive to writers of a puritanical tendency.

3.13 Given its confessional associations, it is not surprising that Senecan prose is exemplified by John Knox's writings. Knox (1514–72) is of course one of the greatest figures in Scottish history, leader of the Protestant reformation. One of his most famous polemical works, *The First Blast of the Trumpet against the Monstruous Regiment of Women*, was composed at a time when Knox felt his ambitions were being hampered on all sides by women rulers whose position were (in his view) unsanctioned by biblical authority: Mary Tudor, a Catholic, ruled in England, while Mary of Guise (or Lorraine), another Catholic and mother of Mary Queen of Scots, was Queen Regent in Scotland. It was not until 1560 that the Protestant religion was formally established in Scotland. The passage below reproduces the punctuation of a contemporary edition, flagging periods, and it will be observed that some periods are shorter, others longer, i.e. such units are deployed **by jirkes**.

[*page 9*] And first, where that I affirme the em-[*page 10*]pire of a woman to be a thing repugna[n]t to nature, I meane not onlie that God by the order of his creation[n] hath spoiled woman of authoritie a[n]d dominio[n], but also that man hath seen, proued and p[ro]nounced iust causes why that it so shuld be. Ma[n], I say, in many other cases blind, doth in this behalf see verie clearlie. For the causes be so manifest, that they can not be hid. For who can denie but it repugneth to nature, that the blind shall be appointed to leade and co[n]duct such as do see? That the weake, the sicke and impotent persones shall norishe and kepe the hole and strong, and finallie, that the foolishe, madde a[n]d phrenetike shal governe the discrete, a[n]d giue counsel to such as be sober of mind? And such be al women, co[m]pared vnto man in bearing of authoritie. For their sight in ciuile regiment, is but blindnes: their strength, weaknes: their counsel, foolishenes: and iudgement, phrenesie, if it be rightlie considered.

3.14 Baroque style represents the culmination of seventeenth-century prose. Baroque writers use Senecan clause-structure, but add simile, metaphor and daring imagery in the manner of contemporary metaphysical poets. It is no coincidence that two of the greatest practitioners of the baroque prose style in English were

John Donne and Jeremy Taylor, both 'high-churchmen' who were associated with the Church of England's 'catholic' wing; Donne, of course, is now better known as a leading practitioner of metaphysical verse. Baroque prose itself inspired an eighteenth-century reaction: an emphasis, since sustained, on ease, pithiness and clarity. These virtues are those, of course, of the Enlightenment.

3.15 Perhaps the most famous – or notorious – practitioner of baroque prose in the Scottish literary 'canon' is Sir Thomas Urquhart of Cromarty (1611–60). Urquhart was a member of the minor gentry, who supported the Royalist cause during the civil wars of the seventeenth century. In 1650, Charles II landed in Scotland and was crowned at Scone in 1651; Urquhart joined Charles's army, and was captured at Worcester in September. He was then imprisoned at Windsor Castle. Conditions seem to have been fairly relaxed, and Urquhart composed at Windsor most of his major works, including a translation of Rabelais and a curious text outlining a universal language which was to work as well when spoken or written backwards as forwards. He was released in 1655 and sent into exile in the Netherlands, where he died in 1660; tradition has it that he died of an apoplexy brought on by laughter on hearing of the restoration of Charles II.

3.16 Urquhart's writing represents the culmination of the baroque style in prose. He published *The Jewel*, from which the well-known passage below comes, in 1652. The passage displays Urquhart's interest in contemporary theoretical linguistics; it comes from about half-way through the work (cf. Jack and Lyall 1983: 124–5). We might note the combination of *double-entendre* with a strong Latinate element and the typically baroque fascination with obscure vocabulary (including several neologisms); some (though not all) of these words were flagged typographically by the printer, using italics. The following words in the passage seem to be unique to Urquhart:

hirquitalliency '?loudly expressed excitement'. The word is cited but not glossed in *OED*, which nevertheless offers an etymology from Latin **hirquitallīre** '(of infants) to acquire a strong voice', from **hircus** 'he-goat' + –**ency**. Urquhart is *OED*'s only source for the citation; *DSL* does not cite the word.

tacturiency 'desire of touching'. The word appears as a headword in both *DSL* and *OED*, but only with this citation.

visotactil 'involving both sight and touch'. The word appears as a headword in *DSL*, but only with this citation; it does not appear in *OED*.

visuriency 'desire of seeing'. The word appears as a headword in *OED*, but only with this citation. *DSL* includes the word within its citation for **tacturiency**, but not as an independent headword.

The word **attrectation** 'touching, handling, feeling with the hands' may also be noted. *OED* has three citations only for the form, all from seventeenth-century sources, none of which is Urquhart. *DSL* includes the word within its citation for **tacturiency**, but not as an independent headword. *DSL* does not cite **luxuriousness**, but *OED* has the word, flagging 'lasciviousness' as an older meaning, which seems, from the citations (Urquhart is not included), to be the dominant meaning in the sixteenth and seventeenth centuries. The term **gnomon** 'rod' is fairly obviously a euphemism here for 'penis'; a possible extra opportunity for double-entendre is that the word was sometimes used 'jocularly' (*OED*) to refer to the human nose (see *OED* meaning (1c)). More poetically, a gnomon is also the term used for the pointer on a sundial, thus the reference to *horizontal* dyal.

For further discussion of Urquhart's rhetorical technique, see Jack and Lyall (1983: 31–7); see also Part II, Text 3(c) and references there cited. Quite sophisticated punctuation, probably introduced by the printer, is deployed fairly thoroughly to flag periods.

> *[page 125]* ... Thus for a while their eloquence was mute, and all they spoke, was but with eye and hand; yet so perswasively, by vertue of the intermutual unlimited-ness of their visotactil sensation, that each part and portion of the persons of either, was obvious to the sight and touch of the persons of both; the visuriency of either, by ushering the tacturiency of both, made the attrectation of both co[n] sequent to the inspection of either: here was it that Passion was active, & Action passive; they both being overcome by other, and each the conquerour. To speak of her hirquitalliency at the elevation of the pole of his Microcosme, or of his luxuriousness to erect a gnomon on her horizontal dyal, will perhaps be held by some to be expressions full of obscoeness, and offensive to the purity of chaste ears: yet seeing she was to be his wife, and that she could not be such without consummation of marriage, which signifieth the same thing in effect, it may be thought, as definitiones logicae verificantur in rebus, if the exerced act be lawful, that the diction *[page 126]* which suppones it, can be of no great transgression, unless you would call it a solæcisme, or that vice in grammar which imports the copulating of the masculine with the feminine gender.

PART II.   TEXTS

List of Texts

Texts 1. Documents
(a) *The Scone Glosses* (1312)
(b) Exemption of the Abbey of Melrose from customs of their wools (1389)
(c) Extracts from a medieval Scottish merchant's handbook (after 1390)
(d) Extract from the vernacular *Leges Burgorum* (before 1424)
(e) *The Excommunication of the Border Reivers* (1525)
(f) Extract from *The Register of Acts of the Privy Council*: Proclamation against the earl of Bothwell (1567): (1) manuscript version, (2) Robert Lekprevik's printed version
(g) Extract from *The Register of Acts of the Privy Council*: Act in favour of St Andrews (1626)

Texts 2. Letters
(a) Letter from George Dunbar, earl of March, to Henry IV of England (1400)
(b) Letter from James Douglas to Henry IV of England (1405)
(c) Letter from Gavin Douglas to Adam Williamson (1515)
(d) Letter from Catherine Bellenden to Mary of Lorraine (1543)
(e) Letter from Henry, Lord Methven, to Mary of Lorraine (1548)
(f) Letter from Marion, Lady Home to Mary of Lorraine (1549)
(g) Letter from John Knox to Robert Dudley, later earl of Leicester (1563)
(h) Letter from John Knox to William Cecil, later Lord Burghley (1570)
(i) Letter from John Knox to Sir William Douglas of Lochleven (1570)
(j) Letter from George Buchanan to Sir Thomas Randolph (1577)
(k) Letter from James VI to Elizabeth I (1587)
(l) Letter from James VI to Jean Douglas, dowager countess of Angus (1589)
(m) Letter from James VI to the earl of Mar and Edward Bruce (1601)
(n) Letter from James VI to the earl of Mar (1618)
(o) Letter from Sir Thomas Urquhart to Robert Farquhar of Mounie (1648)

Texts 3. On Language and Literature
(a) James VI, *Ane Schort Treatise Conteining some Revlis and Cautelis to be obseruit and eschewit in Scottis Poesie* (1584)
(b) Extracts from Alexander Hume, *Of the Orthographie and Congruite of the Britan Tongue* (c. 1617)
(c) Extracts from Sir Thomas Urquhart, *The Jewel* (1652)

Texts 4. Poetry
(a) Extract from John Barbour's *Bruce*, in four versions: (1) John Ramsay's manuscript, (2) Robert Lekprevik (1571), (3) Andro Hart (1616), (4) Robert Sanders (1672)
(b) Extract from *The Kingis Quair*
(c) Robert Henryson, *The Preiching of the Swallow* from *The Morall Fabillis*
(d) Extract from William Dunbar, *The Flyting*
(e) Extract from Dunbar, *The Tua Mariit Wemen and the Wedo*
(f) Extract from Dunbar, *The Goldyn Targe*
(g) Extract from Gavin Douglas, *The Palice of Honour*
(h) Extract from David Lyndsay, *The Dream*
(i) Extract from Elizabeth Melville, *Ane Godlie Dreame*
(j) Alexander Montgomerie, *Against the God of Love*
(k) From John Stewart of Baldynnis, *Roland Furious*
(l) From William Fowler, *The Tarantula of Love*
(m) William Drummond of Hawthornden, *I know that all beneath the moon decays*
(n) James Graham (Marquis of Montrose), *On Himself, upon hearing what was his Sentence*
(o) Lady Grisell Baillie, *Were ne my Hearts light I wad Dye*
(p) Extract from Dunbar, *Discretioun in Taking*, in three versions: (1) Bannatyne Manuscript, (2) Maitland Folio Manuscript, (2) Allan Ramsay, *The Ever-Green* (1724)
(q) Extract from *Christ's Kirk on the Green*, in three versions: (1) Bannatyne Manuscript, (2) broadside (1701), (3) Allan Ramsay, *Poems* (1721)

Texts 5. Prose
(a) Prologue and Conclusion to *The Spectakle of Luf*
(b) Extract from John Gau, *The Richt Way to the Kingdome of Heuine*
(c) Extract from John Knox, *The First Blast of the Trumpet against the Monstruous Regiment of Women*
(d) Extract from Nicol Burne, *Disputation*
(e) Extract from Ninian Winzet, *Buke of Fourscoir-thre Questionis*
(f) Extract from George Buchanan, *The Chamaeleon*
(g) Extract from Robert Lindsay of Pitscottie, *The Historie and Cronikles of Scotland*
(h) Extracts from James Melville, *A Frvitfull and comfortable Exhortation anent Death*
(i) Extract from James VI, *Basilikon Doron*
(j) Extract from Sir Thomas Urquhart's translation of Rabelais

Texts 6. Bible Translation
(a) Extract from Murdoch Nisbet's translation
(b) Extract from *The Bassandyne Bible*

Editorial Principles

The Texts presented here are edited diplomatically directly from the manuscripts (or from good-quality reproductions) and early printed books, following, with some exceptions, principles laid down by Grant Simpson for transcribing the handwriting of Scottish documents: the 'purpose of the transcripts . . . is to show the reader as exactly as possible what the writing in each document was intended to represent' (Simpson 1998: 47).

Simpson's practice with the expansion of contractions is as follows: 'Letters which the writer had left out by using contraction or suspension, or has represented by a symbol, are placed in square brackets' (1998: 47). Thus for instance he represents **nacioū** by **naciou[n]**, where [n] represents an expansion of the macron. I have adopted this usage in editing printed texts. However, in accordance with usual practice, I have not adopted this usage in the transcription of manuscripts, where contractions are very numerous, and where brackets would be therefore both very common and potentially distracting; instead I have used less intrusive italics, e.g. **nacio*un***. My reason for this distinction is that italic type is sometimes employed in printed texts for (e.g.) aesthetic or emphatic reasons, and I wish to retain that distinction. Simpson had difficulties with end-flourishes, which he either expanded or marked with an apostrophe. I have adopted the former procedure when it seems etymologically appropriate but not added apostrophes to mark flourishes, which are very common, especially after ⟨r⟩. These 'otiose strokes' seem to be simply decorative (see further Houwen 1990: 22 and references there cited).

I have departed from Simpson's practice in that ⟨y⟩ is used for both the letter *y* and the letter thorn when the two letters are not distinguished in the handwriting of the texts. In a few texts, the two letters are kept distinct; when this is the case, ⟨y⟩ appears for the letter *y* and ⟨þ⟩ appears for thorn. Distinguishing, or failing to distinguish, thorn from *y* has a philological implication in Older Scots and Middle English, and should therefore be marked in editions such as those provided here (see Benskin 1982).

Simpson uses square brackets to indicate where contraction by superscript letters is carried out (1998: 47); thus he prints **y^t** as **y[at]**. I have not adopted this practice in the transcription of manuscripts, instead reflecting the usage by italics, e.g. **y*at*** 'that', **y*is*** 'this', **w*ith*** 'with' and **y*e*** 'the'.

'Square brackets are . . . used to enclose any letters which have been omitted by the writer in error or which have been inserted conjecturally by the editor on account of damage to the text' (1998: 47). Simpson records such additions in footnotes; I have indicated such changes in the text, e.g. [**vnjust** *supplied*].

'Spelling is given exactly as in the manuscript, and the original usage of *u* and *v*, *i* and *j* has been retained' (1998: 47).

I have departed from Simpson's practice in that I have retained the obsolete letter yogh. In Older Scots texts, yogh can appear as either ȝ or z; I have kept the distinction between the two, since the history of the letter has some interest for philologists (see the *OED* entry for the letter, and also Smith 2000 and references there cited). I have also used ȝ when it appears as a marker of plurality, e.g. **seruauntȝ** 'servants'.

'Capitals are also reproduced exactly' (1998: 47), but again I have departed from Simpson's practice in using long-*I* (i.e. J) whenever it appears, whether it represents the letter *I* or *J*. Sometimes it is hard to tell in handwriting whether a capital letter is intended; if this is the case, I have adopted modern conventions. I have also used ff whenever it appears for the capital form of *f*, not replacing it with F. However, I do not make a distinction between long- and short- *s*, since long-*s* can easily be confused with other letters. After some hesitation, I have not retained the common manuscript-form ß, replacing it with a simple s; ß is fairly common in final position in manuscripts but seems simply to reflect a scribal flourish.

Interlineations and additions by the scribe are shown thus: \cowart/ (cf. Simpson 1998: 48); glosses are offered if the addition is marginal rather than interlinear, e.g. \For Kennedy to the this cedull send*is* [*line inserted in margin*]/. 'Alterations in the text, such as deletions, are . . . given in the transcript within square brackets' (1998: 48), e.g. [rewme *deleted*].

'If two words are written conjoined either accidentally or deliberately, they are so printed' (1998: 48).

'Punctuation is reproduced exactly . . .' (1998: 48). For the *punctus interrogativus* in manuscripts, a question-mark ⟨?⟩ is used. The *punctus elevatus* is reproduced as ⟨:⟩; it appears only rarely in the texts presented here. The *virgula* (virgule) appears as ⟨/⟩; the simple *punctus* appears as ⟨.⟩.

Line divisions in prose texts in manuscripts are marked by a vertical bar, thus |. Verse is treated differently from prose, however, in that the lineation of the original is offered as on the folio or page, and the symbol | is not therefore used. Since facsimiles of prose texts in printed books are almost all available through *Early English Books Online* (*EEBO*) and *Eighteenth-Century Collections Online* (*ECCO*) it has not been thought generally necessary to mark line divisions there, although the practice has been adopted when quoting title-pages or when the texts are not available in *EEBO* or *ECCO*. In printed works, catchwords are not cited. Changes of folio are inserted when relevant in prose, and in the margin in verse texts, e.g. *folio 6v* for 'folio 6 verso (i.e. left-hand side of the opening)', *folio 7r* for 'folio 7 recto (i.e. right-hand side of the opening)' (foliations may also be indicated in the margin of prose at section breaks; marginal foliations omit 'folio', giving just the foliation). Page-breaks are flagged similarly (with 'page' abbreviated to 'p.' when necessary). In some printed books no pagination is given; in these cases signatures are treated as folios, e.g. *folio Kiij r.*

When symbols are used, an attempt is made to reproduce them. The pilcrow or paragraph-mark is quite common, i.e. ¶, as is the sign of the cross †. Crosses with a missing left-hand bar, viz. ⸶, and double-cross symbols ‡ occur in Text 6(a).

In some printed books there is variation between fonts (i.e. italic versus roman, or roman versus black-letter) and differing practices of justification. Variation between italic and roman is represented, but other such practices are not reproduced.

Manuscript references are given in all cases, plus facsimiles when available. For printed books, most texts are available through *EEBO* or *ECCO*, and availability through these resources is indicated here. In a few instances, the text used is not available through *ECCO* or *EEBO*, and in these cases the location of the volume in question is given.

Brief discussions are offered of the handwriting found in manuscripts, and of fonts in printed texts. The terminology adopted for handwriting in manuscripts is that used by Grant Simpson, who distinguishes between *text hand*, *court hand*, *pre-secretary hand*, *secretary hand* and *italic hand*. Fonts in printed books are generally either *black-letter* or *roman*, although sometimes decorative fonts are used, as in the Bassandyne print of Henryson's *Morall Fabillis* (Text 4(c)).

It will be observed, of course, that diplomatic editing is, as much as critical editing, an act of interpretation, and that the conventions listed above represent a series of editorial decisions. There is of course an alternative which some readers might have preferred: to offer facsimiles of the material presented. But facsimiles do not offer *interpretations*, i.e. 'what the writing was supposed to represent'. Eric Dobson's discussion of the diplomatic editor's task deserves quoting in full (Dobson 1972: xii–xiii):

> To publish a photographic facsimile is not the way out. It is true that photographs present the facts (or some of them, and not always truthfully), but they do nothing to interpret them; the interpretation is left to the individual reader ... it is no answer to the editorial problem simply to put a photographic facsimile in the hands of postgraduate students or even of their teachers. What is necessary is that a single editor should spend the time necessary to solve the problems of the manuscript, even those that are themselves trivial and unimportant, and should find a means of presenting his [*sic*] results so that others may benefit from his [*sic*] pains; the job should be done thoroughly once, not superficially by each individual user of a facsimile.

Although readers of this book will judge the thoroughness of the task undertaken here, Dobson's point seems to me still valid. We are however fortunate that many of the texts edited in Part II also appear in facsimile form, allowing for comparisons to be made should that be desired.

Earlier editions of all these texts have, when available, been consulted, but all texts have been approached afresh. Each text is preceded by a contextualising introduction, including references to other standard editions and (where available) facsimiles, so that students can compare and assess editorial decisions. Historical notes draw on a number of sources, especially *The Oxford Dictionary of National Biography* (*ODNB*) and standard historical surveys; Lynch 1991 can be recommended as an authoritative single-volume history of Scotland. Notes on the language of each text are also offered, though readers are also referred to Part I for full discussion of the linguistic systems within which these forms exist.

The texts in this book have been chosen to illustrate the range of linguistic features found in Older Scots writings from the earliest records through the seventeenth century; a few early-eighteenth-century versions of earlier texts are also included. An attempt has been made to give coverage across a range of genres: documents and records, letters, works on language and literature, poetry, prose and Bible translation. An important feature is the inclusion of non-literary texts, making it possible for direct comparisons between these texts and other important collections now becoming available, e.g. Cusack 1998 for Early Modern English, or the diplomatic editions mounted online as part of the Stavanger-Glasgow *Middle English Grammar Project*, the Helsinki VARIENG programme, the Edinburgh *Breadalbane Project*, the London *William Herle* project, or the Glasgow *Bess of Hardwick Project*. Older editions can also be useful, e.g. Donaldson 1970 for documents, or Cameron 1927 for the Scottish correspondence of Mary of Lorraine.

Most texts other than short ones (e.g. letters, sonnets) are represented by extracts. However, a few complete longer texts are offered, because of their intrinsic historical interest or because of their difficulty of access, e.g. the *Excommunication of the Border Reivers*. In order to show how editors have intervened in their texts in the past, and also to show how Older Scots was transmitted to later generations, parallel texts are offered of extracts from some poems: Barbour's *Bruce*, Dunbar's *Discretioun in Taking*, and the anonymous *Christ's Kirk on the Green*.

The texts presented here therefore enable students and researchers whose interests are primarily linguistic and philological to have as direct access as possible to the written forms of Scots and English current in Scotland from the fourteenth to the early eighteenth centuries.

Documents

(a) Lease of Land between the Abbot of Scone and Edmund de Haye of Leys and his son William, 1312 ('The Scone Glosses')

This text, traditionally seen as one of the earliest records of an emerging distinctive Scots linguistic variety, is now MS Edinburgh, National Archives of Scotland, RH6/72. A facsimile appears in James 1870–2, volume II, number XIX; see also Slater 1951. The manuscript is now rubbed in two places, so the nineteenth-century facsimile (carried out by Cosmo Innes, James's highly skilled amanuensis) offers valuable evidence for the readings presented below. *LAOS* also reports an unpublished study by Keith Williamson of the relationship of the Scone Glosses to the Latin text; I am grateful to Dr Williamson for discussion of this item.

The Augustinian abbey at Scone was one of the most significant monastic houses in Scotland. Monarchs were enthroned there on its ceremonial stone, whose removal to Westminster by Edward I in 1296 remained a matter of dispute for several centuries. This document records a transaction between the abbey and a local family (see further Donaldson 1970: 24–6, for an impression of the range of properties and rights granted to religious houses during the medieval period). It would originally have had a seal **hingand** from it; this seal is no longer attached.

A gloss is an interlinear crib to a text in another language, usually Latin. The Latin text of the charter dates from 1312, while the vernacular gloss dates from the middle of the fourteenth century. It has been noted that the vernacular scribe distinguishes between thorn and ⟨y⟩ (see ch. 2, 2.8 above); close re-examination of the manuscript modifies this claim. The scribe seems to have attempted to distinguish thorn and ⟨y⟩ by placing a dot above the latter, but occasionally misplaces a dot over a thorn or omits one over a ⟨y⟩; the distinction is clearly breaking down. Where the scribe uses dotted ⟨y⟩ in the text below, y appears; where the scribe omits the dot I have used thorn (thus apparent curiosities such as **do awaþ** for 'do away'). The script of both lease and gloss is court hand.

The Scots in this text presumably represents the kind of language found in Perthshire during the Early Scots period. Although the materials are fragmentary, features characteristic of Scots may be observed, e.g. **abute** for 'about', with Old English ū reflected in ⟨u⟩, Old English ā reflected in ⟨a⟩ in **halding, lauerd–,** the use of **sal** for 'shall' and **ger** (from Norse **gera**) as an auxiliary, present plural inflexions in –s and present participle endings in **–and**, third person plural pronouns in all cases beginning with thorn (whether written as y or þ). The form **lauerd–** retains the medial ⟨u⟩ for v, subsequently lost in Scots; cf. Old English **hlāford** 'lord', later Scots **laird**. Such features are of course common to Scots and dialects of Northern Middle English, and the vernacular materials in this text therefore demonstrate the continuities between Scots and Northern English during the fourteenth century.

In the text below, glossed items in the Latin are underlined, and followed by numbers referring to the relevant vernacular glosses, listed afterwards. A translation of the Latin text is also supplied (after James 1870–2).

Anno gracie M°ccc° duodecimo facta est conuencio hec inter Religiosos viros Dominum Thomam dei gracia Abbatem de Scona & eiusdem loci conuentum ex vna | parte et Edmundum de Haya del Leys & Willelmum filium eius ex altera parte. videlicet quod dictis Abbas & conuentus concesserunt
5 (1) & ad firmam dimiserunt (2) | totam terram suam de Balgarvi cum omnis pertinencijs (3) & suis rectis diuisis (4) cum quibus (5) Husbandi eandem terram ad formam tenere solebant,(6) dictis Edmundo et Willelmo | filio suo & heredibus dicti Willelmi de corpore suo proprie legitime directe immediate. linialiter (7) & non ex latere procreandis (8) & descendentibus (9) vsque ad
10 terminum triginta (10) annorum | subsequencium plene complendorum. Reddendo inde annuatim (11) dicti Edmundus Willelmus filius suus & heredes dicti Willelmi dictis Abbati & conuentui primo anno duas | marcas bonorum & legalium sterlingorum videlicet medietatem ad festum Pentechostes & aliam medietatem ad festum sancti martini in hyeme (12) Secundo anno
15 duas marcas | ad terminos prenotatos. Tertio anno tres marcas quarto anno quatuor marcas Quinto anno quinque marcas Sexto anno sex marcas per sex vero annos immediate sequentes (13) | videlicet vsque ad finem duodecimi anni quolibet anno soluent Sex marcas ad terminos prenotatos. per octo vero annos immediate sequentes videlicet vsque ad finem vicesimi | anni quolibet anno
20 soluent octo marcas per decem vero annos immediate sequentes videlicet vsque ad finem tricesimi anni soluent quolibet Anno decem marcas bonorum et legalium sterlin|gorum ad terminos prenotatos Termino introitus dictorum Edmundi et Willelmi in dictam terram incipiente ad festum Pentechostes Anni domini M'ccc' Duodecimi. Termino | prime solutionis sue incipiente ad
25 festum Pentechostes anni gracie M'ccc' tercijdecimi. Predicti vero Edmundus Willelmus & heredes dicti Willelmi facient sectam ad Curiam | Abbatis ter in anno ad tria placita capitalia. Husbandi eorum facient sectam ad omnia placita dicti Abbatis tenenda infra Baroniam de Scona. Dicti eciam Edmundus Willelmus & he|redes dicti Willelmi cum omni genere bladi
30 crescentes in dicta terra de Balgarvi quod molent pro sustencione (14) sua; venient ad molendinum (15) dictorum Abbatis & conuentus de | Kyncarroqui & ibi dabunt vicesimum quartum vas (16) ad multuram pro omnibus saluo jure seruientes(17) molendini. Homines vero husbandi & Cottarii eorum prestabunt (18) sextum decimum | vas (19) de omni genere (20) bladi crescentis
35 in dicta terra de Balgarvi sicut alij Husbandi & natiui (21) dictorum Abbatis & conuentus; facient eciam tam ipsi quam tenentes sui ad preparacionem (22) & | sustencionem (23) dicti molendini in omnibus sicut alij husbandi faciunt in circuitu (24). Dicti eciam Edmundus Willelmus & heredes dicti Willelmi facient forinsecum (25) seruicium domini Regis quantum | ad

dictam terram pertinet Et sustinebunt omnia alia onera dictam terram   40
qualitercunque tangencia vsque ad finem termini sui predicti. Dicti eciam
Edmundus. Willelmus. heredes dicti Willelmi ac | homines sui commorantes
in dicta terra de Balgarvi percipient focale (26) de communi ad vsus proprios
tantum. nec inde vendent. dabunt vel aliquo modo alienabunt (27) nisi de
terra | sua arabili quod liceat eis inde percipere (28) dare & vendere Saluo   45
dictis Abbati et conuentui & eorum successoribus in communi (29) pastura
dicte terre vsufructu pro suis animalibus (30). | In moris & mareseis pro
focali percipiendo cum indiguerint (31). Si autem querele minores & non
graues exorte (32) fuerint inter homines dictorum Edmundi Willelmi &
heredum dicti | Willelmi; inter se decidentur (33) & corrigentur; si autem   50
maiores fuerint & ad dominium pertinentes; ad Curiam dicti Abbatis debent
reseruari (34). & ibidem iuste determinari. | Saluo in omnibus dicto domino
Abbati dominio (35). Dicti eciam Edmundus Willelmus & heredes dicti
Willelmi ad consilium. & auxilium dictorum Abbatis & conuentus cum
requisiti (36) fuerint sine | simulacione accedere (37) debent. Et si contingat   55
(38) dominum nostrum Regem donacionem dicte terre a dictis Abbate &
conuentu reuocare (39); dicti Edmundus Willelmus. heredes dicti | Willelmi
ac eorum husbandi absque firma anni sui recessus recedent (40). Dicti eciam
Edmundus, Willelmus. ac heredes dicti Willelmi in dicta terra de Balgarvi
edificia (41) pro se | & husbandis suis construi facient competencia (42)   60
que in fine termini sui sic dimittent edificata (43). In cuius rei testimonium
parti huius scripti in modum Cyrograpphi | confecti. penes (44) predictos
Edmundum & Willelmum residenti (45); Sigillum commune Capituli de
Scona est appensum (46). parti vero penes predictos Abbatem & conuentum
residenti (47); | sigilla predictorum Edmundi & Willelmi sunt appensa (48). | 65

(1) has grantit	(2) has letin	(3) purtenauncis
(4) rithwis diuisis	(5) diuisis	(6) was wont
(7) euin in line	(8) on side to be to gett	(9) descendant
(10) yritti	(11) iere bi iere	(12) wyntir
(13) for vtin oni mene foluand		
(14) þat þai sal grind for yair fode		(15) miln
(16) four and tuentiand fat	(17) .i. cnaueschipe	
(18) sal gif	(19) fat	(20) kynd o
(21) in bornmen	(22) grayting	(23) vphalding
(24) abute þaime	(25) forayn	
(26) sal take fuayl		
(27) do awaþ	(28) to take	
(29) þa þat comis in yair stede	(30) gres watir and oþir profitis	
(31) yay haf mister	(32) haf grouyn	(33) haf fallin
(34) be yemit	(35) ye lauerdscape	(36) requirit
(37) feyning .i. venire	(38) impersonaliter	(39) cal agayn
(40) of yair parting. sal depart	(41) biging	

(42) be made sal ger gaynand   (43) sal leue bigit
(44) hand chartir | made a*n*entis (45) duelland
(46) hinga*n*d   (47) duella*n*d   (48) hingand

Translation (after James 1870–2):

'In the year of grace One thousand three hundred and twelfth was made this
agreement between the religious men Lord Thomas, by the grace of God,
Abbot of Scone and the Convent of the same place on the one part, and
Edmund de Hay of the Leys and William his son on the other part, to wit,
5 that the said Abbot and Convent **has grantit**, and in ferme **has letin**, their
whole land of Balgarvi, with all the **purtenauncis** and its **rithwis diuisis**
with which husbandmen **was wont** to hold the same land in ferme, to the
said Edmund and William his son, and the heirs of the said William, of his
own body lawfully, dire&ctly, immediately **euin in line** and not **on side to be**
10 **to gett** and **descendan*t***, even to the completing of the term of **yritti** years
next following, Paying for the same **iere bi iere** the said Edmund, William
his son and the heirs of the said William, to the said Abbot and Convent,
the fir&st year two merks of good and lawful &sterlings, to wit, one half at
Whitsunday and the other half at Martinmas in **wyntir**; the second year
15 two merks at the terms forenoted; the third year three merks; the fourth
year four merks; the fifth year five merks; the sixth year six merks; and for
the six years **for vti*n* oni mene foua*n*d**, namely, up to the end of the twelfth
year, in each year they shall pay six merks at the terms forenoted; and for
the eight years immediately following, namely, to the end of the twentieth
20 year, they shall pay each year eight merks; and for the ten years immediately
following, namely, up to the end of the thirtieth year, they shall pay each
year ten merks of good and lawful &sterlings at the terms forenoted; the
term of entry of the said Edmund and William to the said land beginning
Whitsunday·of the year of our lord the thirteen hundred and twelfth; the
25 term of the fir&st payment of the same beginning at Whitsunday, the year of
grace One thousand three hundred and thirteenth. And the foresaid Edmund,
William and the heirs of the said William, shall give suit at the Court of the
Abbot three times in the year, at three head courts; their husbandmen shall
give suit at all the Courts of the said Abbot to be held within the barony of
30 Scone. Also the said Edmund, William and the heirs of the said William,
shall come with all kinds of grain growing on the said land of Balgarvi, þ*at*
þai sal gri*n*d for yair fode, to the **miln** of the said Abbot and Convent of
Kyncarroqui, and there shall give the **four a*n*d tuentia*n*d fat** for multure for
all dues, reserving the **.i. cnaueschipe** of the mill. But the husbandmen and
35 their cottars **sal gif** the sixteenth **fat** of every **kynd o** grain growing on the
said land of Balgarvi as the other husbandmen and **in bornmen** of the said
Abbot and Convent also; also, they and the tenants shall do for the **grayting**
and **vphalding** of the said mill in all things, as the other husbandmen round
abute þaim do. Also, the said Edmund, William and the heirs of the said

78

William shall perform the **forayn** service of our Lord the King which to the 40
land effairs; and they shall bear all other burdens of whatever kind affecting
the said land even to the end of their foresaid term. Also, the said Edmund,
William and the heirs of the said William and their men dwelling in the
said land of Balgarvi, **sal take fuayl** from the common for their own use
only; but they shall not thence sell, give or in any other wise **do awaþ**, unless 45
from their own arable land what is lawful for them from the same **to take,**
give and sell. Reserving to the said Abbot and Convent, and **þa þat comis
in yair ſtede**, in the common paſturage of the said land **gres watir and oþir
profitis** for their beaſts; in the moors and marshes for taking fuel when **yay
haf miſter**. But if diſþutes petty and not serious shall **haf grouyn** amongſt 50
the men of the said Edmund, William and the heirs of the said William, they
shall **haf fallin** and corrected among themselves. But if they be more serious
and belonging to the lordship, they ought to **be yemit** to the Court of the
Abbot, and there juſtly determined, reserving in all points **ye lauerdscape**
to the said lord Abbot. Also, the said Edmund, William and the heirs of the 55
said William, when they shall be **requirit**, ought, without **feyning .i. venire**,
to come to the counsel and aid of the said Abbot and Convent. And if it
happen **impersonaliter** that our lord the King **cal agayn** the gift of the said
land from the said Abbot and Convent, the said Edmund, William, the heirs
of the Said William and their husbandmen, **sal depart** without rent of the 60
year **of yair parting**. Also, the said Edmund, William and the heirs of the
Said William, **sal ger be made** on the said land of Balgarvi, for themselves
and their husbandmen, **gaynand biging** which, at the end of their term,
they **sal leue** so **bigit**. In witness whereof, the Common Seal of the Chapter
of Scone is **hingand** to the part of this writing made in the form of a **hand** 65
chartir made anentis duelland in the hands of the foresaid Edmund and
William; but to the part **duelland** in the hands of the foresaid Abbot and
Convent the seals of the foresaid Edmund and William are **hingand**.'

(b) Exemption of the Abbey of Melrose from customs of their wools, 26 May 1389

The text appears in James (1870–2), volume II, number XLVII; the original is MS
Edinburgh, National Archives of Scotland, GD55/480, and is now rather rubbed.
The original seal is still appended.

Robert Stewart, earl of Fife and Menteith, was a son of King Robert II. He was
appointed chamberlain of Scotland in 1382; in 1398 he was created duke of Albany
by his older brother, Robert III. He died in Stirling in 1420, with the reputation
of being 'a man of great expenses and munificent to strangers', according to the
chronicler Walter Bower (Nicholson 1974: 252).

The exemption presented here is a generous one – wool was one of the few Scottish goods available for export, and customs were a major source of government
revenue – but was very necessary; Melrose Abbey, one of the great religious houses

of Scotland which had been particularly favoured by Robert the Bruce, had been set on fire four years previously by the English army of the young Richard II, and the institution was in dire need of financial support.

This document is one of the earliest records in the Scots language, and it exemplifies many common Scots features. Thorn is invariably written as ⟨y⟩. In spellings, the reflex of Old English hw– appears as ⟨qwh-⟩ in **qwhilom**, **qwhilk**, **qwhy**, while the reflex of Old English ō appears as ⟨u⟩ in **gude** 'good' and the reflex of Old English ā appears as ⟨a⟩ in **mare** 'more', **mast** 'most', though cf. **lorde** 'lord' where Scots might have been expected to have **laird**; it seems to be common for this anglicised form to be used, possibly since the term was commonly used as a form of address in cross-border communication. Inflexions characteristic of – although of course not exclusive – to Scots include –**it** in **Shippit** and –**is** in **apperis**. Third person plural possessive and dative pronouns appear with **y**, e.g. **yair**, **yaim**, while the demonstrative system includes **yir** 'these'. The construction **we bid & commandes** exemplifies the Northern Personal Pronoun Rule. The passage also exemplifies loans into Scots from languages with which it came into contact, e.g. **kyrkes** 'churches' and **efter/eftir** 'after' (from Norse) beside **memore** 'memory', **assoilie** 'absolve' (from French). The traditional spelling for the town is **Meuros** (as here); the modern spelling may be a hyperadaptation or 'back-spelling', presuming an older *l*-vocalisation (see ch. 2, 2.22).

The text is written in court hand. Punctuation is light; however, the double virgule //, accompanied by litterae notabiliores before the preposition **To**, is used to mark the transition from the background information to the instruction.

Robert erle of ffyf & of menteth wardane & Chambirlayn of Scotland to ye Custumers of ye grete Custome of ye burows of Edynburgh | hadyntou*n* and Dunbarr greting ffor qwhy yat of gude memore Dauid kyng qwhilom of Scotland yat god assoillie w*ith* his chartir vndre his grete | sele has gyvin

5   to ye Religios men ye Abbot & ye Conuent of Meuros & to yair successours for euere mare frely all ye Custume of all yair | wollys as wele of yair awin growing as of yair tendys of yair kyrkes as it app*er*is be ye forsaid Chartir confermyt be our mast souereigne | & doubtit lorde & fadre our lorde ye kyng of Scotland Robert yat now ys w*ith* his grete Sele// To yow ioyntly &

10   seu*er*ailly be ye | tenour of yis *lett*re fermely we bid & co*m*mandes yat ye forsaid wollys at your Portes yir *lett*res sene ye qwilk *lett*res yhe delyuere to yaim | again yhe suffre to be Shippit & frely to pass w*ith*outyn ony askyng or takyng of Custume or ony obstacle or lettyng in ony point | eftir as ye tenour of ye forsaides Chartir & confirmacioun plen*er*ly askis & p*ur*portis. In wytnes

15   here of to yis *lett*re we haue put our sele | at Edynburgh the xxvj. day of Maij/ ye yhere of God mill. ccc. iiij and nyne |

(c)   *Extracts from a medieval Scots merchant's handbook (after 1390)*

This text comes from MS Edinburgh, National Library of Scotland, Advocates' 34.7.6, a small book which survives in its original binding. A full description and discussion of the manuscript and its contents appears in Hanham (1971); Hanham also offers an annotated edition. The first part of the manuscript, written in what Hanham calls 'a clerkly script' (1971: 108), i.e. a neat court hand, contains a Latin set of penitential prayers with a short introductory rubric, claiming that the prayers are especially efficacious in calming storms at sea and thus useful for a Christian merchant setting out on a perilous journey; the prayers are also useful in cases of childbirth. The second part, 'in a less clerical-looking hand', i.e. a rather less formal version of court hand, is described by Hanham 'primarily as a ready-reckoner for use in the extremely complicated conditions obtaining in the markets of the Low Countries in the late fourteenth and early fifteenth centuries, . . . offering incidental remarks about the means of buying or selling different commodities there' (1971: 109). A faint drawing of a Virgin with Child appears on folio 8 recto. The work is particularly interesting about rates of exchange between various currencies. The book was owned in 1571 by Robert Methuen, who wrote his name on folio 3 recto. Of the original owner, John Messon (for Mason), or indeed of Peter (his brother?), nothing is known. An ownership inscription and humorous letter to the owner's wife, in a very untidy script, appear on folio 2 verso, and are given here below. These inscriptions are clearly later additions, probably from the first quarter of the fifteenth century.

The text presented here contains many Scots features: **qwha** 'who' exemplifies both **qwh–** and ⟨a⟩ as the reflex of Old English ā. Old English ā seems also to be reflected in ⟨ay⟩ in **haym** 'home', and Old English ū is reflected in ⟨wy⟩ in **bwyk** 'book'; in both cases ⟨y⟩ seems to be used as a diacritic flagging the presence of a long vowel. The form **meykyll** 'much' is a Norse-derived form common in Scots; the form **fray** 'from' seems to derive from Norse frá. The form **at** 'that' (conjunction) in **I wald at** might also be noted; there is some evidence that this usage is less formal in Older Scots. There is a good deal of technical vocabulary in the text, e.g. **schorlingis** 'skins from recently shorn sheep' (cf. *DSL* **s(c)horling**), which may related to Flemish **schoorlinc**, and **creyll** 'wicker basket' (of obscure etymology, according to *DSL*). The form **hogvell** is not recorded in either *DSL* or *OED*, either in this form or as **hogfell**, but from the context it seems to mean 'pigskin'; the spelling with ⟨v⟩ may indicate that the word has transferred to Scots from a German dialect (see the *OED* etymology for **fell** (1), though see also *DSL* **vellus** (n)). The text also exemplifies the admission of Middle Dutch vocabulary to the Scots technical lexicon, e.g. **coft** 'bought'; such vocabulary entered Scots through trade, and it is therefore appropriate that it should be seen in this document. We might also note the sporadic use of Latin in the text, commonplace as part of the casual 'macaronic' language adopted by international traders during the Middle Ages, e.g. **vel** 'or'.

The ownership inscription:

> *[folio 2v]* Qwha sum ewer dois on me lwyk
> I am invrite Johann messonis bwyk
> & I be tynt & ȝe me fynd
> I pray ȝow hartly be so kynd
> To tak on ȝow so meykyl pain
> As for to send me haym again
> John vel Peter Messon

Humorous letter to wife (same folio):

Spowis I *com*mend me to 30w & | I wald at 3e dwyd weyll// |
I haif coft mony// yngannis bot | I want ane creyll// preſþylle |
owt ow*er* all thyng rasaif | fray y*is* barer/ v dry herein |
Weyll kneyt on ane ſtreyng |
Jn M |

A typical entry:

*[The word **Nota** appears in the margin of this entry.]*

10v Here begynns ye Reknyng of | ye skyns yat vxx mak*is* ye c yat | is to say woll
skyns schorling*is* & | hogvell/ and ar salde be ye flemis | nobil/ yat is vj s*chillingis* |

(d) Extract from a vernacular version of the 'Leges Burgorum', c. 1424

The *Leges (Quattuor) Burgorum* ('Laws of the (Four) Burghs') formed an important
element in the burghal reforms of David I and his successors (see ch. 1, 3.7). These
laws, based on those current in Newcastle-upon-Tyne in northern England, governed many aspects of life and work in the four royal Burghs of Berwick, Roxburgh,
Edinburgh and Stirling (see Nicholson 1974: 17–18). The *Leges Burgorum* were
originally written in Latin, the language of record for all modern western European states in the twelfth and thirteenth centuries, and several versions survive, e.g.
the Berne and Ayr Manuscripts, images of both of which have been digitised (see
⟨http://www.stairsociety.org/bernems.htm⟩).

This Scots version of the *Leges Burgorum* survives in the Bute Manuscript, a
large volume now in the National Library of Scotland and containing various legal
texts, in both Latin and Scots. The following entry appears in the National Library
of Scotland's typescript *Catalogue of Mss Acquired since 1925*, Volume XIV:

> REGIAM MAIESTATEM. A manuscript of the Regiam Maiestatem, statutes,
> Leges Portum, forest laws, Quoniam attachiamenta, burgh and guild laws, and
> other smaller legal texts, some in Scots, written by two hands in the second half
> of the fourteenth century . . .

The book was completed by 1424, when there is a record (folio 178v) of its being
purchased by Duncan Parker, possibly a burgess of Dundee, from one Cragy of
Edinburgh. By 1565 the book was owned by William Skene of St Andrews; his
brother Sir John used the book as the basis for his edition of the *Regiam Maies-
tatem*, which he published in Edinburgh in 1609. The book later came into the
possession of the Marquess of Bute, and is thus often referred to as the Bute Manuscript; the National Library acquired the book in 1987. It is now MS Edinburgh,
National Library of Scotland 21246.

The *Leges Burgorum Scocie*, as it is called in the manuscript, is item xix. It is
written in the second hand; the script is a formal variety of court hand, with text
hand frequently used for rubrics. The *Leges* begins with the following heading
(folio 155r):

Hic incipiunt leges burgorum Scocie facte apud nouum castrum | super Tynam per daiud regem Scotorum illustrissimum | In primis deleted de redditu domini regis |

There are several Scots texts in the manuscript, representing the kind of Scots current at the end of the fourteenth century; in addition to the *Leges*, these texts include such works as *The Assise of brede and ye payse*, *Of law and ye custume of schippis*, and *Of Wecht in flandrys and reknyns by ye price of ye mone*. The passage below exemplifies several features characteristic of Scots, e.g. the reflex of Old English ā in ⟨a⟩, e.g. **swa**, and of Old English ō in ⟨u⟩, e.g. **gude**. The prepositions **fra** 'from', **til** 'to' and **eftyr** 'after' are all common to Scots and Northern English, and are usually considered to derive from Norse, as does the modal verb **ger** 'cause (to)'; **sal** (cf. Present-Day English 'shall') is also notable. Inflexions in –**yt**, –**it** may also be noted, as is the use of ⟨qwh-⟩ as the reflex of Old English **hw**–, e.g. **qwhen, qwhar, qwhil**. It is interesting that a medieval glossator (it seems from the script later in the fifteenth century) offered an interpretation of **foroth** as **beforn** and **convickyt** as **committit**; cf. the entries in *DSL* for **forouth** (cf. Northern Middle English **for-with**), **convict** (v); clearly these words were already dying out in some parts of the Scots-speaking area. As might be expected, there is some specialist legal vocabulary, e.g. **sykyr borws** 'secure pledges' (cf. the alternative spelling **borch** 'pledge'), **lauch** 'law', **bailies** 'town magistrates' and **somondyng** 'summoning'; the last of these words derives from Anglo-Norman/Old French **somondre**, and according to *OED* is 'Sc. and *north*. Obs.'. Present-Day English **summon** derives from the stem of the word, viz. **somon**–, without the ending in –**dre**.

151r... xxxxiiij. Of thing reft and fundyn in ye market/ |

Gyf ony man fyndys his thyng in ye fayre yat is ſtollyn | or rabbyt fra hym or tynte wyth ony man he aw to lede | *[folio 151v]* hym to ye bailes qwhen ye thyng is fondyn and yar nemmyn | his scath and ask qwhar his dwellyng is and ger hym fynde | borws foroth [beforn *marginal gloss*] ye bayles of ye fayre to ye   5
chalangear yat he | sal hafe hys thyng ye .xv. day eftyr ye fayre in yat ſtede ye | qwhilkys ye bayles lymytis of ye fayre/ And yar sal lauch be | haldyn to ye chalangeoure And gyf he hafe na borch ye bailes | sal hafe ye thyng qwhil he fynd borch to ye chalangeour or | ellys to ye courte eftyr ye fayre And gyf he yat is chalangour cum yan and fynd borch as is beforsaid ye thyng sal be   10
convickyt [committit *marginal gloss*] | til hym and ye chalangear sal follow his ſpeche And gyfe | ye chalangyt man cum nocht at ye courte of ye fayre ye thyng | sal be gyfyn to ye chalangear vndyr sykyr borws swa yat | gyf ony man mak ſpeche yar of eftyrwart he sal furthe | bryng it at somondyng of ye bailes to yat ſtede yat he re | sayvit it in als gude ſtate as it was qwhen he resayvit it | or   15
ellys ye valw of it gyf it be peryſt or ſpylt in his kepyng | to do yat lauch wyl |

(e) 'The Excommunication of Border Reivers' by the archbishop of Glasgow (1525)

This famous 'monition' by Gavin Dunbar, archbishop of Glasgow (*c.* 1490–1547) relates to a turbulent time in the complex and troubled sixteenth-century relationship between Scotland and England. Dunbar had been confirmed as archbishop in 1523, and this monition against banditry in the debatable lands between the two nations formed part of an attempted policy of international pacification. The monition was intended to be pronounced in churches, and also at mercat crosses in various Border towns. Although this example is the most elaborate in the Scots vernacular yet discovered, formal cursings were fairly common. They were regarded as an abuse by reformers, who mocked them for their concern with trivial offences, e.g. 'that a priest would invoke solemn maledictions for the theft of a porridge-stick, a flail and a horn spoon' (Donaldson and Macrae 1942: xi, citing a comment by John Knox).

Dunbar was a prominent public figure in Scottish politics throughout the first half of the sixteenth century. For much of this period he held the office of Chancellor of Scotland, taking a role in (e.g.) reforming the system of justice. He seems generally to have followed the ebb and flow of royal policy rather than to have taken a significant part in its formulation, although in 1543 he led clerical opposition to an act permitting the reading of the New Testament in Scots. His main (and bitter) rival for much of the period was Cardinal David Beaton, archbishop of St Andrews; rivalry between the two archbishops meant that internal church reform was stalled and that there was a lack of consistent action against perceived Protestant heresies. However, both men were present at the notorious burning of George Wishart in St Andrews in 1546 (see Text 5(g)), a key event in the martyrology of the Reformation which was followed shortly afterwards by Beaton's assassination. It is possible that there was an element of personal, and rather petty, revenge in Dunbar's involvement in Wishart's death; the previous year, in Ayr, a congregation had largely deserted Dunbar's preaching in order to hear Wishart, a charismatic speaker, in a nearby market-place (see further Dunbar's *ODNB* entry, and also Easson 1947).

The text edited here is from the *St Andrews Formulare*, now MS St Andrews, University Library 1720, folios 204r–206r; the manuscript dates from the first half of the sixteenth century. Another shorter copy is in MS London, British Library Cotton Caligula B.ii, folio 289r ff. An edition of the *Formulare* appears in Donaldson and Macrae (1942); the *Excommunication* is on pp. 268–71. According to Donaldson and Macrae, the *Formulare Instrumentorum Ecclesiaticorum* ('book of ecclesiastical styles': a later title) was compiled by John Lauder, an ecclesiastical notary who became successively secretary to Andrew Forman, bishop of Moray, an associate of James Beaton of St Andrews, Robert Forman, dean of Glasgow, and archbishop Dunbar. Lauder eventually became David Beaton's secretary.

Lauder's competent secretary hand has been recognised in other documents. He is referred to by John Knox, in his *History of the Reformation*, as a particular persecutor of George Wishart: 'Right against Wishart stood up one of the fed flock, a monster, John Lauder, laden full of cursings, threatening, maledictions and words of devilish spite and malice, saying . . . so many cruel and abominable words . . . that the ignorant people dreaded lest the earth then would have swallowed Wishart up quick . . . When that this fed sow had read through all the lying menacing, his face running down with sweat and frothing at the mouth like a bear, he spat at master George's face' (cited Donaldson and Macrae 1942: vii–viii). There are several monitions in the *Formulare*: 'Lauder may have been famed throughout the land as an expert in malediction' (Donaldson and Macrae 1942: xii).

The language of the passage is a good example of early sixteenth-century Scots. Old English ā is commonly reflected as ⟨a(i)⟩ in **haly** 'holy', **aithis** 'oaths', **lang** 'long', **alanerly** 'alone' (adverb), **ane** 'one'; however, **lord** is usual (cf. **hlāford**). The form **hayme** 'home' may also contain the reflex of Old English ā, cf. Old English **hām**, but cf. also Old Norse **heimr**; the form **geyst** 'spirit' may derive from Norse **geist** rather than from Old English **gāst**. Old Norse **frá** appears as –**fray**, **fra**. Old English ū is reflected in ⟨u(y)⟩ in **gude** 'good', **gud**is 'goods', **tuke** 'took', **fluyde** 'flood'. Old English hw– is reflected as **quh**– in **quhilk**, **quhen**, **quhill** etc., while *l-mouillé* appears in **spulȝeit** 'ravaged'. The form **chalmeris** 'chambers' (cf. French **chambre**) is a back-spelling suggesting that *l*-vocalisation is in progress. **Devill** 'devil' is found in place of a form with *v*-deletion, i.e. **deil**, although the latter form, interestingly, appears in *DSL* only in the later citations derived from *SND*. The form **thunnyr** demonstrates that Scots has not yet developed epenthetic /d/, as in Present-Day English **thunder** (cf. Old English **þunor**); **cummyrles**, conversely, 'unencumbered' may show the assimilation of /b/ to /m/ (cf. Middle English **cumber**, though see the discussion in *OED*). Thorn is written as ⟨y⟩, e.g. **yaim** 'them', but is often replaced by ⟨th⟩, e.g. **thame**. ⟨w⟩ often appears in this text in place of ⟨v⟩, e.g. **wile** 'vile', and ⟨v⟩ sometimes appears for ⟨w⟩, e.g. **varld** 'world', **vardly** (*sic*) 'worldly' alongside **warld**. Norse forms appear, e.g. **kirk**–, **hundr**e**th**, but we might note the use of ȝ- in **ȝettis** 'gates', which is derived from Old English. In Scots, as in Northern English, **gate** (from Norse **gata**) is used with the meaning 'road', 'street', with the cognate native form used for 'gate'; we might compare the place-name **Yetts o' Muckhart** for a pass between hills with **Trongate** for a street in Glasgow. The form **pott** 'pit' seems to be peculiarly Scottish and northern, and may derive from Norse (see *OED pot*, noun (2)). The Norse-derived present participle inflexion in –**and**, e.g. **duelland**, **drynkand** is very common. The Northern Personal Pronoun Rule is also exemplified, e.g. **y**a*t* **thai su**m **to or remanis, I forbyd and Inhibit**is **al preist**is **and kirkme**n. There is, as we might expect in such an elaborate text, a good deal of specialist terminology, largely to do either with property liable to theft or with violent criminality: **cailȝardis** 'cabbage-garden', **Catall** 'goods, chattels', **heirchippes** 'armed incursions', **malysonis and varysonis** 'curses and rewards', **palȝeoun** 'pavilion' (see *DSL pallion*, noun (2)), **reiffis** 'spoliations' (cf. **Reyffaris** 'spoilers'), **resettaris** 'receivers of (stolen) goods' (cf. *DSL* **resait**), **saikles** 'pitiless', **spulȝies** 'spoils', **supplearis** 'collaborators, accomplices'.

204r Gude folkis heir ar my Lorde Archibischop of Glasgews | letteris gevin vnder his rovnde Sele / direkit to me or | ony vthir chaplane Makand mentioun with grete regrait hov | hevilie he beris The pietous lamentable and dolorous com-|plaint that passis our all the reaulme and cu*m*in to his Eris be | oppin voce and fame/ How o*ur* souv*er*ane lordis the king*is* trew | and faithfull liegis/ men/ 5 wyiff*is* and bayrnis/ bocht and re-|demit be the precios blude of o*ur* Salvato*ur* Jh*es*u cri∫te and | levand i*n* his faith and lawis ar saikleslye put dovn and | di∫troyit Part murdrei∫t/ part slane/ vtheris mutilate/ | brynt/ heriit/ ∫pulȝiet and reft oppinlie on day ly*ch*t And | vnder silence of the ny*ch*t/ and thare landis/ takkis/ housis/ | and ∫tedyngis laid vai∫t and di∫troyt and thar 10 self*is* ba*n*ny∫t | th*er*fray Als wele temporale landis as kirklandis/ be commou*n* | traitouris/ Reyffaris/ theyff*is*/ murderiȝaris & men slayar*is* | duelland

within the sowth p*artis* of this reaulme and within | his dioc*es* of glasgw That
is to say In ſpeciale within | the p*artis* of Teviotdaile/ Tuedaile/ Ettrikforeſt/
15 Crau-|furdmure/ Clyddisdaile/ lyddisdaile/ Nithisdaile/ Annan-
|derdaile | Eskdaile/ Eusdaile/ and Vauchopdaile and | diu*ers* vtheris p*artis*
within his said dioc*es* of glasgw Quhilk*is* | has bene diuers vays p*er*sewit and
punyſt be the temp*orale* | swerde and *our* soverane lord*is* auctorite And dred*is*
noc*h*t | the sam*m*yn And tharfore my said lord Archbischop of glasgw | hais
20 thoc*h*t expedi*ent* to ſtryke thame with the t*er*rible suorde | of halykirk/ quhilk
thai ma noc*h*t lang Indure nor resiſt And | hais chargeit me or ony vthir
chaplane/ To denunce declair | And procleme thame oppinlie and generalye
cursit | at this m*ar*ket crois And al vther public plac*is*. Herefore | Throuch the
Auctorite of almyc*h*ty god The fader of hevin/ | his sone *our* salvato*ur* Jhesu
25 chriſt And of the haly geyſt And | throuch the auctorite of the Blissit Virgyne
Sancte marye | his moder/ Sanct Michael/ Sanct gabriell/ Sanct Ra-|phaell
and al the Angellis/ Sanct Jhone the baptiſt and | al the haly patriarchis and
prophet*is*/ Sanct Petir/ Sanct | Paule/ Sanct Androw/ Sanct James/ Sanct Jhon
the | Ewangeliſt And all haly appoſtillis/ Sanct Stevyn/ Sanct | Laurence/ Sanct
30 Sebaſtiane and al haly m*ar*theris/ Sanct | Mongw/ sanct goile/ Sanct Niniane
Sanct Martyne | and al haly c*on*fessour*is*/ Sanct Tan/ Sanct Katheryne | Sanct
Margarete/ Sancte Bryde/ and all haly virginis and | matronis And of all the
sainctis and haly c*um*pany of | hevin/ be the auctorite of *our* maiſt haly fadere
the paipe | And his Cardinalis/ and of my said lord Archibischop of Glasgw | Be
35 the avise and assiſtance of my lord*is* Archibischop | bischoppis/ abbot*is*/
priour*is*/ and vtheris p*re*latis and miniſteris | of haly kirk/ I denunce/
proclemis/ and declaris All and | syndry the c*om*mittaris of the said*is* saikles
Murthuris/ slauchter*is* | byrnyng*is*/ heirchippes/ reiffis/ Thiftis & ſpulȝeis
oppi*n*lie | apon day lyc*h*t/ and vnder silence of the nyc*h*t Alsweile | within
40 temporale landis as kirkland*is*/ togydder w*ith* thare | parttakkaris/ assiſtaris/
supplearis/ wittandlye resettaris | of thar p*er*sonis/ the gud*is* reft ſtollin and
ſpulȝeit be thame | Art or p*ar*t yerof and yar Counsalouris and defendour*is* | [*folio*
205r] of thare euill ded*is* alan*er*lye/ Cursit vareyt Aggregit and Reag-|gregit
with the grete cursing/ I curse thare heid and all the | haris of y*er* heid/ I curse
45 thare face/ Thar Ene/ thar mouth/ thar | neys/ Thar tounge/ Thar teith/ Thare
crag*is*/ Thar schulder*is*/ thar | breyſt*is*/ thare hartis/ Thar ſtomok*is*/ Thar bak*is*/
Thar waymes/ thar | armys/ Thar leggis/ Thare handis/ Thare feyt/ And everilk
p*ar*t | of thar bodys fra the top of y*ar* heides To the sole of y*ar* feyt/ be-|fore
and behynde within and without/ I curs thame gangand | and I curs yaim
50 rydand/ I curs thame ſtandand/ I curs thame sitta*n*d/ | I curs yaim eittand/ I
curs yaim drynkand/ I curs yaim walka*n*d/ | I curs yaim slepand/ I curs yaim
rysand/ I curs yaim lyand/ I | curs yaim at hame/ I curs yaim fra hayme/ I curs
yaim within the | hous*is*/ I curs y*a*m without the hous*is*/ I curs thar wyiff*is*
thar | bayrnis and y*ar* s*er*vandis p*ar*ticipant w*ith* thame In thar evil
55 and | myscheiffis deid*is*/ I vayry thare cornis/ thare Catall/ Thar | woll/ thar
scheip/ thar hors*is*/ thar swyne/ thar geys Thar | he*n*nis/ thar Cokkis And all

yar quyk gudis/ I wayry thar | hallis/ thare chalmeris/ yar beddis/ thar
kechynis/ thar stabillis | Thar bernys/ Thare byris/ Thare berne3ardis/ thar
cail3ardis | Thare pleuchis/ thare harrovis/ And al the gudis and housis |yat ar
necessar for thar sustentatioun and velefare/ All the maly-|sonis and   60
varyesonis that euer gatt vardly creatur/ seyn the | beginnyng of the warld to
this hour/ mot lycht apoun thame | The maledictioun of god that lichtit apoun
lucifer and al his | fallovis/ that straik yame fra the hevin to the deip pott of
hell | mot lycht apoun yame/ the fyre and the suorde that | stoppit Adam our
forefader fra the 3ettis of paradys/ mot stop | yame fra the gloir of hevin quhill   65
thai foirber yar misdedis | and mak amendis/ The malysoun That lychtit on
cursit | Cayn/ quhen he slew his bruther Just Abell saikleslye | mot lycht on
yam for the saikles slauchteris/ murthuris and | *[folio 205v]* Reyffis that tha
commit daylie and nychtlye/ The maledictioun | that lychtit apoun the varld
man woman and beist/ And al | yat euer tuke lyif/ quhen al ves drovnit be the   70
fluyde of Noye | Except Noye and his arch mot lycht apoun thame And | drovne
yame man woman barne & beist And mak this reaulm | cummyrles of yam
for thare vykkit synnys/ The thunnyr | and fyre flauchtis yat 3ett dovne as rayn
apon the | Citteis of Sodoma and gomorra with al the landis about | And brynt
thaim for thar wile synnis/ mot rayn apoun yaim | and byrne thaim for thar   75
oppin synnis & cruel mysdedis | the malysoun and confusioun that lychtit on
the gygantis | for thar oppressioun and pryde biggand the tour of ba-|bilon/
mot confound yame and all thar verkis/ for thar | oppin Reyffis/ spul3eis and
oppressionis/ All the plagis yat fell apoun king Pharao and his peple of Egipt/
thar | landis/ Corne & Catall mot fall apoun thame/ thar takkis | rovmis and   80
stedyngis Cornis Cattall and beystis/ the | Watteris and riveris of Tuede/
Teviot/ Clyde/ Nyth/ | Esk/ Eus and Annande/ and all vtheris watteris
quhare | *[folio 206r]* tha Ryde/ gang or pas Mot drovn yaim As the Reid Sey
drovnit kyng pharao and the peple of Egipt per-|sevande goddis peple of
Israel The 3erd mot oppin | Ryif and cleyf and suelly thame/ quyk to hell/ As   85
It suellit | Cursit dathan and abyron/ yat ganestude Moyses and the | commande
of god/ The vyld fyre that brynt Chovr and | his fallovis to the nomer of Tua
hundreth & fyifty And vtheris | fourtene thousande and sevin hundreth at
Anis vsurpand | aganis Moyses and Aaron servandis of god/ not
suddandly | byrne and consume yaim/ dayly ganestandand the commandis | of   90
god and haly kyrk/ The maledictioun/ yat lychtit suddandlie apoun | fayr
Absalon Rydand contrar his fader kyng David/ seruand | of god throuch the
wod/ quhen the branchis of ane tree fred | him of his hors and hangit him be
the hair/ mot lycht apoun yam | Rydand aganis trew Scottis men And hang
thame siclike yat | all the varld ma see the vengiance of god cum apoun   95
yame | The maledictioun yat lychtit apoun Olofernes lieutennent to
Na-|bogodono3er makand were on goddis peple/ quhen his heide | ves cuttit
of suddandlye in his avn pal3eoun In the myddis of | his grete oist mot lycht
on yame/ Makand plane wer and | heirschippis apoun the cristin men/ The
maledictioun on Judas | Scaryoth/ Poynce Pylot/ kyng Herode and the Jowis   100

87

yat | crucyfeit our Lord Jhe*su* Chri*st* And all the plagis and trublis | *yat* lychtit
on ye Citte of Jherusalem *y*erfore And apon Symon | Magus/ for his symony/
Bludy nero/ Cursit Decius/ Max-|entius/ Olibrius/ Julianus apo*st*ata And the
laif of the cruell | tyrannis/ that slew and m*u*rthirit cryi*stis* haly s*e*ruandis/
105 mot | lycht apoun yai*m* for thar cruel tyra*n*ny and murthur dom done on
Cri*st*in peple And als all the vengean*cis* that eu*er* | vas takin sen the varld
began for oppyn synn*is* and al | the plagis and pe*st*ilence/ that euer fell on
man or bei*st* | mot fall apoun yame for thar oppin Reyf*fis*/ saikles slauch-|teris
and schedding of innoce*n*t blude/ I dissevir and | *p*artis thame fra the kirk of
110 god/ and deliueris thame | quyk to ye Devill of Hell/ thar p*er*petualy to Remane
co*n*damp-|nit In body and Saule/ quhill thai co*n*uert to god | and mak ame*n*dis
for thar cruell tre*sp*asses/ I Inter*dy*te | all and syndry the kyrkis/ Abbais/
Collegis/ chapellis | and orito*u*ris/ Citteis/ burghis/ tovnis/ ca*st*ellis/
villagis | and housis and all and quhatsu*m*eu*er* pla*cis* yat thai cu*m* | to or
115 remanis In/ fra all messis sayng and celebration | *[folio 206v]* of diuine s*e*ruice
and mini*st*ratioun of the sacramentis of haly kirk except | the sacrament of
baptisme alan*er*ly And thar bodeys at happinnis to | dee vnd*er* this cursing
and Inter*di*ctioun tobe ca*st*yn furth to dog*gis* & | bei*st*is And nothir to be erdit
In kirk nor kirk3ard/ bot i*n* myddi*nis* | myris and vthir wile and foull placis
120 And atto*u*r I forbyd and | Inhibit*is* al prei*st*is and kirkme*n* vnd*er* the pane of
the gret cur-|sing to schriyf or absolue yame of y*er* synnis/ quhill thai be
fir*st* | assoil3eit fra this cursing/ I forbid and Inhibitis alsua al cri*st*in | ma*n* and
voman til haue ony cu*m*pany w*ith* yame/ Eittand/ drynkand | *sp*eikand/
prayand/ lyand/ gangand/ *st*andand or ony vthir deid | Doand/ vnder the
125 pane of deidlye sy*n*ne/ I discharge al band*is* | a*ct*is/ contra*ct*is/ aithis/ and
obligationis maid to yame be ony | personis/ othir of lavtie/ kyndnes or
manrent/ sa lang as thai | su*st*ene this cursing and inter*di*ctioun Sua y*at* na
ma*n* be bu*n*din | to yame And that thai be bundin til all men/ I tak fra
thai*m* | and cryis dovne al the gude deid*is* y*at* euer tha did/ or sal | do quhill
130 yai ryse fra this cursing/ I declair thame p*a*rtles | of al matynis/ messis/
Evinsang*is*/ dirig*is* or vther prayer*is* | on buke or beid/ of al pilgramag*is* and
almous deid*is* done | or to be done In haly kirk/ or be cri*st*in peple Induring | this
cursing And fynaly I co*n*dampne thame p*er*petualy | to ye deip pott of hell to
remane w*ith* Lucifer and bael3ebub | and al y*er* fallouis devillis of hell and y*er*
135 bodeys to the gallovs*is* | fir*st* to be hangit/ Syne revyn and ruggit with dog*gis*
svyne | & vther*is* wyle bei*st*is abhominable to al the varld And as the | sovnde
of this bell gais fra 3o*u*r eris And the lych*t* of this candle | fra 3o*u*r sych*t* Sa mot
thar saulis gang fra the visaige of | god almych*ty* And y*ar* gude fame fra the
varld/ quhill tha forbeir | y*er* oppin sy*n*nis/ Reif*fis*/ thyf*tis*/ slauch*te*ris/
140 m*u*rthuris/ *sp*ul3eis/ and | byrnyng*is* forsaid*is* And ryis fra this t*e*rrible cursing
& Inter*di*ctioun | And mak satisfa*ct*ion for y*ar* misded*is* And cu*m* to ye
boissu*m* of haly | kirk to ressaue and do pe*n*nance for ye remission of y*ar*
oppi*n* synnis forsaid*is* |

(f) Extract from 'The Register of Acts of the Privy Council': Proclamation against the earl of Bothwell(1567)

James Hepburn, earl of Bothwell, duke of Orkney, Lord High Admiral of Scotland, seducer of numerous women and probable murderer, is one of the most notorious figures in sixteenth-century Scottish history. The document below accuses him – almost certainly accurately – of playing the principal part in the murder earlier in 1567, at Kirk o'Field in Edinburgh, of Henry Stewart, Lord Darnley, the second husband of Mary Queen of Scots (**king henry stewart of gude memorie**). Subsequent to Darnley's death, Bothwell abducted Mary and, at Dunbar Castle, raped her; she and Bothwell were then married at Holyrood. The other lords of Scotland, jealous and suspicious of Bothwell's power, rose against the couple; Mary abdicated and was imprisoned in Lochleven Castle, and Bothwell fled, first to Dunbar Castle and then, after the appearance of this proclamation, into exile.

Captured by the king of Denmark, Bothwell was imprisoned in conditions of increasing severity. He was eventually placed in solitary confinement, 'allegedly chained to a pillar half his height, so that he could never stand erect. He died . . ., insane, on 14 April 1578, and his mummified remains were displayed in Faarevelje church until finally buried in the late twentieth century' (from Bothwell's entry in *ODNB*).

The *Register of Acts of the Privy Council of Scotland*, the formal record-book of the Privy (**secreit**) Council's meetings dealing with public or state business which was sustained (with a break for the Interregnum) until 1708, is now PC1 in the National Archives of Scotland in Edinburgh. The passage below is in volume 5 (June 1567 – December 1569), p. 2. It is written in a neat secretary hand. An edited/abridged version of the *Register* has been published (Burton *et al.* 1877–1933), though this edition is essentially an historian's tool containing a mixture of quotation and summary. An electronic version of this edition was published in 2004–9. This particular entry was obviously of considerable public significance, and a derived text, printed by Robert Lekprevik and dated 1567 (STC 21931), was issued as a broadside for public display and circulation (a photostat may be consulted in the National Library of Scotland in Edinburgh, F.6.b.7(19)).

The text is in formal prose, with the complex Senecan syntax characteristic of contemporary legal documents. There are numerous features characteristic of Scots. Old English **hw-** is reflected as ⟨quh-⟩ in **quhen, quhilk, vmquhile**, and Old English ō appears as ⟨u⟩ in **gude** 'good'. Old English ā is reflected for the most part in ⟨a(i)⟩, e.g. **maist, lang, nane, ane, knawin, twa**, but we might note **lordis**. Present-Day English –ed appears mostly as –it, though sporadic forms in –ed may be noted, while the present participle inflexion varies between –**and** and –**ing**. Notable closed-class words, distinctively Scots or Northern English by this date, include **fra** 'from', **eftir** 'after', **sensyne** 'since then', **sic** 'such', **vmquhile** 'sometimes' and **sall, salbe** (cf. Present-Day English 'shall'). The verb **vnderly** 'accept, submit to' and the adjective **vnlesum** 'unlawful' are not recorded in *OED*, but are fairly common in Scots, as witnessed by their attestation in *DSL*. An inflected form of the adjective appears in **ye saidis lordis** 'the said lords'. There is hardly any punctuation as such, but litterae notabiliores are deployed in places to mark periods and to emphasise discourse markers such as **That** and **And**, and the virgule / is occasionally used.

89

A copy of Robert Lekprevik's black-letter printed version appears beneath the manuscript text (see for a brief account Dickson and Edmond 1890: 232). Lekprevik was the most significant printer in Scotland in the 1560s and early 1570s, operating in general from the Netherbow in Edinburgh. His surname is variously spelt, e.g. Lekpreuik, Lekprewik; the name is still found in the West of Scotland, often spelt Lapraik. He produced a wide range of religious texts for the reformed kirk, such as *The Forme of Prayers* (1562), and a Protestant service-book containing metrical psalms and Calvin's catechism (1564); he also produced a Gaelic version of the latter, *Foirm na nurruidheadh* (1567), the first Scottish Gaelic print publication. Literary works followed, with copies of Henryson's *Moral Fabillis* (1570), Hary's *Wallace* (1570) and Barbour's *Bruce* (1571), all funded by Henry Charteris. Lekprevik was to become printer to the 'king's party' in the late 1560s and 1570s, and spent some time on the run and in prison for printing – or being rumoured to be printing – controversial works (see Text 5(f) below). His rival Bassandyne, printer to the 'queen's party', was close enough to him personally to leave him a legacy (see Text 6(b) below); as has been pointed out, printers' outputs may indicate their general politico-religious sympathies, but they were primarily businessmen working within a complex network of competitors and customers (see Mann 2000: 150–2; see also Dickson and Edmond 1890, especially 198–272).

Some interesting differences may be observed from the manuscript, notably in Leprevik's fairly sophisticated deployment of punctuation (including the pilcrow ¶) in place of litterae notabiliores. For the most part the range of Scots forms is retained, although we might note **being** in place of **beand** at one point. Although Lekprevik's version is in print, it does not appear on *EEBO*; for that reason, line-breaks are marked in the text below.

p.2   The quhilk day ye lordis of secreit counsale and nobilitie vnderſtanding
That | James erll bothuile put violent handis in oure sourane ladiis maiſt nobill
perſoun | vpoun ye xxiiij day of apprile laſtbipaſt And yaireſtir wardit hir
hienes in | ye caſtell of Dunbar quhilk he had in keping and be a lang ſpace
5 yaireſtir | convoyit hir maieſtie invironned *with* men of weir and sic freindis
and kynnismen | of his as wald do for him euir in sic places quhair he had
maiſt dominioun | and power hir grace beand deſtitute of all counsale and
servandis Into ye quhilk | tyme ye said erll seducit be vnlesum wayis oure said
souerane to ane vnhoneſt | mariage *with* him self quhilk fra ye begy*n*ning is
10 null and of nane effeċt for sindrie | causs knawin alsweill to vyeris nationis
and realmis As to ye inhabitantis of | yis co*m*moun weill And als expres
contrair ye law of god and trew religioun | professit *with*in yis realme quhilk
yai ar in mynd to manteine to ye vttirmeſt point | of yair lyff Attour ye saidis
lordis and nobilitie ar assuredlie informit yat ye same | James erll bothuile
15 for to bring ye mariage betuix oure said souerane ladie and | him till effeċt
wes ye principall authour devysar and inſtrument of ye cruell | and maiſt
abhominabill murthour committit vpoun vmquhile oure souerane lord | king
henry ſtewart of gude memorie quhilk apperis to be of veritie Becaus yat | ye
said James erll bothuile being mariit and co*n*iunit *with* ane wyff ye tyme
20 of | ye murthour foirsaid hes sensyne And ſpecialie quhen he had ye quenis

maiesties | persoun into his handis Causit ane pretendit diuorcement tobe maid and wranguslie | led All ye proces and sentences yairof begun endit and sentence gevin yairintill | within twa dayis/ quhilk confirmis ye informatioun gevin to ye saidis lordis and no|bilitie of ye said erll bothuile Als he nocht being content and satisfiit with ye | cruell murthour done vpoun oure said   25
souerane king henrie stewart Revesing | warding/ and seduceing of ye quenis maiestie to ane vnlauchfull mariage and | halding hir 3it in captiuitie Is now as ye saidis lordis and nobilitie ar informit | Makand sum assembleis of men tyiscing and perswading yame to assist to him | quhilk we luke can be for na vyer effect bot to commit ye lyke murthour vpoun | ye sone as wes vpoun ye   30
fader To ye quhilkis ye saidis lordis and nobilitie | myndis with all yair forceis to resist And als to deliuer ye quenis grace | furth of maist miserabill bondage foirsaid Tharefoir ordanis ane Maser | or officiar of armes To pas to ye marcat croces of Edinburgh perth dunde | sanctandrois striueling glasgow and vyeris places neidfull And yair be | oppin proclamatioun command and charge all   35
and sindrie liegis of yis realme alsweill | to burgh as to land That yai be in reddines vpoun thre houris warning | to pas furthwartis with ye saidis lordis of secreit counsale and nobilitie To deliuer | ye quenis maiesties maist nobill persoun furth of captiuitie and presoun And | vpoun ye said erll bothuile and all his complices yat sall assist vnto him To | bring yame to vnderly ye lawis of   40
yis realme for ye cruell murthour of our | said vmquhile souerane king henrie Revesing and detening of ye quenis | maiesties persoun And to obuiat and resist to yis maist wickit interpryis | quhilk we ar informit he intendis to do againis ye prince Attour We | command all and sindry sic as will nocht assist to the revenge of ye premiss | And to deliuer ye quenis grace persoun furth of   45
thraldome Togidder | with all sic as ar assistaris complices or partakeris with ye said erll bothuile | That yai within four houris eftir ye publicatioun of yis present act void and | red yame selffis furth of yis burgh of Edinburgh With certificatioun in | cais yai fail3e That yai salbe repute and haldin as Ennemeis and pvneist | in body and gudis as effeiris | 50

Lekprevik's version, 1567:

¶Heir followis ane act that the | Lordis of Secreit counsall maid for the Tolbuith of Edinburgh the xii. day | of Iunij. 1567. declaring James Erle Bothwell to be the principall | authour and murtherar of the kingis grace of gude memorie | and rauysing of the Quenis Maiestie. |

THE quhilk day the Lordis of secreit counsale & Nobilitie vnderstanding,   5
That Ja-|mes Erle Bothwell put violent handis in oure Souerane Ladyis maist Nobill per-|soun vpon the xxiiij. day of Aprill last bypast, & thaireftir wardit hir hienes in the Ca-|stell of Dumbar quhilk he had in keping, & be ane lang space thairefter conuoyit hir | Maiestie inuironit with men of weir, and sic freindis and kinnismen of his as wald | do for him euer in sic places   10
quhair he had maist dominioun and powar, hir grace be-|ing destitute of all counsale & seruandis into the quhilk tyme the said Erle seducit be | vnlesum

wayis oure said Soueraine to ane vnhonest mariage with him self, quhilk | fra
the beginning is null & of nane effect for sindrie causis knawin, alsweill to
15 vther | natiounis and Realmes as to the inhabitantis of this commoun weill,
and als expres | contrare to the Law of God and trew Religioun professit in this
Realme quhilk thay | ar in mynde to mantene to the vttermost poynt of thair
lyfe. Attoure the saidis Lord*is* | and Nobilitie ar assuritlie informit, that the
same James Erle Bothwell for to bring | the mariage betuix our said Soueraine
20 Lady and | him till effect was the principall | author devysar and Instrument
of the creuell and maist abhominabill murthur com- | mittit vpone vmquhile
oure Souerane Lord King Henry Stewart of gude memorie | quhilk appeiris
to be of veritie, because that the said James Erle Bothwell being | maryit &
coniunit with ane wyfe the tyme of the murther foirsaid, hes sensyne & spe-
25 | cialie quhen he had the Quenis Maiesteis persou*n* into his handis, causit ane
preten*dit* | diuorsiment to be maid & wrangously led all the proces and sentence
thairof begun en- | dit and sentence geuin thairintill within twa dayis, quhilk
confirmes the informati- | oun geuin to the saidis Lordis and Nobilitie of the said
Erle Bothwell. Als he not | being content and satisfeit with the crewell murther
30 done vpone our said Souerane | King Henry Stewart, rauissing warding &
seduceing of the Quenis Maiestie to ane | vnlauchfull mariage, and halding hir
3it in captiuitie. Is now as the saidis Lordis | and Nobilitie ar informit, makand
sum assembleis of men trysting and perswading | thame to assist to him, quhilk
we luik can be for na vther effect bot for to commit the | lyke murther vpone
35 the Sone as was vpone the Father, to the quhilk the said*is* Lordis | and Nobilitie
myndes with all thair forces to resist, and als to deliuer the Quenis | grace
furth of maist miserabill bondage foirsaid. ¶Tharefoir ordanis ane Masar &
Officiar of Armes to pas to the mercat Croces of Edinburgh, Perth, Dundie,
Sa*n*c- | tandros, Striuiling, Glasgow. &c. and vther places neidfyll, and thair
40 be oppin pro- | clamatioun co*m*mand and charge all & sindrie liegis of this
Realme alsweill in Burgh | as to land, That thay be in reddynes vpone thre
houres warning to pas fordwartis | with the saidis Lordis of secreit counsall
and Nobilitie to deliuer the Quenis maie- | sties maist Nobill persoun furth of
captiuitie and presoun, and vpone the said Erle | Bothwell & all his complecis
45 that sall assist vnto him to bring thame to vnderly the | Lawis of this Realme
for the cruell murther of our said vmquhile Souerane King | Henry, rauissing
and detening of the Quenis Maiesties persoun, and to obuiat and | resist to this
maist wickit interpryse quhilk we ar informit he intendis to do againis | the
Prince. ¶Attour we command all and sindrie sic as will not assist to the
50 reve*n*ge | of ye premissis, and to deliuer the Quenis grace persoun furth of
thraldome, togidder | with all sic as ar assistaris complecis or partakeris with
the said Erle Bothwell, that | thay within four houris efter the publicatioun of
this present act woide and red | thameselfis furth of this Burgh of Edinburgh,
with certificatioun in cais thay fail- | 3e, that thay salbe repuite and haldin as
55 ennemeis, and punist in body and gudis as | effeiris. |

¶Imprentit at Edinburgh be Robert Lekpreuik. 1567.

(g) Extract from 'The Register of Acts of the Privy Council': Act in favour of St Andrews (1626)

The Register of Acts continued to be kept after the Union of the Crowns, and indeed the distinct Privy Council of Scotland was not dissolved until 1708, after the Union of Parliaments in 1707. The following passage, less historically exciting than Text 1(f) but perhaps more representative of the daily business of the Privy Council, is an act in favour of the city of St Andrews relating to the payment of taxes; **acquittance** is a legal term for a 'discharge from a debt or obligation' (*DSL*). The entry dates from 1626, just after the accession of Charles I, and appears in PC1, volume 31, in the National Archives of Scotland, Edinburgh.

It will be observed that the passage is still written in Scots; Scots forms become gradually rarer in the Privy Council Register as the seventeenth century progresses, but until the very end of the records forms such as **Anent** 'concerning' (commonly used to introduce entries), **quheras** 'whereas' and even **ane** 'a(n)' etc. are still found. In this entry, Old English **hw–** is reflected as ⟨quh⟩ in **quhair, Quhilk**, and common closed-class words include **ane** (indefinite article), **sall** (cf. Present-Day English 'shall'). Perhaps the most obviously Scots features are in inflexions, with **–and** for the present participle in **Makand** (beside **being**), present plural in **–is** in **Allowis and acceptis**, agreement between adjective and noun in **the saidis lordis** and the reflex of Present-Day English **–ed** appears as **–it**. The form **adois** 'occupations', 'affairs' seems to be especially common in Scots use, cf. the *DSL* entry for *ado* (noun). *OED* considers the plural form to be rare. Punctuation is sparingly deployed, with only /. to mark the end of the entry, but litterae notabiliores are used carefully to distinguish periods. Some words, in common with the practice in many contemporary legal documents, are *engrossed*, i.e. written slightly larger in comparison with the rest of the words in the passage to help readers distinguish quickly key stages in the document: **Makand mentioun** offers background information, **Hum-|blie** introduces the formal petition, and **The Lordis** introduces the Privy Council's decision. We might note the expression **Like as at|mair lenth is contenit in the said supplicatioun**; like the minutes of many modern business meetings, the passage records a decision rather than deals with every detail of the process. The script adopted in this entry is a formal variety of secretary hand with some italic features.

158r Anent the supplicatioun presentit to the lordis of secreit counsell be|the provoſt bailleis and counsell of St androis Makand mentioun | That quhair the saidis supplicantis for teſtifieing of thair moſt|humble and duetifull affeĉtioun to his Maieſties seruice and to the|furtherance so far as lyis in thair waik poweris of his Maieſties|royall adois ar content to advance in ane   5 sowme the whole foure|yeiris payment of the ordinair taxatioun of thair burgs Hum-|blie desireing thairfore the saidis lordis to accept this thair|offer as a teſtimony and prooffe of thaire affeĉtioun to his Maieſtie|and to grant thame and aĉt thairvpoun with a declaratioun that|thair payment and the acquittance of the Colleĉtouris deputis sall be|vnto thame ane sufficient   10 exoneratioun and discharge Like as at|mair lenth is contenit in the said supplicatioun Quhilk being red|hard and considderit be the saidis lordis and

thay being thairwith | weele advisit The Lordis of secreit counsell Allowis and
acceptis | the offer foirsaid maid be the saidis supplicantis as a testimonie | and
15 prooffe of thare affectioun to his Maiesties seruice And remittis | thame to tak
thare acquittanceis from the Collectouris of the taxa-|tioun in suche forme
as may best secure thame/. |

Letters

(a) Letter from George Dunbar, earl of March, to Henry IV of England, 18 February 1400

This letter claims kinship between the earl of March (i.e. the Scottish borders) and Henry IV, and calls for redress against the duke of Rothesay. The letter was written at Dunbar castle, and was mapped (along with other letters by Dunbar) by *LALME* as LP 401. The language is localised by *LALME* to East Lothian. A facsimile appears in James (1870–2), volume II, number LIII; the original is in MS London, British Library, Cotton Vespasian F.vii (folio 22r). The letter is in court hand.

George Dunbar (*c.* 1336 – ?1416/?1423) was the ninth earl of Dunbar or March. During the fourteenth century, he had taken a key part in Robert II's 'forward' policy in the Scottish/English borders, burning English-controlled Roxburgh in 1377 and blackmailing northern English communities into paying tribute. However, in the 1390s he quarrelled with Robert III over the relationship between David Stewart, duke of Rothesay and heir to the throne, and March's daughter Elizabeth; David's rejection of Elizabeth in favour of the daughter of a rival led to this letter of appeal to Henry IV. March now defected to the English side. Rothesay died, probably murdered, in 1402; March took part in various battles on the English side, notably at Homildon Hill in 1402 where the Scots were comprehensively defeated. Henry IV, however, was unable to reward March financially, and the latter eventually managed to negotiate a return to Scotland in 1408; unluckily for him, his lands were much reduced, and his family never regained its former wealth and power.

It is interesting that Dunbar apologises for his language in this letter: I. **write my *le*ttres in engl*is*/ fore y*at* ys mare clere to myne vnderstandyng yan latyne ore ffraunche./** First, we might note that he is apologising for not writing in some other language, which would have been regarded by Henry as being more suitable for communication between magnates; certainly most of the rest of the letters collected in this manuscript are in French and Latin. Secondly, of course, we might note that Dunbar refers to the language he is using as **engl*is***; at this date **Scottis** would have meant Gaelic (see ch. 1, 3.8 above).

There are several features in the text of linguistic interest. Old English ā is reflected as ⟨a⟩ in (e.g.) **ane, nane, haly, halikirc, mare** and **knawen**, while Old English ō appears as ⟨u⟩ in **gudely**. Old English hw– is reflected in ⟨quh, qw-⟩ in **ye quhilk** and **qware**, and Old English –h– appears as ⟨ch⟩ in **doucht*er***. The Norse-derived form **–kirc** 'church' might be noted, as may be the prepositions **Eft*ir*** 'after' and **tyll** 'to' and the numeral **hundreth** 'hundred', all of which are usually seen as having Norse etymologies. Characteristically Scots/Northern English inflexions in **–es/–is** (third person singular and plural) and **–it** (cf. Present-Day English –ed) may be noted. For the item 'such' **swilk** is used as opposed to **sik** etc.; citations in *DOST* suggest that **swilk** etc. is an early form. The form **dedeyn** 'deign' is according to *OED* 'confined to Scotch' (*sic*), though both *OED* and *DSL* cite an example from the Middle English poet Thomas Hoccleve; the reduplicating prefix **de–** seems to be an intensifying morpheme meaning 'down', 'so as to strengthen the notion of condescension' (*OED*). The form **suppowall** 'support' is similarly found in both Middle English and Older Scots. The figura y is dotted, whether it represents thorn or 'y'. The letter exhibits a fairly sophisticated set of punctuation marks, with ././ and // used to mark changes in *sententiae*, and a punctus elevatus (:) appears after the opening salutation.

Excellent mychty and noble Prince : likis yhour Realte to wit yat I am gretly wrangit be ye Duc of Rothesay ye quhilk ſpousit my douchter and now agayn | hys oblisyng to me made by hys lettre and his seal and agaynes ye law of halikirc ſpouses ane other wif as it ys said./././ of ye quhilk wrangis | and
5 defowle to me and my douchter in swilk maner done/ I/ as ane of yhour poer kyn/ gif it likis yhow requere yhow of help & suppowall | fore swilk honeſt seruice as I may do. Eftir my power. to. yhour noble lordship. and to yhour lande./././ ffore Tretee of ye quhilk matere. Will yhe dedeyn | to charge ye lord ye ffournevalle/ ore ye Erle of Weſtmorland at yhour likyng to ye Marche.
10 with swilk gudely haſte as yhow likis/ qwar yat I may haue | ſpekyng with quhilk of yaim yat yhe will send./ and schew hym clerly myne entent ye quhilk I darr nocht discouer to nane other but tyll ane of | yaim be cause of kyn/ and ye grete lewtee yat I traiſt in yaim/ and as I suppose yhe traiſt in yaim on ye tother part/ Alsa noble Prince will yhe | dedyn to graunt and to
15 send me/ yhour saufconduyt endurand quhill ye feſt of ye natiuite of Seint Iohn ye Baptiſt. fore a hundreth knichtis and | squiers & seruant3 gudes hors and hernais als wele within wallit Town as with owt/ ore in qwat other resonable maner yat yhow likis | fore trauaillyng and dwellyng within yhour land gif I hafe myſter././ And excellent Prince syn yat I clayme tobe of kyn tyll
20 yhow. and it peraventour | nocht knawen on yhour parte I schew it to yhour. lordschip be yis my lettre yat gif dame Alice ye Bowmount was yhour graunde dame/ dame Mariory | Comyne hyrr full siſter was my graunde dame on ye tother syde/ sa yat I am. bot of ye feirde degre of kyn tyll yhow/ ye quhilk in alde | tyme was callit neir// And syn I am in swilk degre tyll yhow I requer
25 yhow as be way of tendirnessis yare of/ and fore my seruice in | maner as I hafe before writyn/ yat yhe will vouchesauf/ tyll help me and suppowell me tyll gete amendes of ye wrangis and ye | defowle yat ys done me/. sendand tyll me gif yhow likis yhour answer of yis/ with all gudely haſte/ And noble prince. mervaile yhe nocht | yat. I. write my lettres in englis/ fore yat ys mare
30 clere to myne vnderſtandyng yan latyne ore ffraunche./ Excellent mychty & noble prince. ye | haly Trinite hafe yhow euermar in kepyng//. Writyn at my Caſtell of Dunbarr ye xviij. day of ffeuerer. |

Le Count de la | Marche Descoce |

(b) Letter from James Douglas to Henry IV of England, 26 July 1405

This letter, written at Edinburgh, justifies the burning of Berwick by the Scots. Mapped by *LALME* as LP 1359, and localised to Midlothian. A facsimile appears in James (1870–2), volume II, number LIV; the original is in MS London, British Library, Cotton Vespasian F.vii (folio 17v). The letter is in court hand.

With Dunbar's defection to the English (see Text 2(a) above), the preeminence of his family in the Scottish borders passed to the Douglas family. James Douglas, now acting warden of the March, took advantage of conflict between Henry IV and various northern English magnates (notably the earl of Northumberland and the archbishop of York) to burn the border town of Berwick. Henry complained; James responded with this aggressively expressed letter which, despite using honorific expressions such as **hee and Excellent prince**, does not offer any concession or apology. We might note the repeated reference to Berwick as a Scottish town, e.g. **berwike y**a**t stand**is **in scotlande**. James went on to play a major role in southern Scottish politics, focusing on family and personal aggrandisement without much reference to broader considerations. Perhaps the most notorious event in his career was the so-called 'Black Dinner' of 1440, at which his great-nephews and rivals were arrested and executed at a feast held at Edinburgh Castle. James died in 1443. At his death, his body was reported to contain four stone of tallow, thus his nickname: 'James the Gross'.

There are many linguistic forms characteristic of Scots in the letter. Old English ā is reflected in ⟨a⟩ in **nane, (al)sua, nathing, knawin, ath(e)** 'oath', **haly gast** 'holy spirit', but we might note ⟨o⟩ in **lorde** (cf. Old English **hlāford**), a regular exception in Older Scots texts. Reflexes of Old English ō are rarer in his text, but we might note **gudly** 'goodly'. Old English **hw-** is reflected as ⟨quh-, qwh-⟩ in **ye quhilk(e), qwhar, qwhat**, while Old English medial **h** is reflected as ⟨ch⟩ in **mycht** (cf. Present-Day English 'might'). The auxiliaries **sall, suld(e)** are also commonplace in Scots and Northern English. The Norse-derived auxiliary **ger(e)** 'cause' might be noted, as might be **til** 'to' and **war** 'were', both of which are again often considered to be derived from Norse. Inflexional endings in **–and(e)** (present participle) and **–it** (cf. Present-Day English **–ed**) are prototypical of Scots; the form **has** as the present plural of 'have' is also notable. The word **ȝhemsall** 'care, charge, custody' is a variant of **ȝemsel**, which is the *DSL* headword form; see also the form **yemsel**, cited in *OED*. *OED* considers the word 'Chiefly Scottish' and obsolete, and derives its etymology from Norse **geymsla**, cf. **geyma** 'watch, guard' followed by the suffix **–sla**. *OED* citations are, as is indicated, from Scottish texts, with the exception of **ȝemsle**, recorded in *The Ormulum* (Lincolnshire, c. 1200). The form **tholyte** 'suffered, endured' seems to have been increasingly restricted to Scots and Northern texts by the fifteenth century, while many of the citations in *OED* for *scathe* (noun), cf. **skathis** 'injuries', come from Scottish texts. The form **punitioun** 'punishment' is now rare in English and Scots. The spelling ⟨yh⟩ is used in **yhu** 'you', presumably as an alternative for yogh, cf. **ȝour** 'your'.

Certain place-names may be noted: **Calkow** (an alternative spelling for 'Kelso', suggesting a distinct pronunciation from that used in modern times), **arane** 'Isle of Arran', **lawadyr dale** 'Lauderdale'. The form **brathwike** 'Borthwick (Castle)' may be noted; the transposition of elements such as ⟨r⟩ and ⟨o⟩ is known as *metathesis*, a fairly common, if sporadic, process in many languages (cf. common Present-Day

English non-standard **aks** 'ask', or Old English **þridda** 'third'). The reference to **Ile malasch** is obscure.

Punctuation is more sparing than in the previous letter, though a range of forms is used. The letter is in a fine court hand.

He Excellent and Rycht mychty prince likit to ʒour henes to wyte me haff resauit/ ʒour honorabile *lett*res to me sende be a Reu*er*end fadir | ye abbot of Calkow. contenand yat it is well knawin yat trewis. war tane & sworne o late betwix ye Rewmys of ingland & scotlande & for yi yhu | mervalis gretly
5 *yat* my men be my wille & assent/ has byrnde ye toun of berwike & in oy*er* *cer*tayne places wythin ye Rewme of inglande in brekyng fully | ye saide trewis in my defaute & nathing in ʒhouris & als agayn myn ath made in ſtreynthing of ye same trewis of ye qwhilke yhe desire rather yat amend*is* | war made yan ony mar harme war done yarfor Requirande me to do yhou to wyte.
10 qwheyn I will gere refourme ye sayde attemptat*is*/ or qwhat my full | will be to do o yat mat*er*// Anence ye qwhilkys hee and Excellent prince qwhar yhe say yhu m*er*valys gretly y*at* my men be my will & assent/ has brennede | ye toun of berwik ye qwhilk is wyth in scotlande & oy*er* places in inglande in brekyng fully of ye sayde trewis I vnd*er*ſtand y*at* giff yhour hee Excellent
15 war | clerly enfourmyte of ye brennyng slachtyr/ & takyng of *pr*isoner*is* & scott*is* schippis y*at* is done by yhour men to scottys men within ye saide trewis i*n* diu*er*s | places of scotlande befor ye brynnyng of Berwike. ye qwhilk skathis our lege lorde ye kyng and his lieg*is* has paciently tholyte in ye kepyng of ye saide | trewis & chargit me til aske & ger be askyte by my deput*is* redress*is* yar
20 of/ ye qwhilk my deput*is* has askyte at day⸍is⸍ of marche & nane has gotyne/ Me think | o resoune yhe sulde erar put blame & punicioun to ye doarys of ye saide treſþas done agayn ye trewis in swilke man*er* & callys yaim rather brekar*is* of ye | trew yan me y*at* has tholyte sa mikylle iniur so lang & nane amend*is* gottyn/ bot it is like y*at* ye gret attemptat*is* y*at* yhour men. dois agayn
25 ye trewis is | well concelyte fra yhour audience for I suppos & yhe wiſt it/ ʒhe wald of ʒhour he worschipe ger it be refourmyte & redressit/ as ye cause requiryt | for lang befor ye bryni*n*g of berwike yhour men com *with*in our lorde ye kyngis awin *pr*opir lande of arane & Ile malasch & til his caſtell of brathwike & | brynt his chapelle & oy*er* diuerse plac*is* of yat lande & tuke &
30 Rawnsounde ye capitain of ye sayde caſtelle & slow his sone. & heryde al y*at* yai mycht our take | and alsua yai hade takyne befor yat tym *cer*tayne scott*is* schippis chargit *with* marchaund*is* & ye marchand*is* yar of/ in ye contrer of ye sayde trewis of ye qwhilk*e* | reparacioun & redress*is* has bene askyte befor ye brennyng of berwike & nane gottyne And qwhar ʒhe say y*at* berwike y*at*
35 ſtand*is* in scotlande ye qwhilk*e* | toun yhe call yhour*is* in yhour sayde *lett*res & *cer*tayne land*is* of yhour*is* wythin inglande was brende be my men my will & myn assent/ brekand y*e* trewis | in my defaute & nocht in yhour*is* & in ye contrar of my*n* athe ./ yar to I answer in yis man*er*. y*at* qwhat tyme it like to our lege lorde ye kyng & to yhour | hee Excellent/ to ordane redress*is* to be
40 made be his Co*m*missaris & yhouris of all attemptat*is* done of aythir side/

I sall *with* ye help of gode make it well | kennyt y*at* I haff trewly kepit my*n*
athe & ye trewis as afferys to me of Resoun And qwha eu*er* enfourmyt yhour
Excellence y*at* I hade brokyn my*n* | athe it hade bene fayrar for him to haffe
sende me y*at* querell in to wyrt vndir his selle & til haff tane answere greable
as afferit to him vnd*er* | my scelle agayne/ yan sua vntrewly in my*n* absence   45
till enfourme yhour excellence. for I tray*st* he has saide mar in my*n* absence
yan he dar awow in | my p*re*sens. for nocht di*s*plece yhour honour. learys
sulde be lytille alowit wyth ony sic worschipfull kyng as ʒhe ar And qwhar
ʒhe say in yhour sayde |lett*re*s. y*at* ʒhe desir rather amend*is* of attemptat*is*
done agay*n* ye trewis yan ony mar harme war done yarfor/ to y*at* I answer   50
in yis man*er* y*at* qwhen | yhour saide lett*re*s come to me. our lorde ye kyng
was passit in ye northe p*ar*tis of scotlande. & I with al gudly ha*st* sende
yhour lett*re*s til him of ye qwhilk*is* | at ye makyng of yir lettris I hade nane
answer// Neu*er* ye latt*er* qwhen I hade vnd*irst*andyne yhour lett*re*s I gert/
cry in diu*er*se plac*is* ye trewis to be kepit/ | tray*st*and yat it suld be sua done   55
on ye toy*er* p*ar*t/ eftyr ye qwhilk crye/ yhour men of Inglande has rydyne
in scotlande wyth gret company like in | fere of were & has heryde lawadyr
dale. Tewydalle & a part of Etryke fore*st*/ ye qwhilke at ye makyng of yir
lett*ri*s was tholyt & nocht don yarfor | And foryi giffe ye trewis sall *st*ande it
lyes to yhour heenes to se for cha*st*yni*n*g of tre*s*passouris & for amend*is* of   60
attemptat*is* done & y*at* be tym | and qwhat yhe wochesaff of ʒour heenes to
do twychand ye forsayde mat*er*is ʒhe walde c*er*tify me be ʒour lett*re*s wyth al
gudly ha*st*. hee almychty | prynce ye haly ga*st* ʒow haff in his ʒhemsall eu*ir*mar
wrytyn at Eddynburgh vnd*ir* my selle ye xxvj day of Julij |

James of douglas wardane | of ye marche. | 65

(c) Letter from Gavin Douglas to Adam Williamson (1515)

Gavin Douglas (*c.* 1476–1522) was both a poet and clergyman. His poetry was written during the earlier part of his career. Text 4(g) is part of his *The Palice of Honour*,
which was completed probably in 1501 or just before (see Bawcutt 2003: xxviii),
and in 1513 he completed his *Eneados*, a translation of Virgil's *Aeneid*. Shortly afterwards took place the disastrous battle of Flodden Field, at which James IV and
many Scottish magnates died.

The subsequent power-vacuum opened up opportunities for the ambitious,
and, supported by Henry VIII of England, Douglas sought the archbishopric of
St Andrews. However, there were other applicants, and the post was awarded to
Andrew Forman, bishop of Moray; the letter below, one of two written to Douglas's agent Adam Williamson in 1515, captures something of Douglas's resentment
at events. Subsequently, Douglas was awarded the bishopric of Dunkeld, but not
without some hostility from rival interests; Douglas was imprisoned for a period,
and had to deal with armed resistance from another contestant for the post. He
sustained his hostility to his rivals, continued to take a role in Scottish politics
and some international diplomacy, and even attempted again to obtain the archbishopric of St Andrews when Forman died; however, David Beaton (subsequent

persecutor of George Wishart; see Text 1(e) above), nominated by the young king James V's chief minister the duke of Albany, was the successful candidate. Douglas, by that time accused of treason by Albany, was in London in 1522 when he died, probably of plague (see Douglas's *ODNB* entry; see also Bawcutt 1994).

The style of the letter is in general terms colloquial, reflecting the 'trailing style' common in contemporary prose (see ch. 4). It is preserved in a collection of correspondence concerned with Anglo-Scottish relations in the first half of the sixteenth century, MS London, British Library, Cotton Caligula B.ii; this letter forms folios 374r–374v. It seems to be written in Douglas's own secretary hand. The postscript after Douglas's signature is in smaller handwriting.

The passage is of considerable linguistic interest. Old English hw– is reflected as ⟨quh-⟩ in **quhairof, quhar;** abbreviated forms are **quhilk** and **quhilkis.** Although abbreviated, the reflex of Old English –h– seems to be ⟨ch⟩, e.g. no*ch*t. Old English ā is reflected in ⟨a(y)⟩ in **bay***th***, knaw, mast, ane, lang,** while the reflex of Old English ō is ⟨u⟩ in **gud.** Modal verbs include **sall, ma***n*, and the form for 'were' is **war** (cf. Norse **váru**). The pronominal and demonstrative systems include **scho, yaj** 'they', **yir** 'these' and **ȝon** 'that/those over there', and the form for 'such' is **syk.** Inflexions are characteristically Scots, e.g. –**it**/–**yt** as the reflex of Present-Day English –**ed** and –**and** for the present participle in **beand** 'being'. Other forms apparently derived from Norse include **eftyr** 'after', **mekyll** 'much, large'; more learned is French-derived **solyst** 'solicit', **solistatiou***n* 'solicitation'. Thorn appears commonly as ⟨y⟩, but slightly curious are two occurrences where it seems to have been replaced by yogh, i.e. **ȝis** 'this', **ȝat** 'that' (beside **yat**). Such usages are fairly common in Middle English, given that ⟨y⟩ and yogh are commonly seen as mapping onto the same sound-equivalent (i.e. *potestas*); yogh therefore is sometimes extended to map onto the same sound as thorn. Something similar seems to have occurred here. The form **bedyttyt** 'endebted' is also interesting; it appears in *DSL*, but both citations are from Gavin Douglas (including this letter). Some expressions are a little puzzling; but **parley** seems to mean 'without argument' (cf. *OED* **parley** (n.(1)). There is no citation of such a form in *OED*. Punctuation is deployed lightly, with a single virgule being used to distinguish clauses, generally but not always in combination with litterae notabiliores.

374r Brothir ma*st*ir Adam I com*m*en*d* me to ȝow in my harty wys/ And ȝe sall | knaw y*at* sen my la*st* writyng of perth ye la*st* day of december quhi*l*k I tra*st* ȝe | hafe gottyn & hard forthar all thyng*is* be sch*ir* James/ The byschop of du*n*kelden | is decessit yis monu*n*day ye xv day of January/ And becaus
5 ȝon | euyll myndyt bischop of m*ur*ray trublys all o*ur* promociones/ & hes *sp*ed | San*ct* andro*is* to hym self wy*th* du*n*fermlyng Arbro*th* legacy & oy*ir* faculteys | quhilk*is* ar nedfull & all ways ma*n* be retretyt/ ȝit no*ch*t ye les so*m* in syk | debat*is* & co*n*trouersyes ar co*st*ly & dissentius/ in all aue*n*tour ye queines grace | my self & frend*is* thynk*is* nedfull/ I be promouyt to y*at* seyt
10 quhi*l*k now | is vacand & but parley/ & an*e* rych*t* gud byschopry of rych*t* & ye thryd | seyt of ye realm/ And to y*at* effe*ct* hes ye quenys grace writi*n* for | me to ye papis halynes/ & cardynal*is*/ quhairof ȝe sall wy*th* yis ressaue | ye copy to soly*st* syk lyke wrytyng*is* fra ye kyng*is* grace hyr | broy*ir*/ And be no*ch*t

hir lettyr*us* obeyt in ye curt of rom. ʒe solyſt|euyll ʒo*ur* memoryall/ les yan
ye kyng wyll do no*ch*t for his syſtyr|as I knaw ye *contra*y/ bayt*h* in deyd 15
& wryt/ I dout no*ch*t bot ʒe wyll|solyſt my mat*er*is als trewly as ʒo*ur* awin
yo*ch*t ye qwenys grace had|no*ch*t wrytyn for me/ And as I wrate to ʒ*ow* laytly
ye promotioun of hyr|s*er*uand*is* & frend*is* is hyr weylfar & autorisyng &
hyndiryng of hyr|adu*er*saryis/ I pray ʒ*ow* at [I *deleted*] a word ſ*p*ed yir lettyr*is*
to flandris as|yaj ar dyre*ct*yt/ & ſ*p*ed wyt*h* yaim ye kyng*is* wrytyng*is*/ And 20
gif ʒe|kowth do so mekyll as caus ye kyng mak a poſt yarfor/ I war|bedyttyt
to hys grace & ʒ*ow* for eu*er*/ a wyse frend is soyn chargeyt/|

Item ʒe sall knaw y*at* me lord Erll of huntlye was heyr at ye quenys|grace &
wyll go hyr way/ & bryng mony of ye oy*ir* lord*is* to hyr opinion|And wyt*h* hys
avys scho hes mayd p*ro*clame a p*ar*lyam*ent* in yis toun|to be haldyn & begyn 25
in yis toun ye xij day of March quhar we|traſt t*il* haf all thyng*is* redressyt.
[*erasure*] I wald no*ch*t ʒe leyt ye|bychop of m*ur*ray nor ʒ*on* duk ſteyll hyddyr
by ʒ*ow*. as now latly|his clerk maſtir John sauquhy has doyn/ & landyt at leyth
furth|of a franch schypp/ & bro*ch*t wyt*h* hym ye bullys of San*ct* andr*ois* &
pub-|lyſt ye samyn by hys man*e* in Edynburgh yis laſt twisday ye|xvj day of 30
Januare/ bot I beleve he sall no*ch*t haf possessyoun yis|ʒeir [*erasure*] Nedfull
it is & yt is a ſ*p*eciall pun*ct* of ʒ*our* memoryall|to caus ye kyng wryt to ye kyng
of frans heyr apon/ to ye|effe*ct* y*at* by hys ways ye kyng o*ur* souerane lord
be no*ch*t hurt in his|*[folio 374v]* priuileg*is* & faculteys/ for yt war to byreif hym
hys croun/ Nor y*at* hys|gud syſtyr ye quenys grace [*erasure*] at all by mynyſt 35
in hyr autorite/ bot|raythar mantenyt & defendyt be hym in ye samin/ And
o*ch*t hes|beiyn doyn by hys wrytyng*is* in ye *con*try othyr in fawir*is* of ʒ*on*
byschop|of m*ur*ray or ony oy*iris*/ y*at* ye saming be hys ways & soliſtation*is*
be|reuersyt agayn/ y*at* yarby na preiudyce may happyn to ye kyng nor
this|hys [ʒ *deleted*] realm/ now in tyme present/ nor ʒit in tyme cu*m*myng 40
by|evyll exemple/ so y*at* syk doyng nor attemptat*is* be na preparatyve|to
oy*ir*is in tyme to cu*m*/ And kowth ye kyng solyſt his brothyr|of frans to haf
y*at* byschop rendyrryt to him othyr be pollycy or|oy*ir* wayis/ y*at* he my*ch*t
yar eftyr war demanyt as effer*is*/ all yir|thre realmys I traſt war bro*ch*t to
grete reſt/ ffor he is in his bein|ye inſtrum*ent* of mekyll harm/ & I dreyd sall 45
ʒit be of mair &|he be no*ch*t snybbyt/ [*erasure?*] Tent to hym & ʒ*on* duyk
[gon *deleted*] \gif/ ye|Kyng thar luffe ye weylfar of hys syſtir & maſt tendir
nevois|& als ye quyet of his awyn realm/ [*erasure?*] Haſt ansuer agayn|& be
solyſt as ʒe haf bey*n* in tyme bypassyt/ And God keip ʒ*ow*|of perth ye xviij
day of January/ wyt*h* ye hand of|ʒ*our* frend|gawin|Douglas| 50

The quein thynk*is* ʒe haf bey*n* ou*er* slawthfull y*at* sa lang tym ʒe beand in
Ingland y*ar* haf bein|no*ch*t doyn noy*ir* in Rome nor ye curt of frans againys
ʒ*on* wykkit|byschop of m*ur*ray/ & bydd*is* ʒ*ow* m*en*d y*at* falt/ Item at ʒe
solyſt ye|kyng hyr broy*ir*/ y*at* na l*e*tter*is* pas*is* throu*ch* hys realm to na fra
y*at*|belang*is* ony scott*is* ma*n* les y*at* he haf hyr ſ*p*eciall wrytyng*is* & remiſt 55
y*ar* for/ ffor syk letter*is* hes|er*ar* doyn gret harm/ & was ye fyrſt caus of all

ye truble ane*nt* ye pr*o*motionis And is | daly a pr*e*paratyve to soly*ſt* ʒon duyk
of Albany to cu*m* hyddyr [*erasure?*] Reme*m*byr my salue *con*duit | & *ſp*ed ye
samyn to me as I wrayt to ʒ*ow* latly/ And gif ony of my wrytyng*is* or ple|nyng
60   ye quen cu*m* furth of flandr*is* or Rome to ʒo*ur* ha*n*de/ na fors y*at* ye kyng se
or | knaw ye *con*tent*is* y*a*rof/ at yaj maybe ye bettyr & mair ha*ſt*yly *ſp*ed to
hyr grace or me | for I wayt hys henes wyll *ſt*op nan*e* of hyr l*ett*r*is* nor myn/
q*uhi*lk sall cu*m* to hys | hous & avaye |

(d) Letter from Catherine Bellenden to Mary of Lorraine (1543)

The correspondence of Mary of Lorraine, now better known as Mary of Guise, is
one of the largest collections of Scottish letters from the sixteenth century. Texts
2(d) through (f) are all drawn from this collection (see further Cameron 1927,
which remains the standard edition of the correspondence). The letters are all in
the National Archives of Scotland in Edinburgh, as SP2, which consists of several
volumes: this letter is item 36 in volume 1, hence number XXXVI in Cameron's
edition. The letter is written in a neat secretary hand; Cameron considers it to be
a holograph.

Mary of Guise, daughter of a French nobleman and wife to the grand chamberlain of France, became on the death of her first husband the wife of James V
and subsequently the queen dowager. When James died in 1542, Mary of Guise
decided to stay in Scotland to protect, insofar as she could, the interests of her
daughter, Mary Queen of Scots. The following letter from Catherine Bellenden,
with its emphasis on money seen as owed, should be seen in this context.

Mary felt herself vulnerable. James had just died; the earl of Arran had been
chosen as regent, and was attempting to arrange the marriage of the infant Queen
Mary to Edward, the son of Henry VIII of England. Mary of Guise and others,
notably Cardinal Beaton, were opposed to the match, and forced Arran to aban-
don the proposed alliance with England, of which the marriage was an expression.
In 1544, Henry VIII attacked Scotland in a series of destructive acts of vengeance
known as the 'Rough Wooing', culminating in 1547 in the battle of Pinkie, the last
open field battle between English and Scottish armies (Merriman 2000).

Catherine Bellenden was the first wife of Sir Oliver Sinclair, a favourite of James
V. Sinclair, it seems (there is some uncertainty, given the confusion of the period),
commanded the Scottish forces at the battle of Solway Moss in Cumberland in
November 1542; captured after the battle, he was not released until early 1543, after
James V's death. Catherine's letter refers to moneys owed to the queen **for orknay
and ʒetland**; Sinclair had been given a *tack* (i.e. the Scots legal term for leasehold
tenure) of lands in Orkney and Shetland (**ʒetland**) in 1541, extended to 1547 (see
ODNB). The Sinclairs were well-established landowners in Orkney; Catherine
refers to their enjoyment of these holdings for three or four hundred years.

The letter contains many Scots features. The reflex of Old English **hw-** is ⟨quh-⟩
in **quhilk, quhill, quhat**; we might also note **quhom**. Old English ā appears as ⟨a(i)⟩
in **haill, maist, lang, na thing, sa** and **wrait**, while Old English ō is reflected in ⟨u⟩
in **gude, guddis**; cf. also **puir** 'poor'. L-mouillé appears as ⟨lʒ⟩ in **assoilʒe**. Significant
closed-class words include **eftir** 'after', **fra** 'from', **sall, suld** (cf. Present-Day English
'shall', 'should'), **gart** 'caused', **hundre*th*** 'hundred'. Present participles are inflected

in –and. The expression **sabeis** '(if) it so be' is unusual; the only citation in *DSL* is to this text. Inflected forms of adjectival **said** are noticeable, e.g. **ye saidis landis, ye saidis frutis.** The form **rowmes** 'rooms, spaces etc.' is of interest; the semantic range of the word, given the evidence of its meanings in *DSL*, seems wider than that of its Present-Day English reflex **room.** The same goes for **geir** 'property'; cf. Present-Day English **gear.** Catherine uses **beltan** 'Beltane' to refer to the ancient Scottish 'quarter-day' at the beginning of May. There is no punctuation, but Catherine repeats **Madame** to flag a further stage in her argument, and the formal conclusion is marked by litterae notabiliores in **And Eternall God.**

Madame eftir maiſt hvmill commendationis of my puir service to 3our | hienes
I am adverteiſt y*at* 3our grace belevis yat my husband and I | ar awand greit
sovmes of money to 3our grace for orknay and 3etland | and wil no*ch*t pay 3our
grace and to yat effe*ct* maiſter thomas | makcal3en your graces ma*n* of law hes
arreſtitt our schip and | guddis [v *deleted*] and haldin ye samyn yis mon*eth*   5
bygane quhairthrow [h *deleted*] we | haif tynt ye mercat y*at* we suld haif maid
money of our pe*nn*y-|worthis to our greit skaith and da*mm*age be ressoun
y*at* I my*ch*t | no*ch*t cu*m* to get soverte to lows ye said arreiſtme*nt* becaus I
haif | bein vnder greit seiknes and wyir trublis yis lang tyme bygane | ye q*uhi*lk
I traiſt and 3o*ur* grace had bein weill informyt 3o*ur* grace | wald no*ch*t haif gart   10
trubill our geir in ye maner as it was | Madame 3our grace sall wnderſtand we
haif no*ch*t tane wp ane | pe*nn*y of orknay or 3etland nor will no*ch*t get quhill
efter yis | next beltan and we ar informyt 3our grace hes set ye said*is* land*is* | to
my lord of huntlie ye q*uhi*lk purposis to be yair or yan and to | tak wp ye said*is*
frutis gif sabeis we suld pay na thing yairfor | will 3o*ur* grace be sa gracious   15
to ws as to ratifie our fyve 3er*is* | tak quhilk our maiſter quhom god assoil3e
set to ws we sall mak | 3o*ur* grace thankfull payment at 3our grace plesour as
I wrait | to 3o*ur* grace of befoir for we think greit lak to gang fra our | native
rowmes q*uhi*lk my husband and his surname hes brukit | yir thre or four
hundre*th* 3er*is* considering y*at* we ar in will to mak als | gude payment to 3o*ur*   20
grace as ony yat ca*n* dissyre it beseikand | 3o*ur* grace to shaw yis gentill ma*n*
ye berar of yis bill quhat | 3o*ur* grace intendis to do to ws and quhat we sall
lyppin to And | Eternall God keip 3our grace and 3o*ur* graces successioun in
all | haill and weilfair writtin at Edinburgh ye xxiij day of | november Be 3our
gracis hvmill s*er*vatr*is* | 25

Katherine Bellenden |

Dorse to the quenis grace |

(e) Letter from Henry, Lord Methven, to Mary of Lorraine (1548)

This letter describes an event during the Rough Wooing (see Text 2(d) above). Henry Stewart, Lord Methven, had been the third husband of Queen Margaret Tudor, widow of James IV; when Margaret died in 1541, he married his long-time mistress, Lady Janet Stewart. Methven was a significant figure at the court of

Mary of Guise. Mary used him as an ambassador and he took a major role, as master of artillery, at the siege of Haddington, East Lothian, in 1548–9, where a lone English garrison held out for eighteen months despite repeated attacks by Scottish troops supported by French allies and German and Italian mercenaries, brought over after the battle of Pinkie in the previous year. The siege is supposed to have been the longest in Scottish history; it is also famous for the use by the English of new-style 'star-fort' or *Trace Italienne* fortifications (see Cooper 2009). The English garrison was relieved in September 1549, and then withdrew unopposed, razing the fortifications as they did so. Mary of Guise is reported to have said that 'they left nothing behind but the plague' (cf. Merriman 2000). The letter below is a somewhat optimistic report to Mary about the progress of the siege, written from the besieging army's encampment. It survives in Edinburgh, National Archives of Scotland, SP2, volume 3, item 186, hence CLXXVI in Cameron's edition (1927: 248–50). It is written in a very careless secretary hand; Cameron considers it to be a holograph.

The reflex of Old English ā appears as ⟨a(i/y)⟩ in **na, an, mair, bayth, ald**, but we might note the usual exception of **lord**. Old English ō appears as ⟨u⟩ in **futtis** (an unusual plural, here used with reference to the measurement). Old English **hw–** appears as ⟨quh-⟩ in **quhilkis** etc., while *l*-mouillé appears as ⟨lʒ⟩ in **bastalʒe**. Present-Day English **–ed** is reflected in **–yt, –it**. Notable closed-class words include **eftir** 'after', **fra** 'from', **till** 'to' and **salbe** (cf. Present-Day English 'shall be'). The forms **northt** 'north', **tolbutht** 'tolbooth' with the common Scots addition of **–t** may also be noted. The form for 'church' is Norse-derived **kirk**, but the most obvious feature of the letter is its large-scale use of technical vocabulary, e.g. **carmosche of hakbuttis** 'skirmish of harquebuses', though both words are fairly well-attested in *DSL*. *DSL* derives **carmosche** from Old French **escarmusche**, 'with irregular dropping of the initial *es-*'; cf. *OED* **skirmish** (n.). Other technical terms include **bastalʒe** 'wooden siege-tower', **gabionis** 'wicker baskets filled with earth, used in fortification', **tolbutht** 'tollbooth' (often used as a prison), **gallions** '?galleons', **peonaris** 'pioneers, soldier-labourers'. The phrase **bagsaif & livis** is of interest; *DSL* gives only this citation for the word **bagsaif**. It seems to be based on the French expression **vie et bagues sauves** 'with life and baggage safe'. The word 'trench' seems to have given Lord Methven some problems; he spells the word as **trenhe, trenche, tryncht** and **trinsche**. The form *presoaris* seems to be a mistake for **presonaris**; possibly a macron above the ⟨o⟩, flagging an abbreviation for ⟨n⟩, was omitted. Discourse units are distinguished fairly regularly by the use of the virgule (/).

Pleis ʒo*ur* graice |

This wednisday ye [northt *deleted*] sut*h*we*st* ba*st*alʒe condamnit yat na | defence is maid in it/ ye ba*st*alʒe at ye freir kirk all | brokin except an litill p*art* to the we*st*/ ye meid ba*st*alʒe | apou*n* yer trenhe at the we*st* p*art* ye an half of ye | gabionis and a p*art* of ye ba*st*alʒe dwung away/ ye | northt we*st* trencht is conda*m*nit all except ye | rovm yat an small peice lyis in quhilk*is* I tra*st* salbe | conda*m*yt all yis day/ daly & nyc*h*tlie is at all ouris | carmosche of hakbutt*is*/ yai vssit noc*h*t sen tuisday ef*t*er | nou*n*/ yis nyc*h*t continwall carmosche fra ye su*n* pa*st* | till yis day at iiij i*n* ye morning ʼwyt*h* hakbutt*is* [*inserted in the margin; place for*

insertion marked with caret]' / & all ny*ch*t [g *deleted*] \'all o*ur*' great | artall3ery   10
lawborit & has dong ye tolbutht & re*ſt* | an pece yat lay betuix it & ye kirk of ye
freyr*is* | / yis ny*ch*t o*ur* peonar*is* has wroucht owr tryncht [w *deleted*] | wyth*in*
ferty futt*is* to yar [*illegible word deleted*] trinsche yat is ry*ch*t befo*r* | yat meid
ba*ſt*al3e/ yer is vc workmen to c*um* out | of ye gallions to ca*ſt* yis ny*ch*t in ye
trensche/ I tra*ſt* | [*illegible word deleted*] yis ny*ch*t salbe sein mair besynes to ye   15
Inglis | me*n*/ or ellis ye morn at ye furri*ſt*/ I belief | yat few Inglis has sleppit yis
[yis *deleted*] la*ſt* xxiiij | hour*is* i*n* *ſ*peciall// ya mak greit defence on yar | fassun
& trewille ya haif fortefeit ye tov*n* in | greit sort at ye begi*n*ing/ & i*n* ye ny*ch*t
work*is* as | ya may/ I put na dout yaj will tyn ye tovn | ha*ſt*ile/ yis Wednisday
lait an [boy *deleted*] Scott*is* boy com | out at ye e*ſt* port of ye tovn & is hald/   20
quhilk*is* | sayis Wil*ſt*rop ye principall [calpiden *deleted*] capiden | is slayn &
his lyutene*n*t bayt*h*/ no*ch*t ye les yar | is na credit gevin yerto/ Madem yar
is | Scott*is* me*n* quhilk*is* *ſ*pak wyt*h* p*art* of yam wyth*out* | [yar *deleted*] owr yar
trenchis quhilk*is* my lord govern*our* has [cas *deleted*] | caussit tak/ quhay sayis
yaj ar all in deidly feyr | & wald randyr bagsaif & livis & no*ch*t to be hald*in* | as   25
presoar*is*/ bot yer is no dout of the wy*n*ing of town | & all yerintill will god
quhay conserve 30*ur* grace evir | of ye camo yis fersday at iiij hour*is* arly |

30*ur* grace ma*ſt* humill & obedie*n*t *s*ervito*ur* Methven |

The following lines are written sideways in the margin

ye boy sayis y*er* is on tuisday & wenisday | la*ſt* iic me*n* slayn wyt*h* o*ur*
artall3ery | 30

Dorse To ye que*n*nis | graice |

(f) Letter from Marion, Lady Home, to Mary of Lorraine (1548–9)

Lady Home's letter, one of a series by her in the correspondence associated with
Mary of Lorraine, reports a concern that Englishmen at **beryk** (i.e. Berwick) were
about to join with the Haddington garrison (see Text 2(e) above) to attack the Scottish headquarters at **Inaresk** (i.e. Inveresk), the fort there at that time being under
construction. The letter survives in Edinburgh, National Archives of Scotland, SP2,
volume 3, item 201, thus CCI in Cameron's edition (1927: 291–2). It is written in
secretary hand; Cameron considers it to be a holograph.

    Marion (or Mariota) Lady Home (or Hume) was the wife of George Home,
who died in 1549. The Homes were a major family in the borders, with properties
focused on Hume Castle in Berwickshire, a strategic strong-point in the eastern
marches; as a result (it seems) of this letter, Hume Castle was taken over by a French
garrison, securing it not only for Scotland but also for the family. Husband and wife
seem to have worked together as a team in negotiating the complex border politics
of the period to the advantage of their family (*ODNB*).

    The letter is quite short, but several interesting Scots features might be noted.
Old English **hw–** is reflected as ⟨quh-⟩ in **quhill**. Old English **ā** appears as ⟨a⟩ in **ane**,
ma, **s(u)a**, **bath(t)** 'both', and the reflex of Old English **ō** is ⟨u⟩ in **gud**. Present-Day
English **–ed** is reflected in **–it**; we might note the form **cumit** 'come' (past participle),

the verb being transferred from the strong to the weak conjugation. The characteristically Scots and northern English auxiliary **maun** 'must' might also be noted. The reflex of Present-Day English –th appears sporadically as ⟨-tht⟩ in **furtht** 'forth', **batht** 'both'. The pronoun **hem** 'them' beside **tham** is, however, unusual for Scots; it may represent a reduced stress form. The form **besyns** seems to be an error for **besynes** 'business'. Marion uses a mixture of marks of punctuation, including the virgule, the punctus and (not especially systematically) litterae notabiliores.

Madem I comend my hartly ser*wis* to ʒo*ur* grace. pleis ʒou to | be adu*er*teisit
y*at* thar is cu*m*it/ s*er*ten of Inglis me*n* to beryk | ma nor wes of befor/ bot I be
lief tha well not all | be thre thousand men/ Caus wait one ye fortht of | Inaresk
sa mony as is nedfull/ & maik for suir | adu*er*tisement in tha partt*is*/ y*at* tha
be not ſtoun on | als sua I be seik ʒo*ur* grace to caus/ my son/ and | all vd*er*
scott*is* men y*at* ʒe ma for ga to cu*m* in yis | cu*n*tre for ther welbe besyns
about yis toun or ellis | in som vder pairt in yis cu*n*tre/ ye french men y*at* wes
heyr | cald not agre *with* ye capeden wes sent to tham | and said to hem/ tha
aucht na s*er*uis to ye king and | we haf caussit hem/ to send for vd*er*is/ sa mony
as | plissis hem/ and pout tham away/ yis laſt Rad | was mad In Ingland/ has
doun na gud bot maid | our Inimeis harde/ and quhill it be mendit ye | Inglis
men/ well neu*er* traſt to geit skath/ ʒo*ur* | grac maun/ be v*er*e scherp batht
on ye franch men | and on ye scott*is* men | or it will not be weill | ʒet ad*er*
to do as aferis to tham/ or lat it be | tha mecht neu*er* getin sa gud ane tym/
p*ar*don | me y*at* writt*is* sa hamly to ʒo*ur* grac for in | gud feth it cu*m*is of ane
gud hart [*illegible word deleted*] as than | y*at* loif*is* bath ye honou*r* of scotland
and frans ford*er* | god keip ʒo*ur* grace wrytin of hom ye | ix. day of merch be
ʒo*ur* gracis s*er*uetou*r* |

mariune |

Dorse   to ye quenis gras
21   om. the ix. day of Merch be

(g) *Letter from John Knox to Lord Robert Dudley (1563)*

The next three letters are all from John Knox (1514–72) to various English and Scottish magnates. For a short biography of Knox, see ch. 4, 3.13; a recent full-length biography is Marshall 2000. The standard edition of Knox's correspondence remains that edited in the nineteenth century by the antiquarian David Laing (1846–64), though see also an important edition of newly discovered material by Jane Dawson and Lionel Glassey (2004). Laing's transcriptions are in general accurate, though he imposes modern punctuation and expands contractions silently.

The first letter (Laing 1848: LXXII) dates from 1563, and is written in Knox's English, i.e. in English for the most part but with sporadic Scotticisms which betray Knox's origins, e.g. **man** 'must', a characteristic Scots modal auxiliary, or **faschious** 'angry', a word not found in contemporary Early Modern English texts (see further Aitken 1997, Smith 2010). The Scots form **spreit** 'spirit' might also be noticed, as might the ending –**eht** as the present tense third person singular inflexion for more usual Early Modern English –eth (see ch. 2, 2.8). Punctuation is deployed lightly, with the simple punctus being used often where we would write a comma, though Knox does use parentheses, e.g. (**saieht the et*er*nall**).

The letter is written to Lord Robert Dudley, the favourite of Elizabeth I of England; Dudley was created earl of Leicester the following year. Dudley traditionally favoured and protected Protestants, and Knox's friend, Christopher Goodman, took refuge on Dudley's estates after he had angered Elizabeth I with his companion-piece to Knox's *First Blast*.

Elizabeth had proposed Dudley as a suitable match for Mary Queen of Scots, and Knox writes to encourage Dudley in his suit, since he sees this marriage as an opportunity to **advance the | puritie of religio*n***. However, Dudley's candidacy puzzled many contemporaries, not only because he was widely considered – however unfairly – to have murdered his previous wife but also because he was equally widely perceived to be Elizabeth's lover. It is perhaps for these reasons that Knox adds the polite rider: **yf vprightlie ye will apply | your witt*is* and power yerto**. The marriage did not take place; Mary married Henry Stewart, Lord Darnley, instead: an ill-fated match.

The letter survives in the State Papers referring to Scotland in the National Archives, Kew, SP52/8, number 68. The letter has been damaged by damp, but is still mostly legible; certain phrases are rubbed, and may have been legible in Laing's time. For that reason certain readings are supplied from Laing's edition, and are marked thus below in square brackets, ending in an asterisk *. The letter is written in Knox's own secretary hand. A transcript of the letter, in what appears to be Laing's hand, has been pasted into the manuscript immediately after the original.

The Father of al mercies mack you feall | the sweet odour of his grace wh*ic*h by his | holie ſpreit floweht to mankynd from Jesus | chriſt &c.

Seing that it hath pleased y*our* hono*ur* to call me to | that familiaritie that by writeing I may conferr | w*ith* y*our* l*or*d*ship* men myg*h*t Judge me more foolish | yf I should lyg*h*tlie eſteame so great a benefitt | or yit negleᵈt the   5
opportunitie so liberallie offered. | o*n*e thing I fear. that my writeing*is* att all tymes | shallbe vnto you more faschious nor confortable. but | as [att comand I begyn*] so vpon the sam I shall | gladly desiſt. and yit befor I enter in any farther | familiarite I man proteſt that it be in Jesus Chriſt for | [w*ith*out him | ye shall eſteam | no fauo*ur* of man *in margin*]] God hath placed you in   10
fauo*ur*, credith, and in some | authoritie, by wh*ic*h ye may greatlie advance the | puritie of religio*n*, yf vprightlie ye will apply | y*our* witt*is* and power yerto. I am not ignorant that | ye shall haue many hinderar*is*, and that many terri|ble block*is* shalbe caſt befor y*our* feitt yf you ones | purpos openly to walk in that ſtraitt way that | leadeht to lyef; but my lord yf this sentence of | y*our*   15
god shalbe printed in y*our* hart. farr be it from | me (saieht the et*er*nall) but that I shall glorifye | such as glorifye me: yf this sentence I say be | surelie persuaded vnto y*our* hart, and oft remembred | as it [becomeht*] ye shall easely ouercome, tenta|tions and dangers that appear moſt difficill. and | thus for my proteſtacion. Becaus the sufficiencye | of the bearer Is able faythfully   20

to reaport the estate | of all commoun effares feir [I shall*] trouble your
Lordship | for this present only with tuo headis, the on | *[dorse]* concerneht
our nobilitie, the other the faythfull diligence | of my dear brethren the trew
preacheris, with yow. | Trew it Is my lord, that ȝeall Joyned with knowledg | ones
25 appeared in a great part of our nobilitie but | allace to the greif of many hartes
it Is now Judged | to be waxen cold, whether it be be reasson | of this laitt calme
and tranquilitie in the which | euery man seakeht to build his own hous and | to
mack him selfe great having small cayr | to reedify [the hous of god.*] whether
this I say | be the caus [or whether*] because from the begynnyng | thei sought
30 not [the treuht*] but their owen advantage | I know not, god knoweht: but
this Is most certen | that there appearis no suche feruencye in the most
part | of our nobilitie (our courteours ar coldest) as | somtymes I haue sein.
yea I am eschamed and | confounded within my self when I considder so
great | mutacion within so schort a space and yet my | hope Is that for his
35 mercies saik god shall | preserue some euen vnto the end. I prase | my god
throught Jesus Christ that it pleaseht | him to mack his woord to be effectuall
in the | mouhtes of many within [this yle but*] allace my | lord [when that I
hear that grosse*] superstition is | manteaned [and vane cere*] monies ar
required | in this greatte [tyme of Christs*] evangill I can | not [but lament
40 doubting in whome the |falt consisteht. For the*] present I will | compleane
no farther, but concluding I |pray my God, that for Christ Jesus his | *[new leaf]*
sones saik that it will please him so to assist all | that travell in the gospell of
Jesu Christ | that thei may leave of testimony to this present | most wicked
generation and vnto the posteritie | to cvm that the ȝeall of his hous eateht | vp
45 in thame all carnall affections. It | may be that heirafter I comprehend your
lordship | my lord president of wales and my lord | secretary in on letter. for I
suppos that in | the publict effares ye all be of on mynd | and of on secrecye.
but heirintill I will | vse your lordships owen advysses. of Capitaine | Cockburn
his larg commission, of his articles | and ansuer I suppos the bearer [can*]
50 sufficiently | instruct your lordship. [Mentime . . .*] |promessed and our fooles
and [murderars . . .*] |

And thus I hartlie wishe vnto your honour prosperitie | and stabilitie in jesus
Christ to whose | protection I committ your lordship Of edenburgh | *the 6th*
of October 1563 |

55 Your Lordship to | commaund in Jesus | Christ, |

John Knox |

(h) Letter from John Knox to William Cecil, Lord Burghley (1570)

The addressee of this letter (Laing 1848: LXXXVIII) is Sir William Cecil, later Lord
Burghley, principal minister to Elizabeth I of England. Cecil, always a Protestant
sympathiser but primarily a famously astute politician with a long-term ambition
for a united defensive polity in Britain, had corresponded with Knox for more than

a decade by this time. The original is in the collection of State Papers referring to Scotland at the National Archives at Kew, SP52/17, number 3. The date given below (1569) is 'old-style'; according to modern practice the letter dates from 1570.

The letter makes a useful contrast with the earlier letter to Dudley. It is much more blunt and direct, and has a clear political message for a tangled time; it also demonstrates Knox's depressed views about contemporary events (he signs it, with mordant humour, **with his one foote in the grave**: probably a reference to his own physical frailty).

In 1567 Mary Queen of Scots had been forced to abdicate in favour of her infant son, and the regent of Scotland was her half-brother the earl of Moray, a Protestant lord who rose against her in 1565, but who had fled Scotland to England without a battle (thus the 'Chaseabout Raid', as his rising was called). Moray, supported by the English regime, now returned from exile to take power as Regent. Mary was imprisoned in Lochleven Castle, but escaped and raised an army, only to be defeated by Moray's forces at Langside, near Glasgow; she fled to England, where she was imprisoned once more. Mary's presence in England was a problem for Elizabeth and her ministers, as she immediately became a focus for Roman Catholic discontent with the English authorities.

Knox, who by now believed that the only way forward was to have Mary executed, was deeply concerned by rumours of plots against Regent Moray, rumours which were fulfilled when Moray was assassinated as he left Linlithgow, shortly after the date of this letter. A former friend of Knox's, William Kirkcaldy of Grange, had declared for the queen and now occupied Edinburgh Castle. Knox was under threat, and he knew it. The following year, there was an assassination attempt on Knox himself, and he was persuaded to leave the capital for St Andrews. He continued to preach there, denouncing Mary Queen of Scots and her supporters. When a truce was called between the supporters of the infant James VI ('the King's Party') and of Queen Mary ('the Queen's Party'), he returned to Edinburgh, where he died towards the end of 1572.

The letter is written in English, in Knox's own secretary hand. The word **fremmedly** is notable, since it does not appear in this form in *OED*; it seems to be an anglicisation (through replacement of –it with –ed) of Older Scots **fremmitly** 'strangely, in an unfriendly manner'. (The word was not known in Early Modern English – neither **fremmedly** nor **fremmitly** are recorded in *OED*, and only forms with –it–, –yt– appear in *DSL* – and presumably would have appeared odd to Cecil.) The forms **ryght**, **knyght** in the address are of course expanded abbreviations, which could equally easily be expanded as **rycht**, **knycht**; however, the expanded form **weght** 'weight' suggests that ⟨gh⟩ was intended in all such contexts.

Benefeit*is* of godd*is* handis receaved, crave that men*n* be thankfull & | daunger knowen wold be awoided. yf ye ſtrik not att the | roote, the branchis that appear to be brocken will budd againe | (and that mor quickly then men*n* can beleve) w*ith* greattar | forse then we wold*e* wishe. Turn*e* yo*ur* Eie vnto yo*ur* god, | foryett y*our* self and youre*s* when consultation Is to be had | in mater*is* of   5 such weght as presently lye vpon you. | Albeit I haue bein fremmedly handilled yet was I never | Enemy to the quietnis of England. god grant you | wisdome – in haiſt of Edinburgh the 2 of Januar | 1569 |

Youres to commaund in | god |

10 John Knox *with* his | one foote *in* the | grave – |

Mo daies then one | wold not suffice to expres | what I think |

The address appears on a scrap of paper pasted onto the back of the sheet on which the letter is now mounted:

To the ry*ght* worschipfull sir | Williame Cicill kny*ght* princi|pall secretary to the quenis ma*jestie* | and consall of Englande | Deliuir this |

(i) *Letter from John Knox to Sir William Douglas of Lochleven (1570)*

This letter (Laing 1848: XCII, with facsimile) was written in March 1570, and is thus roughly contemporary with Text 2(h). It is now folio 79r in MS Edinburgh, National Library of Scotland 76, the *Registrum de Honoris de Morton*.

Sir William Douglas, a staunchly Protestant lord and half-brother to Regent Moray, was Queen Mary's (reluctant) gaoler at Lochleven Castle; the warrant committing her to the castle, signed by the principal Scottish magnates, also survives in the register (folio 52r). William's brother George was involved in Mary's escape from Lochleven, but Sir William was not charged with any complicity, and indeed took part in the action against Mary at Langside. He later became sixth earl of Morton. The letter below, in secretary hand, was written not long after Moray's assassination in early 1570; Sir William was one of those who had called for the summary execution of the assassin, James Hamilton of Bothwelhaugh.

Knox this time, when addressing a Scotsman, uses many Scots features, e.g. **rycht** and **nycht**, **quhilk**, **sick** 'such', **gude**, **tacken** 'taken', **sall** (cf. Present-Day English 'shall') **tua** 'two', **gude** 'good' and even **lard** 'lord'. The vocabulary of the passage, however, contains many forms common to Older Scots and Early Modern English, e.g. **bruite** 'rumour', and Knox has adopted not only –ed in place of Scots –it (e.g. **receaved**) but also the present participle in –ing, e.g. **perceiving**. The form **tack** 'attack' (verb) is not recorded in *DSL*, and citations in *OED* date from the eighteenth century. Interestingly, punctuation is not used, contrasting with Knox's usage in his letters to the two English magnates.

After harty commendatiou*n* of my se*r*vice vnto you ry*cht* wyrshipfull I | receaved yo*ur* missive this la*st* of march *per*ceaving tharby the bruite that | ye hear of the purpose of some to tack the ca*st*ell of San*ct*androis | q*uhi*lk bruite I easely beleve be not alltogidder vane for men will | not faill to hurt what thei
5   can the quietnes of this realme and | to reenter in thare vsurped possessiou*n* and In iu*st* vplifting of the | fruit*is* that never ju*st*lie did apperteane to sick Idill bellies | how sick trublar*is* may be *st*ayed of thare Int*er*prises I remitt | to god to whose counsall I co*m*mitt yow in that and all other cases | worldly for I have tacken my gude ny*cht* of it and y*er* for bear *with* | me gude sir albeit I writ
10 not to the superintendent of fyff in the | a*ct*ioun that ye desyr as conce*r*nyng the excuse of the | tua mini*st*er*is* to *our* super*in*tendent I sall do the be*st* that

I | can when I meitt *with* him and thus *with* my harty commendatiou*n* | I
commit*t* you to the prote*ct*iou*n* of the omnipotent of Edinburgh | the sam
hour I receaued your*is* this friday att 5 after | none 1570 |

your*is* to power in god | trubled in body | 15

Johne Knox |

To the ryght worshepfull | the lard of loghlevin |

(j) *Letter from George Buchanan to Sir Thomas Randolph (1577)*

George Buchanan was one of the leading humanists of his day; for a short biography, see ch. 4, 3.11, and see also Text 5(f). Thomas Randolph was Elizabeth I's
highly trusted agent at Queen Mary's court; the title **maister of postes** underplays
his significance. Numerous letters from Randolph survive in the Elizabethan
archives, ranging from polite formal messages to Mary Queen of Scots to confi-
dential dispatches to London on Scottish affairs. Mary distrusted Randolph, not
least because of a widely circulated satirical poem, *Maister Randolphes Phantasey*,
which described how **the Quene was bent . . . to subyect to the thristie sworde
the blood of Innocente** (Cranstoun 1891: 9). Randolph denied his authorship of
the poem, but it has been ascribed to one of his more disreputable servants, the
'literary cockroach' Thomas Jenye (Cranstoun 1891: xxiv).

The following letter is one of two surviving sent by Buchanan to Randolph. This
example is both longer and less formal than the other; Buchanan teases Randolph
about his recent marriage.

Many Scots features may be noted in the letter, e.g. the reflex of Old English
hw– in ⟨quh-⟩ in **quhylk(s)**, **quhair** and Old English ā reflected in ⟨a⟩ in **ald** 'old',
ane, **bath** 'both', **lang**, **twa**. Old English –h– is generally abbreviated, but has been
expanded here as ⟨ch⟩ in **rycht** etc. The prototypically Scots auxiliaries **sal**, **suld**
might be noted, as may be the third person present singular form **has** (cf. contemporary southern Early Modern English **hath**). The forms for 'if', 'such' are Scots-
type **geif**, **sic**. However, we might note **muche** 'much' (cf. Scots **mekill** etc.), and
the present participle in –**ing**, –**yng** (cf. Scots –**and**). The form **stermes** 'storms'
seems to be a northernism, according to *OED* (see *OED* **storm** n.); in *DSL* the form
is cited only from this text. The word **naufrage** 'shipwreck' (from Middle French
naffrage), here used figuratively, is fairly commonly cited in *DSL*; **scabie poetica**
seems to be a jocular usage, i.e. 'poetic itch'. Buchanan's reference to his historical
project – **I am besy *with* our story of Scotland to purge it of sum Inglis lyis and
Scottis vanite.** – refers to his last, most ambitious work: the *Rerum Scoticarum
Historia*. Also interesting are the references to other writers, e.g. **maister knoks** (i.e.
John Knox), and the eleventh-century Irish chronicler **Marinus Scotus**; presumably this reference is to the Basel print of Scotus's chronicle, dating from 1559.

The references to Randolph's marriage, to Knox's history and to Buchanan's illness suggest a fairly precise date for the letter. Randolph's first marriage was in 1571,
to Anne Walsingham, a connexion of Elizabeth I's spymaster Francis Walsingham.
The Walsingham family was a leading group of Protestant gentry in north-west
Kent: thus presumably the jocular reference to a **kentys man**. (The curious refer-

ence to such folk being **ane centaure half man, half beast** refers to the ancient tradition that Kentish men had tails, a widespread belief in the Middle Ages. Various explanations for this odd belief have been offered; the best-known is that it was a punishment inflicted by God on people from the Kentish village of Stroud, strong supporters of Henry II in his quarrel with Thomas à Becket, who were alleged to have cut off the tail of Becket's horse. See the discussion in Brown 1892.) However, Anne died in childbirth quite soon after the marriage took place, and – although he sustained his close relationship with the Walsingham family – Randolph was married again, in 1575, to Ursula Copinger. It seems likely that this later marriage is that referred to here, even though a pencilled '1572' has been added by the archivist who put the manuscript together. Knox had died in 1572, but his *History of the Reformation*, supplemented and revised, was not published until 1587. Buchanan himself became increasingly ill during the 1570s, suffering from what he called (as here) **gut** 'gout'; he died in 1582. The reference to Buchanan's sickness suggests the later date, as does his somewhat tasteless statement **bot you deliuerit of ane wyfe castis | your self in the samyn nette**; one is reminded of the view that Buchanan was 'a sour, mean-minded misogynist' (Akrigg 1984: 5). It is worth noting, though, in fairness, that Buchanan had also composed a rather affecting Latin poem on Anne Walsingham's death in childbirth (see Ford and Watt 1982: 172–3).

The most convenient collection of Buchanan's vernacular writings remains that edited by P. Hume Brown for STS (1892), who prints both letters to Randolph as well as a longer one from Randolph to Buchanan (1892: 54–9). A facsimile of the letter presented here appears in H. James (ed), *Facsimiles of the National Manuscripts of Scotland* volume III (no. LXVI) (1870–2). The original is in MS London, British Library Lansdowne 15 (item 24); the manuscript is a collection of various letters on Scottish matters (Burghley Papers 1572). The letter forms folio 49; the address is on a covering sheet, folio 50. It is written in Buchanan's own fine secretary hand, with some italic features (e.g. ⟨f⟩). The punctuation is Buchanan's own, with careful use of the comma and punctus, and sporadic use of the virgule to mark a change of topic.

49r   I resauit twa pair of lettres of you sens my latter wryting | to you. wyth the
first I resavit Marinus Scotus, of quhylk | I thank you greatly, and specialy that
your ingles men ar | fund liars in their cronicles allegyng on hym sic thyng*is*
as | he never said. I haif beyne vexit wyth seiknes al the tyme | sens, and geif I
5   had decessit [ye *deleted*] ye suld haif lesit bath than|kis and recompens/ now
I most neid thank you, bot geif wear | brekk*is* vp of thys foly laitly done on the
border, [for *deleted*] than I | wyl hald the recompense as Inglis geir, bot geif
peace | followis and nother ye die [of *deleted*] seik of mariage or of the | twa
symptomes following on mariage quhylk*is* ar Jalo3ie | and cuccaldry, and the
10   gut cary not me away, I most | other ʼfindʼ [*inserted in margin*] sum way to pay
or ceise kyndnes, or ellis geifing vp kynd|nes pay 3ow wi*th* evil wordis, and geif
thys fasson of dealing | pleasit me I haif reddy occasion to be angry wyth you
that | haif wissit me to be ane kentys man, quylk in a [mer *deleted*] maner | is
ane centaure half man, half beast. and yit for ane cer|taine consideration
15   I wyl pas over that iniury, imputyng it | erar to your new foly, than to ald
wysdome. for geif ye | had beine in your ry*ch*t wyt. ye being anis escapit the

tempeſtu|ous ſtormes and naufrage of mariage had never enterit|agane in
the samyng dangeris. for I can not tak you|for ane Stoik philosopher, having
ane head inexpug[h *deleted*]nable|*with* the frenetyk torme*n*tis of Jaloʒie
or ane cairles hart|[skeptik *marginal gloss*] that tak*is* cuccaldris as thing   20
indifferent/ In thys caise|I moſt neidis præfer the [s *deleted*] rude scottis wyt
of capitane Cocburne|to your inglis solomonical sapience, quhylk wery of
ane wyfis deliue|rit hir to the queyne againe, bot you deliuerit of ane wyfe
caſtis|your self in the samyn nette, et ferre potes dominam saluis tot|reſtibus
ullam. and so capitane cocburne is in better case than you|for his seiknes   25
is in the feitte and ʒowris in the heid. I pray ʼyouʼ geif I be|out of purpose
think ʼnotʼthat I suld be maryit. bot rather consider your|awyn dangerous
eſtait of the quhylk the ſpeking as thus troublit|my braine and put me sa
far out of the way. as to my occupation|*[folio 49v]* at thys present tyme, I am
besy *with* our ſtory of Scotland to purge it|of sum Inglis lyis and Scottis   30
vanite. as to maiſter knoks|his hiſtorie is in hys freindis handis, and thai ar
in co*n*sultation to|mitigat sum part the acerbite of certaine wordis and sum
taintis|quhair in he has followit to muche su*m* of your inglis writaris|as M.
hal et suppilatorem eius Graftone, *&c*. As to M. beza|I fear *yat* eild quhylk
has put me from vers making sal de|liure him sone a Scabie poetica, quhylk   35
war ane great pitye|for he is ane of ʼtheʼ moſt singular poetes that has beine
this lang|tyme. as to your great prasyng gevin to me in your *le*tt*re* geif |ye
scorne not I thank you of luif and kyndnes towart me|bot I am sorie of your
corrupt iugement. heir I wald say mony|iniuries to yow war not yat my [gvt
deleted] gut co*m*mandis me to cesse|and I wyl als ſpair mater to my nixt   40
writing*is*. Fairweal|and god keip you at ſterling the sext of auguſt.|

Be youris at al a power|

G Buchanan|

50v To his singular freynd|M. Randolf maiſter of|poſtis to the queinis g.
of|Ingland.|In london.| 45

(k) *Letter from James VI to Elizabeth I (1587)*

The next four letters were written by James VI (and I of England), and survive in
his own distinctive italic handwriting. The most up-to-date edition of selections
from James's correspondence, both holograph (i.e. completely written by him) and
autograph (i.e. scribal, with the king adding his signature), with selective finding-
aids including partial references to current manuscript-locations, is Akrigg 1984.
However, Akrigg's edition, though in many ways valuable for historians, is largely
useless for philological work; the letters are supplied with modern punctuation and
the spelling is generally anglicised rather than reproduced in what the editor refers
to as 'good homely Lallan' (which James habitually used, according to Akrigg,
when writing to Scottish persons). Akrigg does not cite *DOST* (for items to date)
or *SND*, and his only reference to any linguistic authority is to Smith 1902. He does

however retain some items of Scots vocabulary and a few grammatical features, and there are some helpful – if tantalisingly brief – comments in his introduction about variation and changes in James's spelling-practices.

The standard old-spelling editions of much (not all) of James VI's correspondence therefore remain John Bruce's *Letters of Queen Elizabeth and King James VI of Scotland* (1849) and *Correspondence of King James VI. of Scotland with Sir Robert Cecil and others in England* (1861). Bruce's transcriptions are generally accurate, though he does omit deletions and miscopy a few minor features, and he also introduces modern punctuation. For a discussion of the political and personal dynamics of the Elizabeth-James correspondence, see Allinson 2007 and references there cited. For a short characterisation of James's letters, see Simpson 2000.

A facsimile, with transcript, of a further letter from James VI to the earl of Mar appears as plate 21 in Simpson 1998, derived from MS Edinburgh, National Archives of Scotland, GD 124 (Mar and Kellie Muniments).

James was twenty-one when he wrote the following letter to Elizabeth I of England, apparently about a month after his mother's execution in 1587. The text below is a draft, written in James's own hand and with various corrections. It is unsigned. It survives in MS London, British Library Additional 23240, folio 65r; a useful illustration appears in Akrigg's edition (1984: 28, Plate II). The letter is number 27 in Akrigg's collection and (coincidentally) number XXVII in Bruce's edition; neither editor reproduces the deletions. In this draft, James did not bother to add his signature or complete the formal complimentary closing phrase; Akrigg supplies '*ng and dearest brother*', and the signature.

It is, as might be expected, a careful letter. Although he was at this difficult time, it seems, 'floundering amidst the conflicting pressures upon him' (Doran 2002: 592), James's corrections demonstrate his concern for diplomatic nuance. Thus the definite **proofe of youre honorable & kynde dealing touar|dis me** is replaced by the vaguer **satisfaction in all respectis**; James is aware that to require a fellow-monarch to offer **proofe** is potentially face-threatening. Even as a young man, James had developed (as the whole correspondence with Elizabeth shows) an ability to write fulsome prose while pursuing his own agenda. He was, it is now known (see Doran 2002: *passim*), deeply offended by the execution, even though he had hardly been close to his mother, who was rumoured to have left her crown and titles to Philip II of Spain; James refers to her in the draft obliquely as **the defunct**. It seems to have been for James an issue not so much of family affection as of honour, touching national sovereignty and his own sense of kingship. As soon as the news of her death reached Scotland James went into mourning, and worried reports were sent to London that he was unleashing the notorious Border Reivers (see Text 1(e) above) onto the English marches. In this letter James ostensibly accepts Elizabeth's claims of **innocentie**, although we know that simultaneously he was pursuing negotiations with France, Spain and Denmark about an anti-English alliance.

Elizabeth responded by taking various military measures, and by showing favour to Lady Ar(a)bella Stewart, granddaughter of Bess of Hardwick and James's eleven-year-old first cousin, who herself had a claim on both the English and Scottish thrones (Arbella eventually died in 1615, imprisoned in the Tower of London after an unfortunate marriage; see Akrigg 1984: 320–1, letter 151). Eventually both sides climbed down; James was always worried that conflict would jeopardise his claim to both kingdoms, whereby he might **unite this yle**. But James continued to dabble in cross-border politics; see Text 2(m) below, for example.

James kept Scotland and subsequently England at peace, and out of foreign entanglements, for some forty years. 'That this was not a simple achievement is eloquently illustrated by the bloody histories of both nations before and after his reign' (Jack and Rozendaal 1997: 460). It is worth recalling that both James's mother, Mary Queen of Scots, and his son, Charles I, were beheaded after taking part in vicious civil wars.

Robert Carey, referred to in the first line of the draft, seems to have made a good impression on James. Although the king at first excluded him from Scotland in retaliation for his mother's execution, Carey boasted in his later memoirs that James had written to Elizabeth asking for him to be granted leave to come back to Scotland. When Elizabeth died in 1603 Carey rode non-stop to Holyrood to give the news to James; he subsequently took on various court roles in James's reign, including a period as guardian to James's son Charles (later Charles I). He was created first earl of Monmouth a few days after the coronation of Charles in 1626 (*ODNB*).

The letter contains a few Scots forms, most notably ⟨quh-⟩ in place of Old English hw–, e.g. **Quhairas, sumquhat, quhom** (cf. more prototypical Scots **quham**) and **quhole**. The form **quhole** 'whole' is interesting; despite deriving from Old English hāl, the Older Scots reflex always seems to have ⟨o⟩, cf. *DSL* **quhole** (the form **quhale** means 'whale' in Older Scots). James seems to have sustained the Scots ⟨quh-⟩ spelling throughout his career, though Akrigg states that 'By 1623 King James was beginning to waver even in his allegiance to "quh" and, meeting the English halfway, addressed a letter from "qwhitehall"' (1984: 32), though such a spelling for the king's London administrative centre would be entirely acceptable for a Scot (seeText 2(n) below). Old English ā appears generally as ⟨o⟩ in **knou, longe, one** and Old English ō is reflected as ⟨oo⟩ in **good**; Present-Day English –ed, –ing appear in their English form. In closed-class words, however, Scots forms are more noticeable, e.g. **sall** (cf. Present-Day English 'shall'), **yone** 'that (over there)' beside **hath, heirafter**. A curiosity is that James habitually placed an acute accent over the indefinite article, thus **á**; in general he does not use Scots **ane** (although see **ane aulde horne** in Text 2(l)). How this accent is to be interpreted is uncertain, and it has thus been retained here. The form **uas** 'was' appears as **war** in Bruce's edition; the final ⟨s⟩ seems a little darker in the manuscript, and may represent a corrected form. James uses commas, but sparingly.

There is some evidence that James retained his Scots accent even after moving to London. In their collaborative play *Eastward Hoe* (1605, Act 4, Scene 1) George Chapman, Ben Jonson and John Marston notoriously had a James-based character say **I ken the man weel, hee's one of my thirty pound Knights**: a reference to a practice, begun by James, of allowing men to purchase their nobility.

Madame & deareſt siſter, ʼQuhairas byʼ [I haue receaued *deleted*] your lettir & bearare [harde *deleted*]|ʼrobert careyʼ youre seruand & ambassadoure [Robert carey *deleted*] ye purge|youre self of yone unhappy faċt as on the one pairt|considdering your rank & sexe, consanguinitie, & longe pro|fessed good uill to the defunċt together uith youre many|and solemne atteſtationis of youre innocentie I darr not|[& *rubbed out*] uronge you so farre as not to iudge honorablie of youre un|ſpotted pairt thairin so on the other syde   5

I uishe that | youre honorable behauioure in all tymes heir after may | fully
persuaide the quhole uorlde ˈof the sameˈ [of youre innocent *deleted*] | [pairt
10 thairin *deleted*], & as for my pairt I looke [*single letter deleted*] that ye uill | [at
this tyme guue *deleted*] geue me at this tyme suche á | full ˈsatisfactionˈ in all
respectisˈ [proofe of youre honorable & kynde dealing touar *deleted*] | [dis
me *deleted*] as sall be á meane to strenthin & unite this | yle, establishe &
maintaine the treu religion, & obleig | me to be as of befoire I uas youre most
15 loui - |

Inserted in bottom left-hand corner:

this bearare | hath sumquhat | to informe you | of in my name | quhom I neid
not | desyre you to credit | for ye knou I loue him |

(l) *Letter from James VI to Jean Douglas, dowager countess of Angus (1589)*

Jean Douglas (née Jean Lyon, daughter of Lord Glamis) was the widow of Archibald
Douglas, eighth earl of Angus, who had died in 1588; she gave birth to a daughter
after the earl's death. Angus, an ultra-protestant, had had a somewhat chequered
political career, but ended in favour with the king and possessing a reputation as a
significant administrator in the Scottish Borders. In 1590, shortly after the date of
this letter, his widow married James's then favourite Alexander Lindsay, later Lord
Spynie, who had loaned James substantial sums of money; this letter encourages
the lady. The reference to **my auin bedd** may relate to Lindsay having shared a bed
with James; Akrigg (1984: 93) quotes a contemporary reference to Lindsay as 'the
King's only minion . . . his nightly bed-fellow' (see also Lindsay's *ODNB* entry).
Akrigg transcribes **bedd** as '"bedl" bed?'; examination of the original manuscript
indicates a faint lobe at the foot of the last letter of the word which suggests that
James intended to write **d** – which of course makes sense in context. The reference to **my sonnet** is to a poem which now seems to be lost. This letter is number
32 in Akrigg's collection. It is now item 13 in MS Edinburgh, National Library of
Scotland, 33.1.1 (volume I).

James was successful in persuading Jean to marry Lindsay; they lived in some
style at Aberdour Castle and had four children together. Lindsay was killed in a
street-brawl in 1607; Jean died in 1610.

The language of the passage is more markedly Scots than Text 2(k). Old English
ā appears as ⟨a(i)⟩ in **baith**, **sa**, **na(thing)**, and as ⟨au⟩ in **auld** 'old'. James's liking for
initial ⟨quh⟩ in **quhaire**, **quhaise**, **quhilke** etc. may be noted, as may also characteristically Scots forms such as **sall** (cf. Present-Day English 'shall'), **sen** 'since' and
sicc 'such', and James's characteristic form for the indefinite article, **á**. However, we
might note a single occurrence of **ane**, in what seems to be a proverbial expression,
i.e. **á neu | tout in ane aulde horne as thay saye**. James uses little or no punctuation,
except in splitting up a list: **quhaise bloode, quhaise affection, & quhaise credit**.
Akrigg glosses **acsistaire** as 'assister', and **inlayke** as 'be lacking'; *DSL* has **inlaik**,
inlake 'deficit', and *OED* considers **inlaik** to be only a Scottish word. The reading **not
to | to doute** is in the original; James repeated the word **to** when he started a new line.

Madame as I haue na neu occasion sa haue I na neu thing to uritt at this present
excepe á neu | tout in ane aulde horne as thay saye thairby to reneu unto you that
quhilke I euer uishe to be | neu in youre breist quhill the parformance thairof
I can use na other argumentis | unto you then I used at my last speiking uith
you & I trust I neid not to repeat | the same sen I take you to be als ueiluilling   5
in that maitter as euer ye uas & in á uord | as he merites quhaise bloode,
quhaise affection, & quhaise credit uith me I hope be | nathing inferioure
to any that can suite you & in á thing ame I suire he ouir pasis | thaime all
that [q *deleted*] quhaire in other folkis bestouing I ame but á consentair or
ac-|sistaire in this I ame the onlie actoure solistaire & bestouaire quhom as   10
I haue | out of my auin bedd beine uilling to bestou upon youris sa neid [ye
neid *deleted*] ye not to | to doute I uill aduance him to sicc degree as that place
meritid Madame as my | sonnet sayes I ame & man contineu best freind to
you baith sen sa is for all otheris | ye neid the les to caire ye are cum to parfit [it
deleted] aage & can gouuerne yourself | nou sen I ame sa constant in this   15
maitter & his affection sa laisting I looke | the constancey sall not inlayke at
the thridd hande quhilke otheruayes as | godd forbidd this maitter being sa
publicklie brokkin furth as it ‘is’ [it *deleted*] ualde | [totu *deleted*] turne to my
skorne, his skaith & youre small honoure. fair ueill |

he that uill & can best in this cause | 20

James R. |

(m) Letter from James VI to the earl of Mar and Edward Bruce (1601)

These informal notes to his two ambassadors to the English court, the second earl
of Mar and Edward Bruce (later Lord Kinloss), relate to a time of particular delicacy in Anglo-Scottish relations. The earl was one of James's closest friends (they
had been fellow-pupils of George Buchanan), and later became High Treasurer
of Scotland; Bruce was a highly trusted legal administrator. James had had covert
dealings with the earl of Essex, who was plotting his notorious coup d'état (**this
accident**) against Elizabeth. James determined to send a mission to spy out the
land; but the ambassadors arrived too late, after Essex's rebellion had been crushed
and Essex himself executed. They focused their efforts, therefore, on building a
close relationship between James and Elizabeth's principal minister, Sir Robert
Cecil. A later lengthy coded correspondence between James and Cecil (addressed
by James cryptically in various letters as **my dearest 10**) on political matters also
survives; examples are printed in modernised form in Akrigg's edition (1984: 178–
205), and in old-spelling in Bruce's edition (1861). The text below is item 7 (*olim* 6)
in MS Edinburgh, National Library of Scotland, 33.1.7 (volume XXI); it appears as
number 76 in Akrigg's collection. The marginal numbering is James's own.

Several features characteristic of Scots appear in the passage. The forms **kythe,
kything** 'reveal' seems, from citations in *OED*, to have been restricted to Scots and
northern English usage by the early modern period; the English writer Francis
Palgrave states in 1530 that **This terme is nat vsed in comen spetche**. The preposition **anent** 'concerning' is similarly restricted to northern/Scots use. Other forms

of interest include **gif** 'if' (beside **if**), **man** 'must' and **sall** (cf. Present-Day English 'shall', beside **shall**). Old English ā is reflected in ⟨o⟩ for the most part (e.g. **nothing**), but we might note **aulde** 'old' and also **langer** corrected to **longer**. Old English ō appears as ⟨oo⟩ in **goode, looke**. Old English **hw–** appears as ⟨quh⟩ in **quhilke** etc. Akrigg glosses **redding** as 'saving, relieving, clearing'; *DSL* gives 'clearing from encumbrances etc.', and *OED* cites the form as originally and chiefly Scottish. Akrigg interprets **tua** as 'thitherward', which seems to make sense in context; the latter may be a back-spelling of **to**, suggesting that the word **tua** 'two' was pronounced by James without medial /w/ (see Dobson 1968: 981–2). *DSL* gives a 1646 citation for **two** 'to'. The curious reference to **litle lomini** is probably to Antoine de Loménie de Brienne (1559–1638), a French minister of state with antiquarian interests who at one time had been French ambassador to England. Akrigg considers that the 'allusion here is probably irrecoverable' (1984: 171).

Notes [to *deleted*] for my ambasadouris anent this accident |

1 if turnes be remediable & that my freindis thinke it the beſt appearance for | [my *deleted*] thaire safetie that I lye ſtill & that ye kythe not follow thaire aduys | bot beuaire to be preeuentid or ye looke for it. |

5   2 bot gif thay thinke youre kything in it maye doe goode ſtande not then | upon termis & I sall auow you brauelie. |

3 & gif thay be resoluit that thay lakke nothing bot á heade to enter in | plaine aÄ±tion uith it asure thame I shall be as uilling & readdie to suplee | that place as thay can be to desyre me onelie with that ꞌauldeꞌreseruation of | the safetie
10   of the quenis personne quhilke ye man take thaime suorne to |

4 bot gif as god forbidde it be paſt redding or ye cum thaire use ꞌthenꞌall the | meanis ye can to gett me á pairtie thaire & asure thaime that I cane | nather uith honoure nor suretie disguyse my self any longer [*corrected from* langer]. |

5 & gif quhen ye cum to berwike ye finde any perrell of præuenting
15   youre | cumming poſte up uith all ſpeid tua & youre self & be not á ble[. . .] | ambasadoure bot remember of litle lomini |

James R. |

(n) Letter from James VI to the earl of Mar (1618)

This note to the earl of Mar, by this time High Treasurer of Scotland, requests a payment to the Marquess of Hamilton. The letter (number 175 in Akrigg 1984) is GD 124/10/149 in the National Archives of Scotland, Edinburgh. On the dorse of the letter appear two notes: the first, in the king's own italic hand, addresses the letter **To our right trustie & right | welbeloued cosen**, while the second, in a distinct and rather scruffier hand, gives the place and date of composition.

    James Hamilton (1589–1625), second marquess, was another of James's favourites and a prominent courtier; he was a commissioner charged with negotiating the abortive plans for the marriage of Prince Charles to the Spanish Infanta. He was created earl of Cambridge in 1619. The clause **I knowe well the present wa⟨ntis′⟩|in my estate thaire** refers to James's chronically chaotic finances.

The language of the passage shows a few changes from James's earlier practice, e.g. his use of ⟨w⟩ alongside ⟨u⟩ as the reflex of Present-Day English ⟨w⟩ in **new, wrytte** etc. Apart from his retention of ⟨quh⟩ in **quhiche, quhy** there is little to betray James's use of Scots here. Punctuation is much more elaborate in this letter than in the others edited here; we might note how brackets are reinforced by commas, for instance. The second hand on the dorse retains Scots usage, with **aun** 'own' (cf. James's **owin**); we might also note the spelling **quhythall** 'Whitehall' (i.e. Whitehall Palace, London).

Milorde it is nou many monethes agoe since I signed á precept|to milorde hammilton of three thousande poundis sterling,|to be payed him ⟨out′of⟩ my resettis thaire, & nou by these|presentis, I haue thoght goode to reuiue it againe & giue it|new strenthe & uigoure, my pleasure is that it maye be|[[paye to *deleted*] paied unto him, with as conuenient speede, as the|urgent   5
necesitie of my owin particulare effaires (, quhiche|muste be preferrid before all things,) maye permitte &|withall, that it maye be kept as secreate, as posiblie|maye be, for eschewing the inportunitie of á number|of suters, & this is the reason quhy I wrytte this unto|you with my owin hande, I knowe well the present wa⟨ntis′⟩|in my estate thaire, but I ame so fullie saitisfied & so   10
mu⟨che′⟩|reioiced, at the conquest I haue made, in drawing this man|to wayte upon me, nou that I knowe him, as he doeth me,|that I asure my selfe, his [*illegible deletion*]⟨seruice′⟩ will repaye my libera-|litie with á double interest & thus I biddle you hairtelie|fairwell.|

James R.| 15

Dorse To our right trustie & right|welbeloued cosen & counsellou*r*|The earle of Mar & c.|

his maiestis letter concer|ning ⟨and in fauore′⟩my Lord hamilton|all vryttin vith his aun|hand.|[*? datitt uncertain*] quhythall the xxvi|of maij 1618|

(o) Letter from Sir Thomas Urquhart to Robert Farquhar of Mounie, 18 December 1648

For a biography of Urquhart, see ch. 4, 3.15. An edition of this letter is printed in Jack and Lyall (1983: 42); it is now MS New Haven, Yale University, Beinecke Library, Gordonstoun Papers, Box I, folio 6. The letter's plain, workmanlike expression can usefully be compared with the baroque public prose found in Urquhart's *The Jewel* and in his translation of Rabelais. In this letter, Urquhart uses many forms that are protypically Scots or quasi-Scots, e.g. **hundreth** 'hundred', **quhich** (cf. prototypically Scots **quhilk**), **salbe, suld** etc., though we might note **tuo** (cf. Scots **twa**) 'two' beside **ane** 'one'/indefinite article 'a(n)'. The present participle inflexion, though, is **–ing**. Urquhart retains ⟨y⟩ in **yat** 'that' (commonly) and **broy*er*** 'brother', but we may also note **the**.

Urquhart writes in a neat secretary hand with some italic features; he deploys a mixture of punctuation and litterae notabiliores (notably with **And**) to disambiguate grammatical and rhetorical units. His signature is a complex one, adopted to make forgery difficult, with the **Ur–** of his surname imposed upon Tho with elaborate decorative flourishes.

Much honoured freind, wnderſtanding by Mr tho|mas mcKen3ie yat you haue his band for four | hundreth merks for his entrie to the lands | off ballacuth, quhich he thinkes too much | being bot a compryser *with*out possessione, | for a litle somme off money not haueing a pur|pose to enjoy the land. and besyds
5   because | not long since my wmq*uhi*ll ˋfathyrˊ gott ane entre | from the present heritor theroff: and being | certainly [fo *deleted*]informed be Mr thomas yat you pro|meised him quhateuer ease off the sayde | somme I wald giue him you wald condiscend | to it, I will requeſt you to accept off | tuo hundreth merks And to giue him his | band off four hundreth for besyds diuerse oy*er* | reſþeċts
10   in my absence off the Cuntrey he | was at paines and charges in our affaires | as my broy*er* Dunlugus knoues, so yat we suld | deale courteously vith him And so exſþeċt|ing you will doo me this favour quhich | in accompt salbe taken from yor by your |

   wery lowing frend |
15   to doe you service |

   Tho *U*rquhart |

Cromerty yis Monday |
The 18th of Decemb |
1648 |

3

On Language and Literature

(a) James VI, 'Ane Schort Treatise Conteining some Revlis and Cautelis to be obseruit and eschewit in Scottis Poesie' (1584)

James VI's *Reulis and Cautelis* (**Cautelis** = 'tricks, strategems') appeared in 1584, at the very beginning of his personal reign as King of Scots, as part of his *The Essayis of a Prentise in the Divine Art of Poesie*. The *Essayis*, for all their occasional naiveté as literary criticism, are a bid by James for credibility as head of a courtly renaissance; they were thus a significant component in his self-fashioning as a new kind of ruler for Scotland, comparable to other contemporary humanist magnates. Famously, the *Essayis* formed a manifesto for the poets who became associated with James's reign including figures such as Alexander Montgomerie, Robert Ayton and William Fowler (traditionally referred to as the 'Castalian band', although this usage is now outdated; see Bawcutt 2001). James uses Montgomerie as a source of illustrative verse. The *Reulis and Cautelis* are thus more significant in political terms than meets the eye (see also the introduction to Text 2(k)). For further discussion of the significance of *The Reulis and Cautelis*, see the edition in Jack and Rozendaal 1997; see also Jack 1988, Lyall 1991.

The book was printed in Edinburgh by Thomas Vautrollier, a printer who – as a Huguenot – linked Protestant credentials with a French cultural range. Vautrollier had begun his career in London, but there are records of his being fined by the London Stationers' Company for printing without licence works such as the sermons of Martin Luther and *A learned and very profitable exposition made vpon the cxi Psalme*. By 1580, he was in Scotland, and the General Assembly of the Kirk, meeting in Dundee, referred to him as **a stranger banischit for religioun . . . quho offers to imploy his labour** in the **vocation** of printer (Dickson and Edmond 1890: 378–9). Vautrollier seems to have shuttled between London and Edinburgh for the remainder of his career, but continued to suffer from the attentions of the Stationers' Company until his death in London in 1587; the Court of Assistants of the Company forbade his widow from printing **anye manner of book or books whatsoever, aswell by reason that her husband was noe printer at the tyme of his decease, as alsoe for that by the decrees sette downe in the Starre Chamber she is debarred from the same** (Dickson and Edmond 1890: 382–3). His son Monasses or Manasses – it was common practice for Protestants to use Old Testament names – succeeded to the Scottish arm of his business, which continued until at least the 1630s (Mann 2000: 132, 201). (For further discussion of Vautrollier's career, see Dickson and Edmond 1890: 377–93; see also Corbett 2010.)

In 1584 Vautrollier received two royal commissions from James VI: a printing of a translation of Du Bartas' *History of Judith*, and the *Reulis and Cautelis*. The title-page of the latter reads as follows: **Imprinted at Edinbrugh | by Thomas | Vautrollier. | 1584. | CVM PRIVILEGIO | REGALI.** No reference is made on the title-page to the royal author. The work is not paginated, but signatures are supplied in place of folios, and are thus used here, e.g. *[folio Kij r]* means 'second leaf in quire K, recto'.

Many Scots forms might be noted in this edition; from the following statement it is clear that James conceives of his language as being distinct from English albeit closely related: **For albeit sindrie hes written of it in English,** *quhilk is lykest to our language* [my italics], **zit we differ from thame in sindrie reulis of Poesie, as ze will find be experience.** It might also be noted that James identifies certain forms of language as being rustic and presumably therefore to be stigmatised, an interesting parallel with the sociolinguistic concerns flagged by (e.g.) contemporary English orthoepistical writers such as John Hart and Alexander Gil; we might note James's reference to **vplandis wordis** which he deems appropriate for what he calls **land-wart effairis** 'rustic matters'. Old English ā is reflected in ⟨a(i)⟩ very regularly, with forms such as **sa, twa, baith, lang(est), maist, haill, ane, knaw(ledge)**, while Old English ō appears with ⟨u(i)⟩ in **gude, fute, buikis** 'books'. The form **auld** 'old' may also be noted (cf. Old Anglian āld). Old English **hw–** is reflected almost always as ⟨quh-⟩, e.g. **quhilkis**, although the form **why** appears once. Old English medial/final **h** is reflected as ⟨ch⟩ in **heich** 'high', **nocht, aucht** etc. Characteristically Scots inflexions in –is appear in **vsis** 'use', **hes, dois**; however, the present participle is generally in –ing, e.g. **vsing, eating, seming** except in what seems to be an idiomatic expression in 'tumbling' (i.e. alliterative) verse, **hurland ouer heuch** 'rushing over [the] precipice'. Present-Day English –ed is generally reflected in –it. The characteristically Scots formal Latinate **dedicat** 'dedicated', **mentionat** 'mentioned' may also be observed. The auxiliary verbs **man** 'must', **gar** 'cause', **sall** and **sould** are characteristic of late-sixteenth-century Scots; the form for 'were' is usually **wer**, but **vvar** (cf. Norse **váru**) appears in one of James's verse-passages. The form for 'such' is **sic** (see also **siclyke** 'suchlike'), which, according to *DSL*, is the dominant form for this item in Middle Scots; **efter, fra** and **abone** appear for 'after', 'from' and 'above'. The forms for 'those', 'these' are **thais, thir** respectively. Forms for 'six' are **six** and **sex**. Characteristically Scots words include **kythe** 'show', 'make known' described by *OED* as 'Now Sc[ottish] and *north. dialect*', and **sensyne** 'since then' (*OED* records as '*Sc[ottish], Obs[olete]*'). The form **pantoun** 'slipper/soft shoe' has an obscure etymology according to both *DSL* and *OED*; with this meaning the word is now, according to *OED*, restricted to Scots (the word seems to have had a wider use, now obsolete, in farriery). The expression *moylie and coylie* 'meekly and coyly' might be an example of James's liking for proverbial sayings, as witnessed in his letters; the form *moylie* (derived according to *OED* from Middle Dutch) seems to be a Scottish/Northern English expression. Yogh is represented – as is common – in this printed text as ⟨z⟩; thorn has been replaced by ⟨th⟩.

Kij r   THE PREFACE TO *the Reader.*

THE cause why (docile Reader) I haue not dedicat this short treatise to any particular personis, (as co[m]mounly workis vsis to be) is, that I esteme all thais quha hes already some beginning of knawledge, with ane earnest
5   desyre to atteyne to farther, alyke meit for the reading of this worke, or any

vther, quhilk may help thame to the atteining to thair foirsaid desyre. Bot
as to this work, quhilk is intitulit *The Reulis and cautelis to be obseruit &*
eschevvit in Scottis Poesie, ze may maruell parauenture, quhairfore I sould
haue writtin in that mater, sen sa mony learnit men, baith of auld and of late
hes already written thairof in dyuers and sindry languages: I answer, That 10
nochtwithstanding, I haue lykewayis writtin of it, for twa caussis. The ane
is, As for the[m] that wrait of auld, lyke as the tyme is changeit sensyne, sa
is the ordour of Poesie changeit. For then they obseruit not *Flovvyng*, nor
eschewit not *Ryming in termes*, besydes sindrie vther thingis, quhilk now
we obserue, & eschew, and dois well in sa doing because that now, quhe[n] 15
the warld is waxit auld, we haue all their opinionis in writ, quhilk were
learned before our tyme, besydes our awin ingynis, quhair as they then did
it onelie be thair *[folio Kij v]* awin ingynis, but help of any vther. Thairfore,
quhat I speik of Poesie now, I speik of it, as being come to mannis age and
perfectioun, quhair as then, it was bot in the infancie and chyldheid. The 20
vther cause is, That as for thame that hes written in it of late, there hes neuer
ane of thame written in our language. For albeit sindrie hes written of it in
English, quhilk is lykest to our language, zit we differ from thame in sindrie
reulis of Poesie, as ze will find be experience. I haue lykewayis omittit dyuers figures, quhilkis are necessare to be vsit in verse, for twa causis. The 25
ane is, because they are vsit in all languages, and thairfore are spokin of be
Du Bellay, and sindrie vtheris, quha hes writte[n] in this airt. Quhairfore
gif I wrait of thame also, it sould seme that I did bot repete that, quhilk
thay haue written, and zit not sa weil as they haue done already. The vther
cause is, that thay are figures of Rhetorique and Dialectique, quhilkis airtis 30
I professe nocht, and thairfore will apply to my selfe the counsale, quhilk
Apelles gaue to the shoomaker, quhe[n] he said to him, seing him find falt
with the shankis of the Image of *Venus*, efter that he had found falt with the
pantoun, Ne *sutor vltra crepidam*.

    I will also wish zow (docile Reidar) that or ze cu[m]mer zow with reid- 35
ing thir reulis, ze may find in zour self sic a beginning of Nature, as ze may
put in practise in zour verse many of thir foirsaidis preceptis, or euer ze sie
them as they are heir set doun. For gif Nature be nocht the cheif worker in
this airt, Reulis wilbe bot a band to Na- *[folio Kiij r]* ture, and will mak zow
within short space weary of the haill airt: quhairas, gif Nature be cheif, and 40
bent to it, reulis will be ane help and staff to Nature. I will end heir, lest my
preface be langer nor my purpose and haill mater following: wishing zow,
docile Reidar, als gude succes and great proffeit by reiding this short treatise, as I tuke earnist and willing panis to blok it, as ze sie, for zour cause.
Fare weill. 45

I Haue insert in the hinder end of this Treatise, maist kyndis of versis quhilks
are not cuttit or brokin, bot alyke many feit in euery lyne of the verse, and
how they are commounly namit, with my opinioun for quhat subiectis ilk
kynde of thir verse is meitest to be vsit.

50 To knaw the quantitie of zour lang or short fete in they lynes, quhilk I haue
put in the reule, quhilk teachis zow to knaw quhat is *Flovving*, I haue markit
the lang fute with this mark, – and abone the heid of the short fute, I haue
put this mark *v*.

L r THE REULIS AND CAVTELIS TO BE OBSERVIT and eschewit in Scottis
55 *Poesie*.

CAP. 1

FIRST, ze sall keip iuſt cullouris, quheirof the cautelis are thir.

That ze ryme nocht twyse in ane syllabe. As for exemple, that ze make
not *proue* and *reproue* ryme together, nor *houe* for houeing on hors bak,
60 and *behoue*.

That ze ryme ay to the hinmeſt lang syllabe, (with accent) in the lyne,
suppose it be not the hinmeſt syllabe in the lyne, as *bakbyte zovv*, and *out
flyte zovv*, It rymes in *byte* & *flyte* because of the lenth of the syllabe, &
accent being there, and not in *zovv*, howbeit it be the hinmeſt syllabe of
65 ather of the lynis. Or *queſtion* and *digeſtion*, It rymes in *oues* & *ges*, albeit
they be bot the antepenult syllabis, and vther twa behind ilkane of thame.

Ze aucht alwayis to note, That as in thir foirsaidis, or the lyke wordis, it
rymes in the hinmeſt lang syllabe in the lyne, althoucht there be vther short
syllabis behind it, Sa is the hinmeſt lang syllabe the hinmeſt fute, suppose
70 there be vther short syllabis behind it, quhilkis are eatin vp in the pronoun-
ceing, and na wayis comptit as fete.

l v Ze man be war likewayis (except necessitie compell yow) with *Ryming
in Termis*, quhilk is to say, that your firſt or hinmeſt word in the lyne, exceid
not twa or thre syllabis at the maiſt, vsing thrie als seindill as ye can. The
75 cause quhairfore ze sall not place a lang word firſt in the lyne, is, that all lang
words hes ane syllabe in them sa verie lang, as the lenth thairof eatis vp in the
pronouncing euin the vther syllabes, quhilks are placit lang in the same word,
and thairfore ſpillis the flowing of that lyne. As for exe[m]ple, in this word,
Arabia, the secound syllabe (*ra*) is sa lang, that it eatis vp in the pronouncing
80 (*a*) quhilk is the hinmeſt syllabe of the same word. Quhilk (*a*) althocht it be in a
lang place, zit it kythis not sa, because of the great lenth of the preceding syllabe
(*ra*). As to the cause quhy ze sall not put a lang word hinmeſt in the lyne: It is,
because, that the lenth of the secound syllabe (*ra*), eating vp the lenth of the
vther lang syllabe, (*a*) makis it to serue bot as a tayle vnto it, together with the
85 short syllabe preceding. And because this tayle nather seruis for cullour nor
fute, as I ſpak before, it man be thairfore repetit in the nixt lyne ryming vnto it,
as it is set doune in the firſt: quhilk makis, that ze will scarcely get many wordis
to ryme vnto it, zea, nane at all will ze finde to ryme to sindrie vther langer
wordis. Thairfore cheifly be warre of inserting sic lang wordis hinmeſt in the
90 lyne, for the cause quhilk I laſt allegit. Bisydes that nather firſt nor laſt in the
lyne, it keipis na *Flovving*. The reulis & cautelis quhairof are thir, as followis.

L ij r CHAP. II

FIRST, ze man vnderſta[n]d that all syllabis are deuydit in thrie kindes: That is, some schort, some lang, and some indifferent. Be indifferent I meane, thay quhilk are ather lang or short, according as ze place thame. 95

The forme of placeing syllabes in verse, is this. That zour firſt syllabe in the lyne be short, the second lang, the thrid short, the fourt lang, the fyſt short, the sixt lang, and sa furth to the end of the lyne. Alwayis tak heid, that the nomber of zour fete in euery lyne be euin, & nocht odde: as four, six, aucht, or ten: & nocht thrie, fyue, seuin, or nyne, except it be in broken 100 verse, quhilkis are out of reul and daylie inuentit be dyuers Poetis. But gif ze wald ask me the reulis, quhairby to knaw euery ane of thir thre foirsaidis kindis of syllabes, I answer, Zour eare man be the onely iudge and discerner thairof. And to proue this, I remit to the iudgement of the same, quhilk of thir twa lynis following flowis beſt, 105

$v - \quad v \quad - \quad v \quad - v - v \quad -$

Into the Sea then Lucifer vpsprang.

$v \ - \quad v \quad - \quad v - v - v \quad -$

In the Sea then Lucifer to vpsprang.

I doubt not bot zour eare makkis zou easilie to persaue, that the firſt lyne 110 flowis weil, & the vther nathing at all. The reasoun is, because the firſt lyne keips the reule abone written, To wit, the firſt fute short, the secound lang, and sa furth, as I shewe before: quhair as the vther is direct contrair to the same. Bot ſpecially tak heid, quhen *[folio Lijv]* zour lyne is of fourtene, that your *Sectioun* in aucht be a lang monosyllabe, or ellis the hinmeſt syllabe of 115 a word alwais being lang, as I said before. The cause quhy it ma[n] be ane of thir twa, is, for the Musique, because that quhen zour lyne is ather of xiiij or xij fete, it wilbe drawin sa lang in the singing, as ze man reſt in the middes of it, quhilk is the *Sectioun*: sa as, gif zour *Sectioun* be nocht ather a mono-syllabe, or ellis the hinmaſt syllabe of a word, as I said before, bot the firſt 120 syllabe of a polysyllabe, the Musique sall make zow sa to reſt in the middes of that word, as it sall cut the ane half of the word fra the vther, and sa sall mak it seme twa different wordis, that is bot ane. This aucht onely to be obseruit in thir foirsaid lang lynis: for the shortnes of all shorter lynis, then thir before mentionat, is the cause, that the Musique makis na reſt in the 125 middes of thame, and thairfore thir obseruationis seruis nocht for thame. Onely tak heid, that the *Sectioun* in thame kythe something langer nor any vther feit in that lyne, except the secound and the laſt, as I haue said before.

  Ze man tak heid lykewayis, that zour langeſt lynis exceid nocht fourtene fete, and that zour shorteſt be nocht within foure. 130

Remember also to mak a *Sectioun* in the middes of euery lyne, quhether the lyne be lang or short. Be *Sectioun* I mean, that gif zour lyne be of four-tene fete, zour aucht fute, man not only be langer then the seuint, or vther

short fete, bot also langer nor any vther lang fete in *[folio L iij r]* the same lyne,
135 except the secound and the hinmeſt. Or gif your lyne be of twelf fete, zour
Sectioun to be in the sext[.] Or gif of ten, zour *Sectioun* to be in the sext also.

The cause quhy it is not in fyue, is, because fyue is odde, and euerie odde fute
is short. Or gif zour lyne be of aucht fete, zour *Sectioun* to be in the fourt. Gif
of sex, in the fourt also. Gif of four, zour *Sectioun* to be in twa.

140 Ze aucht lykewise to be war with oft composing zour haill lynis of
monosyllabis onely, (albeit our language haue sa many, as we can nocht weill
eschewe it) because the maiſt pairt of thame are indifferent, and may be in
short or lang place, as ze like. Some wordis of dyuers syllabis are lykewayis
indifferent, as

145   *Thairfore, reſtore,*

           I thairfore, then.

In the firſt, *thairfore,* (*thair*) is short, and (*fore*) is lang: In the vther, (*thair*)
is lang, & (*fore*) is short, and zit baith flowis alike weill. Bot thir indifferent
wordis, composit of dyuers syllabes, are rare, suppose in monosyllabes,
150 co[m]moun. The cause then, quhy ane hail lyne aucht nocht to be composit
of monosyllabes only, is, that they being for the maiſt pairt indifferent, nather
the secound, hinmeſt, nor *Sectioun,* will be langer nor the other lang fete in
the same lyne. Thairfore ze man place a word co[m]posit of dyuers syllabes,
and not indifferent, ather in the secound, hinmeſt, or *Sectioun,* or in all thrie.

L iij v   Ze man also tak heid, that quhen thare fallis any short syllabis efter the
156 laſt lang syllabe in the lyne, that ze repeit thame in the lyne quhilk rymis
to the vther, evin as ze set them downe in the firſt lyne: as for exempill, ze
man not say

           Then feir nocht
160   *Nor heir ocht.*

     Bot

           Then feir nocht
           Nor heir nocht.

Repeting the same, *nocht,* in baith the lynis: because this syllabe, *nocht,*
165 nather seruing for cullour nor fute, is bot a tayle to the lang fute preceding,
and thairfore is repetit lykewayis in the nixt lyne, quhilk rymes vnto it, euin
as it set doun in the firſt.

There is also a kynde of indifferent wordis, asweill as of syllabis, albeit few
in nomber. The nature quhairof is, that gif ze place thame in the begynning
170 of a lyne, they are shorter be a fute, nor they are, gif ze place thame hinmeſt
in the lyne, as

           Sen patience I man haue perforce,
           I liue in hope vvith patience.

Ze se there are but aucht fete in ather of baith thir lynis aboue written. The cause quhairof is, that *patience*, in the firſt lyne, in reſpect it is in the beginning thairof, is bot of twa fete, and in the laſt lyne, of thrie, in *[folio Liiijr]* reſpect it is the hinmeſt word of that lyne. To knaw & discerne thir kynde of wordis fro[m] vtheris, zour eare man be the onely iudge, as of all the vther parts of *Flovving*, the verie twicheſtane quhairof is Musique. 175

I haue teachit zow now shortly the reulis of *Ryming*, *Fete*, and *Flovving*. 180 There reſtis yet to teache zow the wordis, sentences, and phrasis necessair for a Poete to vse in his verse, quhilk I haue set doun in reulis, as efter followis.

CHAP. III.

FIrſt, that in quhatsumeuer ze put in verse, ze put in na wordis, ather *metri causa*, or zit, for filling furth the nomber of the fete, bot that they be all sa 185 necessare as ze sould be conſtrainit to vse thame, in cace ze were ſpeiking the same purpose in prose. And thairfore that zour wordis appeare to haue cum out willingly, and by nature, and not to haue bene thrawin out conſtrainedly, be compulsioun.

That ze eschew to insert in zour verse, a lang rable of mennis names, or names 190 of tounis, or sik vther names. Because it is hard to mak many lang names all placit together, to flow weill. Thairfore quhen that fallis out in zour purpose, ze sall ather put bot twa or thre of thame in euerie lyne, mixing vther wordis amang thame, or ellis ſpecifie bot twa or thre of thame at all, saying (*VVith the laif of that race*) or (*VVith the reſt in thay pairtis*) or sic vther lyke wordis: 195 as for exemple,

> *Out through his cairt, quhair Eous vvas eik*
> *VVith other thre, quhilk Phaeton had dravvin.*

Ze sie thair is bot ane name there ſpecifeit, to serue for vther thrie of that sorte.

Ze man also take heid to frame zour wordis and sentencis according to 200 the mater: As in Flyting and Inuectiues, zour wordis to be cuttit short, and hurland ouer heuch. For thais quhilkis are cuttit short, I meane be sic wordis as thir,

> *I is neir cair*

for 205

I sall neuer cair, gif zour subiect were of loue, or tragedies. Because in thame zour words man be drawin lang, quhilkis in Flyting man be short.

Ze man lykewayis tak heid, that ze waill zour wordis according to the purpose: As, in ane heich and learnit purpose, to vse heich, pithie, and learnit wordis.

Gif zour purpose be of loue, To vse commoun language, with some passionate 210 wordis.

127

Gif zour purpose be of tragicall materis, To use lamentable wordis, with some heich, as rauishit in admiratioun.

Gif zour purpose be of landwart effairis, To vse corruptit, and vplandis
215 wordis.

And finally, quhatsumeuer be zour subiect, to vse *vocabula artis*, quhairby ze may the mair viuelie represent that person, quhais pairt ze paint out.

This is likewayis neidfull to be vsit in sentences, als *[folio M r]* weill as in wordis. As gif zour subiect be heich and learnit, to vse learnit and infalllible reasonis,
220 prouin be necessities.

Gif zour subiect be of loue, To vse wilfull reasonis, proceding rather from passioun, nor reasoun.

Gif zour subiect be of landwart effaris, to vse sklender reasonis, mixt with grosse ignorance, nather keiping forme nor ordour. And sa furth, euer
225 framing zour reasonis, according to the qualitie of zour subiect.

Let all zoue verse be *Literall*, sa far as may be, quhatsumeuer kynde thay be of, bot speciallie *Tumbling* verse for flyting. By *Literall* I meane, that the maist pairt of zour lyne, sall rynne vpon a letter, as this tumbling lyne rynnis vpon F.

Fetching fude for to feid it fast furth of the Farie.

230 Ze man obserue that thir *Tumbling* verse flowis not on that fassoun, as vtheris dois. For al vtheris keipis the reule quhilk I gaue before, To wit, the first fute short the secound lang, and sa furth. Quhair as thir hes twa short, and ane lang throuch all the lyne, quhen they keip ordour: albeit the maist pairt of thame be out of ordour, & keipis na kynde nor reule of *Flovving*,
235 & for that cause are callit *Tumbling* verse: except the short lynis of aucht in the hinder end of the verse, the quhilk flowis as vther verses dois, as ze will find in the hinder end of this buke, quhair I giue exemple of sindrie kyndis of versis.

M v CHAP. IIII.

240 MARK also thrie speciall ornamentis to verse, quhilkis are, *Comparisons*, *Epithetis*, and *Prouerbis*.

As for *Comparisons*, take heid that thay be sa proper for the subiect, that nather they be ouer bas, gif zour subiect be heich, for then sould zour subiect disgrace zour *Comparisoun* nather zour *Comparisoun* be heich quhen zour
245 subiect is basse, for then sall zour *Comparisoun* disgrace zour subiect. Bot let sic a mutuall correspondence and similitude be betwixt the[m], as it may appeare to be a meit *Comparisoun* for sic a subiect, and sa sall they ilkane decore vther.

As for *Epithetis*, It is to descryue brieflie, *en passant*, the naturall of euerie

thing ze speik of, be adding the proper adiectiue vnto it, quhairof there are   250
twa fassons. The ane is, to descryue it, be making a corruptit worde, composit
of twa dyuers simple wordis, as

    Apollo gyde-Sunne

The vther fasson, is, be *Circumlocution,* as

    Apollo reular of the Sunne,   255

I esteme this last fassoun best, Because it expressis the authouris meaning
als weill as the vther, and zit makis na corruptit wordis, as the vther dois.

M ii r   As for the *Prouerbis,* they man be proper for the subiect, to beautifie it,
chosen in the same forme as the *Comparisoun.*

CHAP. V.   260

IT is also meit, for the better decoratioun of the verse to vse sumtyme the
figure of Repetitioun, as

    Quhylis ioy rang.

    Quhylis noy rang, &c.

Ze sie this word *quhylis* is repetit heir. This forme of repetition sometyme   265
vsit, decoris the verse very mekle, zea quhen it cu[m]mis to purpose, it will
be cumly to repete sic a word aucht or nyne tymes in a verse.

CHAP. VI.

Ze man also be warre with composing ony thing in the same maner, as hes
bene ower oft vsit of before. As in speciall, gif ze speik of loue, be warre ze   270
descryue zour *Loues* makdome, or her fairnes. And siclyke that ze descryue
not the morning, and rysing of the Sunne, in the Preface of zour verse: for
thir thingis are sa oft and dyuerslie writtin vpon be Poetis already, that gif
ze do the lyke, it will appeare, ze bot imitate, and that it cummis not of zour
awin *Inuentioun,* quhilk is any of the cheif properteis of ane Poete. *[folio M ij v]*   275
Thairfore gif zour subiect be to prayse zour *Loue,* ze sall rather prayse her
vther qualiteis, nor her fairnes, or hir shaip: or ellis ze sall speik some lytill
thing of it, and syne say, that zour wittis are sa smal, and zour vttera[n]ce so
barren, that ze can not discryue any part of hir worthelie: remitting alwayis
to the Reider, to iudge of hir, in respect sho matches, or rather excellis *Venus,*   280
or any woman, quhome to it sall please zow to compaire her. Bot gif zour
subiect be sic, as ze man speik some thing of the morning, or Sunne rysing,
tak heid, that quhat name ze giue to the Sunne, the Mone, or vther starris, the
ane tyme, gif ze happin to wryte thairof another tyme, to change thair names.
As gif ze call the Sunne *Titan,* at a tyme, to call him *Phoebus* or *Apollo* the   285
vther tyme, and siclyke the Mone, and vther Planettis.

CHAP. VII.

BOT sen *Inuention*, is ane of the cheif vertewis in a Poete, it is beſt that ze inuent zour awin subieĉt, zour self, and not to compose of sene subieĉtis.
290 Eſpecially, translating any thing out of vther language, quhilk doing, ze not only essay not zour awin ingyne of *Inuentioun*, bot be the same meanes, ze are bound, as to a ſtaik, to follow that buikis phrasis, quhilk ze translate.

Ze man also be war of wryting any thing of materis of co[m]moun weill, or vther sic graue sene subieĉtis (except *[folio M iij r]* Metaphorically, of manifeſt
295 treuth opinly knawin, zit nocht withſtanding vsing it very seindil) because nocht onely ze essay nocht zour awin *Inuentioun*, as I ſpak before, bot lykewayis they are to graue materis, for a Poet to mell in. Bot because ze can not haue the *Inuentioun* except it come of Nature, I remit it thairvnto, as the cheif cause, not onely of *Inuentioun*, bot also of all the vther pairtis
300 of Poesie. For airt is onely bot ane help and a remembraunce to Nature, as I shewe zow in the Preface.

CHAP. VIII. tuiching the kyndis of versis, mentionat in the Preface.

FIrſt, there is ryme quhilk seruis onely for lang hiſtoreis, and zit are nocht verse. As for exemple,

305
    In Maii vvhen that the blisseful Phœbus bricht,
    The lamp of ioy, the heauens gemme of licht,
    The goldin cairt, and the etheriall King,
    With purpour face in Orient dois ſpring.
    Maiſt angel-lyke ascending in his ſphere,
310
    And birds vvith all their heauenlie voces cleare
    Dois mak a svveit and heauinly harmony,
    And fragrant flours dous ſpring vp luſtely:
    Into this season svveiteſt of delyte,
    To vvalk I had a luſty appetyte.

315 And sa furth.

M iij v   ❡ For the descreptioun of Heroique aĉtes, Martiall and knichtly faittis of armes, vse this kynde of verse following, callit *Heroicall*, As

    Meik mundane mirrour, myrrie and modeſt,
    Blyth, kynde, and courtes, comelie, clene, and cheſt,
320
    To all exemple for thy honeſtie,
    As richeſt rose, or rubie, by the reſt,
    VVith gracis graue, and geſture maiſt digeſt,
    Ay to thy honnour alvvayis hauing eye,
    VVere fassons fleimde they micht be found in the:
325
    Of blissings all, be blyth, thovv hes the beſt,
    VVith euerie berne belouit for to be.

❡ For any heich & graue subiectis, specially drawin out of learnit authouris, vse this kynde of verse following, callit *Ballat Royal*, as

> *That nicht he ceist, and vvent to bed, bot greind*
> *Zit fast for day, and thocht the nicht to lang:* 330
> *At last Diana doun her head recleind,*
> *Into the sea. Then Lucifer vpsprang,*
> *Auroras post, vvhome sho did send amang*
> *The leittie cludds, for to foretell ane hour,*
> *Before sho stay her tears, quhilk Ouide sang* 335
> *Fell for her loue, quhilk turnit in a flour.*

❡ For tragicall materis, complaintis, or testamentis vse *[folio M iiij r]* this kynde of verse following, callit *Troilus* verse, as

> *To thee Echo, and thovv to me agane,*
> *In the desert, amangs the vvods and vvells,* 340
> *Quhair destinie hes bound the to remane.*
> *But company, vvithin the firths and fells,*
> *Let us complein, vvith vvofull zoutts and zells,*
> *A shaft, a shotter, that our harts hes slane:*
> *To thee Echo, and thovv to me agane.* 345

❡ For flyting, or Inuectiues, vse this kynde of verse following, callit *Rouncefallis* or *Tumbling* verse.

> *In the hinder end of haruest vpon Alhallovv ene,*
> *Quhen our gude nichtbors rydis (nou gif I reid richt)*
> *Some bucklit on a benvvod, & some on a bene,* 350
> *Ay trottand into troupes fra the tvvylicht:*
> *Some sadland a sho ape, all grathed into grene:*
> *Some hotcheand an a hemp stalk, hovand on a heicht.*
> *The king of Fary vvith the Court of the Elf quene,*
> *VVith many elrage Incubus rydand that nicht:* 355
> *There ane elf on ane ape ane vnsell begat:*
> *Besyde a pot baith auld and vvorne,*
> *This bratshard in ane bus vvas borne:*
> *They fand a monster on the morne,*
> *VVar facit nor a Cat.* 360

For compendious praysing of any bukes, or the authouris thairof, or ony argumentis of vther historeis, quhair sindrie sentences, and change of purposis are re- *[folio M iiij v]* quyrit, vse *Sonet* verse, of fourtene lynis, and ten fete in euery lyne. The exemple quhairof, I neid nocht to shaw zow, in respect I haue set doun twa in the beginning of this treatise. 365

❡ In materis of loue, vse this kynde of verse, quhilk we call *Commoun* verse, as

> *Quhais ansvver made thame nocht sa glaid*
> *That they sould thus the victors be,*
> *As euen the ansvver quhilk I haid*
> *Did greatly ioy and confort me:*
> *Quhen lo, this spak Apollo myne,*
> *All that thou seikis, it sall be thyne.*

❡ Lyke verse of ten fete, as this foirsaid is of aucht, ze may vse lykewayis in loue materis: as also of all kyndis of cuttit and brokin verse, quhairof new formes are daylie inuentit according to the Poetis pleasour, as

> *Quha vvald haue tyrde to heir that tone,*
> *Quhilk birds corroborat ay abone*
> *Throuch shouting of the Larkis?*
> *They sprang sa heich into the skyes*
> *Quhill Cupide vvalknis vvith the cryis*
> *Of Naturis chapell Clarkis.*
> *Then leauing all the Heauins aboue*
> *he lichted on the eard.*
> *Lo! hovv that lytill God of loue*
> *Before me then appeard,*
> *So myld-lyke*
> *And chyld-lyke*
> *VVith bovv thre quarters skant*
> *So moylie*
> *And coylie*
> *He luckit lyke a Sant.*

[folio Nr]

And sa furth.

❡ This onely kynde of brokin verse abone writtin, man of necessitie, in thir last short fete, as *so moylie and coylie*, haue bot twa fete and a tayle to ilkane of thame, as ze sie, to gar the cullour and ryme be in the penult syllabe.

❡ Any of thir foirsaidis kyndes of ballatis of haill verse, and not cuttit or brokin as this last is, gif ze lyke to put ane owerword to ony of thame, as making the last lyne of the first verse, to be the last lyne of euerie vther verse in that ballat, will set weill for loue materis.

Bot besydis thir kyndes of brokin or cuttit verse, quhilks ar inuentit dayle be Poetis, as I shewe before, there are sindrie kyndes of haill verse, with all thair lynis alyke lang, quhilk I haue heir omittit, and tane bot onelie thir few kyndes abone specifeit as the best, quhilk may be applyit to ony kynde of subiect, bot rather to thir, quhairof I haue spokin before.

(b) From Alexander Hume, 'Of the Orthographie and Congruite of the Britan Tongue; a Treates, noe shorter then necessarie, for the Schooles' (c. 1617)

For a discussion of Alexander Hume, see above, ch. 2, 2.3, which includes a brief biographical sketch. *Of the Orthographie . . .* was not printed in Hume's lifetime, and survives only in MS London, British Library, Royal 17 a.xi, *c.* 1617, written in a neat italic hand which seems to be the author's own. The manuscript is currently bound with two other items: MSS Royal 17 A.ix and Royal 17 A.x. The most recent edition of the work is Wheatley 1865, for the Early English Text Society.

For a discussion of Hume's significance in a wider context, see Dobson 1968: 316–21. Dobson's account is critical of Hume's abilities as a phonetician, and cites the Bath anecdote (in (4) below) as demonstrating 'how deplorable an ear he must have had' (1968: 321); Dobson's view – which is somewhat coloured by his own focus on the evolution of standard English accents – is that the **doctour of divinitie** replied 'neatly and justly'. However, Dobson allows that Hume 'does give an impression of the nature of Scottish speech at the beginning of the seventeenth century and its differences from English, and also of its ability to resist – at least in his own case – the influence of English pronunciation during sixteen years spent in the South' (1968: 321). Hume's discussion of orthography does not go much beyond the classical distinctions between *figura* (written manifestation) and *potestas* (sound symbolised), which he sees as linked by mental **congruence**. Hume has clearly read some of the key spelling-reformers ('orthoepists'), e.g. Sir Thomas Smith, a polymath who had contributed with Sir John Cheke to the notorious Cambridge controversy on the pronunciation of Greek. Hume's reference to **Barret's alvearie** is to John Baret's AN ALVEARIE OR | Quadruple Dictionarie, con-|taining foure sundrie tongues: | namelie, English, Latine, Greeke, | and French. | Newlie enriched with varietie of Wordes, | Phrases, Prouerbs, and diuers lightsome ob-|seruations of Grammar, which was published around 1580. Baret was the first lexicographer to focus on 'hard words', the standard approach used in early monolingual English dictionaries (see further Landau 1984).

The excerpts below contain many features characteristic of Scots, although forms more characteristic of English may also be noted. Old English ā is reflected as ⟨a(e)⟩ in **knau** 'know', **knawlege, maest, nae, tuae, fand,** but we might also note **both, one, soe, moe** 'more' and **noe more;** the form **quho** 'who' appears beside **quhae.** Old English ō is reflected as ⟨u⟩ in **gud,** but also as ⟨oo⟩ in **foot.** Inflexions are largely anglicised, e.g. **doeth** 'doth', present participles in –ing, e.g. **seeing, refyning;** the Scots reflex of Present-Day English –ed in –it has been replaced by –ed. There are one or two prototypically Scots/northern English words, e.g. **mikle** 'much', and **spering** 'asking' (cf. *OED* **speer** v.(1)). The form **stiddies** 'anvils' has been transferred from farriery to mean 'the passive articulator' (*DSL*); **mynt,** which seems to be a northern/Scottish word, means here 'a purposive movement of the body' (*DSL*).

Probably the best-known section in Hume's study is his discussion of the reflexes of Old English **hw–,** which appear regularly as ⟨quh-⟩, e.g. **quhae** (and **quho**), **quhilk, quhaer, quhaerbe** etc. Hume's view is that the Scottish spelling is more appropriate since it reflects the heavily velarised pronunciation which he thinks is more correct. However, he is unable to persuade his English contemporaries, who no longer pronounced such words in the same way; the **doctour of divinitie**'s reply is therefore, for a speaker of southern English, an apt one for his own accent. It is interesting that Hume himself forgets on occasion to use ⟨quh-⟩ in e.g. **whither**.

(1) From the dedication

1r To the maeſt excellent | in all princelie wis-|dom, learning, and he-|roical artes JAMES | of great Britan, | France, and | Ireland | King | Defender of the faeth | grace, mercie, peace, | honoure here, and | glorie herafter. |

May it please your maeſt, | excellent M*ajeſtie*, I your grace's | humble servant,
5 seeing sik un-|certentie in our men's wryting, | as if a man wald indyte one | letter to tuentie of our beſt wry-|teres, nae tuae of the tuentie | without conference wald agree; | and that they quhae might per-|hapes agree, met rather be cuſtom, [then *catchword*] | *[folio 1v]* then knawlege: set my selfe about | a yeer syne to seek a remedie | for that maladie. Quhen I had | done, refyning
10 it I fand in Bar-|ret's alvearie, quhilk is a dictio-|narie Anglicolatinum, that S*ir* | Thomas Smith a man of nae | less worth, then, learning, Secreta-|rie to Queen Elizabeth had left | a learned, and judiciouse monu-|ment on the same subject. Heer | consydering my aun weaknes, | and meannes of my person, be-|gan to fear quhat might betyed | my sillie boat in the same seas | quhaer
15 sik a man's ship was | sunck in the gulf of oblivion. | For the printeres, and wryteres | of this age caring for noe more | arte, then may win the pennie, | wil not paen them selfes to | knau whither it be orthographie | or skaieographie, that doeth the [turne *catchword*] | *[folio 2r]* turne: & schoolmaſteres, quhae's | sillie braine will reach no farther | then the compas of their cap, con-|tent them
20 selfes with αυτος εφη | my maſter said it. Quhil I | thus houered betueen hope & de-|ſpare; the same Barret in the | letter E myndes me of a ſtar, & | conſtellation to calm al the | tydes of these seaes; if it wald | please the supreme Majeſtie | to command the universitie | to censure, and ratifie, and the | schooles to teach the future | age right, and wrang, if | the present will
25 not rectius sape-|re.

(2)

7r Of the groundes | of Orthographie | Cap. 1. |

1. To wryte orthographicallie | ther are to be considered the sym-|bol, the thing symboliȝed, and their | congruence. Geve me leave | gentle reader in a new art to | borrow termes incident to the | purpose, quhilk being defyned
5 wil | further underſtanding. |

2. The symbol then I cal the writ-|ten letter, quhilk representes to | the eie the sound that the mouth | sould utter. |

3. The thing symboli3ed I cal the | sound, quhilk the mouth utteres, | quhen the eie sees the symbol. |

4. The congruence between them [I cal *catchword*] |*[folio 7v]* I cal the instrument   10
of the | mouth, quhilk quhen the eie | sees the symbol utteres the sound. |

5. This is the ground of al ortho-|graphie leading the wryter | from the sound
to the symbol, | and the reader from the sym-|bol to the sound. As for exem-
|ple, if I wer to wryte, God, the | tuich of the midle of the tongue | on the roofe
of the mouth befoir | the voual; and the top of the | tongue on the teeth behind   15
the | voual myndes me to wryte it | g. o. d. The voual is judged | be the sound, as
shal be shaued | herafter. This is the hardest | lesson in this treates and may | be
called the key of orthogra-|phie. |

(3)

From Of Consonantes | cap. 4 |

2. A consonant is a letter symbo-|li3ing a sound articulat, that is | broaken
with the tuiches of the | mouth. |

3. The instrumentes of the mouth | quherbe the vocal soundes be broa-|ken
be in number seven. The nether | lip, the upper lip, the outward | teeth, the   5
inward teeth, the top of | the tongue, the midle tong, and | roof of the mouth.
Of these thre | be as it wer ham*m*eres stryking, | and the rest stiddies kepping
the strakes of the ham*m*eres. |

4. The ham*m*eres are the nether [lip, the *catchword*] | *[folio 15r]* lip, the top of
the tongue, and | the midle tongue. The stiddies | the overlip, the outward   10
teeth, | the inward teeth, and the | roofe of the mouth. |

(4)

Of the rules | to symboli3e | cap. 7. |

1. To symboli3 right, the sound of | the voual is first to be observed, | quhither
it be a simple voual or a [compound *catchword*] |*[folio 23r]* compound, and
qu*h*ilk of them is to | be chosen, for quhilk no rule | can be geven, but the
judgeme*n*t | of the ear. | 5

2. Next the consonantes are to | be marked. and first quhither | they break
the voual befoer, or | behind: then quhither they be | one or moe: and lastlie
with | quhat organes of the mouth | they be broaken. |

3. For be the organes of the | mouth, quherwith the syllab | is broaken, the   10
consonantes are | discerned, be quhilk the syllab | must be symboli3ed, qu*h*ilk
we | have said, cap. 1. sect. 5. |

4. The consonantes may dif-|fer in hammar (as we called|it, cap. 4. sect. 3.) and stiddie as b, and, d. Or they may a-|gre in hammer and differ in stid-|die as b, and, v. Or they [may *catchword*]|*[folio 23v]* may agre in both, and differ in|the tuich as f, and v, m, and, p|c, and, g.|

5. The tuich befoer the voual, is|be lifting the hammer af the stiddie|as da, la, pa: and behind be stry-|king the hammer on the stiddie.|as ad, al, ap. And quhen the ham-|mer, and the stiddie are ane; the|difference is in the hardnes, and|softnes of the tuich. as may be|seen in ca, and ga, ta, and, da.|But, w, and, y, maekes sae soft a|mynt, that it is hard to perceave|and therfoer did the latines symbo-|li3 them with the symbol of the vou-|ales. They are never used but be-|foer the voual. as we, ye, wil, you.|behynd the voual thei make noe con-|sonant sound, nor sould be written.|and therfore now, and vow with|sik otheres are not be written *with*|w, as is said befoer.|[of this *catchword*]

6. Of this quhilk now is said may be|gathered that general, quhilk|I called the keie of orthographie|cap. 1. sect. 5. that is the con-|gruence of the symbol, and sound symboli3ed: that is that|bathe must belang to the same|organes, and be tuiched after|the same form.|

7. And be the contrarie here|it is clere that soundes pronun-|ced with this organ, can not be|written with symboles of that.|as, for exemple a labiel symbol|can not serve a dental, nor a|guttural sound. nor a guttu-|ral [sound *deleted*] symbol a dental, nor|a labiel sound.|

8. To clere this point, and|alsoe to reform an errour bred|in the south, and now usurped|be our ignorant printeres,|I wil tel quhat befel my self [quhen *catchword*]|*[folio 24v]* quhen I was in the south, with a|special gud frende of myne.|Ther rease upon sum accident|quhither quho, quhen, quhat, &c.|sould be symboli3ed with, q, or, w,|a hoat disputation betuene him|and me. After manie conflictes|(for we oft encountered) we met|be chance in the cite of baeth *with*|a doctour of divinitie of both our|acquentance. He invited us to|denner. At table my antagonist|to bring the question on foot amangs|his awn condisciples began that|I was becum an heretik. and the|doctour spering how, ansue-|red that I denyed quho to be spel-|led with a, w. but with qu.|Be quhat reason, quod the Doctour.|Here I beginning to lay my grundes|of labial, dental, and guttural|soundes, and symboles. he snap-|ped me on this hand and he|[on that *catchword*] *[folio 25r]* on that, that the doctour had mikle|a doe to win me room for a|syllogisme. Then (said I) a|labial letter can not symbo-|li3 a guttural syllab. But|w, is a labial letter, quho a|guttural sound. And therfoer|w, can not symboli3 quho, nor|noe syllab of that nature.|Here the doctour staying them a-|gain (for al barked at ones)|the proposition said he I un-|derstand, the assumption is|Scottish, and the conclusion|false. Quherat al laughed|as if I had bene dryven from|al replye: and I fretted to see|a frivolouse jest goe for a solid|ansuer. My proposition is|grounded on the 7 sectio of this|same cap., quhilk noe

man I | [trow *catchword*] *[folio 25v]* trow can denye, that ever suked | the paepes   55
of reason. and soe the | question must rest on the assumption | quhither, w,
be a labial letter, and | quho a guttural syllab. As for w, | let the exemples of
wil, wel, wyne, | juge, quhilk are sounded befoer the | voual with a mint of the
lippes as is | said the same cap. sect. 5. As for | quho, besydes that it differes
from | quo onelie be aspiration, and that | w, being noe perfect consonant   60
can | not be aspirated: I appele to al ju-|diciouse eares, to q*uhilk* Cicero
attribu-|ted mikle, quhither the aspiration | in, quho, be not ex imo gutture,
and | therfoer not labial. |

(c) Extracts from Sir Thomas Urquhart, 'The Jewel' (1652)

For an outline of Sir Thomas Urquhart's biography, see ch. 4, 3.15. A full discussion
of Urquhart's extraordinarily colourful career appears not only in his *ODNB* entry
but also, much more fully, in the standard edition of *The Jewel* (Jack and Lyall 1983),
a work which 'resolutely defies any attempt at generic classification' (Jack and Lyall
1983: 17). *The Jewel* is not Urquhart's title; the first part of title-page reads, in characteristically flamboyant fashion, as follows:

> Εκσκυβαλαυρον: | OR, | The Discovery of | A most exquisite JEWEL, | more pre-
> cious then Diamonds | inchased in Gold, the like whereof | was never seen in any
> age; found in the | kennel of Worcester-streets, the day | after the Fight, and six
> before the Au-|tumnal Æquinox, anno 1651. | Serving in this place, | To frontal a
> VINDICATION | of the honour of SCOTLAND, | from that Infamy, whereinto the
> Rigid | Presbyterian party of that Nation, | out of their Covetousness and | ambi-
> tion, most dissembled-|ly hath involved it. |

(The reference to **the Fight** and to *Worcester*-streets refers to the Battle of
Worcester, during the so-called 'second Civil War': an abortive attempt by Charles
II to reclaim his throne.) Εκσκυβαλαυρον (i.e. *Ekskubalauron*) is a coinage by
Urquhart, 'made up from Greek *ek skubalou* ('out of dung') and the Latin *aurum*
('gold') modified by the substitution of the Greek noun ending *–on* for the Latin
–um' (Jack and Lyall 1983: 215). A copy of the 1653 edition, published in London, is
mounted on *EEBO*.

The passage cited in ch. 4 above comes from about half-way through the work.
The first extract below is from the opening *Epistle Liminary*, written by a fictional
persona called **Christianus Presbyteromastix** ('Christian the hater of Presbyte-
rians/Priesthater' – an intentional ambiguity); the suffix –**mastix** seems to have
been commonly used in seventeenth-century religious controversy, and might just
conceivably be an echo of the notorious pamphleteer William Prynne's *Histrio-
Mastix* of 1633, a puritan attack on stage-plays which had been famously burned in
public (see Purkiss 2006: 200).

The second extract below deals with one of Urquhart's interests, viz. contemporary linguistic ideas. His discussion of linguistic universals relates to a current topic
of concern amongst intellectuals, although the reference to **Words are the signes of
things** goes back at least to Aristotle; such interests are also found in the writings of
(e.g.) John Wilkins and other 'Royal Society' luminaries (see further Dobson 1968,

especially 253–61, and Corbett 2007; for the wider intellectual background, see e.g. Jardine 1999). References to the **copiousness** of discourse in different languages, and also to the relationship between Latin and the varieties descended from it (French, Spanish and, perhaps through the use of the plural form signifying its dialects, **Italians**) are also interesting. The passages below are in English, and thus contrast with Urquhart's private writing. See also Texts 2(o) and 5(i).

Urquhart's delight in vocabulary and technical terminology is evident, cf. words such as **comprehended, discourse, composition, agglutinative, incorporating, compendiousness, conducible, conform** (adjective), **dignosced, ubiquitary, copiousness, variety, conciseness.** Urquhart was, however, not alone in enjoying such polysyllabic display; many of these words are cited in *OED* as dating from Middle English times or from the sixteenth century, e.g. **comprehend, discourse, composition** (with a philological meaning), **conducible, conform** (adjective), **ubiquitary, compendiousness.** Some seem to be fairly recent coinages, though Urquhart is not the first to use them, according to *OED*; we might note, e.g. **copiousness** meaning 'abundance of words' (attested by *OED* from 1642), or **dignosced,** used since 1639 (it is interesting that *OED*'s citations for **dignosced** seem all to come from Puritan writers on religion). However, Urquhart's use of **conciseness** predates the first attestation in *OED* (1659). *OED* cites Urquhart as the earliest to use the adjective **agglutinative** in the philological sense, meaning 'characterised by agglutination; using it as the appropriate process of word-building'; the next attestation dates from 1861, in the writings of the linguist and student of comparative religion, Max Müller. Urquhart's use of **incorporating** in relation (apparently) to word-formation is also well in advance of its time; the *OED* gives references only to nineteenth-century philological writings.

(1) From the introductory *Epistle Liminary* (see Jack and Lyall 1983: 49)

THE scope of this Treatise is (for the weal of the publick, in the *A 2r* propagation of learning & vertue throughout the whole Isle of great *Britain*) in all humility to intreat the honorable Parliament of this Commonwealth, with consent of the Councel of State thereof, to grant to Sir *Thomas Vrquhart* of *Cromarty* his former liberty and the enjoyment 5 of *[folio A 2v]* his own inheritance, with all the immunities and priviledges thereto belonging. The reasons of this demand in an unusual (though compositive) way, are so methodically deduced, that their recapitulation here (how curt soeuer I could make it) would afford but little more compendiousness to the Reader; unless all were to be summed up in 10 this, that seeing the obtaining of his desires would be conducible to the whole Land, and prejudicial to no good member in it, he should therefore be fauoured with the benefit of the grant thereof, and refusal of nothing appertaining to it.

(2) *On the Universal Language* (see Jack and Lyall 1983: 61–5)

p. 7 *An introduction to The Universal Language; wherein, whatever is uttred in other Languages, hath signification in it, whilst it affordeth expressions, both for copiousness, variety, and conciseness in all manner of subjects, which no language else is able to reach unto: most fit for such as would with ease attaine to a most expedite facility of expressing themselves in all the Learned Sciences,* 5 *Faculties, Arts, Disciplines, mechanick Trades, and all other discourses whatsoever, whether serious or recreative.*

p. 8 The matter of the Preface begun after this manner, as it was divided into several Articles.

1. Words are the signes of Things; it being to signifie that they were instituted 10 at first; nor can they be, as such, directed to any other end, whether they be articulate or inarticulate.

2. All things are either real or rational: and the real, either natural or artificial.

3. There ought to be a proportion betwixt the signe and thing signified; therefore should all things, whether real or rational, have their proper words 15 assigned unto them.

4. Man is called a *Microcosme*, because he may by his conceptions and words containe within him the representatives of what in the whole world is comprehended.

5. Seeing there is in nature such affinity *[page 9]* 'twixt words and things, as 20 there ought to be in whatever is ordained for one another; that language is to be accounted most conform to Nature, which with greatest variety expresseth all manner of things.

6. As all things of a single, compleat being, by *Aristotle* into ten Classes were divided; so may the words whereby those things are to be signified, be set 25 apart in their several store-houses.

7. Arts, Sciences, Mechanick Trades, notional Faculties, and whatever is excogitable by man, have their own method; by vertue whereof, the Learned of these latter times have orderly digested them: Yet hath none hitherto considered of a mark, whereby words of the same Faculty, Art, Trade, or 30 Science should be dignosced from those of another by the very sound of the word at the first hearing.

8. A Tree will be known by its leaves, a Stone by its grit, a Flower by the smel, Meats by the taste, Musick by the ear, Colours by the eye, the several Natures of things, with their properties and essential qualities, by the Intellect: and 35 accordingly as the things are in themselves diversified, the Judicious and Learned man, after he hath conceived them aright, *[page 10]* sequestreth them in the several cels of his Understanding, each in their definite and respective places.

9. But in matter of the words whereby those things are expressed, no Language ever hitherto framed, hath observed any order relating to the thing signified by them: for if the words be ranked in their Alphabetical series, the things represented by them will fall to be in several predicaments; and if the things themselves be categorically classed, the word whereby they are made known will not be tyed to any Alphabetical rule.

10. This is an imperfection incident to all the Languages that ever yet have been known: by reason whereof, Foraign Tongues are said to be hard to learn; and, when obtained, easily forgot.

11. The effigies of *Jupiter* in the likeness of a Bull should be liker to that of *Io* metamorphosed into a Cow, then to the statue of *Bucephalus*, which was a horse: and the picture of *Alcibiades* ought to have more resemblance with that of *Coriolanus*, being both handsome men, then with the image of *Thersites*, who was of a deformed feature: just so should things semblable in Nature be represented by words of a like composure: and *[page 11]* as the true, intelligible speices do present unto our minds the similitude of things as they are in the object; even so ought the word expressive of our conceptions so to agree or vary in their contexture as the things themselves which are conceived by them do in their natures.

12. Besides this imperfection in all Languages, there is yet another. That no Language upon the face of the earth hath a perfect Alphabet; one lacking those letters which another hath, none having all, and all of them *in cumulo* lacking some. But that which makes the defect so much the greater, is, that these same few consonants and vowels commonly made use of, are never by two Nations pronounced after the same fashion; the French A with the English being the Greek Hτα; and the Italian B with the Spanish, the Hebrew Vau.

13. This is that which maketh those of one dominion so unskilful in the *idiome* of another; and, after many yeers abode in a strange land, despaire from attaining at any time to the perfect accent of the language thereof, because, as the waters of that stream cannot be wholesome, whose source is corrupted; nor the superstructure sure, whereof the ground- *[page 12]* work is ruinous: so doth the various manner of pronouncing one and the same Alphabet in several Nations, produce this great and most lamentable obstruction in the Discipline of Languages.

14. The G of the Latin word *legit*, is after four several manners pronounced by the English, French, Spanish, and Dutch: the Ch likewise is differently pronounced by divers Nations; some uttering it after the fashion of the Hebrew Shin, as the French do in the word *chasteau, chascun, chastier, chatel*; or like the Greek Kappa, as in the Italian words, *chiedere, chiazzare, chinatura*; or as in *Italy* are sounded the words *ciascheduno, ciarlatano*; for so do the Spanish and English pronounce it, as in the words *achaque, leche; chamber, chance*: other Nations of a guttural flexibility, pronounce it after the fashion of the Greek χ. Nor need we to labor for examples in other letters; for there

is scarce any hitherto received, either consonant or vowel, which in some one and other taking in all Nations, is not pronounced after three or four several fashions.

15. As the alphabets are imperfect, some having but 19 letters, others 22, and some 24, few exceeding that number: so do *[page 13]* the words composed of those letters in the several Languages, come far short of the number of things, which to have the reputation of a perfect tongue, ought to be expressed by them. 85

16. For supply of this deficiencie, each Language borrows from another; nor is the perfectest amongst them, without being beholden to another, in all things enuncible, bastant to afford instruction: many Astronomical and Medicinal terms have the Greeks borrowed from the Arabians, for which they by exchange have from the Grecians received payment of many words naturalized in their Physical, Logical, and Metaphysical Treatises. As for the Latin, it oweth all its Scientifick dictions to the Greek and Arabick: yet did the Roman Conquest give adoption to many Latin words, in both these languages, especially in matters of military discipline, and prudential Law. 90 · 95

17. And as for all other Languages as yet spoke, though to some of them be ascribed the title of original Tongues, I may safely avouch there is none of them which of it self alone is able to afford the smattring of an elocution fit for indoctrinating of us in the precepts and maximes of moral and intellectual vertues. 100

p. 14 18. But, which is more, and that which most of all evinceth the sterility of all the Languages that since the Deluge have been spoke, though all of them were quintescenced in one capable of the perfections of each, yet that one so befitted and accommodated for compendiousness and variety of phrase should not be able, amidst so great wealth, to afford, without circumlocution, the proper and convenient representation of a thing, yea of many thousands of things, whereof each should be expressed with one single word alone. 105 · 110

19. Some Languages have copiousness of discourse, which are barren in composition: such is the Latine. Others are compendious in expression, which hardly have any flection at all: of this kinde are the Dutch, the English, and Irish. 115

20. Greek hath the agglutinative faculty of incorporating words; yet runneth not so glib in Poesie as doth the Latine, though far more abundant. The Hebrew likewise, with its auxiliary dialects of Arabick, Caldean, Syriak, Æthiopian, and Samaritan, compoundeth prettily, and hath some store of words; yet falleth short by many stages of the Greek. 120

21. The French, Spanish, and Italians, are *[page 15]* but Dialects of the Latine, as the English is of the Saxon Tongue; though with this difference, that the mixture of Latine with the Gaulish, Moresco and Gotish Tongues make up

the three firſt Languages; but the meer qualification of the Saxon with the old
125   British, frameth not the English to the full, for that, by its promiscuous and
ubiquitary borrowing, it consiſteth almoſt of all Languages: which I ſpeak
not in diſpraise thereof, although I may with confidence aver, that were all
the four aforesaid Languages ſtript of what is not originally their own, we
should not be able with them all, in any part of the world, to purchase so
130   much as our breakfaſt in a Market.

4

Poetry

(a) Extract from Barbour, 'Bruce', from
(1) John Ramsay's manuscript, (2) Robert Lekprevik 1571,
(3) Andro Hart 1616, (4) Robert Sanders 1672

John Barbour (*c*. 1330–95), Archdeacon of St Machar's Cathedral in Aberdeen, seems to have written *The Bruce* for King Robert II, completing the main section of the work in 1375. His reward was a pension, which passed to his legatees on his death.

Barbour's *Bruce* survives in two fifteenth-century manuscripts, probably both copied by the scribe John Ramsay (see Cunningham 1973: 247): Edinburgh, National Library of Scotland Advocates' 19.2.2 (transcribed in 1489), and Cambridge, St John's College G.23 (transcribed in 1487). However, the poem was printed and read throughout the sixteenth and seventeenth centuries. Robert Lekprevik, the most important printer of the 1570s, printed the work in 1571 for Henry Charteris, the publishing impresario and literary enthusiast who patronised several early printers (for Charteris, see Dickson and Edmond 1890, especially 348–76). Andro Hart printed the work at least twice (Edinburgh, 1616 and 1620), and STC records copies by Gedeon Lithgow (Edinburgh, 1648), Andrew Anderson (Edinburgh, 1670) and Robert Sanders the older (Glasgow 1672); there are also records of an earlier edition by Sanders (1665) (Geddie 1912: 61–3). The standard modern edition of Barbour's *Bruce* is McDiarmid and Stevenson (1980–5). A useful single-volume student edition is Duncan (1997).

The rhyme **maner: wer** in the text below suggests that Barbour's form for 'were' was **wer** (cf. Old English **wære**); in mid-line, however, the common form for 'were' is **war** (cf. Old Norse **váru**). The change perhaps reflects Ramsay's (or an earlier copyist's) intervention in the language of his exemplar. The phrase **aulde storys** is also interesting; the appearance of –**e** where an unstressed syllable might be expected suggests that Barbour may – just possibly – have retained the inflected form of the adjective which seems to be indicated by certain pre-literary Scots place-names, e.g. **Blake Burn** 'Blackburn'. Otherwise, the text below is a fairly good representation of Early Scots, with Old English ā reflected in ⟨a⟩ in s(w)a, **haly, na**, and Old English ō reflected in ⟨u⟩ in **suth(fast), gud**. The present participles in –**and** may also be noted; these inflexions probably derive from Norse, as, probably, does **tyll** 'to'; we might also note the causative auxiliary **ger** (cf. Norse **gera**). The French-derived form **stour** 'battle' (cf. Old French **estour**) is commonly cited in *OED* from Middle English and Older Scots romances. The form for 'should' is **suld**. Thorn appears as ⟨y⟩ in **yai, yat** etc. Expressions such as **carpyng** 'talking' remind us of how this text is poised between oral and literate cultures.

(1) The Edinburgh Manuscript

[folio 1r] Storys.to rede ar delitabill
Suppos *y*at yai be no*ch*t bot fabill/
yan suld ſtorys *y*at suthfaſt wer
And yai war said on gud maner
Hawe doubill plesance in heryng   5
ye fyrſt plesance is ye carpyng
And ye toy*ir* ye suthfaſtn*es*
Y*at* schawys ye thing ry*ch*t as it wes
And suth thyng*is* *y*at ar likand
Tyll ma*n*nys heryng ar plesand   10
Yarfor I wald fayne set my will
Giff my wyt my*ch*t suffice y*art*ill
To put in wryt A suthfaſt ſtory
That it leſt ay furth in memory
Swa *y*at na tyme of lenth It let   15
Nor ger it haly be forʒet
For aulde ſtorys *y*at men redys
Represent*is* to yaim ye dedys
˙Of ſtalwart folk *y*at lywyt ar
Ry*ch*t as yai yan in *pr*esence war   20
And cert*is* yai suld weill hawe prys
Yat in yar tyme war wy*ch*t and wys
And led *y*ar lyff in gret t*r*awaill
And oft in hard ſtour off bataill
Wan ri*ch*t gret *pr*ice off chewalry   25
And war woydyt off cowardy
As wes king Robert off Scotland
Yat hardy wes of hart and hand
And gud schyr James off douglas
Yat in hys tyme sa worthy was   30
Yat off hys price & hys bounte
In fer land*is* renownyt wase he
Off yaim I thynk yis buk to ma
Now god gyff grace *y*at I may swa
Tret it and bryng It till endyng   35
Yat I say no*ch*t bot suthfaſt thing

˙ From this point onwards the initial letter in each line is hard to read because of the tight binding of the manuscript.

(2) Robert Lekprevik's edition (1571)

Robert Lekprevik rivalled Thomas Bassandyne as the most successful printer of the 1560s and 1570s. Lekprevik printed *The Bruce* for Henry Charteris in 1571; one imperfect copy of this edition, lacking a title-page and part of a preface, survives from the collection of the nineteenth-century antiquarian David Laing and is now in the Pierpont Morgan Library in New York (a photostat copy is held in the National Library of Scotland, and has been consulted for this edition). There are several differences from Ramsay's edition, suggesting that it may have been derived from a different manuscript. The text is wholly in black-letter. A running-head appears from fol. 1v, reading ¶ **The Buik of** (verso) **King Robert Bruce.** (opposite recto). The book is foliated from the beginning of the text, with signatures on each folio in sequence **A.j.**, **A.ij.** etc., although these are often cropped. There does not seem, unfortunately, to be a facsimile on *EEBO*.

In comparison with the Edinburgh manuscript, the work is punctuated with commas, colons and the punctus fairly carefully, to reflect periods. Scots forms are also common. We might note the replacement of Ramsay's **Storys** with the expanded form **HIstoryis**, and that Hart in (3) below reverted to the older form.

1r ¶The actis and | Lyfe of the maist Victorious Conque-|rour, Robert Bruce, King of Scotland. | Quhairin alswa ar co[n]tenit the martiall | deidis of the Vailȝeand Princes: Ed-|ward Bruce, Schir James Dowglas: | Erle Thomas Randell, Walter | Stewart, and sundrie | vtheris. |

> HIstoryis to heir ar Delectabill,
> Suppois yat nocht co[n]tenit, bot fa=
> Tha[n] suld Historyis y[at] suithfast wer, (bill
> Gif thay be spokin in gude maner,
> Haue dowbill plesour in heiring.   5
> The first is: thair plesand carping:
> The vther is, the suithfastnes,
> That schawis the thing richt as it wes.
> And suith thingis that ar lykand,
> To mennis heiring ar plesand.   10
> Thairfoir I wald fane set my will,
> Gif my wit micht suffice thairtill,
> To put in writ ane suithfast Historie,
> That it may lest in Memorie.
> Swa that na lenth of tyme may let,   15
> Nor gar it haillie be forȝet.
> For all Historyis that men reidis,
> Representis to thame the deidis
> Of stalwart folk that leifit air,
> Richt as thay than present wair.   20
> And Certes, thay suld well haue pryis,
> *[folio 1v]* That in thair tyme wer wicht, & wyse:

And led thair lyfe in greit trauell:
And oft intill richt hard battell,
Wan richt greit praise of Cheualrie, 25
And was voyde of all Cowartrie.
As was King Robert of Scotland,
That hardy was of hart, and hand.
And gude Schir James of Dowglas,
That be his tyme sa worthie was. 30
That of his Praise, and his bountie,
In sindrie landis honour wan he.
Of thame I think this buke to ma.
Now God gif grace, that I may swa
Treit it, and bring it to gude ending, 35
That I say nocht bot suthfast thing.

(3) Andro Hart's edition (1616)

The following appears on the title page:

THE | ACTES | AND LIFE OF | THE MOST VICTO- | RIOUS CONQVEROVR, | ROBERT BRVCE, | KING OF *SCOTLAND*, | WHEREIN | also are contained the Mar- | tiall deedes of the valliant Princes, | EDWARD BRVCE, Sir IAMES | DOWGLAS, Erle THOMAS RANDEL, | WALTER STEWART, and | sundrie others. | *Newly corrected, and conferred with the best* | and most ancient Manuscripts. | EDINBURGH, Printed by ANDRO HART, 1616. |

Andro Hart (d. 1621) was probably the most successful printer in Scotland in the first half of the century; other poetry printed by him included the English verse of Drummond of Hawthornden (see Text 4(m) below). His edition of *The Bruce* demonstrates an interesting blending of fonts; the introductory material, and the names of persons within the text, are all printed in roman fonts, while the body of the text is in black letter. Roman type appears sans serif in the following passage. Scots forms are retained (e.g. **sould, hailly, gude** etc.), although clearly many of the forms found in the Edinburgh manuscript – and even Lekprevik's print – have been replaced. Punctuation has been introduced throughout, although it is interesting that it occurs almost entirely at the end of lines.

Stories to read are delectable,
Supose they noght co[n]tain but fable
Then sould Stories y[at] soothfast wer,
If they be spoken in good maner,
Haue double pleasure in hearing: 5
The first is their pleasant carping.
The other is, the soothfastnes,
That shawes the thing right as it wes,
And soothfast things that are likand,
To mens hearing are pleasand: 10

Therefore I would faine set my will,
If my wit might suffice theretill.
To put in write a soothfaſt ſtorie,
[page 2] That it may laſt in memorie:
Sa that no length of time may let,   15
Nor gar it hailly be forȝet,
For ald Stories that men reides,
Represents to them the deides
Of ſtalward folke that liued air,
Right as they then present wair.   20
And certes they sould weill haue prise,
That in thair time were wicht and wise:
And led thair life in great trauell:
And oft intill hard ſtoure of battell.
Wan richt greit praise of Cheualrie,   25
And was voyde of all Cowartrie:
As was king **Robert of Scotland**,
That hardy was of hart and hand:
And gude Schir **Iames of Dowglas**,
That in his time sa worthie was: 30
That of his praise and his bountie,
In sindrie lands honour wan he.
Of thame I thinke this buke to ma,
Now God of grace, that I may swa
Treit it, and bring it to gude ending,   35
That I say nocht but suithfaſt thing.

(4) Robert Sanders's edition (1672)

The following appears on the title page:

THE|ACTS AND LIFE|OF|The most Victorious Conqueror|Robert Bruce, King of|Scotland.|*Wherein also are contained the mar-|tial deeds of the valiant Princes,|Edward Bruce, Sir James Dow-|glas, Earl Thomas Randel, Wal-|ter Stew-art, and sundry others.*|*GLASGOW,*|by ROBERT SANDERS, Printer|to the City and University, and are|to be sold in his Shop, 1672.|

This book is a much simpler production than Hart's. There is no introduction, and apart from the title and running heads in roman type, the text is printed entirely in a black letter font. No distinction is made between names and the rest of the text. Unlike Hart, Sanders does not make any claim of textual authority. Most Scots features have been removed except (for the most part) in rhyming position, though we might note **gar it hailly** in line 16. A reproduction of this edition appears on *EEBO*.

Stories to read are deleċtable,
Suppose they nought contain but fable;
Then should ſtories that soothfaſt were,

147

If they be ſpoken in good manner,
Have double pleasure in hearing: 5
The firſt is their pleasant carping.
The other is their soothfaſtness,
That shows the thing right as it was:
And soothfaſt things that are lykand,
To mens hearing are moſt pleasand: 10
Therefore I would fain set my will,
If my wit might suffice theretill,
To put in write a soothfaſt ſtory,
That it may laſt in memory:
Sa that no length of time may let,   15
Nor gar it hailly be forget,
For old ſtories that men reads,
Represents to them the deeds
Of ſtalward folke that lived air,
Right as they then present were.   20
And certes they should well haue the prise,
That in their time were wight and wise,
And let their life in great travel:
And oft in hard ſtour of battel.
Wan right great praise of chevalry,   25
And was void of all cowartry,
As was king Robert of Scotland,
That hardy was of heart and hand:
And good Sir James of Dowglas,
[page 4]   That in his time so worthie was: 30
that of his praise and his bountie,
In sundrie lands honor wan he.
Of them I think this book to ma:
Now God of grace, that I may sa
treat it, and bring it to good ending,   35
That I say nought but suithfaſt thing.

(b) Extract from 'The Kingis Quair'

The Kingis Quair is traditionally ascribed to James I of Scotland (1394–1437), and thought to have been composed by him while he was a prisoner in England between 1406 and 1424. James's marriage to Henry VI's second cousin Joan Beaufort, which preceded his release and return to Scotland, may be connected with the poem's composition. The Kingis Quair is an accomplished work, demonstrating its author's acquaintance with English models, notably Chaucer, and a concern with Boethian notions of transience. James's reputation as a poet led him also to be considered the author of Christ's Kirk on the Green (see Text 4(p) below), but this attribution is no longer considered correct.

The Kingis Quair survives in one manuscript: MS Oxford, Bodleian Library, Arch. Selden. B.24 (see Boffey, Edwards and Barker-Benfield 1997). The manuscript was probably written for the Sinclair earls of Orkney during the reign of James IV (Boffey *et al.* 1997: 11–12). The first part of the manuscript, which includes the lines copied here, was written, it has been claimed, by the scribe who also copied a manuscript of the *Historia Norwegiae* (the Dalhousie Manuscript, once at Brechin Castle and now Edinburgh, National Archives of Scotland, GD 45/31/I-II), the Haye manuscript from Roslin (in the Scott Collection, now Edinburgh, National Library of Scotland MS Acc. 9253; see Chesnutt 1985), and a manuscript of Mirk's *Festial* and the *Quattuor Sermones* (Cambridge, St John's College G.19)(see Boffey *et al.* 1997: 9–10).

The language of the text presented here consists of a mixture of forms characteristic of Scots and others that are more common in English. Thus the reflex of Old English **hw–** is regularly ⟨quh-⟩, e.g. **quhat, quhen, quhile**, but we might note the form **quhich** (cf. more prototypically Scots **quhilk**). Old English ⟨h⟩ appears as ⟨gh⟩ in **thoughtis**; the contraction has therefore been expanded as ⟨gh⟩ in **noght, myght**. Old English ā is reflected in ⟨o⟩ in **allone, long**, but we might also note **lang**er, while the reflex of Old English ō appears as both ⟨u⟩ and ⟨o⟩, e.g. **buke, boke**. English rather than Scots forms appear for 'shall', 'she', i.e. **schall, sche** (cf. prototypically Scots **sall, scho**), while inflexional endings again vary between English-type forms, e.g. the present participle in –ing/–yng, e.g. **twynklyng**, and forms more characteristic of Scots, e.g. the ending –**it** (beside –**ed**) as the reflex of Present-Day English –**ed**. English-type forms for 'such' and 'not', i.e. **suich, nat**, may reflect the influence of 'Chaucer'-type spellings; cf. **swich, nat** in the Ellesmere manuscript of the *Canterbury Tales*; however, we might note **eftir** 'after', presumably the Scots form of the word, derived from Norse. Present-Day English 'them' is reflected by **tham**; however, this form was already appearing in some varieties of London English by the end of the fourteenth century, alongside 'Chaucer'-type **hem**. It is noticeable that rhyming practices seem to flag English-type pronunciations; thus **quharfor**, cf. contemporary southern wherfore, rhymes with **more** (the latter with ⟨o⟩ as the reflex of Old English ā, cf. Scots **mare, mair**), **waking** (present participle) rhyming with **thing**, and **long** rhyming with **tong** 'tongue'. A notable feature of the script is that thorn appears as both þ and y, in both cases in the word 'that' (abbreviated to **þat, yat**). The distinction is recorded in the text below. The punctuation of the text is of interest; the scribe uses /. to indicate some periods, in combination with discourse markers such as **And** etc. Word-division is sometimes different from that common in Present-Day English, e.g. **alyte** 'a little'.

191v Heirefter followis the quair Maid be | King James of Scotland ye firſt | callit ye kingis quair and | Maid quhan his Majeſtee wes In | Ingland |

[folio 192r]   Heigh in the hevynnis figure circulere
The rody ſterres twynklyng as the fyre
And In Aquary Citherea the clere
Rynsid hir tressis like the goldin wyre
That late tofore in fair and fresche atyre   5

Through capricorn heved hir hornis bright
North northward approchit the myd nyght

Quhen as I lay In bed allone waking
New partit out of slepe alyte tofore
ffell me to mynd of many diu*er*s thing
Off this and that/. can I no*gh*t say quharfor
Bot slepe for craft in erth my*gh*t I no more
ffor quhich as tho coude I no bett*er* wyle
Bot toke a boke to rede apon a quhile

Off quhich the name Is clepit prop*er*ly
Boece/. eftir him y*at* was the compiloure
Schewing counsele of philosophye
Compilit by that noble senatoure
Off rome/. quhilom þ*at* was the warldis floure
And from estate by fortune a quhile
fforiugit was to pou*er*t / in exile

And th*ere* to here this worthy lord and clerk
His metir suete full of moralitee
His flourit pen so fair he set awerk
Discryving first of his prosperitee
And out of that his infelicitee
And than how he in his poetly report
In philosophy can him to confort

ffor quhich tho*gh*t I in p*ur*pos at my boke
To borowe a slepe at thilke tyme began
Or eu*er* I stent my best was more to loke
Vpon the writing of this noble man,
That in him self the full recou*er* wan
Off his infortune pouert and distress
And in tham set his verray sek*er*ness

And so the vertew of his ȝouth before
[folio 192v] Was in his age the ground of his delytis
ffortune the bak him t*ur*nyt/. and therfore
He makith ioye and confort þ*at* he quitis
Off their vnsekir warldis appetitis
And so aworth he takith his penance
And of his vertew maid it suffisance

With mony a noble resou*n* as him likit
Enditing in his fair latyne tong
So full of fruyte and rethorikly pykit

Quhich to declare my scole is ouer ʒong
Therfore I lat him pas/. and in my tong
Procede I will agayn to my sentence
Off my mater/. and leve all incidence

The long nyght beholding as I saide   50
Myn eyne gan to smert for studying
My buke I schet/. and at my hede It laide
And doun I lay but ony tarying
This mater new in my mynd rolling
This Is to seyne how þat eche Estate   55
As fortune lykith/ thame will translate

ffor sothe it is yat on hir tolter quhele
Euery wight cleuerith In his stage
And failyng foting oft quhen hir lest rele
Sum vp/. sum doun./ Is noun estate nor age   60
Ensured/ more the prynce than the page
So vncouthly hir werdes sche deuidith
Namly In ʒouth. that seildin ought prouidith

Among thir thoughtis rolling to and fro
ffell me to mynd of my fortune and vre   65
In tender ʒouth how sche was first my fo
And eft my frende/. and how I gat recure
Off my distress/. and all myn auenture
I gan our hayle/. þat langer slepe me rest
Ne myght I nat/. so were my wittis wrest   70

For wakit and forwalowit thus musing
[folio 193r]   Wery forlyin I lestnyt sodaynlye
And sone I herd the bell to matyns ryng
And vp I ras no langer wald I lye
Bot now how trowe ʒe suich a fantasye   75
ffell me to mynd þat ay me thoght the bell
Said to me/. tell on man quhat thee befell

Thoght I tho to my self quhat may this be
This is myn awin ymagynacioun
It is no lyf þat spekis vnto me   80
It is a bell/. or that impressioun
Off my thoght/. causith this Illusioun
That dooth me think so nycely in this wis
And so befell as I schall ʒou deuis

(c) Robert Henryson, 'The Preiching of the Swallow' (Bassandyne, 1571)

Robert Henryson (d. *c.* 1490) is one of the greatest figures in Older Scots poetry, and a complete text of one of his *Morall Fabillis*, based on Aesop's *Fables*, is provided here: *The Preiching of the Swallow*. Henryson's biography is uncertain; he seems to have been employed as a lecturer in canon law at Glasgow University, but subsequently lived, probably as a schoolmaster, in Dunfermline. His works in addition to the *Morall Fabillis* include *Orpheus and Erudices* and, most famously, *The Testament of Cresseid*.

The text of *The Preiching* below is a diplomatic edition of the print made by Thomas Bassandyne in 1571; *The Preiching* was also printed for Henry Charteris in 1569 and by Andro Hart in 1621. Bassandyne was well-known in the late sixteenth century as a printer, bookbinder and bookseller, publishing an accurate translation of the New Testament in 1579 (see Text 6(b) for a fuller account of his career). Bassandyne's printing of the *Morall Fabillis* is of high quality, demonstrating the experimental developments in printing characteristic of the period; the narrative sections were printed using an elaborate ligatured font resembling handwriting, while the *Moralitas* with which each story ended was printed in a roman type. Latin expressions and other passages within the text which are printed in roman type are rendered in sans serif font in the text below. A copy of the text appears in *EEBO*. The standard critical edition, which offers a comprehensive editorial apparatus, is that by Denton Fox (Fox 1981).

For a discussion of some stylistic features of the language, see ch. 4 above, 2.2–2.3. The text demonstrates the range of registers available in Older Scots at the height of the language's prestige; for Henryson, Scots is clearly elaborated (the contemporary term is **copious**), available for the discussion of complex philosophical notions as well as for more unadorned narratives. Words such as **omnipotent**, **Ingenious, Corporall, Celestiall, consuetude** 'custom', **Concorddand** are clearly part of a high philosophical register, but all are well attested in English and Scots during the fifteenth and sixteenth centuries.

In contrast with his edition of the Bible, Bassandyne prints the *Morall Fabillis* in Scots. Old English ā appears for the most part as ⟨a(i)⟩ in numerous words, e.g. **ane, baith, hame, knaw, lang, maist, Saull, s(w)a**, although **moir** appears in rhyming position with **befoir** (cf. **mair** elsewhere). There is some variation in forms for 'from', with **ffrom(e)** beside **(f)fra**; and we might note the rhyme **mo: ffro: go**, although as all these words contain reflexes of Old English ā/Old Norse á the rhyme does not offer any conclusive evidence about authorial practice. Old English ō is reflected as ⟨u⟩ in **fude, fule, gude, (vnder)stude, forsuith, tuke**. Old English hw– is reflected commonly as ⟨quh-⟩, e.g. **quhy, quhen, quhilk, quhidder**, and Old English medial and final ⟨h⟩ appears as ⟨ch⟩ in **sicht, aneuch** 'enough', **almychtie**. The inflexional system is consistently Scots, with –**it** as the reflex of Present-Day English –**ed** and the present participle inflexion almost always in –**and**, e.g. **ferliand** 'marvelling', **makand, scheddand, stilland, sawand** 'sowing'; **mouing** is an exception. The past participle **distribute** seems, however, a characteristically Scots usage (cf. Present-Day English **distributed**); citations in *OED* are from Scottish and northern English texts. That Henryson's own practice with the present participle inflexion was to use –**and** is confirmed by rhymes between **appeirand/sittand** (present participle) and **vnderstand**. Scots demonstratives are used, i.e. **thir** 'these', **thay** 'those', and the pronoun system includes **scho** 'she', and **thair, thame**. Present-Day English 'shall', 'should' appear as **sall, suld**. We might also note the words **mirk** 'dark', **gloming** 'evening twilight', **speldit** 'split open', **crag** 'neck', which *OED* identifies as characteristic of Scots and northern English, and **linget** 'linseed', **thusgait** 'thus', which *OED* considers to be characterisically Scots. The form **tume** 'vacant time, spare time' is recorded in *OED* only in Scottish texts from the sixteenth century onwards. **Mauis** 'song-thrush' is regarded by *OED* as more broadly regional, with citations from Northern Irish and US texts. The form **Magre** 'in spite of' is a rare example of a closed-class word in Scots derived from French. Capital ⟨i⟩ generally appears as J in this font, e.g. **Jnfinite**, but occasionally a distinct form is used, as in **Ingenious**.

Bassandyne's text contains comprehensive, modern-style punctuation, and comparison with modern editions reveals many similarities. It may be that the 'knotty' syntax characteristic of rhyme-royal demanded grammar-based punctuation in the modern manner in order to resolve uncertainties for readers (as opposed to listeners). More research on such practices would be worth pursuing. I have reproduced the pilcrow ¶; the *hedera* or ivy-leaf, a mark of punctuation used in antiquity but reintroduced by early printers (see Parkes 1992), is reflected here by ❧.

¶ The Preiching of the Swallow

The hie prudence, and wirking meruelous,
The profound wit off God omnipotent,
Is sa perfyte, and sa Ingenious
[page 67] Excellent ffar all mannis Jugement.
For quhy to him all thing is ay present,   5
Rycht as it is, or ony tyme sall be,
Befoir the sicht off his Diuinitie.

Thairfoir our Saull with Sensualitie,
So fetterit is in presoun Corporall,
We may not cleirlie vnderstand, nor se   10
God, as he is, nor thingis Celestiall,
Our mirk and deidlie corps Naturall,
Blindis the Spirituall operatioun,
Lyke as ane man wer bundin in presoun.

In Metaphisik Aristotell sayis,   15
That mannis Saull is lyke ane Bakkis Ee,
Quhilk lurkis still, als lang as licht off day is,
And in the gloming cummis furth to fle.
Hir Ene ar waik, the Sone scho may not se.
Sa is our Saull with fantasie opprest,   20
To knaw the thingis in nature manifest.

For God is in his power Jnfinite:
And mannis Saull is febill, and ouer small,
Off vnderstanding waik, and vnperfite
To comprehend him that contenis all.   25
Nane suld presume be ressoun naturall
To seirche the secreitis off the Trinitie,
Bot trow fermelie, and lat all ressoun be.

3yt neuertheles we may haif knawlegeing
[page 68] Off God almychtie, be his Creatouris.   30
That he is gude, ffair, wyis and bening,
Exempill tak be thir Jolie flouris,
Rycht sweit off smell, and plesant off colouris.
Sum grene, sum blew, sum purpour, quhyte, and reid,
Thus distribute be gift off his Godheid.   35

The firmament payntit with sternis cleir,
From eist to west rolland in cirkill round.
And euerilk planet in his proper Spheir,
In mouing makand harmonie and sound.
The fyre, the Air, the watter, and the ground.   40
Till vnderstand it is aneuch, J wis,
That God in all his werkis wittie is.

Luke weill the fische that swimmis in the se.
Luke weill in eirth all kynd off bestyall.
The foulis ffair sa forcelie thay fle.   45
Scheddand the air with pennis grit and small.
Syne luke to man, that he maid last off all,
Lyke to his Jmage, and his similitude,
Be thir we knaw, that God is ffair and gude.

All Creature he maid ffor the behufe   50
Off man, and to his supportatioun,
Jn to this eirth, baith vnder and abufe,
Jn number, wecht, and dew proportioun.
The difference off tyme, and ilk seasoun,
Concorddand till our opurtunitie.
[page 69] As daylie be experience we may se.   56

The Somer with his Jolie mantill off grene,
With flouris fair furrit on euerilk fent.
Quhilk Flora Goddes off the flouris Quene,
Hes to that Lord as ffor his seasoun lent.   60
And Phebus with his goldin bemis gent,
Hes purfellit and payntit plesandly.

With heit and moysture stilland ffrom the sky

Syne Haruest hait, quhen Ceres that Goddes
Hir barnis benit hes with abundance.   65
And Bachus God off wyne renewit hes
The tume Pyipis, in Jtalie, and France,
With wynis wicht, and liquour off plesance.
And **Copia temporis** to fill hir horne,
That neuer wes full off quheit, nor vther corne

Syne wynter wan, quhen Austerne Eolus,   70
God off the wynd with blastis boreall,
The grene garment off Somer glorious,
Hes all to rent, and reuin in pecis small.
Than flouris fair faidit with froist, man fall.
And birdis blyith changeis thair noitis sweit,   75
Jn styll murning, neir slane with snaw, and sleit.

Thir dalis deip with dubbis drounit is.
Baith hill and holt heillit with frostis hair.
And bewis bene laifit bair off blis,
Be wickit windis off the winter wair.   80
All wyld beistis than ffrom the bentis bair
[page 70]   Drawis ffor dreid vnto thair dennis deip,
Coucheand ffor cauld in coifis thame to keip.

Syne cummis ver, quhen winter is away,
The Secretar off Somer with his Sell.   85
Quhen Columbie vp keikis throw the clay,
Quhilk fleit wes befoir with froistes fell.
The Mauis, and the Merle, beginnis to mell:
The Lark on loft, with vther birdis smale,
Than drawis furth ffra derne, ouer doun and Daill. 90

That samin seasoun, in to ane soft morning,
Rycht blyth that bitter blastis wer ago,
Vnto the wod to se the flouris spring,
And heir the Mauis sing, and birdis mo
J passit ffurth, syne lukit to and ffro   95
To se the Soill, that wes richt sessonabill,
Sappie, and to resaue all seidis abill.

Mouing thusgait grit myrth J tuke in mynd
Off lauboraris to se the besines.
Sum makand Dyke, and sum the pleuch can wynd, 100
Sum sawand seidis fast ffrome place to place.

The harrowis hoppand in the saweris trace.
Jt wes grit Joy to him that luifit corne,
To se thame laubour, baith at euin and morne.

And as J baid vnder ane bank full bene,   105
Jn hart gritlie reiosit off that sicht.
Vnto ane hedge, vnder ane Hawthorne grene
Off small birdis thair come ane ferlie flicht.

[page 71]

And doun belyif can on the leifis licht,
On euerilk syde about me quhair I stude,   110
Rycht meruellous ane mekill multitude.

Amang the quhilks, ane Swallow loud couth cry,
On that Hawthorne hie in the croip sittand.
O 3e Birdis on bewis, heir me by,
3e sall weill knaw, and wyislie vnderstand,   115
Quhair danger is, or perrell appeirand,
It is grit wisedome to prouyde befoir,
It to deuoyd, for dreid it hurt 3ow moir.

Schir Swallow (quod the Lark agane) and leuch,
Quhat haue 3e sene, that causis 3ow to dreid?   120
Se 3e 3one churll (quod scho) be3ond 3one pleuch.
Fast sawand hemp, and gude linget seid
3one lint will grow in lytill tyme in deid,
And thairoff will 3one Churll his Nettis mak,
Vnder the quhilk he thinkis vs to tak.   125

Thairfoir J reid we pas quhen he is gone,
At euin, and with our naillis scharp and small,
Out off the eirth scraip we 3one seid anone,
And eit it vp, ffor giff it growis, we sall
Haue cause to weip heirefter ane and all.   130
Se we remeid thairfoir ffurth with Jnstante,
Nam leuius laedit quicquid praeuidimus ante.

For Clerkis sayis, it is nocht sufficient,
To considder that is befoir thyne Ee.

[page 72]

Bot prudence is ane inwart Argument,   135
That garris ane man prouyde and foirse,
Quhat gude, quhat euill is liklie ffor to be,
Off euerilk thing behald the fynall end.
And swa ffra perrell the better him defend.

The Lark lauchand the Swallow thus couth scorne 140
And said scho fischit lang befoir the Net.

The barne is eith to busk that is vnborne.
All growis nocht, that in the ground is set.
The nek to ſtoup quhen it the ſtraik sall get,
Js sone aneuch: deith on the fayeſt fall.   145
Thus scornit thay the Swallow ane and all.

Deſþysing thus hir helthsum document
The foulis ferlie tuke thair flicht anone,
Sum with ane bir thay braidit ouer the bent:
And sum agane ar to the grene wod gone.   150
Vpon the land quhair J wes left allone,
J tuke my club, and hamewart couth I carie
Swa ferliand, as I had sene ane farie.

Thus passit furth quhill Iune that Iolie tyde,
And seidis that wer sawin off beforne,   155
Wer growin hie, that hairis mycht thame hyde:
And als the Quailȝe craikand in the corne.
J mouit furth betuix midday and morne,
Vnto the hedge vnder the hawthorne grene,
[page 73] Quhair J befoir the said birdis had sene.   160

And as J ſtude be auenture and cace,
The samin birdis as I haif said ȝow air,
J hoip, because it wes thair hanting place,
Mair off succour, or ȝit mair solitair,
Thay lychtit doun: and quhen thay lychtit wair,   165
The swallow swyth put furth ane pietuous pyme,
Said, wo is him can not bewar in tyme.

O blind birdis, and full off negligence,
Vnmyndfull off ȝour awin prosþeritie.
Lift vp ȝour sicht, and tak gude aduertence,   170
Luke to the Lint, that growis on ȝone le.
Ȝone is the thing J bad forsuith, that we
Quhill it wes seid suld rute furth off the eird.
Now is it Lint: now is it hie on breird.

Go ȝit, quhill it is tender and small,   175
And pull it vp, let it na mair Jncres.
My flesche growis, my bodie quaikis all,
Thinkand on it I may not sleip in peis.
Thay cryit all, and bad the Swallow ceis.
And said, ȝone Lint heirefter will do gude,   180
For Linget is to lytill birdis fude,

We think quhen that ʒone Lint bollis ar ryip,
To mak vs feiſt, and fill vs off the seid,
Magre ʒone Churll, and on it sing and pyip.
Weill (quod the Swallow) freindes hardilie
    beid.

[page 74]
Do as ʒe will, bot certane sair J dreid,   186
Heirefter ʒe sall find als sour, as sweit,
Quhen ʒe ar ſpeldit on ʒone Carlis ſpeit.

The awner off ʒone lint, ane fouler is,
Richt cautelous, and full off subteltie.   190
His pray full sendill tymis will he mis,
Bot giff we birdis all the warrer be.
Full mony off our kin he hes gart de
And thocht it bot ane ſport to ſpill thair blude.
God keip me ffra him, and the halie Rude.   195

Thir small birdis haueand bot lytill thocht
Off perrell that mycht fall be auenture,
The counsell off the swallow set at nocht,
Bot tuke thair flicht, and furth togidder fure.
Sum to the wode sum markit to the mure.   200
J tuke my ſtaff, quhen this wes said and done,
And walkit hame, ffor it drew neir the none.

The Lynt ryipit, the Carll pullit the Lyne:
Rippillit the bollis, and in beitis set.
It ſteipit in the burne, and dryit syne: 205
And with ane bittill knokkit it, and bet.
Syne swingillit it weill, and hekkillit in the flet.
His wyfe it ſpan, and twynit it in to threid.
Off quhilk the Fowlar nettis maid in deid.

The wynter come, the wickit wind can blaw: 210
The woddis grene wer wallowit with the weit.
[page 75]
Baith firth and fell with froiſtys wer maid faw,
Slonkis and slaik maid slidderie with the sleit.
The foulis ffair ffor falt thay ffell off feit.
On bewis bair it wes na bute to byde,   215
Bot hyit vnto housis thame to hyde.

Sum in the barn, sum in the ſtak off corne,
Thair lugeing tuke, and maid thair residence.
The Fowlar saw, and grit aithis hes sworne,
Thay suld be tane trewlie ffor thair expence.   220

His Nettis hes he set with diligence,
And in the snaw he schulit hes ane plane,
And heillit it all ouer with calf agane.

Thir small birdis seand the calff wes glaid.
Trowand it had bene corne, thay lychtit doun.   225
Bot of the Nettis na presume thay had,
Nor of the Fowlaris fals Jntentioun.
To scraip, and seik thair meit thay maid thame boun,
The Swallow on ane lytill branche neir by,
Dreiddand for gyle, thus loud on thame couth cry.230

Jnto that calf scraip quhill ȝour naillis bleid,
Thair is na corne, ȝe laubour all in vane.
Trow ȝe ȝone Churll for pietie will ȝow feid.
Na, na, he hes it heir layit for ane trane.
Remoue J reid, or ellis ȝe will be slane.   235
His nettis he hes set full priuely.
Reddie to draw: in tyme be war ffor thy.

[page 76]   Grit fule is he that puttis in dangeir
His lyfe, his honour, ffor ane thing off nocht.
Grit fule is he, that will not glaidlie heir   240
Counsall in tyme, quhill it auaill him mocht.
Grit fule is he, that hes na thing in thocht,
Bot thing present: and efter quhat may fall,
Nor off the end hes na memoriall.

Thir small birdis ffor hunger famischit neir,   245
Full besie scraipand ffor to seik thair fude.
The counsall off the Swallow wald not heir.
Suppois thair laubour dyd thame lytill gude.
Quhen scho thair fulische hartis vnderſtude
Sa Indurate, vp in ane tre scho flew.   250
With that this Churll ouer thame his Nettis drew,

Allace it wes grit hart sair for to se
That bludie Bowcheour beit thay birdis doun.
And ffor till heir, quhen thay wiſt weill to de,
Thair cairfull sang and lamentatioun.   255
Sum with ane ſtaf he ſtraik to eirth on swoun:
Off sum the heid he ſtraik: off sum he brak the crag:
Sum half on lyfe, he ſtoppit in his bag.

And quhen the Swallow saw that thay wer deid.
Lo (quod scho) thus it happinnis mony syis,   260

159

On thame that will not tak counsall nor reid
Off prudent men, or Clerkis that ar wyis.
This grit perrell J tauld thame mair than thryis.
[page 77] Now ar thay deid, and wo is me thairfoir.
Scho tuke hir flicht, bot I hir saw no moir.   265

⸋ Moralitas.

Lo worthie folk Æsope that Nobill clerk,
Ane Poet worthie to be Lawreate.
Quhen that he waikit from mair autentik werk,
With vther ma, this foirsaid Fabill wrate.
Quhilk at this tyme may weill be applicate,   270
To gude morall edificatioun,
Haifand ane sentence, according to ressoun.

This Carll, and bond of gentrice spoliate,
Sawand this calf, thir small birdis to sla.
It is the feind, quhilk fra the Angelike state,   275
Exylit is, as fals Apostata.
Quhilk day and nycht weryis not for to ga,
Sawand poysoun and mony wickit thocht,
In mannis saull, quhilk Christ full deir hes bocht.

And quhen the saull, as seid in to the eird,   280
Geuis consent vnto delectatioun,
The wickit thocht beginnis for to breird,
In deidlie sin, quhilk is dampnatioun.
Ressoun is blindit with affectioun.
And carnall lust grouis full grene and gay,   285
Throw consuetude hantit from day to day.

Proceding furth be vse and consuetude,
The sin ryipis, and schame is set on syde.
The Feynd plettis his Nettis scharp and rude,
And vnder plesance preuilie dois hyde.
[page 78] Syne on the feild he sawis calf full wyde,   291
Quhilk is bot tume and verray vanitie,
Of fleschlie lust, and vaine prosperitie.

Thir hungrie birdis, wretchis we may call,
Ay scraipand in this warldis vane plesance.   295
Greddie to gadder gudis temporall,
Quhilk as the calf, ar tume without substance.
Lytill of auaill, and full of variance.

Lyke to the mow, befoir the face of wind
Quhiskis away, and makis wretchis blind.   300

This Swallow quhilk eschaipit is the snair.
The halie Preichour weill may signifie.
Exhortand folk to walk, and ay be wair
Fra Nettis of our wickit enemie.
Quha sleipis not, bot euer is reddie,   305
Quhen wretchis in this warld calf dois scraip,
To draw his Net, that thay may not eschaip.

Allace quhat cair, quhat weiping is and wo,
Quhen Saull and bodie departit ar in twane?
The bodie to the wormis Keitching go: 310
The Saull to Fyre to euerlestand pane.
Quhat helpis than this calf, thir gudis vane?
Quhen thow art put in Luceferis bag,
And brocht to hell, and hangit be the crag.

Thir hid Nettis for to persaue and se,   315
This sarie calf wyislie to vnderstand:
Best is bewar, in maist prosperitie,
For in this warld thair is na thing lestand.
Is na man wait how lang his stait will stand,
His lyfe will lest, nor how that he sall end: 320
Efter his deith nor quhidder he sall wend.

[page 79]

Pray we thairfoir quhill we ar in this lyfe,
For four thingis: the first, fra sin remufe.
The secund is, fra all weir and stryfe,
The thrid is, perfite cheritie and lufe.   325
The feird thing is, and maist for our behufe,
That is in blis with Angellis to be fallow.
And thus endis the preiching of the Swallow.

(d) Extract from William Dunbar and Walter Kennedy, 'The Flyting of Dunbar and Kennedy' (Bannatyne Manuscript)

The Flyting of Dunbar and Kennedy represents a genre of poetry recognised by James VI:

Ze man also take heid to frame zour wordis and sentencis according to the mater: As in Flyting and Inuectiues, zour wordis to be cuttit short, and hurland ouer heuch.

Flytings (defined by *DSL* as 'a contest between poets in mutual abuse') were opportunities to demonstrate linguistic virtuosity; 'seriousness' was clearly not expected. Other examples of flytings include *The Flyting of Montgomerie and Polwart* (from about 1585), and (in other languages) the Old Norse *Lokasenna* and the Middle English *The Owl and the Nightingale*. That contemporaries valued the élan of *The Flyting of Dunbar and Kennedy* is demonstrated by its survival in both printed and manuscript-form; a fragmentary print by Chepman and Myllar survives (?1508), and texts also appear in the Bannatyne and Maitland Folio Manuscripts; see ch. 1 above, 5.3 and 5.4. The text here is taken from the Bannatyne version of the poem. For a comprehensive parallel-text edition of the poem, see Meier 2008. A useful facsimile of the Bannatyne Manuscript is Fox and Ringler 1980.

We now know a fair amount about George Bannatyne (1545–1607/8), a business-man with connexions to a range of élite groups – legal, court, church, mercantile – in sixteenth-century Edinburgh. Bannatyne's interests seem to have been prima-rily 'ethical and utilitarian' (*ODNB*); he was also seemingly a tolerant man, who though a Protestant allowed Catholic-flavoured elements from his copy-texts to come through (see also van Heijnsbergen 2010).

The two poets involved in *The Flyting* were William Dunbar (1460?–1513?/1530?), and Walter Kennedy (1455?–1518?), both prominent versifiers (**makars**) at the court of James IV. Of the two, Dunbar is famous as an adept stylist in numerous poetic forms. He is represented in this book by passages from three of his best-known poems: his section of *The Flyting*, *Ane Tretis of the Twa Mariit Wemen and the Wedo*, and *The Goldyn Targe*. Kennedy, though overshadowed by Dunbar, was admired by contemporaries; Gavin Douglas called him **greit Kennedie**, and David Lyndsay praised his grasp of aureate diction. Dunbar himself refers to Kennedy elsewhere as **gud maister Walter Kennedie**.

The language of the passage exemplifies the range of usage available in early six-teenth-century Scots. Old English ā is commonly reflected in ⟨a(i)⟩, e.g. **laith**, **ane**, **baith**, **sa**, **hame** and **mair** (the last rhyming with the morpheme –**ar**), although see **no thing**; Old English ō appears as ⟨u⟩ in **fule**, **rute**. Old English **hw**– appears com-monly as ⟨quh-⟩, e.g. **quhat**, **quhair**. The forms **quho** 'who' and **quhome** 'whom' may be noted, in that they combine Scots ⟨quh-⟩ with 'English' ⟨o⟩; however, these forms appear fairly frequently in Scots texts and may not therefore necessarily have been seen as Anglo-Scottish 'blends'. The item 'devils' appears as **diuillis**, without *v*-deletion. Scots modals **sall** and **s(o)uld** may be noted, as may the Norse-derived causative verb **gar**, The form **salbe** is, during the sixteenth century, very commonly written or printed as one word, both in Scots and English texts; it may therefore have been perceived as one word rather than two. Third-person plural pronouns are **thay**, **thame**, **thair/yair**; verbal inflexions in –**it** (cf. Present-Day English –**ed**) and –**and** (present participle) may also be noted. The form **fra** appears for 'from', cf. Norse **frá**; other Norse-derived core vocabulary includes **hundreth** 'hundred', **sternis** 'stars' (Old Norse **stjarna**). The verb **thoill** 'suffer' survives longest in Scots, and may therefore be derived from Old Norse **þola** rather than Old English **þolian**. The form **kinrikis** 'kingdoms' is also of interest, cf. Old English **cynerice**, which in English was eventually replaced by **kingdom**. *DSL* records this form as the usual word for 'kingdom' in Scots, with **kingrik** (cf. Old English **cyningrice**) a less com-mon variant. The ⟨k⟩ may be the result of influence from Norse, though it may be derived from Old Northumbrian (see *OED* **riche**, n.). Other forms of interest in core vocabulary include **sax** 'six'. The second-person singular pronoun in **thow**, **the(e)** is of course deployed for purposes of insult, cf. Present-Day French use of **tu** as opposed to **vous**.

However, perhaps the most obvious linguistic characteristic of the passage is its 'copiousness' (to use the contemporary term) in vocabulary beyond the commonplace. Fifteenth- and sixteenth-century writers, in English at any rate, complain of the 'injured' (**apeyred**) nature of the vernacular in contrast with Latin or even French, and William Caxton, the late-fifteenth-century English printer, literary impresario and essayist, famously attempted to extend the lexicon through the adoption of what he called **curious termes**. **Curious termes** are used widely in *The Flyting*, and in many cases Dunbar and Kennedy offer the first (sometimes the only) attestation in *DSL/OED* for such words. The poets' aim is clearly not only to insult each other (humorously); they are also displaying their virtuosity. Bawcutt has commented that Dunbar at least is a 'precise and discriminating user of words' (1987: 94). The following examples might be noted:

cuntbittin crawdoun: **crawdoun** is fairly widely attested in *DSL*, meaning 'coward'; however, **cuntbittin** '? poxed' is only cited in *DSL* from *The Flyting*. Neither form occurs in *OED*, although the form **counte beteyne** 'impotent' appears in *MED*; Bawcutt (1987: 85) suggests that glossing the word as 'impotent' rather than 'poxed' fits the context better.

Similarly debated is the form **glengoir loun**: **glengoir**, glossed 'venereal disease, syphilis' in *DSL* and described there as an 'alteration' of **grandgore**; the etymology in *OED* is given as Old French **grand gore** ('*grand* great + *gore* syphilis'). The usage is fairly commonly cited in *DSL*, mostly from burgh records, but the attributive use with **loun** is uniquely cited in *DSL* from *The Flyting*. The word **loun** has an obscure etymology; *DSL* cites early modern Dutch **loen** as the source for the form, but this etymology is disputed by *OED*. The form is widely cited in *DSL* and (as **loon** (1)) in *OED*. However, Bawcutt (1987: 84) has also challenged this interpretation, and suggests that a better reading in place of **glengoir loun** is that found in the Maitland Folio manuscript, viz. **ganȝelon**, i.e. Ganelon, the traitor who betrayed Roland at Roncesvalles.

Bawcutt notes as follows: 'It is usually assumed that Dunbar depicts Kennedy as suffering from syphilis, and that this rules out a date for *The Flyting* earlier than the late 1490's, when the disease is thought to have entered Scotland. But this argument is somewhat flimsy, since the two phrases under discussion constitute the most precise and definite pieces of evidence in its support' (1987: 85).

gulesnowt 'yellow snout': the combination is unique to *The Flyting*, though **snowt** is fairly well-attested. The adjective **gule** however is rare; only two citations are given in *DSL*, one of which is to *The Flyting*.

iersche brybour baird 'Irish (or Highland) vagabond minstrel/buffoon': the combination is unique to *The Flyting* in *DSL*, though the forms individually are quite commonly cited

mandrag 'mandrake' (= poisonous plant): the word is cited in *DSL* only from the Bannatyne manuscript and from Montgomerie's *Flyting*, where its appearance may be an echo of its use in the Bannatyne manuscript.

myꬃmerkin 'dwarfish creature': rare in *DSL*, being cited only from the Bannatyne manuscript and from the legendary narrative of *Prester John*.

scheild trumpir is an obscure construction which in *DSL* is only cited from here. **Trumpir** 'deceiver' is fairly well-attested; *DSL* suggests that **scheild** is here a 'metaphorical application' of **schelit** 'exposed, revealed'. *DSL* would thus interpret the phrase as 'exposed deceiver'.

skaitbird is Scots for the 'Arctic skua', so-called because it was believed that 'it ate the excreta of other birds' (*DSL*). The word is given only two citations in *DSL*, one of which is from *The Flyting*.

rebald 'one of low birth, whore' etc.: fairly well-attested in *DSL*.

[folio 147r]   . . .

        The Flyting of Dumbar and Kennedie
        here efter followis Iocound and mirrie

        Schir Iohine ye Ross, ane thing thair is compild
        In generale be kennedy and quinting
        Quhilk hes thame self aboif ye sternis styld
        Bot had thay maid of mannace ony mynting
        In speciall Sic stryfe sould rys but stynting   5
        howbeit with bost yair breistis wer als bendit
        As Lucifer yat fra ye hevin discendit

[folio 147v] Hell sould nocht hyd yair harnis fra harmis hynting

        The erd sould trymbill the firmament sould schaik
        And all ye air in vennaum suddane stink   10
        And all ye diuillis of hell for redour quaik
        To heir quhat I suld wryt with pen and ynk
        For and I flyt sum sege for schame sould sink
        The se sould birn the mone sould thoill ecclippis
        Rochis sould ryfe The warld sould hald no grippis 15
        Sa loud of cair The commoun bell sould clynk

        Bot wondir laith wer I to be ane baird
        Flyting to vse soir gritly I eschame
        For it is nowyir wynnyng nor rewaird
        Bot tinsale baith of honour and of fame   20
        Incress of sorrow, sklander, and evill name.
        3it mycht thay be sa bald in yair bakbytting
        To gar me ryme and rais the feynd with flytting
        And throw all cuntreis and kinrikis thame proclame

        Quod Dumbar to Kennedy

        Dirtin Dumbar quhome on blawis thow thy boist 25
        Pretendand the to wryte sic skaldit skrowis
        Ramowd rebald thow fall doun att ye roist
        My [laul *deleted*] laureat lettres at the and I lowis

Mandrag My*m*merkin maid mai*s*ter bot in mows
Thrys scheild trumpir *with* ane threid bair goun   30
Say Deo m*er*cy or I cry thee doun
And leif thy rymi*ng* rebald and thy rowis

Dreid dirtfa*s*t dearch yat thow hes dissobeyit
My cousing qui*n*tene and my co*m*missar
Fanta*s*tik fule tre*s*t weill thow salbe fleyit   35
Ignorant elf aip owll Irregular
skaldit skaitbird and co*m*moun skamelar
Wan fukkit funling yat nato*ur* maid ane yrle
Baith Iohine the Ross and thow sall squeill & skirle
And evir I heir ocht of ʒour making mair   40

Heir I put sylence to ye in all p*ar*tis
Obey and ceis the play that thow prete*n*dis
Waik walidrag and werlot of ye cairtis
Se sone thow mak my co*m*missar amendis

[folio 148r] And lat him lay sax leichis on thy lend*is*   45
Meikly in recompansing of yi scorne
Or thow sall ban the tyme that thow wes borne
ˈFor Kennedy to the this cedull send*is* [*line inserted in margin*]ˈ

Quod ke*n*nedy to dumbar
Iuge in ye nixt quha gat the war

Iersche brybo*ur* baird wyle beggar *with* thy brattis
Cuntbittin crawdoun kennedy coward of kynd   50
Evill farit and dryit as densema*n* on ye rattis
Lyk as the gledd*is* had on thy gulesnowt dynd
Mismaid mon*s*tour ilk mone owt of thy mynd
Renu*n*ce rebald thy rymy*n*g thow bot [rois *deleted*] royis
Thy trechour tung hes tane ane heland *s*trynd   55
Ane lawland ers wald mak a bettir noyis

Revin raggit ruke and full of rebaldrie
Scarth fra scorpione scaldit in scurrilitie
I se the haltane in thy harlotrie
And into vyir science no thing slie   60
Of every vertew woyd As me*n* may sie
Quytclame clergie And cleik to the ane club
Ane baird bla*s*þhemar in brybrie ay to be
For wit and wisdome ane wi*s*þ fra the may rub

165

Thow speiris dastard gif I dar *with* the fecht   65
3e dagone dowbart thairof haif thow no dowt
Quhair evir we meit yairto my hand I hecht
To red thy rebald rymy*ng* *with* a rowt
Throw all Bretane it sal be blawin owt
How yat thow poysonit pelo*ur* gat thy paikis   70
With ane doig leich I schepe to gar the schowt
And nowy*ir* to the tak knyfe swerd nor aix

Thow crop and rute of traito*uris* tressonable
The fayir and moder of mortho*ir* and mischeif
Dissaitfull tyrand *with* serpentis tung vnstable   75
Cukcald cradoun \cowart/and co*m*moun theif
Thow purpest for to vndo our lord*is* chief
In paislay *with* ane poysone y*at* wes fell
For quhilk brybour 3it sall thow thoill a breif
Pelo*ur* on the I sall it preif my sell   80

Tho*ch*t I wald lie Thy frawart phisnomy
Dois manifest thy malice to all me*n*
ffy tratour theif ffy glengoir loun fy fy
ffy feyndly front far fowlar than ane fen
My freyind*is* thow reprovit *with* thy pen   85
Thow leis tratour quhilk I sall on the preif
Suppois thy heid war armit tymis ten
thow sall recryat or thy croun sall cleif

Or thow durst move thy mynd malitius
Thow saw the saill abone my heid vp draw   90
Bot Eolus full woid and neptunus
Mirk and moneless wes met *with* woundis waw
And mony hundreth myll hyne cowd us blaw
By holland seland 3etland and northway Coist
In Desert quhair we wer famist aw   95
3it come I hame fals baird to lay thy boist

Thow callis the rethory with thy goldin lippis
Na glowrand gaipand fule thow art begyld
Thow art bot gluntoch *with* thy giltin hippis
That for thy Lounry mony a leisch hes fyld   100
Wan wisaged widdefow out of thy wit gane wyld
Laithly and lowsy als lathand as ane leik
Sen thow *with* wirschep wald sa fane be styld
Haill soverane sen3eour Thy bawis hingis throw thy
    breik

[folio 148v]

(e) Extract from Dunbar, 'Ane Tretis of the Tua Mariit Wemen and the Wedo' (Maitland Folio Manuscript)

Dunbar's *Tretis of the Tua Mariit Wemen and the Wedo* is another text displaying the poet's virtuosity in the mastery of a range of distinct poetic forms. It represents a tradition of verse going back to the earliest Germanic period: alliterative poetry.

The text here is taken from the Maitland Folio manuscript; see ch. 1, 5.3. Sir Richard Maitland (1496–1586), for whom the manuscript was copied, was a prominent mid-sixteenth century courtier. He had been a counsellor to Regent Moray, and in 1562 Mary Queen of Scots made him her Keeper of the Great Seal, a significant office. However, in 1567 he resigned his office in favour of his son, John. All his sons were prominent supporters of Queen Mary; his son William, the subject of George Buchanan's satire in *The Chamaeleon* (see Text 5(f)), died in prison, having surrendered Edinburgh Castle in 1573 along with William Kirkcaldy of Grange (see Text 2(h)). Sir Richard by this time seems to have devoted himself to literary and antiquarian interests, which he sustained until he died. The manuscript is written in a secretary hand; it has been given modern pagination rather than foliation. (See further Martin and McClune 2009.)

Old English ā appears as ⟨a⟩ in **allane, ane, sang, tha** 'those', but we might note **so**. Old English ō appears as ⟨u(i)⟩ in **gudlie, luikit**. Reflexes of Old English **hw–**, **–h–** are **quhyt, quhairon, quhat, quhill** and **hicht, nichtis** respectively, while Present-Day English **–ed** is reflected in **–it**. Notable closed-class forms are **efter** 'after' and **war** 'were' (indicative plural). Dunbar's use of **did gleme** reflects the developing use of the *do*-auxiliary in Older Scots. The word **inthrang** 'pushed in' seems to be comparatively rare in Older Scots; *DSL* only gives two citations, one of which is from this text. However, the verb from which the form derives, **thring**, is much more common. For the style of the passage, see ch. 4 above. The most recent authoritative critical edition of Dunbar's verse is Bawcutt 1998.

<table>
<tr><td>p. 81 ...</td><td>Apon the Midsummer evin mirriest of nichtis</td><td></td></tr>
<tr><td></td><td>I muvit furth allane [in]* meid as midnicht wes past</td><td></td></tr>
<tr><td></td><td>Besyd ane gudlie grein garth full of gay flouris</td><td></td></tr>
<tr><td>p. 82</td><td>Hegeit of ane huge hicht with hawthorne treis</td><td></td></tr>
<tr><td></td><td>Quhairon ane bird on ane bransche so birst out</td><td></td></tr>
<tr><td></td><td>   hir notis</td><td>5</td></tr>
<tr><td></td><td>That neuer ane blythfullar bird was on the beuche harde</td><td></td></tr>
<tr><td></td><td>Quhat throw the sugarat sound of hir sang glaid</td><td></td></tr>
<tr><td></td><td>And throw the savour sanative of the sueit flouris</td><td></td></tr>
<tr><td></td><td>I drew in derne to the dyk to dirkin efter mirthis</td><td></td></tr>
<tr><td></td><td>The dew donkit the daill and dynnit the feulis</td><td>10</td></tr>
<tr><td></td><td>I hard under ane holyn hevinlie grein hewit</td><td></td></tr>
<tr><td></td><td>Ane hie speiche at my hand with hautand wourdis</td><td></td></tr>
<tr><td></td><td>With yat in haist to the hege so hard I inthrang</td><td></td></tr>
<tr><td></td><td>That I was heildit with hawthorne and with heynd leveis</td><td></td></tr>
<tr><td></td><td>Throw pykis of the plet thorne I presandlie luikit</td><td>15</td></tr>
<tr><td></td><td>Gif ony persoun wald approche within yat plesand garding</td><td></td></tr>
<tr><td></td><td>I saw thre gay ladeis sit in ane grein arbeir</td><td></td></tr>
</table>

All grathit in to [ger *deleted*] garlandis of fresche gudlie flouris
So glitterit as the gold wer thair glorius gilt tressis
Quhill all the gressis did gleme of the glaid hewis   20
Kemmit was yair cleir hair and curiouslie sched
Attour thair schulderis doun schyre schyni*ng* full bricht
With curches cassin y*ar* abone of kirſþ cleir and thin
Thair mantillis grein war as the gres that grew in may sessoun
ffetrit *with* yair quhyt fingaris about yair fair sydis   25
Off ferliful fyne favour war yair faceis meik
All full of flurisſt fairheid as flouris in June
Quhyt seimlie and soft as the sweit lillies
New vpſþred vpon ſþray as new ſþynisſt Rose
Arrayit ryallie about *with* mony rich vard*our*   30
That nature full nobillie a*n*namalit [f *deleted*] *with* flouris
Off alkin hewis vnder hewin yat ony heynd knew
ffragrant all full of fresche odo*ur* fynesſt of smell
Ane cumlie tabil coverit wes befoir tha cleir ladeis
With ryalle cowpis apon rawis full of ryche wynis   35
And of thir fair wlonkes tua weddit war *with* lordis
Ane wes ane wedow I wis wantoun of laitis
And as thai talk at the tabill of many taill sindry
Thay wauchtit at the wicht wyne and waris out wourdis
And syne thai ſþak more ſþedelie and ſþarit no matiris   40

p. 83

ˈ[in] added from Bawcutt's edition (1998: 41).

(f) Extract from Dunbar, 'The Goldyn Targe' (Chepman and Myllar, ?1508)

This text illustrates another aspect of Dunbar's skill: his ability as an aureate poet (see ch. 4, 2.0). *The Goldyn Targe* is a dream allegory, reflecting the heightened court culture of James IV. The text given here derives from that in the black-letter print made by Walter Chepman (?1471–1528) and Andro Myllar (fl. 1503–8), and was a direct result of the patent issued by James IV in 1507:

> to furnis and bring hame ane prent, with all stuff belangand tharto, and expert men to use the samyne, for imprenting within our Realme of the bukis of our Lawis, actis of parliament, croniclis, mess bukis, and portuus efter the use of our Realme, with addicions and legendis of Scottis sanctis, now gaderit to be ekit tharto, and al utheris bukis that salbe sene necessar, and to sel the sammyn for competent pricis (cited Dickson and Edmond 1890: 8).

Chepman and Myllar undertook their printing at a shop in Edinburgh's Cowgate, but their enterprise does not seem to have lasted very long. The press's 'best-seller' was Bishop William Elphinstone's two-volume *Breviarium Aberdonense* ('Aberdeen Breviary') of 1510, but by then the partnership was no longer active; the breviary was printed by Chepman alone. Scottish printing had stalled, and did not really resume until at least the middle of the sixteenth century.

The inscription **Here begynys ane litil tretis intitulit the goldyn | targe compilit be Maister Wilyam dunbar |** appears on the front page of the book, with Chepman's device and name (**Walterus + chepman**) at the foot of the page. A copy is mounted on *EEBO*. The most recent authoritative critical edition of Dunbar's verse is Bawcutt 1998.

The language of this passage makes a useful contrast to the copious usage demonstrated in *The Flyting*. Old English **hw–** is reflected as ⟨quh-⟩ in **quhen, quhilk, quhill, quhite**; however, for prototypically Scots ⟨ch⟩, ⟨gh⟩ appears in **ryght**. Inflexions show a similar mixture of Scots forms (e.g. **–it** as the reflex of Present-Day English **–ed**) and forms usually considered by philologists to be more characteristic of southern English, e.g. **glading** (present participle), cf. more prototypically Scots **–and**. The plural auxiliary **war**, cf. Norse **váru**, might be noted; forms such as **intill** 'into' and **stern** 'star' also have Norse etymologies. The system of demonstratives and pronouns is again prototypical for Scots, e.g. **thair** 'their', **thir** 'these'. The form **happis** (line 19) seems to be an error for **hoppis**.

However, what is particularly notable about the passage is its handling of aureate diction, for which see ch. 4, 2.0. Dunbar's use of expressions such as **depurit bemes cristallyne** (**depurit** = 'purified'), **goldyn candill matutyne** (**matutyne** = 'of the morning') and **purpur cape revest** derives from the same kind of impulse that drove him to the use of 'low' language in *The Flyting*; both **rude** 'low' and **aureat** diction represent attempts to make Scots 'copious', i.e. to elaborate the variety. The phrase **our scailit in silvir sloppis** has puzzled commentators; it may be glossed 'scattered with silvery trailing clouds' (see Kinsley 1979: 247).

Ryght as the ſtern of day begouth to schyne
Quhen gone to bed war veſþer and lucyne
I raise and by a rosere did me reſt
Wp ſþrang the goldyn candill matutyne
With clere depurit bemes criſtallyne   5
Glading the mery foulis in thair neſt
Or phebus was in purpur cape reueſt
Wp raise the lark the hevyns menſtrale fyne
In may/ intill a morow myrthfulleſt

Full angellike thir birdis sang thair houris   10
Within thair courtyns grene in to thair bouris
Apparalit quhite and rede wyth blomes suete
Anamalit was the felde wyth all colouris
The perly droppis schuke in silvir schouris
Quhill all in balme did branch and leuis flete   15
To part fra phebus did aurora grete
Hir criſtall teris I saw hyng on the flouris
Quhilk he for lufe all drank up wyth his hete

For mirth of may wyth skippis and wyth happis
The birdis sang upon the tender croppis   20

With curiouse note as venus chapell clerkis
The rosis yong new ſþreding of thair knopis
War powd[er]it bry[ch]t with hevinly beriall droppis
Throu bemes rede birnyng as ruby ſþerkis
The skyes rang for schoutying of the larkis   25
The purpur hevyn our scailit in silvir sloppis
Ourgilt the treis branchis lef & barkis

(g) Extract from Gavin Douglas, 'The Palice of Honour' (c. 1553)

This passage from the beginning of Douglas's *The Palice of Honour* is taken from
the London edition of about 1553, for which see the discussion by Priscilla Bawcutt
(2003: xvi–xviii). The extract offered here is designed as simply illustrative of Douglas's work, and serious students should consult Bawcutt's authoritative diplomatic
edition. Bawcutt offers an edition of the three early authorities for the text: the London edition of *c.* 1553, printed by William Copland; the Edinburgh edition of 1579,
Imprentit at Edin-|burgh be Iohne Ros,|for Henrie Charteris; and fragments of
an edition probably by the Edinburgh printer Thomas Davidson, *c.* 1530–40. For
Douglas's career, see the introduction to Text 2(c) above.

The text below comes from Copland's black-letter edition, which is available on
EEBO. The title-page reads as follows (with ꝕ for the *hedera*):

> ꝕ THE|PALIS OF|Honoure Compeled by|Gawyne dowglas Bys-|shope of
> Dunkyll.|¶Imprinted at London in|fletstret, at the sygne of|the Rose garland
> by|wyllyam|Copland.|¶God saue Quene Marye.|

It is interesting that the London text contains more features regarded as prototypical of Scots than do the Scottish editions; it is important to recall that written Early Modern English, though undergoing standardisation, still allowed of
variation in a way which modern readers find puzzling, while prestigious forms of
spoken English were still in the process of emerging during the sixteenth century.
George Puttenham's famous reference to prestigious language being that spoken
in London and its environs dates from the second half of the sixteenth century
(*The Arte of English Poesie*, 1588). In the text below, Old English hw– is commonly
reflected in ⟨quh-⟩, e.g. **quhois, quhilk(is), quhen, quhil/quhyll**; Old English
medial –h– appears as ⟨ch⟩ in **wrocht** but as ⟨gh⟩ in **right**. Old English ā appears
as ⟨ai⟩ in **baith** but ⟨o⟩ in **so**, and the reflexion of Old English ō is ⟨u⟩ in **gudlyheid**.
Probable Norse-derived forms include **till** 'to', **fra** 'from', **war** 'were' and the present
participle inflexion in –**and**, e.g. **blomand, makand**.

The rhyming words **emerant, fragrant, distillant** and **reflectant** are part of the
elaborated language which entered Scots through aureation. *DSL*'s citations of
emerant, are many fewer than of **emeraud(e)**, and mostly poetical. The remaining
rhyming words are all rare and poetical. The word **fragrant**, though in Present-
Day English a common word, is cited only in poetry in *DSL*; **distillant** is again
rare and poetical; and **reflectant**, apparently a 'nonce'-word meaning '? deflecting,
? retreating', is cited by *DSL* only from *The Palice of Honour*, as is the form **vmbrate**
'shady'. Other rare forms include **gnappit** (from **gnap** 'bite in a snapping fashion'
– 'of imitative origin' *DSL*), cited only from here and in one other text in *DSL*, and

pungitiue 'having the quality of pricking', which is rather more commonly cited but seems to be restrictied to early Scots texts.

QVhen pale Aurora with face lamentable
Hir russat mantill borderit all with sable
Lappit about be heuinlye circumstance
The tender bed and arres honorable
Of Flora quene till flouris amyable   5
In may I rays, to do my obseruance
And entrit in a garding of plesance
With Sole, depaint as paradys amyable
And blisfull bewes, with blomed variance.

§ So craftely dame flora had ouer fret   10
Hir heuinly bed, powderit with mony a set
Of Ruby, Topas, Perle, and emerant.
With balmy dewe, bathit, and kyndly wet,
Quhil vapours hote right fresche and wele ybet
Dulce of odour, of flewour most fragrant   15
The silver droppis on dayseis distillant.
Quhilk verdour branches ouer the altars ʒet,
With smoky sence the mystis reflectant.

§ The fragrant flouris blomand in their seis,
Overspred ye leues of naturis tapestries.   20
Aboue the quhilk with heuinly armoneis
The birdes sat on twistis and on greis
Melodiously makand thair kyndely gleis
Quhois schill notis fordinned al the skyis
Of reparcust ayr the eccon cryis.   25
Amang the branches of the blomed treis.
And on the laurers silver droppis lyis.

§ Quhyll that I rowmed in that paradice
Replennessed and full of all delice
Out of the sea, Eous alift his heid.
[folio A. iii.] I meyne the hors quhilk drawis at device   31
The assiltre and goldin chaire of pryce
Of Tytan, quhilk at morowe semis reid.
The new colowr that al the night lay deid
Is restored, baith fowlis, flowris, and ryce   35
Reconfort was, throw Phebus gudlyheid.

§ The dasy and the Maryguld onlappit
Quhilkis all the nicht lay with thair leuis happit
Thaim to preserue fra rewmes pungitiue

The vmbrate treis that Tytan about wappit   40
War portrait, and on the erth yschappit.
Be goldin bemes viuificatiue.
Quhois amene hete is moſt reſtoratiue.
The gershoppers amangis the vergers gnappit
And beis wrocht materiall for thair hyue   45

(h) Extract from David Lyndsay, 'The Dream' (1528)

Sir David Lyndsay 'of the Mount' in Fife (c. 1486–1555) is, along with Henryson, Dunbar and Gavin Douglas, one of the major early older Scots **makars**. As a herald, he was an important figure at court, in charge of aspects of court ceremonial that were a crucial part of a renaissance prince's **magnyfycence**. Heralds, moreover, undertook important missions on behalf of their monarchs; Lyndsay seems to have acted as a negotiator for James V in arranging his first (short-lived) marriage with Princess Madeleine of France. However, he did not help negotiate the king's marriage with Mary of Guise, since he was involved in setting up the welcoming ceremonies, which included an address by him to Mary emphasising the importance of wifely obedience. Lyndsay ended his public career as Lyon King of Arms (still the principal post in Scotland's heraldic court). His views were reformist; he seems to have disliked Cardinal Beaton's policies and to have been moderately sympathetic to the Cardinal's assassins (who seem to have been known to him as neighbours in Fife). He died in 1555.

Lyndsay wrote many works, including a flyting accusing the king of lasciviousness, a long poem of moral instruction from a reformist perspective called *Ane dialogue betuix experience and ane courteour*, and perhaps most famously a play, *Ane Satire of the Thrie Estaitis*, which was performed both in his home town of Cupar in Fife and on Calton Hill in Edinburgh, the latter performance being before Mary of Guise. Lyndsay's works were widely printed throughout the sixteenth and seventeenth centuries, testifying to the demand for his works. Janet Hadley Williams's selection (2000) is the best introduction to the study of Lyndsay. Lyndsay's *The Dreme*, a work of moral instruction addressed to James V, seems to be his earliest surviving work; it dates from around 1526 (Hadley Williams 2000: 207). The passage below is the opening petition in which, following time-honoured models, Lyndsay emphasises how he has served the king faithfully and how there is an important link between good service and the gracious giving of favours by the recipient of that service. The text of *The Dreme* below comes from the Jascuy edition, printed in Paris (Geddie 1912: 276–7; see also Hadley Williams 2000: 207):

> ¶Heir followis the dre|me of Sir Dauid Lindsay of the | mont knyt, alias Lion kyng of armes | derecket onto our souerane Lord | kyng James the fyft. |

Below this title is a woodcut showing Lyndsay in an heraldic tabard with a raised left hand, presumably declaiming. At the foot of the page appears the following:

> ¶And Imprentit at the command, and | expenses of maister Samuel | Jascuy, In Paris. | 1558. |

A copy of the edition is lodged on *EEBO*.

The language of the passage exemplifies the sophisticated range of usages possible in mid-sixteenth century Scots. Old English **hw-** is reflected in ⟨quh-⟩ in **quhen, quhilk**, and Old English medial **-h-** appears as ⟨ch⟩ in **rycht, hecht**. The reflex of Old English ā is generally ⟨a(i)⟩ in **gaist, ane, schaw, knawin**, but the forms **moir** 'more' and **moist** 'most' are interesting developments, with ⟨i⟩ used, in the Scots manner, as a diacritic flagging a long vowel but where ⟨o⟩ appears for more usual Scots ⟨a⟩, cf. prototypically Scots **mair, maist**. Tokens with reflexes of Old English ō are rare in the passage, but we might note **gudlye**. The form **chalmer** 'chamber' represents a characteristic Scots back-spelling; *l*-vocalisation meant that there was a concomitant tendency to introduce an unhistorical ⟨l⟩ in places. We might note the usual present participle inflexion in **-and**, and Present-Day English **-ed** reflected in **-it**; the past participle form **disfigurate** 'disfigured' is again prototypical of Scots. The auxiliary verb **sal** (cf. Present-Day English 'shall') is notable, as are forms such as **tyll** 'to' and **sic** 'such'.

However, perhaps the most notable feature of the passage is its use of specialised 'court' vocabulary, e.g. **cubiculare** 'bed-chamber attendant', **celsitude** 'highness, majesty', **thesaurare** 'treasurer', **sewar** 'attendant at dining-table', and **yschar** 'usher' (this last word recorded by *DSL* and *OED* as a specifically Scots form), although all these words are fairly well-attested in *DSL*. Lyndsay is not attempting, it seems, the conscious elaboration which seems to have preoccupied Dunbar; such expressions are part of his natural discourse deriving from his own cultural context. This specialised courtier's vocabulary contrasts, in the same text, with 'folk' usages and references, e.g. **Of the reid eitin and the gyir carling**. The phrase **gyir carling** is given several citations in *DSL*, which offers a derivation from Old Norse **gýgr** 'ogress', used attributively, followed by **carling** 'old woman' (see also *OED* **carline**(1)). The phrase **reid eitin** 'red giant' includes the reflex of Old English **eoten**. The Red Etin is referred to in *The Complaynt of Scotland*, while the Gyre Carlin appears in numerous Scottish folk tales; it is referred to by Sir Walter Scott in *The Antiquary*. The reference to **rymour**, **beid** and **marlyng** is to collections of folk prophecies, the most famous of which were those ascribed to Thomas the Rymour.

> [*folio 146r*] Rycht potent prince, of hie Imperiall blude
> Onto thy Grace I traiſt it be weill knawin
> My seruice done onto your celsitude
> Quhilk neidis nocht at lenth for to be schawin
> And thocht my ʒowtheid now be neir ouerblawin   5
> Excerſt in seruice, of thyn excellence
> Hope hes me hecht, ane gudlye recompence.
>
> ¶Quhen thow wes ʒowng I bure the in myne arme
> Full tenderlye tyll thow begowth to gang
> And in thy bed oft happie the full warme   10
> With lute in hand syne softlye to the sang
> Sum tyme in dansyng ferely I flang
> And sumtyme playand farsis on the flure
> And sumtyme on myne office takand cure

¶And sum tyme lyke ane feind transfigurate   15
And sum tyme lyke the gryisly gaiſt of gye
In diuers formis oftymes disfigurate
And sum tyme disagysit full plesandlye
So sen thy birth I hefe contine wallye
Bene occupyit and ay to yi plesoure   20
And sum tyme sewar copper and carvoure.

¶Thy purs maiſter, and secreit thesaurare
Thy yschar ay sen thy natiuite
And of thy chalmer cheif cubiculare
Quhilk to this hour hes keipit my laute   25
Loving be to the blissit trynite
That sic ane wracheit worme hes maid so habill
Till sic ane prince to be so aggreabill

[folio 146v]   ¶Bot now thow arte be influence naturall
Hye of ingyne and rycht inquisityve   30
Of antique ſtoreis and deidis marciall
Moir plesandlye the tyme for tyll ower dryve
I hef at lenth the ſtoreis done discryve
Of Hectour, arthour, and gentill Julius
Of Alexander, and worthy Pompeyus.   35

¶Of Jasone and media all at lenth
Of Hercules the honorabill
And of sampsone the supernaturall ſtrenth
And of leill lufears ſtoreis amiabill
And oftymes hef I feinƺeit mony fabill   40
Of troyelus the sorow and the ioy
And seigis all of tyre thebes and troy.

¶The prophiteis of rymour beid and marlyng
And of mony wther plesand ſtorye
Of the reid eitin and the gyir carlyng   45
Confortand the quhen that I saw the sorye
Now wyth the support of the kyng of glorye
I sal the schaw ane ſtorie of ye new
The quhilk affoir I neuer to the schew.

¶But humilye I beseik thyne excellence   50
Wyth ornat termis thocht I can nocht expres
This simpill mater for laik of eloquence
Zit nochtwythſtandyng all my besynes
Wyth hart and hand my pen I sal addres

As I beſt can and moiſt compendious   55
Now I begyne the mater hapnit thus

(i) Extract from Elizabeth Melville, 'Ane Godlie Dreame' (1603)

Elizabeth Melville (fl. 1599–1631), daughter of the diplomat Sir James Melville (1535/6–1617), married John Colville, who was probably a Presbyterian minister in Culross on the north shore of the Firth of Forth, in Fife. Her Calvinist faith under-pins her writing. Her poem **Ane godlie Dreame compy-|lit in Scottish Meter be M. M. Gentelwoman in|Culros, at the request of her freindes.**|'reflects medieval and Renaissance conventions of female spiritual 'autobiography', but is an allegory moulded by the doctrinal exigencies of [her] Calvinism' (*ODNB*). The word **godlie** in the title might be noted (see Text 5(c) below). The work was frequently reprinted in the seventeenth century, and both Scots and anglicised versions survive. The following extract is from an Older Scots version, printed in 1603 by Robert Char-teris (Henry Charteris's son) in Edinburgh; a copy appears on *EEBO*. The poem's heading is in roman type, but the rest of the text is in black-letter.

The language of the passage is Scots, with some features which may be seen as more prototypical of English. Old English **hw–** appears as ⟨quh-⟩ in **quhilk, quhen, quhy** and **quhat**, and Old English **–h(-)** is reflected as ⟨ch⟩ in **micht, nocht, thocht** and **sich(s)** 'sigh(s)'. Old English ō is reflected as ⟨ui⟩ in **luik** 'look' (cf. Old English lōcian); the form **puir** derives from Anglo-Norman **pover** etc., but it may be pre-sumed that the spelling ⟨ui⟩ represents a fronted reflex of Middle English ō. There are many examples of the reflex of Old English ā in the passage, some with ⟨a(i)⟩ and others with ⟨o(i)⟩, e.g. **saull(is), nane, maist** beside **alone, moir, so**. Rhyming practice varies, but in some cases is of uncertain significance since some rhyming words in question all contain reflexes of Old English ā/Old Norse á, and are thus self-rhymes, although we might note the sporadic retention of ⟨i⟩ as a diacritic flag-ging length, e.g. **soir: moir**, beside **fro: go: so: wo**. However, we might also note the rhyme-sequence **lang: sang: strang: wrang**, where the forms **sang** and **wrang** (with reflexes of lengthened Old English a) rhyme with **lang** and **strang**, traditionally seen as Scottish or northern English forms (although **lang/long** and **strang/strong** are widely recorded variants in all Old English dialects; cf. *OED*). Inflexions are a mixture of Scots and English, with **–it** as the reflex of Present-Day English **–ed** but the second person singular present tense is **–est** in **sleipest thou**. We might note the Scots auxiliary verbs **sall** (cf. Present-Day English 'shall') and **war** (cf. Old Norse **váru**); interestingly, Melville exemplifies the Early Modern English habit of using the auxiliary 'do' with French-/Latin-derived verbs, e.g. **did sa molest, did still incres, dois . . . infest**. The adjective **sillie** 'innocent' (e.g. **The sillie Sancts**) may also be noted; the Present-Day English reflex 'silly' has of course a distinct meaning.

[folio A2r]   VPON ane day as I did mourne full soir,
With sindrie things quhairwith my saull was
My greif increasit and grew moir & moir (grefit
My comfort fled and could not be releifit,
With heauines my heart was sa mischeifit,   5

I loathit my lyfe, I could not eit nor drink,
I micht not speik nor luik to nane that leifit,
Bot musit alone and diuers things did think.

The wretchit warld did sa molest my mynde,
I thocht vpon this fals and Iron age. 10
And how our harts war sa to vice inclynde,
That Sathan seimit maist feirfullie to rage.
Nathing in earth my sorrow could asswage,
I felt my sin maist stranglie to incres,
I greifit my Spreit that wont to be my pledge, 15
My saull was drownit into maist deip distres.

All merynes did aggrauate my paine,
And earthlie joyes did still incres my wo:
In companie I na wayes could remaine,
Bot fled resort, and so alone did go. 20
My sillie saull was tostit to and fro,
With sindrie thochts quhilk troublit me full soir:
I preisit to pray, bot sichs overset me so,
I could do nocht bot sich, and say no moir.

[folio A2v] * The twinkling teares aboundantlie ran down,
My heart was easit quhen I had mournit my fill: 26
Than I began my lamentatioun,
And said, O Lord, how lang is it thy will,
That thy puir Sancts sall be afflictit still?
Allace, how lang sall subtill Sathan rage? 30
Mak haist O Lord, thy promeis to fulfill,
Mak haist to end our painefull pilgramage.

Thy sillie Sancts are tostit to and fro,
Awalk, O Lord, quhy sleipest thou sa lang?
We have na strenth agains our cruell fo. 35
In sichs and sobbis now chaingit is our sang,
The warld preuails, our enemies ar strang,
The wickit rage, bot wee are puir and waik:
O shaw thy self, with speid rejenge† our wrang,
Mak short thir days, euen for thy chosens saik. 40

Lord Jesus cum and saif thy awin Elect,
For Sathan seiks our simpill sauls to slay:
The wickit warld dois stranglie vs infect,
Most monsterous sinnes increasses day be day,
Our luif grows cald, our zeill is worne away, 45

Our faith is faillit, and we ar lyke to fall:
The Lyon roares to catch vs as his pray,
Mak haiſt, O Lord, befoir wee perish all.

Thir ar the dayes, that thou sa lang foretald,
Sould cum befoir this wretchit warld sould end: 50
Now vice abounds and charitie growes cald,
And euin thine owne moſt ſtronglie dois offend,
The Deuill preuaillis, his forces he dois bend,
Gif it could be to wraik thy children deir:
Bot wee ar thine, thairfoir sum succour send,   55
Resaue our saullis, wee irk to wander heir.

[folio A3r] * Quhat can wee do? wee cloggit ar with sin,
In filthie vyce our sensles saules ar drownit:
Thocht wee resolue, wee neuir can begin,
To mend our lyfes, bot sin dois ſtill abound.   60
Quhen will thou cum? quhen sall thy trumpet sound?
Quhen sall wee sie that grit and glorious day?
O saue vs, Lord, out of this pit profound,
And reif vs from this loathsum lump of clay.

* = line cropped at the top of the page.
† for **reuenge**

(j) Alexander Montgomerie, 'Against the God of Love'

Alexander Montgomerie (early 1550s–1598) was a soldier, courtier and poet: the **maister poete** of James VI's coterie (see further the introduction to Text 3(a); see also his *ODNB* entry). The king regarded Montgomerie as **his gude servitour**, and even exchanged poetic nicknames with him (James was William Mow, while Montgomerie was either Rob Stene or 'beloved Sanders'). However, Montgomerie's Catholic sympathies led eventually to involvement in plots; he was outlawed in 1597, having failed to respond to a summons to trial for treason. He died soon afterwards. However, the king never lost his affection for Montgomerie; he granted a request for the poet to be buried in consecrated ground, provided a royal cortege, and even commemorated him in verse:

> Though to his buriall was refused the bell,
> The bell of fame shall aye his praises knell.

The most authoritative modern edition of Montgomerie's works, which survive in many manuscripts and early prints, is by David Parkinson (2000). Montgomerie's range is wide; he wrote short lyrics (some with surviving music), flytings, and a long work on human happiness (*The Cherrie and the Slae*). He also wrote sonnets, one of which appears here (Parkinson 2000: 135); an attack on Cupid, the sonnet combines classical learning with the old flyting tradition of ingenious invective.

The use of alliteration and rhythm is notable (see ch. 4 above).

The sonnet below survives in the Ker Manuscript. This collection was put together by a Catholic sympathiser in the late 1590s, in an italic hand; the manuscript subsequently passed to William Drummond of Hawthornden (see Text 4(m) below), who donated it, along with other books, to Edinburgh University Library in 1627. It is now MS Edinburgh, University Library, De 3.70. The text below is slightly cropped at the edges on folio 80 recto, and thus two suggested readings are supplied, as marked. The text includes certain Scots features, e.g. **Gok** 'fool' (cf. Present-Day Scots **gowk**), **stirk** 'stupid fellow' (an extended meaning; the literal meaning is 'young bullock'), and **Playmear** 'play-mare, hobbyhorse' (the word is according to *DSL* unique to Montgomerie in this text, and *OED* has citations only from Montgomerie and Sir Walter Scott). The obscure term of abuse **bluiter** 'fool, oaf' is also, according to *OED*, 'chiefly' Scots. Scots forms include **maist** 'most', **sik** 'such' and the inflexion in –**it**; however, we might also note forms such as **waving** (present participle), **these** and **vhom** 'whom'; the reflex of Old English ō appears as ⟨oo⟩ in **good**. The second-person and third-person singular inflexions in –**es**/–**is**, e.g. **chuisis, refuises, begylis** proven by the rhymes with the nouns **Muses, stylis** are also worth noting; both inflexions are more characteristic of Scots than Early Modern English, where –**est**/–**eth** might be regarded as more prototypical.

   [folio 80r]   Against the God of Love.

                   Blind brutal Boy that *with* thy bou abuses
                   Leill leisome Love by Lechery & Lust,
                   Judge Jakanapis & Jougler maist vnj[ust *supplied*]
                   If in thy rageing RESONE thou refuise[s *supplied*]
[folio 80v]   To be thy Chiftanes changers ay thou chuisis   5
                   To beir thy baner so they be robust
                   fals Tratur Turk betrayer vnder trust
                   Quhy maks thou Makrels of the Modest Muses?
                   Art thou a God, no, bot a Gok disguysit
                   A bluiter buskit lyk a belly blind   10
                   With wings and quaver waving with the Wind
                   A plane Playmear for Vanitie devysit
                   Thou art a stirk for all thy staitly stylis
                   And these good Geese vhom sik a God begylis

                   Finis

(k) John Stewart of Baldynneis: from 'Roland Furious' (a partial translation of Ariosto, 'Orlando Furioso')

John Stewart (*c.* 1545–*c.* 1605) was a courtier and poet who spent much of his career attempting to assert his family's claims to property. His mother Elizabeth, once James V's mistress, had subsequently married John Stewart, Lord Innermeith; the poet was her second son. On his father's death around 1570, Elizabeth remarried, but this second marriage was not a success, being dissolved in 1581. John Stewart took his mother's side, and the conflicts over property became violent; they seem to have been settled only in 1585 (*ODNB*). John had inherited the estate of Baldynneis in Perthshire in 1580, on the death of his elder brother. A major new edition of Stewart's work is in preparation (see McClune forthcoming).

John Stewart seems to have become another of James VI's court poets, producing a range of courtly and occasional poems: sonnets, lyrics, a religious allegory and this translation of Ariosto (see further Jack 1972: 57–74, Corbett 1999: 68–71, Spiller 2010, and McClune forthcoming). The poems survive in one manuscript (MS Edinburgh, National Library of Scotland 19.2.6), which seems to be a presentation volume for the king (to whom it is dedicated). It is copied in a fine italic hand; some items are in red ink (indicated here by sans serif font). The original cover survives, stamped **IR**, surmounted by a crown. An account of the poem, and of the other texts in the volume, appears on folio 6 recto of the manuscript, as follows:

ANE ABBREGEMENT OF ROLAND | FURIOUS TRANSLAIT OVT OF | ARIOST. TOGITHER VITH | SVM RAPSODIES OF THE AVTHors | ZOUTHFVLL BRAINE AND | LAST ANE SHERSING OVT | OF TREW FELICITIE | COMPOSIT IN SCOTIS | MEITER BE | J Stewart of Baldyneis. |

The following inscription appears on folio 7 recto:

TO THE RYCHT EXCELLENT RYCHT | HICH AND MYCHTIE PRENCE | IAMES THE SEXT KYNG OF Scotland | His maiesteis most humyll Seruant | J Stewart of Baldynneis wishith | long And most prosperous reigne | In the continewall fauor | And feir of God. |

The dedication letter which follows begins with an allusion to the *Reulis and Cautelis*, which suggests a date after 1584; Stewart claims (folio 7 recto) that he began this work **haifing red** *zour maiesties* **maist prudent | Precepts in the deuyn art of poesie.** Stewart also, interestingly, refers in his dedication to his **Inept orthographie.**

The language of the manuscript is consistently Scots, with forms such as **quhan** and **quha, thocht** and **knycht, suld, scho, maist** (though we might note the form **most** in the dedication above), **na,** inflexions in **–it, varps** 'throws', **fra** 'from' (beside **from**) and **till** 'to', although we might note **both, non** 'none' (cf. more prototypically Scots **baith, nane**), and **thois** 'those' rhyming with **repois**. The form **scherst** 'searched' is of interest; *DSL* gives three citations of this spelling, all from Stewart of Baldynneis. The following passage comes from the second canto of the poem. The form **deray** 'disturbance, revelry', derived from Old French **desrei**, is cited fairly frequently in *DSL*; it also occurs in the Bannatyne version *Christ's Kirk on the Green* (see Text 4(q) below), and is kept there by eighteenth-century redactors, both in the broadside version and in Allan Ramsay's edition. The form is also given in *OED*, although there, interestingly, its citations from non-Scottish authors end with Caxton's translation of Ovid. The form **formois** 'beautiful', derived from Latin **formōsus**, is rarely attested in *OED*; *DSL* gives references only to Lyndsay, Stewart and Alexander Scott.

[folio 13v] . . .

Quhan both the armeis suld the gither chak.
Helas for than succedit all his vrak
for at deray Quhow soone the vangard gois
On horse scho lop And did hir Journay tak
And vald be thrall scho thocht to non of thois   5
This lustie dame obteine culd na repois
for hote persute of euerie vordie knycht

[folio 14r] Hir person peirles And hir face formois
Oft hir constrains to tak the feirfull flycht
And now supposing till escaipe be slycht   10
At this hir voyage vtheruayis did chans
for In the vod befoir hir visage Rycht
Ane knycht Scho spyde on fute in armeur glans,
Than dreid of dainger varps hir in ane trans
As tender **faune**, vithin ane darnit den   15
Quhan It persaifs the **Leopard** Auans,
Or compast close about be craft of men,
for **Rennault** heir scho did perfytlie ken
Quha scherst his **Bayard** bendit from his hand,
Bot to his feit, his zeill did suiftnes len   20
fast for to rin fra he the fairrest fand,
He plaints, he cryis, Scho vill not stay nor stand
Bot fleis in feir as from ane **Serpent** fell,
Scho gifs hir horse both brydle, chak, and vand,
And muifs hir heils, his speid for to compell: 25
It is vncertan to my toung to tell
Quhilk of the tuo maist feruent zelus beine
Scho for to flie, or he to Intermell,
Thay both assay so schairplie to preueine:
As **Daintie Daphne**, fleing **Phebus** scheine   30
Vith Lustie lyms so luiflie squair and quhyt
Quha vas transformit \In/ the **laurell greine**
Quhan he approtchd hir persone maist perfyt:
So **Rennault** Raidgeing vith na les delyt
Sped vith sic speid Quhill scho vas skairslie frie.   35

(l) *William Fowler, Sonnet from 'The Tarantula of Love'*

William Fowler (1560/61–1612) had a colourful career. He was born into a family
of prominent Edinburgh burgesses; his sister was the mother of William Drummond of Hawthornden. He was educated in St Andrews and Paris; a convinced
Protestant, he published in 1581 a polemic attack on the **erroneous propositions**
of the Scottish Jesuit John Hamilton. He subsequently had a brief career as a spy
(employed by Elizabeth I's spymaster, Francis Walsingham, see Text 2(j)), but by

1584 he was part of the courtly and literary circle around James VI. He helped negotiate James VI's marriage, and was later involved emotionally, in a rather vague way, with James's cousin Ar(a)bella Stewart (1575–1615; see Text 2(k)); Fowler records the relationship in various love poems. He travelled extensively in Italy, ending his career as secretary to James's queen Anne.

Fowler was a substantial poet, though comparatively little was published in his lifetime; his verse largely survives in manuscript. The sonnet below is from his sequence *The Tarantula of Love*, which survives in MS Edinburgh, University Library, Drummond De.3.68; another, less authoritative manuscript also survives, MS Edinburgh, National Library of Scotland, Hawthornden 2063 (*olim* XI) in the National Library of Scotland. (For a discussion of the manuscripts, see the important essay by Verweij 2007; see also Elliott 2010.) The Drummond manuscript is written in a secretary hand, and there are some corrections in places, which seem to be authorial 'second-thoughts'; as Verweij points out, these changes are much more substantial in the Hawthornden manuscript. A later scribe in the Drummond manuscript, in a different ink and in what looks like an eighteenth-century hand, has offered a translation of the last line of the poem, reading as follows: **ye will me grant to harbour in your heauen**. The language of the poem is a mixture of Scottish and English forms; we might note **quhen, gif** 'if' and **thole** 'suffer' beside **whils, whome** and **which, sore** and **so** (cf. prototypically Scots **sair, s(u)a**) and the third-person present tense inflexion in the form **rekendleth** 'rekindles'. For a thorough study of the language, see James Craigie's essay in the third volume of the STS edition (in Meikle 1940: li–lxxix).

The title *The Tarantula of Love* is bizarre to a modern eye, but would be explicable to contemporaries. Fowler's travels in Italy may have introduced him to the word. Sir Thomas Hoby, in his translation of Castiglione's *The Courtier* (1561), felt he needed to offer a gloss: **Them that are bitten with a Tarrantula.** [*margin*] **A kind of spiders, which being diuers of nature cause diuers effectes, some after their biting fal a singing, some laugh [etc.]** (cited from *OED tarantula* n.). It was believed that the bite of the tarantula could be cured by music; the Neapolitan dance, the *tarentella*, seems to derive from this belief.

[*folio 24v*]	Schip brokken men whome ſtormye seas
	[off *deleted*] sore toss
	proteſts with oaths not to adventur more
	yet all there perrells promeses and loss
	they quyte forgett quhen they come to the schore
	Euen so ffair dame whils sadlye I deplore 5
	the schipwrak of my witts proceurd by yow
	your lookes rekendleth love as of before
	and dois reviue which I did disavowe
	so all my former voues I disallowe
	and buryeis in oblivions grave my grones 10
	yea I forgiue herefter euen as now
	my feares my teares my cares my sobbs and mones
	in hope gif I agane \on'[oo *deleted*] roks be dreven
	ʒe will me thole to ancer in your heaven.

(m) William Drummond of Hawthornden, 'I know that all beneath the Moon decays'

William Drummond (1585–1649), the son of a gentleman-usher to James VI, was a graduate of the new Edinburgh University (**the tounis college**, as it was then known); he visited Paris and studied law in Bourges, but spent most of his life on his estate of Hawthornden just to the south of Edinburgh.

Drummond collected a library, large for his time, covering philosophy (in those days including not just logic and moral philosophy, but also physics, mathematics, astrology, alchemy), law, theology, Latin poetry and prose and also vernacular literature. He left many of these books to Edinburgh University Library (see Macdonald 1971 for a full account). Works of English or Scottish literature in Drummond's library included William Alexander's *Elegie on the death of prince Henrie* (1613) and *The monarchicke tragedies* (1607 and 1616 editions), William Bullokar's *Book at Large* (1580), Gavin Douglas's translation of Virgil (printed in London, 1553), Sir Thomas Hoby's translation of Castiglione's *The Courtier*, the works of Samuel Daniel and Michael Drayton, the Jesuit James Gordon's treatise of the written word of God (translated), John Heywood's works, the works of Ben Jonson (Jonson visited Drummond in 1618), James VI/I's *Daemonologie*, plays by George Chapman and Thomas Middleton, Golding's translation of Ovid, plays by Shakespeare (*Love's Labour's Lost, A Midsumer Night's Dream, Romeo and Juliet*) and the poems *Venus and Adonis* and *The Rape of Lucrece*, and (above all, because most influential on him) Philip Sidney's works (*Apology, Countess of Pembroke's Arcadia*).

As this list suggests, Drummond's library of British literature is largely English-focused, including, interestingly, a work on spelling-reform (Bullokar's *Book at Large*, although he does not adopt Bullokar's somewhat eccentric recommendations). It is therefore perhaps not surprising that his work is published in English, though we might note **Spright** in the text below; the word seems to have its Scots meaning ('spirit') rather than its English one ('demon').

The text here is taken from POEMS | BY VVILLIAM DRVMMOND, | of | *Hawthorne-denne* | The second Impression | EDINBVRGH, | Printed by ANDRO HART, 1616. |. A copy appears in *EEBO*.

> *[A3v]* I Know that all beneath the *Moone* decays,
> And what by Mortalles in this World is brought,
> In *Times* great Periods shall returne to nought,
> That faireſt States have fatall Nights and Dayes:
> I know how all the *Muses* heavenly Layes,   5
> With Toyle of Spright which are so dearely bought,
> As *idle Sounds* of few, or none are sought,
> And that nought lighter is than airie Praise.
> I know frail *Beautie* like the purple Flowre,
> To which one Morne of Birth and Death affords,   10
> That Loue a Jarring is of Mindes Accords,
> Where *Sense* and *Will* inuassall *Reasons* Power:
>   Know what I liſt, this all can not mee moue,
>   But that (ô mee!) I both muſt write, and loue.

(n) James Graham (Marquess of Montrose), 'On Himself, upon hearing what was his Sentence'

James Graham, first marquess of Montrose (1612–50), is one of the most glamorous figures of the Civil Wars of the mid-seventeenth century. He initially supported the presbyterian Covenanters, but came to distrust the Covenanters' leaders, notably Archibald Campbell earl of Argyll, and changed sides. In 1644, Charles I appointed Montrose his lieutenant-general in Scotland; in this capacity, Montrose won a series of major victories across Scotland over the Covenanters, beginning with Tibbermore in September 1644 and culminating in the battle of Kilsyth in August 1645. However, his army was defeated at Philiphaugh in September, and he was forced into temporary exile. After the execution of Charles I in 1649, he returned to Scotland where, after defeat in the far north, he was captured in Assynt, taken to Edinburgh, and there hanged; his corpse was dismembered and his head displayed on Edinburgh's Tolbooth. After the restoration of monarchy in 1660, his body was reassembled and buried in St Giles's Cathedral.

Montrose is supposed to have written the poem below on the eve of his execution; its contents indicate that he was only too aware of the details of the fate he was about to suffer. A legend – of unknown origin – has it that he inscribed the poem on a pane of glass in his cell, using a diamond in his ring to do so. Some well-founded doubt has been expressed, however, as to whether the poem was written precisely at that time, or even whether it is by Montrose at all (see Harvey Wood 1991: 287, 292, and references there cited).

Various versions of the poem survive; the text here is that given in James Watson's *Choice Collection* of 1706: A |Choice Collection|of|COMIC and SERI-OUS|Scots Poems|BOTH|ANCIENT and MODERN|By several Hands|. . . EDINBURGH,|Printed by *James Watson*: Sold by *John Vallange*.|M. DCC. VI. |. The work appeared in three parts, spanning the period between 1706 and 1711. Watson, a significant figure in Scottish publishing and a prominent Jacobite, produced his collection as an assertion of Scottish traditional culture in the period preceding the Union of 1707, to which he was opposed. A report to the Edinburgh Burgh Council in 1694 had referred to him as a **printer and a profest papist**, and he was later in trouble with the authorities for his production of works with titles such as *Scotland reduced by force of arms and made a province of England*, and *A Pil for Pork-eaters or a Scots Lancet for an English Swelling together with The Englishman's address to his pock-pudding* (Harvey Wood 1991: xii, xv).

Watson included seven poems ascribed to Montrose in the *Choice Collection*, including the *Epitaph upon King Charles I*, beginning **Great, Good and Just, could I but rate / My Grief to Thy too Rigid Fate!** Two manuscript versions of the poem printed here survive: MS London, British Library Additional 10422, folio 110v, and MS Edinburgh, National Archives of Scotland, RH 13/40. The BL manuscript dates from the seventeenth century and mostly consists of poems, letters and prose by the sixteenth-century Jesuit Robert Southwell; its version of *Let them bestow* has been added, somewhat clumsily, on the verso of the last folio by a later hand, followed by what appears to be the signature of 'an unidentified Will. Wartters' (Harvey Wood 1991: 292). The NAS manuscript is a verse miscellany whose contents range in date from the sixteenth to the end of the seventeenth centuries.

The poem is written in English, though the word **Airth** 'quarter, direction of the compass' seems at this date to be restricted, with this meaning, to Scots and northern English; a common alternative later spelling is **airt** (see *DSL* **airth**, *OED* **airt**). The BL manuscript, according to Harvey Wood, replaces **Airth** with **earth**, while the NAS manuscript replaces **Airth** with **wind**: both seem weaker readings than that in the *Choice Collection* (see further Harvey Wood 1991: 292–3). A copy of the *Choice Collection* appears on *ECCO*.

> *[page 116]* Let them bestow on ev'ry Airth a Limb;
> Open all my Veins, that I may swim
> To Thee my Saviour, in that Crimson Lake;
> Then place my purboil'd Head upon a Stake;
> Scatter my Ashes, throw them in the Air: 5
> Lord (since Thou knowest where all these Atoms are)
> I'm hopeful, once Thou'lt recollect my Dust,
> And confident Thou'lt raise me with the Just.

The BL text is clumsily written, and the beginning of the word Harvey Wood reads as **earth** is obscured at the beginning by a small stain. My own reading of the opening line in the BL text is as follows:

> Let them bestow on euiry [. . .]rd a limb

(o) Lady Grisell Baillie, 'Were ne my Hearts light I wad Dye'

Lady Grisell Baillie (other spellings are also used) is aptly described by David Murison as a 'heroine and business woman' (*ODNB*). If Montrose represents a royalist martyr, Lady Baillie represents a later generation of persecuted covenanters, though she herself had a successful career despite early vicissitudes.

Grisell was born in 1665. Her future father-in-law, Robert Baillie, was hanged during the 'Killing Time', the suppression of presbyterianism in Scotland during the 1670s and 1680s, the last years of the Stewart (or, by this time, Stuart) monarchy. Grisell, then aged 11, had smuggled a letter into Baillie's cell during an earlier imprisonment. Her father, Patrick Hume, had been a close associate of Baillie's, and, with Grisell's assistance, went into hiding when Baillie was arrested, first in the family vault and subsequently in a specially constructed refuge underneath the family house; Grisell kept him supplied with food and drink. When her father escaped to the Netherlands, Grisell and the rest of the family followed; since her mother was ill, Grisell ran the household. She returned with her father in the train of William of Orange in 1688. She turned down the offer of the position of maid of honour to Queen Mary, instead preferring to marry George Baillie, Robert's son. She then took on the running of large estates, supporting the rise of her husband who became a lord of the Treasury in 1717. She amassed a large fortune, and also found time for developing her literary interests. She died in 1746.

Were ne my Hearts light I wad Dye is probably Lady Baillie's best-known poem, with many Scots features, and it supplies an interesting bridge between the Older Scots poets and the poetry of the post-1700 so-called 'vernacular revival', represented by the verse of Allan Ramsay, Robert Fergusson and Robert Burns. Various versions are recorded; the text below is that surviving in *Orpheus Caledonius*, a book of songs with music, collected by William Thomson and dating from 1726. The text is engraved, written in an italic script throughout. There seems to be no copy on *ECCO*; the copy used for the edition below is from the Euing Collection in Glasgow University Library, Sp. Coll. N.a.2. The book, which was dedicated to the Princess of Wales, was sold by subscription; **The Right Hon. the Lady Grisel Bailie** is recorded as a subscriber, as well as many others, including the Prime Minister Robert Walpole (who ordered two copies).

The title-page of *Orpheus Caledonius* reads as follows:

Orpheus Caledonius | or | a Collection of the best | Scottish songs | set to Musick | by | W. Thomson | London, Engrav'd and Printed for the Author at | his house in Leicester fields | Enter'd at Stationers Hall according to Act of Parliament |

Were ne my Hearts light I wad Dye appears on page 40. The first stanza is accompanied by music. Much of this material, comparatively neglected until recently, is now being reassessed by scholars (see Perry 2008).

The language of the poem demonstrates the remaking of the ballad tradition in the eighteenth century. The so-called 'ideological apostrophe' is noticeable, flagging a perceived lack even in words where historic sound-changes would mean that the form in question would have been a genuine Scots form, e.g. **lo'ed**, flagging *v*-deletion, and **fu'** 'full' with *l*-vocalisation. It is interesting that there is variation between **wad** and **wou'd** for 'would', the latter clearly flagging that pronunciation of ⟨l⟩ would have been regarded as more prestigious by at least some in the early eighteenth century (cf. the Present-Day English pronunciation), cf. also **shou'd**. Old English ā is reflected in ⟨a(i)⟩ in **ane, na, baith** and **lang**, but cf. **so**. Old English hw– appears as ⟨wh-⟩ in **when** etc., and Old English –h– is reflected in ⟨gh⟩ in **light** etc. The third person singular feminine pronoun is **she**. However, some closed-class words are prototypically Scots, e.g. **sick** 'such', **till** 'to' and **yon** 'those over there'. We might note **appose** 'although, albeit', cited by *DSL* only from this text and seen as a variant of **albuist** conflated with **suppose**. Distinctively Scots open-class forms include **Bigged** (see *DSL* **big** 'build'), **bra** (see *DSL/OED* **braw** 'fine', derived from **brave** with *v*-deletion), **gang** (from Norse **ganga** 'go'), **Titty** ('sister' – 'Perhaps a childish pronunciation . . .' – *DSL*) and **Tykes** ('(ill-bred) dogs'). The word **bing** 'pile', from Norse **bingr**, is of interest; the *DOST* section of *DSL* notes that the word was used especially by Gavin Douglas with reference to 'a funeral pile' [*sic*]. Most inflexional endings are as in Present-Day English, e.g. present participle in –**ing**, but we might note **Een** 'eyes', cf. Old English **eagan**; the inflexion in –**n** lasted longer in Scots than in English (see *DSL* **ee**).

[page 40]   1

There was ance a May and she lo'ed na men,
She Bigged her bonny Bow'r down in yon Glen,
But now she cryes dale and a-well-a-day,
Come down the Green gate and come here away.
But now she cryes dale and a-well-a-day,   5
Come down the Green gate and come here away.

2

When bonny young Johnny came o'er y[e] sea,
He said he fan nathing so bonny as me,
He haight me baith Rings and mony bra things,
And were ne my Hearts light I wad dye.   10

3

He had a wee Titty that lo'ed na me,
Because I was twice as bonny as she,
She rais'd sick a Pother twixt him & his mother,
That were ne my Hearts light I wad dye.

4

The day it was set and the Bridal to be,   15
The wife took a Dwalm and lay down to dye,
She maip'd and she grain'd out of Dollor & pain,
Till he vow'd that he ne'er wou'd see me again.

5

His Kin was for ane of a higher degree,
Said what had he do with the likes of me,   20
Appose I was bonny I was ne for Johnny,
And were ne my Hearts light I wad dye.

6

They said I had neither Cow nor Calf,
Nor drops of drink runs thro' the drawf,
Nor Pickles of Meal runs thro' the mill Eye,   25
And were ne my Hearts light I wad dye.

7

The maiden she was baith wylly and slye,
She ſpyed me as I came o'er the Lee,
And then she ran in and made sick a din,
Beleive your ain Een an ye trow ne me.   30

8

His bonnet ſtood ay fu' round on his Brow,
His auld ane lookt ay as well as his new,
But now he lets't gang ony gate it will hing,
And caſts himsell down on the Corn bing.

9

And now he gaes drooping about the Dykes,   35

And a' he dow do is to hund the Tykes,
The live lang night he ne'er bows his Eye,
And were ne my Hearts light I wad dye.

10

But young for thee as I ha' been,
We shou'd ha' been galloping down in yon Green,   40
And linking out o'er yon lilly white Lee,
And wow gin I were young for thee.

(p) Extract from William Dunbar, 'Discretioun in Taking': (1) Bannatyne version, (2) Maitland Folio version, and (3) Allan Ramsay's version

These three versions of the opening of the same poem are offered here to demonstrate the way in which Older Scots texts were transmitted to future generations, and how they were modified in the eighteenth century in response to contemporary criteria of taste. Two sixteenth-century versions are offered, transcribed from the Bannatyne and Maitland Folio manuscripts, followed by Allan Ramsay's eighteenth-century edition. For further discussion of the issues raised, see Smith and Kay 2011; the most recent authoritative critical edition of Dunbar's verse is Bawcutt 1998.

It will also be observed that the two versions of the poem in the Bannatyne and Maitland Folio manuscripts also differ. There is no punctuation as we would understand it in either Bannatyne or Maitland Folio texts. In both texts, other strategies are used to indicate the structure of verse and argument. In Bannatyne, features of layout are used, such as an initial rubric to mark the poem's beginning, and *litterae notabiliores* (capitals) to mark sense-divisions in lines 4 and 8. Capitals are used interestingly at the beginning of lines; we might compare their presence and absence at the beginnings of lines 4 and 14. In Maitland Folio too, features of layout are used. However, there is no title marking off the poem from that which precedes it. Capitals are not used in the same way in mid-line; they occur initially, though we might note their absence in lines 8 and 14. Maitland Folio introduces a further communicative strategy by using features of discourse grammar to flag steps in the argument, notably the deictic **Thir** in lines 6 and 11. Such demonstratives are usually glossed 'these', which is generally adequate in etymological terms although the semantics of demonstratives in Older Scots and Middle English is subtly distinct from that in Present-Day English. Maitland Folio emphasises the strategy by adding an extra stanza beginning **Thir merchandis**, thus completing the three estates into which society was divided (cf. **Thir clarkis ... Thir baronis**) and adding a new theme to the poem. Some spelling differences between Bannatyne and Maitland Folio are linguistically interesting, e.g. line 1 **geving** (Bannatyne), **giffing** (Maitland Folio); line 2 **gud** (Bannatyne), **gude** (Maitland Folio); line 5 **sowld** (Bannatyne), **suld** (Maitland Folio).

Allan Ramsay's *The Ever-Green* was published in 1724. Ramsay (1686–1758) was a Jacobite sympathiser, and his antiquarian interest in Older Scots poetry stemmed from his traditionalist views. *The Ever-Green* ('a Collection of Scots Poems, Wrote by the Ingenious before 1600') was based on the Bannatyne manuscript but very considerably modified. Despite this acknowledgement, *Of Discretioun in Taking* is presented according to eighteenth-century practices. Semi-colons are introduced at line-endings, and in place of B's capitals marking a sense-change, Ramsay – or of course his printer – has introduced mid-line commas. Capitalision is used according to incipient early eighteenth-century conventions, whereby key words in discourse, usually nouns, appear with capitals: **Giving, Taking, Gude, Autoritie, Discration, Gersomes**. Ramsay intervened too in the text's discourse grammar, pointing up the contrast with the previous poem in the series by adding **Now** at the outset, as well as adopting, in modified form, Bannatyne's connecting rubric as the italicised title for the poem (though, interestingly if understandably, **Follows** is dropped in the running-head). Layout of the text has been changed to create a more interesting appearance on the page and emphasise the refrain. Spellings are partially modernised, e.g. **Giving**, but other interventions have been made to accord the text with Ramsay's own version of Scots, e.g. **Deil** 'devil' in line 9, for Bannatyne's **diuill**. Ramsay's form is a hyper-Scotticism; *v*-deletion, i.e. the dropping of [v] with compensatory lengthening of the vowel, is common in Scots after *c*. 1450, but is clearly not reflected in Bannatyne's or Maitland Folio's spellings. Inflexions which are syllabic in Older Scots are removed, e.g. **taks** (line 3) for B's **takkis**. Further, Ramsay generally drops the characteristically Scots and Northern Middle English present plural verb-inflexion in –s (e.g. **The Clerks tak** for Bannatyne's **The clerkis takis** in line 6), save in line 14 (**gars**), where it is possible that he has failed to note concord between the verb and the subject (i.e. **Barons**, cf. Bannatyne's **Barronis**) (see ch. 3, 3.6).

(1) The Bannatyne Manuscript

[folio 62v]   ffollowis discretioun in taking

Eftir geving I ſþeik of taking
Bot littill of ony gud forsaiking
Sum takkis our littill awtoritie
And sum our mekle And yat is glaiking
In taking sowld discretioun be   5

The clerkis takis beneficis w*ith* brawlis
Sum of sanƈt petir and sum of sanƈt pawlis
Tak he the rentis No cair hes he
Suppois the diuill tak all thair sawlis
[folio 63r]   In taking sowld discretioun be   10

Barronis takis fra the tenne*n*tis peure
all fruƈt yat growis on ye feure
In mailis and gersomes rasit ouirhie
and garris thame beg fra dur to dure
In taking sowld discretioun be   15

(2) The Maitland Folio Manuscript

[page 261]   . . .

Eftir giffing we will ſpeik of taking
Bot litle of na gude giftis forsaiking
Sum takis *our* litle authorite
And sum *our* mekle and yat is glaiking
In taiking suld discretioun be   5

Thir clarkis takkis benefices *with* bralis
Sum of sanct Petir and sum of S. paulis
sett he ye rent na cure giffis he
Suppois ye dewill tak all yair saulis
In taking ‖ –   10

Thir baronis takis frome yair tenne*n*tis pure
All fructis yat growis in ye fure
Males and gressowmes ar raisit so hie
and garris yame beg fra dur to dure
In taking ‖ –   15

Thir merchandis takis vnlesum win
Q*uhi*lk makis yair pakkis oftymes full thin
Be yair successioun ȝe may see
That ill won geir Riches not ye kin
In taking ‖ –   20

(3) Ramsay (1724): *The Ever Green, being a Collection of Scots Poems, Wrote by the Ingenious before 1600*

Follows Discration in Taking.

I

NOw after Giving I ſpeik of Taking,
But litill of ony Gude forsaiking;
Sum taks owre scrimp Autoritie,
And sum owre-mekle, and that is glaiking;
In Taking suld Discration be.   5

II

THE Clerks tak Benifices with Brawls,
Sum of Saint *Peter*, sum of Saint *Pauls*,
Take he the Rents, nae Cair hes he,
Abeit the Deil tak all thair Sauls;
In Taking suld Discration be.   10

III

BARONS tak frae thair Tennants pure
All fruit that grows upon the Feure,
In Mails and Gersomes raiſt owre hie,
And gars them beg frae Dore to Dore;
In Taking suld Discration be.

(q) Extract from 'Christ's Kirk on the Green': (1) Bannatyne Manuscript, (2) broadside, 1701, (3) Allan Ramsay's version, 1721

Christ's Kirk on the Green was part of a genre of poetry with a considerable afterlife; the tradition, for instance, underpins Robert Burns's satiric The Ordination. George Bannatyne ascribed the poem to James I, the probable author of The Kingis Quair, but this attribution seems unlikely; in the seventeenth century the attribution was shifted, equally implausibly, to James V. The rhyme **bowdin** 'swollen': **browdin** 'stained' in the Bannatyne text (after the extract given here) suggests a date after the middle of the fifteenth century; the form **bowdin** derives from an earlier **boldin**, and the rhyme would only work if *l*-vocalisation had taken place (see ch. 2, 2.22). Moreover, there are many words which *DOST* records only after 1500, e.g. **chat** 'hang' (MacLaine 1996: 156, citing advice by A. J. Aitken). Other notable forms are **gaitis** 'goats', **gympt** 'dainty', **kitteis** 'Kittys (i.e. young women)', **lynkome** 'Lincoln (i.e. green cloth)', **raffell** 'deer-skin', **schone** 'shoes', **straitis** 'cloth of single width'. For **deray** 'disturbance, disorderly revely', see Text 4(k) above.

Three parallel texts are offered here. (1) is from the Bannatyne Manuscript, already discussed (see Text 4(d) above). (2) is from a broadside of 1701 (NLS Ry.III.a.10(004)); broadsides were single sheets which were printed cheaply and circulated very widely (see further ⟨http://www.nls.uk/broadsides/index.html⟩, from which this text is taken). (3) is the version of the poem edited by Allan Ramsay in 1721; Ramsay went on to add two continuations of his own composition, cantos II and III, with the (modified) original forming canto I. For a full discussion of the texts of (1) and (3), see MacLaine 1996, which is a comprehensive study of the genre with edited texts.

The events described in Christ's Kirk on the Green take place at a fair, and several places have laid claim to being the original location.

(1) The Bannatyne Manuscript

[folio 99r]   Was nevir in scotland hard nor sene
Sic dansing nor deray
Nowthir at falkland on the grene
Nor peblis at the play
As wes of wowaris as I wene   5
At chryſt kirk on ane day
Thair come our kitteis weschin clene
In thair new kirtillis of gray full gay
At chryſtis kirk of the grene

To dans thir damysellis thame dicht 10
Thir lassis licht of laitis
Thair gluvis wes of ye raffell rycht
Thair schone wes of ye straitis
Thair kirtillis wer of lynkome licht
Weill prest *with* mony plaitis 15
Thay wer so nys quhen men thame nicht
Thay squeilit lyk ony gaitis / so lowd
    At chrystis kirk of ye grene *yat* day

Off all thir madynis myld as meid
Wes nane so gympt as gillie 20
As ony ros hir rude wes reid
he lyre wes lyk the lillie
fow ȝellow ȝellow wes hir heid
bot scho of lufe wes sillie
Thocht all hir kin had sworn hir deid 25
Scho wald haif bot sweit willie / Allone
    At chrystis kirk etc.

Scho skornit Iok and skraipit at him
and mvrionit him *with* mokkis
he wald haif luvit scho wald nocht lat him 16
for all his ȝalow loikkis
he chereist hit scho bad ga chat him
Scho compt him not twa clokkis
So schamefully his schortgoun set him
His lymmis wes lyk twa rokkis / Scho said
    At chrystis kirk etc.

(2) Broadside (1701)

The National Library of Scotland holds several broadside versions of *Christ's Kirk on the Green*, attesting to the popularity of the work as street entertainment. This example dates from 1701.

    Chrits Kirk on the Green,

Composed (as was supposed) by King *James* the fifth,
Newly Corrected according to the Original Copy.

    Was never in Scotland heard or seen,
    Such dancing and deray;
    Neither at Faukland on the green,
    nor Peebles at the play,
    As was of Woers as I ween; 5

at Chriſts Kirk on a day:
For there came Kittle washen clean,
with her new Gown of Gray,
    Full gay that day

To dance these damsels them dight,   10
these lassies light of laits
these Gloves were of the raffal right,
their shoes were of ſtraits
Their kirtles were o' linco'u light
well preſt with many plaits 15
They were so nice when men them neigh'd
they squell'd like any gaits,
    Full Loud that day.

Of all these Maidens, wild as weed,
was none so gimp as Gillie: 20
As any rose her rude was red,
her lire was like the Lillie,
But yellow, yellow was her head,
and she of love so silly;
Though all her kin had sworn her dead   25
she would have none but Willie.
    Alone that day,

She scorned Jack and scripp'd at him,
and murgeond him with mocks;
He would have loved her, she would not let him   30
for all his yellow locks.
He cherisht her, she bad go chat him
she counted him not two clocks:
So Shamefully his short jack set him,
his legs were like two rocks, 35
    or rangs that day

(3) Allan Ramsay, Poems (Ruddiman: Edinburgh, 1721)

Ramsay places a note at the foot of the page:

This Edition of the first Canto is taken from an old Manuscript Collection of Scots Poems written 150 Years ago, where it is found that James, the first of that Name, King of Scots, was the author; thought to be wrote while that brave and learned Prince was unfortunately kept Prisoner in England by Henry VI. about the Year 1412. Bellenden in his Translation of H. Boece's History, gives this Character of him, He wes weil lernit to fecht with the Swerd, to iust, to turnay, to worsyl, to syng and dance, was an expert Medicinar, rycht crafty in playing baith of Lute and

Harp, and sindry othir Instrumentis of Musik. He was expert in Gramer, Oratry and Poetry, and maid sae flowand and sententious Verses, apperit weil he was ane natural and borne Poete.

As already noted, Ramsay also added two further cantos of his own composition. Comparison of his usages with those of the other two texts is illuminating; Ramsay's interventions (or of course those of his printer) can be compared with those he undertook in Text 4(p). *Fakland* for 'Falkland' is the spelling that appears in the printed text, and may be an attempt to reflect *l*-vocalisation.

> WAS ne'er in Scotland heard or seen
> Sic Dancing and Deray;
> Nowther at *Fakland* on the Green,
> Nor *Peebles* at the Play,
> As was of Woers, as I ween, 5
> At *Christ's Kirk* on a Day;
> There came our Kitties washen clean,
> In new Kirtles of Gray,
>   Fou gay that Day.
>
> TO dance these Damesels them dight, 10
> Thir Lasses light of Laits,
> Their Gloves were of the Raffel right,
> Their Shoon were of the Straits
> Their Kirtles were of *Lincome* light,
> Well prest with mony Plaits, 15
> They were so nice when Men them nicht,
> They squeel'd like ony Gaits
>   Fou loud that Day.
>
> OF all these Maidens mild as Mead,
> Was nane sae jimp as *Gilly,* 20
> As ony Rose her Rude was red,
> Her Lire was like the Lilly:
> Fou yellow, yellow was her Head,
> But she of Love was silly;
> Tho a' her Kin had sworn her dead, 25
> She wald have but sweet *Willy*
>   Alane that Day.
>
> SHE scorned *Jack*, and scraped at him,
> And murgeon'd him with Mocks;
> He wad have loo'd, she wad na lat him, 30
> For a' his yellow Locks.
> He cherisht her, she bade gae chat him,
> Counted him not twa Clocks;

Sae shamefully his short Gown set him,
His Legs were like twa Rocks,   35
   Or Rungs that Day.

Prose

(a) Prologue and Conclusion to 'The Spectakle of Luf'

The Spectakle of Luf is an anonymous prose work surviving uniquely in the Asloan
Manuscript (MS Edinburgh, National Library of Scotland 16500); see ch. 1, 5.3 for
a discussion. John Asloan or Sloan has been identified as a notary public in Edinburgh, attested there between 1518 and 1530, and he is the main scribe of the manuscript (see Craigie 1923–5). However, Ian Cunningham has argued, on the basis of
some differences in handwriting, that *The Spectakle of Luf* was copied by M G Myll,
referred to at the end of this text and usually taken as the translator of the (lost)
work from which the text is derived (see Cunningham 1994: 130). Cunningham
suggests that this scribe could be possibly either the Gilbert Myln who appeared
as a witness in 1520, or the man of the same name who worked as a notary public
in Lanarkshire in 1545–50 (Cunningham 1994: 131); these two records, of course,
could refer to the same person. The script adopted throughout the manuscript
is 'pre-secretary hand'. For further discussion of the Asloan manuscript, see van
Buuren 1966, 1982 and Houwen 1990.

Two extracts from *The Spectakle* are offered here: the Prologue and the Conclusion. They show that the author – perhaps more correctly the translator – practised
the 'trailing' style in the manner of other late-fifteenth-/early-sixteenth-century
prose writers, such as William Caxton (see ch. 4, 3.8–3.9).

The language of the passage is consistently Scots. Old English **hw–** is reflected in
⟨quh-⟩ in **quhilk*is*, ye quhilk, quhar** and **quhy**; we might note **quhom**, sometimes
seen as a 'blend' Anglo-Scots form, but in this context probably a genuine Scottish
variant. Old English **–h–** is reflected as ⟨ch⟩ in **nocht**, and thus contracted forms
have been indicated thus, e.g. **tho*ch*tis**. Reflexes of Old English ā in ⟨a(i)⟩ and ō in
⟨u⟩ are common in the passage, e.g. **ald** 'old', **alswa, ane, hair** 'grey, hoary', **haly,
hushald, lang, mair, sa, twa** and **buk, gud**. The form **tuk** 'took' contains the reflex
of Old Norse ó, which merged with Old English ō. Thorn and 'y' are generally
undistinguished and are all recorded as ⟨y⟩ here.

The demonstrative and pronominal system of the passage is consistently Scots,
with **scho** 'she', **yai** and **yar** for 'they, their' and **yir** 'these'. Other closed-class words
prototypical of Scots include **sic** 'such', **fra** 'from'. The Norse-derived numeral
hundredth may be noted. Inflexions are also typically Scots, with **–it** as the reflex of
Present-Day English **–ed** and **–and** (present participle) in **Besekand**. The present
plural inflexion in **–ys, –is** might be noted, e.g. **cu*m*mys, apperis**, as might the
modal auxiliaries **sall, suld**.

The vocabulary of the passage contains some notable features. *DSL* records **transla-
tory** 'transitory, subject to alteration/change' only from this text. The form occurs in

OED, but with somewhat distinct meanings, and only from the eighteenth century until 1881; the citations are few, and in the nineteenth century restricted to scientific contexts, meaning 'Of or pertaining to physical translation'. The form **habound** 'abound' with initial **h–** was common in both Scots and English (alongside **abound** etc.); the initial **h–** arose, it seems, as the result of association with classical Latin **habēre** 'have'. The form **maternall** is interesting, in that in *DSL* by far the majority of citations use the word metaphorically in relation to **toung**, **langage** etc.; the only citation in *DSL* with its literal use is from Gavin Douglas's translation of the *Aeneid*. It may be noted that the earliest citation in *OED* (1481, in Caxton's *Myrrour of the Worlde*) is similarly metaphorically applied to language. The form **spreit** 'spirit', derived from Old French **esprit** rather than from Latin **spīritus**, is similarly prototypical, with this meaning, of Scots and northern English. Finally, the expression **naturall philosophy** might be noted, referring to what we would now call natural science, i.e. 'The study of natural bodies and the phenomena connected with them' (*OED*).

(1) The Prologue

137r   As I was musing vpone ye reſtles besynes of this | *[folio 137v]* translatory warld quhilk*is* tho*ch*t*is* and fantesyes tru|blit my ſpreit And for to devoyd me of sic ymagy-|nationis I tuk a lytill buk in latyn to pass myn | tyme ye quhilk as I had red and consederit me | tho*ch*t the mater gud and proffitable to
5   be had in | to our wulgar and maternall toung, for to caus | folk*is* to mair eschew ye deleᴄtatioun of the flesche | quhilk is ye modir of all vicis Tharfor be ye suf|ferans of god I purpois to endur me to the trans-|latioun of ye samyn becaus of ye gud and prof-|fitable mater It treitis of/ yat was How a gud | anceant kny*ch*t yat in his ȝouthheid had frequentit | his body in ye deid*is*
10   of chevalrye to the encressing | of his name to hono*ur* no*ch*twithſtanding his gret bes-|ynes in ye faᴄtis merciall Inlykwys he had occupijt | him self in ye ſtudy of naturall philosophy to ye | end yat he suld eschew vice The quhilk gud | ald kny*ch*t opnyt and declarit vnto a ȝoung squy|ar his sone yat was to gretly amorus ye evillis | and myshappis yat me*n* cu*m*mys to throw
15   ye gret | plesans yai haif in weme*n* be ye deleᴄtatioun of | ye flesche except ye luf quhilk Is detfully vsit in | ye haly band of matermoney tuiching ye quhilk I | will no*ch*t ſpeik in my sempill translatioun bese|king all ladyes and gentillweme*n* quhar It Is said | in ony poynt to yar disſpleso*ur* yai put no*ch*t ye blai*m* | yerof to me bot to myn auᴄto*ur* yat was ye fyrſt compylar | of yis buk
20   ye quhilk is Intitillit & callit ye ſpec-|takle of luf for in it apperis & schawis su*m* evillis & | myshappis yat cu*m*mys to me*n* yerthrow as ye filth or | ſpottis of ye face schawis i*n* ye myrro*ur* of glas. |

(2) Conclusion

149v   The conclusion of yis lytill buk and ye | excusatioun of ye translato*ur* |

  MY sone I haif in entent to caus ye to abſtene | fra sic fleschly deleᴄtationis quhilk yow callis | luf firſt schawyn ye diᴄtis & saying*is* of diuers

haly|doctouris & gret philosophouris Secundly I haif schawin ye|quhy ye
foull lust generalye Is to be forborne with all|wemen excepe ye haly band   5
of matermoney And yera-|pone I tald ye mony notable examplis Alswa
I|haif schawyn ye quhy yat delectatioun Is to be eschewit|with madynis
or wemen of 3oung age I haif Inlykwys|schawyn ye quhy ye foull syne &
delectatioun of adultre|Is to be eschewit quharapone I haif schawin ye
diuers|& famous historijs Consequentlye I haif schawyn ye|quhy ye luf   10
of wedowis & agit wemen Is to be for-|borne All yar last I haif schawyn ye
quhy the delec-|tatioun of nunnis or relegious wemen Is to be|eschewit
with sum notable examplis quhilk suld gyf ye|or ony man of wysdom
occasioun to abstene yarfra|Quharfor my sone gyf yow will pleis god
Incres|in honour & richeis in yis warld to cheis ye a wyf|cummyn of a gud   15
hous & lynage yat hir parentis and|frendis has bene honest & chaist & of
gud gouernans yat|Is of 3ung age & vnbrocht in evill techis & thewis &
kepe hir yar in vnder ye dreid of awe or ellis scho|sall neuer dreid ye nor
set bye ye bot throw ye|evill Inclynatioun yat wemen Is of quhar yai haif
ye|maistrye or brydill at yar will grow to ye maneris|of yir wemen befor   20
wrytyn And yus leif with hir|[folio 150r] Vnder ye haly band of matermoney
And happines|sall habound to ye And skaipe and be [. . . illegible]|yir And
mony vyar perrellis Wrytyn in yis lytill|buk quhilk Is entetillit or callit
ye spectakle of|luf or delectatioun of wemen translatit out of|latyn in to
our wulgar and maternall toung at|The cyte of Sanctandrois The x day of   25
Julij The 3er|of god ane thowsand four hundreth nyntye and|twa 3eiris
be ane clerk quhilk had bene In to|Venus court mair yan ye space of xx
3eris quhill|I mycht nocht mak ye seruice yat I had bene accustomyd|to
do quharfor I was put out of hir byll of hus-|hald howbeit to gyf example
till all vyeris to|perseveir in ye seruice of luf at my deperting scho|gaif me   30
thre gyftis lyk as scho dois to all yaim|yat contynewis in to hyr cowrt That
Is an|ald hair and dotand heid ane emptyff and|twme purs And ane pair of
beidis of sabill|To caus me for to haif remembrans yat I had|bene sa lang
in to hyr seruice Besekand [Besekand deleted]|heirfor all ladyes damesellis
And gentill we-|men of ane gud fame quhat at yis lytill sober|tretys Is   35
said in ony thing vyerwayes na weill|To haif me excusit As I wate at yair
will|ffor I wate weill yair Is nane yat will haif|disdene heir at bot gyf yai be
of ye condici-|onis of yir ladyes yat Is befor wrytyn|considerand my gud
intensioun And quhair|[folio 150v] [. . . torn page] said or to 3our displesour
in ony poynt yat|[. . . torn page] emput ye falt to yame that commyttit   40
sic|[. . . torn page] And him yat was ye first compylar herof|and nocht to
me yat bot translatit yat I fand befor|wrytyn to ye effect yat euery man and
woman suld|eschew vyce and pleis ye glorius lord quhom mot|bryng ws
to his blys withoutyn end Amen|

Explicit the spectakle of luf per|M G Myll| 45

(b) Extract from John Gau, 'The Richt Vay to the Kingdom of Heuine'

John Gau or Gaw died *c.* 1553. Little is known of this Protestant reformer, who wrote one of the first texts in Scots from the reformed point of view. He may have been a graduate of the University of St Andrews, where in 1528 Patrick Hamilton was burned for heresy at the gates of St Salvator's College; Gau may have gone into exile as a result of this event. He spent the rest of his life in Scandinavia, first in Sweden and then in Denmark, where he became Lutheran chaplain in Copenhagen. *The Richt Vay to the Kingdom of Heuine*, which was printed in Malmö, was a translation of Christiern Pedersen's Danish *Den rette vey till hiemmerigis rige* (1531), itself based on a German work (see Gau's *ODNB* entry for further information). The book contains extracts from the Bible translated into Scots, and is therefore discussed in Graham Tulloch's history of the Scots Bible (see Tulloch 1989). It was probably composed in about 1533.

The work is printed, like many early printed books, in black-letter; a facsimile may be found on *EEBO*, and there is also a nineteenth-century edition published by STS (Law and Mitchell 1888). There is no pagination. The title page reads as follows: The richt|vay to the kingdome of he|uine is techit heir in the X co[m] |mandis of God/ And in the|Creid/ and Pater noster/|In the quhilk al chrissine me[n]|sal find al thing yat is ned|ful and requirit to onderstand|to the saluation of|the saul|. Gau's book thus engages with the doctrinal 'kit' shared by all Catholics and Protestants during the sixteenth century: the *Ten Commandments*, the *Apostles' Creed*, the *Lord's Prayer*, and the *Ave Maria* or 'Hail Mary' (see further MacCulloch 2003: 709–11). The passage below is part of Gau's discussion of the role of the Virgin Mary, demonstrating his distinctively restricted, Protestant view of her function in the Christian narrative; it may be noted that there is no reference to the *Ave Maria* on the title page.

Several forms characteristic of Scots appear in the text, e.g. **quhilk, quhair** and **quhen**; the form **quhom** also appears. Old English ō is reflected in ⟨ui⟩ in **guid(nes)**, and Old English ā is reflected in ⟨a⟩ in **ane, sua** and **alanerlie**. The form **alene** 'alone' is a little puzzling; *DSL*'s citation of the form is from Gau's text. *DSL* sees the form as 'north-eastern Sc[ots]', representing the extra raising of Middle Scots /eː/ in the environment of a following nasal (see also Text 5(j) below); see also **neyne** 'none'. Also common in Scots are the modal verbs **sal, suld** (cf. Present-Day English 'shall', 'should'), third person pronouns in the oblique cases in ⟨th-⟩, e.g. **thair, thayme**, and inflexions in in –**it**, e.g. **blissit**. The form **schw** 'she' (cf. more prototypically Scots **scho**) is distinctive; *DSL* cites Gau as the main source, but also the *Glasgow Diocesan Register* of 1521. The text's Scots has been influenced in places by German and Danish practice; Graham Tulloch notes the use of **s3** for s(s) in places, which may reflect German practice, and common use of **v** for **w** which may be influenced by Danish use (e.g. **ves3** 'was'), although v for w and vice versa are fairly common in sixteenth-century Scots; cf. **veilbelouit** 'wellbeloved' alongside **weilbelowit**, **lowe** 'love', **vardill** 'world'. However, Gau often models his vocabulary on Danish, e.g. **leirfeders** 'masters of learning' (cf. Danish **lerefedre**) (not in the passage given here; see further Tulloch 1989: 10–11, Corbett 1999: 60–1). There are of course many words which seem to be restricted to Older Scots or Northern Middle English, e.g. **sternis** 'stars'. In stylistic terms Gau's work prefigures the 'plain style' favoured by John Knox and other reformed writers (see further Lyall 1988). The form **3eird** 'earth' derives from an Old English by-form with intial **ge-**.

Of the Aue Maria

HEir euerie man sal mark that neyne sal put thair hop in the virgine Maria or
trow that schw cane saiff ony man for prayer or seruice dwne to hir Thairfor
euerie man sal put thair hop alanerlie in Jesu Chriſt for thair is na oder
saluiour bot he alene/ quhilk gaiff hime selff in redemptione for al/ as S. Paul   5
vritis in ye ii chaiptur of ye firſt epiſtil to Thimothe/ This is ye greitaſt seruice
a[n]d honour that man cane dw to God to trow in his sone quhome he send in
ye vardil as our saluiour sais inye vi chaiptur of S. Jhone Thairfor euerie man
sal lowe and thank God for the greit grace quhilk he gaiff to *[new page]* hir/
nay man sal lowe hir oderwis3 bot that schw gat that greit grace of ye guidnes   10
of God without hir meritis that he maid hir vorthty to beir his veilbelouit
sone as hir selff said in ye Magnificat/ god hes lukit apone ye powerte of his
madine or seruand/ schw extollit notht hir selff of hir humilite or meiknes
(as mony sais without onderſta[n]di[n]g) for yat haid beyn prid a[n]d fine
and schw haid dwne sua/ bot schw lowit God quhilk maid hir vorthty of his   15
guidnes and grace and chosit hir to beir his sone quhair schw ves3 pwir and
lichtlit in the vardil/ quhen ane man seis the sone or the mwne or the ſternis
or ony oder plesand creaturs thane thay giff occasione to lowe and thank God
quhilk maid thayme and to say blissit be thow almichtine God of al thy angels
and sanctis and of al thy creaturs quhilk thow hes maid in heuine and 3eird/   20
sua suld we dw and say of the virgine Maria O almichtine and merciful God
blissit be thow quhilk maid that plesand crea-*[new page]*tur ye virgine Maria
and gaiff hir sa greit grace and honour to be the Moder of thy weilbelowit
sone our saluiour/ giff ws3 al grace yat we may thank the thair for without
ony end/ we suld sua think in our hart of hir in our prayer/ yat we put notht   25
our hop in hir bot in Jesu chriſt our lord and saluiour and mediatur betuix
ws3 and the fader/ we may sua remember of hir and of oder sanctis in our
prayer/ O almichtine God quhilk gaiff the virgine Maria and Peter and Paul
and N N. say greit faith and grace yat thay trowit alanerlie in the/ giff vs3 pwir
sinners grace yat we may alsua trowe in ye and lowe and thank ye for euer   30
in the heuine/ sua we may pray for al thingis quhilk ar neidful to ws3 and
traiſt alanerlie in God That he may giff ws3 thayme/ Thairfor chrissine reder
consider the Aue Maria perfitlie and thow sal find yat is* giffis the lowine of
al guid quhilk wes3 in hir to God

sic; error for **it**.

(c) Extract from John Knox, 'The First Blast of the Trumpet against the Monstruous Regiment of Women'

Knox's arguably most famous work, published in 1558, has the following on its title-page:

THE FIRST | BLAST OF THE | TRUMPET AGAINST |
THE MONSTRVOVS | regiment of | women. | Veritas temporis filia. |
M. D. LVIII. |

No indication is given on the title page of author, place or printer, but the evidence is that the work was printed in Geneva, by James Poullain and Antoine Rebul. The book is printed throughout in roman type; a facsimile appears on *EEBO*. The book is foliated rather than paginated. Several marginal notes are supplied, in italics; since these have some interest, I have supplied them here at the end of the passage, inserting numbers to indicate their approximate position.

The work was revolutionary. The term **regiment** has, of course, its older meaning, i.e. 'rule'. Knox's book was interpreted by contemporaries as an attack on Mary Tudor in England and Mary of Guise in Scotland: two Catholic queens. John Calvin regretted that the notoriety of the work had harmed Geneva's reputation; Knox himself held later that he had been misinterpreted, in that his arguments were general rather than particular, and he later explained to Elizabeth I and Mary Queen of Scots that divine providence could over-rule the general law of God which forbade female rule. Neither queen seems to have been convinced by this argument (*ODNB*).

The text as printed below is written in English, and there are no distinctively Scots forms; **suppostes** 'servants' is also found in (for instance) Caxton's writings. It is provided here as an example of part of the 'linguistic landscape' available in writing in sixteenth-century Scotland. However, there are linguistic features which Knox's contemporaries would have noticed as signs of his Protestant ideology, e.g. the use of the term **godlie** (see Text 4(i)). For a discussion of Knox's style in this passage, see ch. 4, 3.13. Marginal notes in the original are marked by numbers in the text, e.g. (1) etc.

2r THE KINGDOME APPERTEINETH TO OVR *God.*

VVonder it is, that amongeſt so many pregnant wittes as the Ile of greate Brittanny hath p[ro]duced, so many godlie and zelous preachers as England did somtime norishe, and amongeſt so many learned and men of graue
5 iudgement, as this day by Iesabel are exiled, none is found so ſtowte of courage, so faithfull to God, nor louing to their natiue countrie, that they dare admonishe the inhabitantes of that Ile how abominable before God, is the Empire or Rule of a wicked woman, yea of a traiteresse and baſtard. And what may a people or nation left deſtitute of a lawfull head, do by the authoritie of
10 Goddes worde in electing and appointing common rulers and magiſtrates. That Ile (alas) for the contempt and horrible abuse of Goddes mercies of- *[folio 2v]* fred, and for the shamefull reuolting to Satan frome Chriſt Iesus, and frome his Goſþell ones professed, doth iuſtlie merite to be left in the handes of their own counsel, and so to come to co[n]fusion and bondage of ſtrangiers. But

yet I feare that this vniuersall neglige[n]ce of such as somtimes were estemed   15
watchemen (1), shall rather aggrauate our former ingratitude, then excuse
this our vniuersall and vngodlie silence, in so weightie a mater. We se our
countrie set furthe for a pray to foreine nations, we heare the blood of our
brethren, the me[m]bres of Christ Iesus most cruellie to be shed, and the
monstruous empire of a cruell woman (the secrete counsel of God excepted)   20
we knowe to be the onlie occasion of all these miseries: and yet with silence
we passe the time as thogh the mater did nothinge appertein to vs. But the
co[n]trarie examples of the auncient prophetes (2) moue me to doubte of
this our fact. For Israel did vniuersalie decline frome God by embrasing
idolatrie vnder Ie- *[folio 3r]* roboam. In whiche they did continue euen vnto   25
the destruction of their common welthe (3). And Iuda withe Ierusalem did
followe the vile superstition and open iniquitie of Samaria (4). But yet ceased
not the prophetes of God to admonishe the one and the other: Yea euen after
that God had poured furthe his plagues vpon them (5). For Ieremie did write
to the captiues of Babylon, and did correct their errors, plainlie instructing   30
them, who did remaine in the middest of that idolatrouse nation. Ezechiel
(6) frome the middest of his brethren prisoners in Chaldea, did write his
vision to those that were in Ierusalem, and sharplie rebukinge their vices,
assured them that they shuld not escape the vengeance of God by reason of
their abominations committed.   35

    The same prophetes for comfort of the afflicted and chosen saintes of
God, who did lie hyd amongest the reprobate of that age (7) (as co[m]mon-
lie doth the corne amongest the chaffe) did pro-*[folio 3v]* phecie and before
speake the changes of kingdomes, the punishmentes of tyrannes, and the
vengeance (8) whiche God wold execute vpon the oppressors of his people.   40
The same did Daniel and the rest of the prophetes euerie one in their season.
By whose examples and by the plaine precept, which is geuen to Ezechiel,
commanding him that he shall say to the wicked: Thou shalt die the death.
We in this our miserable age are bounde to admonishe (9) the world a[n]
d the tyra[n]nes thereof, of their sodeine destruction, to assure them, and   45
to crie vnto them, whether they list to heare or not. That the blood of the
saintes, (10) which by them is shed, co[n]tinuallie crieth and craueth vengeance in the presence of the Lorde of hostes. And further it is our dutie to
open the truthe reueled vnto vs, vnto the ignorant and blind world, vnlest
that to our owne co[n]demnation we list to wrap vp and hyde the talent   50
committed to our charge. I am assured that God hath reueled to some in
this our age, that it is more *[folio 4r]* then a mo[n]stre in nature, that a woman
shall reigne a[n]d haue empire aboue man. And yet with vs all, there is
suche silence, as if God therewith were nothing offended. The naturall man,
ennemy to God shall fynd, I knowe, many causes why no suche doctrine   55
oght to be published in these our dangerous dayes (11). First, for that it
may seme to tend to sedition: secondarilie, it shal be dangerous not onlie
to the writer or publisher, but also to all such as shall read the writinges,

or fauor this truth ſpoken: and laſt it shall not amend the chief offend-
60 ers, partlie because it shall neuer come to their eares, and partlie because
they will not be admonished in such cases. I answer, yf any of these be a
sufficient reason that a truth knowen shalbe co[n]celed, then were the auncient prophetes of God very fooles, who did not better prouide for their
owne quietnes, then to hasard their liues for rebuking of vices, and for the
65 opening of such crimes, as were not knowen to the world. And Chriſt Iesus
did iniurie to *[folio 4v]* his Apoſtles, comma[n]ding them to preache repentance and remission of synnes in his name to euerie realme and nation. And
Paule did not vnderſtand his owne libertie, when he cried, wo be to me, if I
preache not the Euangile (12). Yf feare, I say, of persecution, of sclander, or
70 of any inconuenience before named might have excused, a[n]d discharged
the seruantes of God, from plainlie rebuking the sinnes of the world, iuſte
cause had euerie one of them to haue ceased frome their office (13). For
sodeinlie their doctrine was accused by termes of sedition, of newe learning,
and of treason: persecution and vehement trouble did shortlie come vpon
75 the professours with the preachers: kinges, princes and worldlie rulers did
conſpire againſt God and againſt his anoynted Chriſt Iesus. But what? Did
any of these moue the prophetes and Apoſtles to faynt in their vocation? no.
But by the resiſtance, whiche the deuill made to them by his suppoſtes, were
they the more inflamed to publishe the truthe reueled *[folio 5r]* vnto them
80 and to witnesse with their blood, that greuous condemnation and Goddes
heuie vengeance shuld folowe the proude contempt of graces offred. The
fidelitie, bold courage, and co[n]ſtancie of those that are passed before vs,
oght to p[ro]uoke vs to folowe their footſteppes, onles we loke for an other
kingdome then Chriſt hath p[ro]mised to such as perseuere in p[ro]fession
85 of his name to the end. Yf any think that the empire of women, is not of such
importance, that for the suppressing of the same, any ma[n] is bounde to
hasarde his life, I answer, that to suppresse it, is in the ha[n]d of god alone.
But to vtter the impietie and abomination of the same, I say, it is the dutie of
euerie true messager of God, to whome the truth is reueled in that behalfe.
90 For the eſpeciall dutie (14) of Goddes messagers is to preache repenta[n]ce,
to admonishe the offenders of their offenses, and to say to the wicked, thou
shalt die the death, except thou repent. This, I truſt, will no man denie to be
the propre office of all Goddes messa- *[folio 5v]* gers to preache (as I haue said)
repentance and remission of synnes. But nether of both can be done, except
95 the co[n]science of the offenders be accused and conuicted of transgression.
For howe shall any man repe[n]t not knowing wher in he hath offended?
And where no repentance is founde (15), there can be no entrie to grace.
And therfore I say, that of necessitie it is, that, this monſtriferouse empire of
women, (which amongeſt all enormities, that this day do abound vpon the
100 face of the hole earth, is moſt deteſtable and damnable) be openlie reueled
and plainlie declared to the world, to the end that some may repent and be
saued. And thus farre to the firſt sorte.

Marginal notes:

(1) *Negligence of watchemen.*
(2) *The dilige[n]ce of the olde prophetes of God.*
(3) *1. Reg. 12.*
(4) *Ezech. 16.*
(5) *Ierem. 29.*
(6) *Ezech. 7, 8, 9.*
(7) *God alway has his people amongest the wicked, who neuer lacked their prophetes and teachers.*
(8) *Isaie 13, Ierem. 46, Ezech. 36.*
(9) *Examples what teachers oght to do in this time.*
(10) *Ezech. 2, Apoca. 6.*
(11) *These chef reasons, that do stay man from speaking the truthe.*
(12) *1 Cor. 9.*
(13) *Mat. 26, Act. 18, 21.*
(14) *It is necessarie for euerie ma[n] to ope[n] the impietie, whiche he knoweth to hurt his co[m]monwelth.*
(15) *No man can repe[n]t except he knowe his synne.*

(d) Extract from Nicol Burne, 'Disputation'

The next two texts are placed together as examples of the kind of language used by Catholic controversialists writing for a Scots-reading audience during the middle and later years of the sixteenth century. Facsimiles of both are on *EEBO*.

Burne's *Disputation,* **Imprented at Parise the first day of**|October. | **1581.** |, has a lengthy autobiographical text on the title-page:

> THE | DISPUTATION | CONCERNING THE | CONTROVERSIT HEADDIS | of Religion, haldin in the Realme of | Scotland, the zeir of God ane thou- | sand, fyue hundreth fourscoir | zeiris. Betuix. | The prætendit Ministeris of the deformed Kirk | in Scotland. | And, | Nicol Burne Professor of philosophie in S. | Leon-ardis college, in the Citie of Sanctan- | drois, brocht vp from his tender eage in the | peruersit sect of the Caluinistis, and nou be | ane special grace of God, ane membre of the halie and Catholik kirk. | Dedicat | To his Souerane the kingis M. of Scotland, | King Iames the Saxt. | Nisi conuersi fueritis, gladium suum vibrabit: arcum | suum tetendit, & parauit illum. I. | Vnles ze be conuerted, God vil draw his suord: he hes | bendit his bovv, and preparit it | Psalm.7. |

The title-page demonstrates rather well the attempt to assert the author's Catholic faith but also, through the dedication to the king, to refute accusations of treason. When *The Disputation* was published, Burne had just arrived in Paris, banished from Scotland; he seems never to have returned. (For a text of the poem attached to some copies of the text and usually ascribed to Burne, *Ane Admonition to the Anti-christian Ministers in the Deformit Kirk of Scotland,* see Cranstoun 1891: 333–45).

The Disputation is, according to *ODNB,* 'not a work of sophisticated theological argument. It is, rather, a piece of vigorous polemical writing, shrewd, scurrilous, and occasionally obscene.' It is also written in Scots, and there are several notable features in the passage below. Old English **hw–** is reflected in ⟨quh-⟩ in **quha, quhilk, quhairof**, while the reflex of Old English –h– appears as ⟨ch⟩ in **brocht, nocht, socht**. There are many words containing the reflex of Old English ā in ⟨a(i/y)⟩, e.g. **ane, bayth, haldin, halie, maist, saulis** and **salang** (*sic*) 'so long', although we might note **onlie** 'only'. Reflexes of Old English ō are less frequent, but we might note **blude, gude**. Inflexions are less prototypical of Scots, with the present participle inflexion in –**ing**, and reflexes of Present-Day English –ed in –**ed**, beside more common –**it**. The prototypically Scots auxiliary **sal** (cf. Present-Day English 'shall') appears, as does **sic** 'such and **thair** 'their'. The Norse-derived forms **hundreth** 'hundred' and **kirk** may be noted. The form **mentenar** 'upholder' is of interest; the word had courtly connotations in Older Scots, as witnessed by the citations in *DSL*.

The opening sentence from the dedicatory epistle appears below.

a ij TO THE MAIST NOBIL, POTENT AND GRATIOVS *king of Scotland king Iames the saxt.*

SIndrie and vechtie reasonis (My Souerane) mouis me not onlie to haue Zour M. in gude remembrance in my daylie prayeris, bot also to confess
5 my verie erneaſt affectione in offering my humil seruice bayth be vord and vritt salang as the æternal God sal prolong my dayis in this vail of miserie: This I am bund to do alsueil be command of the æternal God, quha inioynis to inferiore subiectis al deu obedience touardis thair Souerane pouaris and Magiſtratis: as be the inæſtimable benefeit quhilk I receauit of zour hienes
10 clemencie aganis the traitorous dealing of sik malitious personis, as cruellie socht the schedding of my innocent blude: For being impresoned firſt in the caſtel of Sanctandrois, and nixt in the tolbuith of Edinburgh, nocht for onie euil doing, bot for oppin professione of the treu and Catholik Religion, quhilk nocht onlie al kingis and Quenis hes euer mentenit in zour hienes impyre,
15 bot thairin also zour M. (be the maiſt sollicit cair of zour darreſt mother our Souerane the Quenis grace, ane maiſt conſtant mentenar of the treuth) vas maid participant of the sacramentis of Baptisme and Confirmation: And quhairof lykuyse God of his infinit gudnes granted me knaulege to my æternal saluatione, deliuering me out of the thraldome and bondage of that
20 idolatrous Caluinisme, vith the quhilk (alace) manie be ane blind zeal ar fraudfullie deceauit to the lamentabill perdition of thair auin saulis, except be earneſt repentance ſpedelie that returne to thair ſpiritual mother the halie Catholik kirk.

(e) *Extract from Ninian Winzet, 'Buke of Fourscoir-thre Questionis'*

Like Burne's *Disputation*, Winzet's *Buke* has a lengthy title-page, printed in an italic font:

The buke of fourscoir-|thre questions, tueching doctrine, ordour,|and maneris proponit to ye prechouris of|ye Protestants in Scotland, be ye Catholiks|of ye inferiour ordour of clergie and layt|men yair, cruelie afflictit and dispersit, be | persuasioun of ye saidis intrusit precheours. | Set furth be Niniane VVinzet a Catholik | Preist, at ye desyre of his faythfull affli-|ctit brethir, and deliuerit to Iohne Knox | ye .xx. of Februar or yairby, in ye zere | of the blissit birth of our Saluiour, 1561. | Ne sis sapiens apud temetipsum. Prouerb .iij. | Sed interroga patres tuos, & annunciabunt | tibi: maiores tuos, & dicent tibi. Deu .xxxij. | ANTVVER-PIÆ | Ex officina Ægidij Dicst. M. D.lxiij.xiij Octob. | Cum Gratia & Priuilegio. |

As with Text 5(d), the opening sentence from the preface *to ye Christiane Reidar*, again printed in an italic font, is given here.

Winzet was a well-known controversialist, and his argument with Knox, which included an accusation that Knox had discarded his handling of Scots, is often cited (see ch. 1, 3.11 above). *The Buke of Fourscoir-Thre Questions* was published in Antwerp in 1563, as part of a long-running programme of publication against Protestants, notably Knox (whom he does not seem to have met). He returned to England, and briefly Scotland in 1571, but eventually settled as abbot of the Scots monastery of Regensburg (Ratisbon), in Bavaria, dying there in 1592. Winzet's career began in Linlithgow, where he taught at the grammar school, and was a parish chaplain and notary public; the passage below is biographical.

The passage contains several Scots features. Old English **hw**– is reflected in ⟨quh-⟩ in **quhen, quhais**, and –h– in ⟨ch⟩ in **nocht, micht, thocht**. Old English ā/Old Norse á appears as ⟨a⟩ in **fra, na**. Present-Day English –**ed** appears as –**it**. Other notable forms include **sik** 'such' and **yair, yame** 'their, them'. The construction **yai suffer** is good Scots; according to the Northern Pesonal Pronoun Rule, the present plural inflexion –**is** is added only when the personal pronoun is not immediately adjacent.

The form **tribules** is worth noting; *DSL* would derive the form (not cited from here) from Old French **trubler**, late Latin **turbulare**, but *OED* gives a different etymology, deriving the form from the verb **tribul**, both noun and verb being flagged as 'Chiefly Sc[ottish]. Obs[olete]'. *OED* derives the verb from Old French **triboler**, Latin **trībulāre**. *OED* glosses the noun **tribule** as 'tribulation, distress, affliction', citing only Gavin Douglas's translation of the *Aeneid*, *The Complaynt of Scotland*, and (twice) Winzet's tract.

A ij *Niniane Winzet a catholik Preist to ye Christiane Reidar wisshis grace, and peace. AT the command of Dene Patrik Kinloquhy precheour in Linlythqow and of his superintendent, gentil Reidar, quhen I, for denying only to subscriue yair phantasie and factioun of faith, wes expellit and Schott out of yat my kyndly toun, and fra my tender Freindis yair, quhais perpetuall Kyndnes I* 5
hoipit yat I had conquest, be ye spending about ten zeris of maist flurissing aige, nocht without manifest vtilitie of yair commoun welth, and be all apperance had obtenit sik fauour of yame, as ony sik man micht haif of ony communitie: I thocht I had na cause to be eschameit, bot to reiose and glorifie my God (according to S. Petiris reull) for yat I sufferit nocht, as a wickit persoun, or 10
an ewill doar, bot as an wnfenziet and faithfull Christiane: for ye tyme is now (as ye samin Apostill writtis) yat ye terribill iugement tocum, in a manere in yis lyfe beginnis at ye houss of God: yat is, at ye faithfull catholikis, yat first for yair awin sinnis, and syne for ye trewthis saik yai suffer in yis lyfe with Christe yair heid, yat be diuers tribules yai mot enter with him ye lyfe eternall. 15

(f) Extract from George Buchanan, 'The Chamaeleon'

For a biography of Buchanan and an account of the background to *The Chamaeleon*, see ch. 4, 3.11. The work, composed in 1570, survives in a single sixteenth-century text in the Cotton collection: MS London, British Library Cotton Caligula C.iii, a composite manuscript containing various items of correspondence, including indictments, letters between Elizabeth I and Mary Queen of Scots, and notes by the 'intelligencer' William Herle. The text of *The Chamaeleon* begins on folio 280r. It is written in a neat but faint variety of secretary script, distinct from Buchanan's own clear hand (for which see Text 2(j)).

Buchanan wished to have the work printed by Robert Lekprevik, but it was suppressed, not being printed until 1710; the work does, however, seem to have circulated '*sub rosa*' (McFarlane 1981: 337). An account survives, from 1571, of how far Maitland of Lethington, the target of Buchanan's satire, was prepared to go to secure the manuscript. The reference to **Robert Lekprevickis hous** may be noted (cited Brown 1892: 39; see also Cranstoun 1891: liv–lix).

> This nycht at ewin, about xj houris, captane Meluine comes vnto Robert Lekprev-
> ickis hous, and socht him (as he had done twyse of befoir), and louket all the hous
> for the Camelione, which the Secretar fearit that he had prentit; bot he, beand
> wairned befoir, escapit, and went out of his hous with sic thingis as he feared sould
> have hurt him, gif thai had bein gottin.

Lekprevik seems to have been given sufficient warning about Captain Melvin's plans to allow him to leave with his printing equipment. He moved first to Stirling and later to St Andrews; he returned to Edinburgh in 1573 (Dickson and Edmond 1890: 204–5).

The passage cited in ch. 4 is near the opening of the work. The passage below, from later in the text, deals with the Chamaeleon's (i.e. Maitland's) role – in Buchanan's view, a despicable one – during Mary's deposition and imprisonment in Lochleven Castle. As well as being written in Buchanan's Ciceronian prose, it contains many Scots forms, e.g. **efter**, **–it**, **gar**, **quhen**, **quhilk**, **scho** etc.; **–in**, which may be deemed a reduced form derived from **–and**, is used alongside **–ing** for the present participle inflexion (although note **–eth** in the passage in ch. 4, e.g. **clymeth** 'climbs'). The French expression **ane ligue defensive** may also be noted. The passage is printed in Brown's edition of Buchanan's vernacular writings (1892: 47–8). The page is slightly damaged on the right-hand side, and I have supplied some readings, placed in square brackets just before line-endings, from Brown's edition. For Bothwell, see Text 1(f); for a letter by Buchanan, see Text 2(j).

282r Now to returne agane to o*ur* propose efter ye deid of ye king | devysit be him/
executit be ye erll boithuile/ for feir of ye s*aid* | erll he lurkit ʾa quhileʾout of
court vntill ye tyme ye quene at Carberrie [Hill *supplied*] | come to ye lordis.
and ye erll boithuile fled to Dunbar/ Than [he *supplied*] | come to p*ar*liament/
5 and w*ith* sum otheris p*ar*ticipant of the kingis sl[aughter *supplied*] | wald haif
had ye quene slane be a*ct* of p*ar*liament/ And not finding | mony consenting
yairto/ and s̷pecialie ye erll of murray yan c[hosen *supplied*] | regent beyng in
ye contrair/ [h *deleted*] he sollicitat some prevue men [to *supplied*] | gar hang

hir on hir bed with hir awin belt that be yat way he | and his partinaris in ye
kingis murthour mycht be deliuerit of an | witnesse/ knawing weil ye quenis   10
nature yat quhen scho wes | misscontent of ony man scho wald tell all sic
secreittis as scho [did *supplied*] | knaw of him/ This propose not proceeding
as he desyrit/ he t[urnit *supplied*] | [firſt *deleted*] him ˈfirſtˈin flatteryng with
ye quene and send to hir being in Lo[ch *supplied*] | levin ane piᴄture of ye
deliuerance of ye lyoun by ye mouse/ and | nixt turnit his haill wit to ye   15
diſtruᴄtion of ye erll of murray | Thinking yat ye wickit could not proffeit
greitlie so iuſt a man | having ye supreme power And als seing yat ye quenis
craftynes | wes abill at ye lang. to owerthraw ye erll of murrayis sempilnes | So
he bendit all his wittis to ye said erllis eversioun and ye quenis | reſtitutioun
and procedit in yis caise partlie be making ane faᴄtioun | of ye counsalleris   20
and partakeris of ye kingis murthoure of men lycht | of fantase and covatous of
geir partlie be corrupting of my lord | of murrayis freindis and seruandis/ and
travellit princypallie with ye | Laird of grange/ thinking yat it sould be ane greit
ſtrenth to ye | faᴄtioun to haue ye caſtell of Edinburgh at yair command. | The
regent being diuers tymes aduertisit of yir praᴄtiȝis wes | of so upricht nature   25
yat he wald beleif na thing of ony yat he had | takin in freindschip/ quhilk he
wald not haif done him self/ And | als mony of ye faᴄtioun in ye begynning
thocht it had bene bot ane | [b *deleted*] ligue defensive aganis ye power of ye
great yat is accuſtumat | to owerthraw the small in tyme of troubill. |

(g) *Extract from Robert Lindsay of Pitscottie, 'The Historie and Cronikles of Scotland'*

For Robert Lindsay of Pitscottie (*c.* 1532–*c.* 1592), see ch. 4, 3.9 above. Pitscottie's
history, probably composed in the 1570s, survives in several manuscripts from the
sixteenth, seventeenth and early eighteenth centuries (see Mackay 1899: lix–xciii);
MS I (*olim* Phillipps 1023, now Edinburgh, National Library of Scotland Acc. 9769)
seems to have been marked up for printing, although no printed edition is known
until 1728. The basis of the text given here is MS A (MS Edinburgh, University
Library Laing III.218), which dates from the end of the sixteenth century. (For a
recent discussion of MS I, see Hadley Williams 2010.)

The passage is from chapter 12 of the *Historie and Cronikles*, and describes the
burning of George Wishart at St Andrews in 1546. Wishart's death, as already noted
in Text 1(e), was a key event in the Scottish Reformation. Although his martyrdom
left Scottish Protestantism temporarily without a leader – a vacuum eventually to
be filled by John Knox – Wishart's example impressed many, not least because of
his earlier career as a charismatic preacher. The cardinal referred to below was
Cardinal Beaton, who was shortly afterwards assassinated; see references in Text
1(e) above.

The text contains many Scots features, though there are variants where Old
English **hw-** is generally reflected in **quh-** in this text, even if often as part of a
contracted form, e.g. **quhene, quhilk, quho**; we might note the more prototypically
English **whome**. Old English –h– is generally reflected in ⟨ch⟩ in this text, though

here in contracted forms, e.g. **brocht**; see also **might**. The reflex of Old English ā is ⟨a(i)⟩ in **ane, stane** and **taiken** 'token', but we might note **botht** 'both'; 'poor' (cf. Anglo-Norman **pover** etc.) appears as **poore, poure**. Old English ō appears as ⟨u⟩ in **clude, fute**. ⟨w⟩ appears for ⟨v⟩ in **winam** 'venom'. Pronouns and demonstratives of interest include **ȝone** 'that/those over there' and **thame/yame** 'them'. The Scots **sic** appears for 'such'. Auxiliary verbs are of interest, with **sall** (cf. Present-Day English 'shall'), and **was** (present plural), the latter demonstrating the operation of the Northern Personal Pronoun Rule.

The vocabulary of the passage is also of interest. Notable closed-class words are **fornent** 'in front of, over against' and **abone** 'above' (exemplifying *v*-deletion), both distinctively Scots and northern English. The form **tumpatis** seems to be a simple error for **trumpatis** 'trumpets', but **ȝeitt** 'gate' is of interest, showing the retention of the Old English form **geat** (with initial palatalised consonant) in Scots, with the forms **gate, gait** from Old Norse **gata** reserved for the meaning 'road'. The Scots form **spreit** 'spirit' (derived from French **esprit**) may be noted, as might **kirk** 'church', from Old Norse. The etymology of **targe** 'shield' is complex, since it is found in Romance as well as Germanic languages; it is probably a loan from Old Norse. Finally, **bobe of wind** 'gust of wind' might be noted; **bobe** is a variant of **bub**. *DSL* considers the etymology of the form to be 'obscure'; *OED*, glossing **bub** as 'a storm, a blast', offers the view that the form is 'Prob[ably] imitating the sound of a dull blow as in *thud*'. *OED* considers the usage to be distinctively Scottish, and obsolete.

160v   … be yis ye offiecers & torment*ar*is was chargit to | proceid all fordwart Then
ye tumpatis blew & ye | officear*is* & tormentar*is* bro*ch*t fourt*ht* this poore
Innoce*nt* | ma*n* to ye fyre q*uhi*lk was buldit & prepairit befor ye ca*st*ell | ȝeitt
on the wa*st* syde fornen*t* ye wa*st* blok house q*uhai*r ye bischop*is* | might ly on

5   ye wall*is* & sie ye sacrifice & q*uh*ene mai*st*er | george was put on ye skaffald
& bund to it wit*ht* Irone | chennȝies he desyrit licence to mak his *sp*etiall
prayer*is* | To allmightie god for support of his kirk q*uhi*lk was in | danger of
wollfis y*at* was lyk to devoir ye sami*n* noc*ht*|wit*ht*standing godis promise was
ane sicker targe to all | yame y*at* wald beleif y*er*in and at lenth wald confound

10   ye | [enemeis *catchword*] *[folio 161r]* Enemeis q*uh*ene he thoc*ht* tyme at ye la*st*
q*uh*ene mai*st*er george | had maid ane end of his prayer*is* & wriesouns to
allmightie | god & had Randerit his *sp*reit in ye handis of ye Lord then | They
laid fyre into him & gaif him ye fir*st* bla*st* of | pulder q*uhi*lk was werie terribill
& odieous to sie for y*er* | Raise so great ane bobe of wind out of ye sie & so

15   great | ane clude of Raine of ye heavnis y*at* q*uh*ene ye wind & weit | mett
to gither it had sic noyis & sound y*at* all me*n* was | affrayit y*at* saw or hard
it had sic force & *st*rength y*at* it | blew doune ye *st*ane wall*is* & ye me*n* y*at*
sat y*er*in to ye nu*m*ber | of ijc p*er*sous q*uhi*lk fell on ye bischop*is* ȝaird
abone ye wall | y*er*of q*uhi*lk so money of thame fell y*er*in y*at* ane of thame

20   was | drowinitt Inmediatlie & so y*er* was sacrifice bot*ht* of fyre and | watter
Then ye captane of ye ca*st*ell exortit mai*st*er george | wischart to remember
on god & ask forgivenes of his sinns he | ansu*er*it againe *st*outlie howbeit
ye fyre had p*er*turbit him & | said captane god forgif ȝone man y*at* lyis so

glorieous on | The wall & with*t*in few dayis he sall ly all*is* schamfullie | as he
lyis glorieous now with*t* y*at* they put ye tow & lute | him *ʃ*peik no more bot   25
buldit ye great fyre Round about him | and q*uh*ene he was brunt all fre the
wai*ʃ*t doune they bad | him Remember on god & mak ane signe y*er*of To y*at*
taikin | he bend Into ye fyre ane fute of height q*uhi*lk was great | ReIoyssing
to thame y*at* faworit godis worde bot ye bischopis & | prei*ʃ*tis dischargit all
men wnder ye paine of curssing to | pray for him because they said he was ane   30
herretick he aught | no*ch*t to be prayit for ffor we will lat him Re*ʃ*t with*t* god
& Iesus | chri*ʃ*t his m*ai*ʃ*t*er whome he sufferit patient and marterdome | ffor
his evangell & we will Returne to ye bischopis & prei*ʃ*tis | quho become so
glorious & sa proud of y*at* sacrifice y*at* no | m*a*n might hald wpe heid with*t*
thame heirefter bot all y*er* glorie | & pryd was turnit in dollo*u*r & mischeif   35
with*i*n ane schort | *ʃ*pace howbeit y*at* day in ane winam aganis ye poure m*a*n
q*uhi*lk | sufferit & In *ʃ*petiall ye cardinall & ye bischope of glasgow | was great
y*at* day at y*at* poure mans bloode scheding lyk as | pylat and caiaphas was at
ye death of chri*ʃ*t this marter | of god sufferit on this wyse as I haue schawin
to 3ow ye | day of ye moneth of [*gap in MS*] In the 3eir of god Im vc | [ffourtie   40
catchword] *[folio 161v]* ffourtie sex 3eiris at san*ct*androis befor all ye clargie | and
wniverssitie of scottland was y*er* for ye tyme with*t* money | wy*er* gentillm*e*n
q*uhi*lk saw y*at* s*er*vant of god suffer marterdome | patientlie

(h) Extract from James Melville, 'Ane Frvitfull and comfortable Exhortatioun anent Death'

The title-page of James Melville's *Exhortatioun* reads as follows:

> Ane FRVIT-|FVL AND COM-|FORTABLE | Exhortatioun a-|nent Death. | Gif
> thou wald lead a godly life, | Think daylie thou man die: | Gif thou wald die a
> blessed dead, | Liue weill I counsell thee. | EDINBVRGH | PRINTED BY RO-|bert
> Walde-graue, Printer | to the Kings Maiestie. | Anno Do. 1597. | Cum Priuilegio
> Regio. |

This Protestant text, though a little later in date, makes a useful contrast with the
Catholic works by Burne and Winzet. Two passages are provided here: (1) the
opening and first three sentences of the dedicatory epistle, and (2) the first three
paragraphs from the body of the text. The citation of **APOC.** (= Apocalypse, i.e. the
Book of Revelation) correlates with increasing millennarian concerns among the
godly (see further Gribben 2000). The distinction between italic and roman type is
kept in this extract. A copy appears in *EEBO*.

James Melville (1556–1614) was a Church of Scotland minister who was Mod-
erator of the General Assembly in 1589; he also taught at both Glasgow and St
Andrews universities. He took a prominent part in church affairs, and published
widely on matters of contemporary controversy; he also completed, in 1602, an
Autobiography and Diary which was not published until the nineteenth century.
According to his *ODNB* entry, 'his writings have made a profound impression on
the historiography of the kirk'.

Robert Waldegrave (*c.* 1554–1603/4) began his career as a printer in London, but fled England after producing pamphlets as part of the 'Martin Marprelate' controversy; Martin Marprelate was the pseudonymous author of a series of tracts advocating radical presbyterianism. By 1590 Waldegrave was in Edinburgh, and subsequently became King's Printer; but he continued to be involved in controversy. In 1596/7, he was charged with **tressonabill imprenting of ane alledgeit Act of his hienes Parliament . . . intitulat** *for the abolisching of the Actis concerning the Kirk*. He escaped punishment on a technicality (see Mann 2000: 142–3), and continued to print for the king; he followed James to England in 1603 but died there shortly afterwards (see further Dickson and Edmond 1890: 394–404).

Scots features are still fairly common in this text of the *Exhortatioun*, though forms more prototypical of contemporary English writings are also to be found. Old English **hw–** is reflected in ⟨quh-⟩ very regularly, e.g. **quhilk, quhen, quhair**; the form **quhome** may also be noted. However, Old English **–h–** appears as ⟨gh⟩ in **might, right**. Old English ā is reflected as ⟨a⟩ in **ane, haly, mair, sa, twa**, but we might also **both**. Old English ō appears as ⟨u⟩ in **gude, vnderstude**, but see also **soone**. Inflexional endings seem to be regularly anglicised, with –**ing** as the present participle inflexion and –**ed** as the reflex of Present-Day English –**ed**. Perhaps most notable is the form **hath** 'has', which at this date is very definitely prototypically southern English. However, prototypically Scots modal auxiliaries appear, viz. **sall, suld** and **man**; also Scots are the forms **sic** 'such' and –**efter** 'after', beside **after**.

There are some characteristically Scots words. *OED* considers the form **recognosce**, which it derives from Latin **recognōscere**, to be 'Chiefly Sc[ottish]. Now hist[orical]'; there are numerous citations for the word in *DSL*. The form **anent**, here meaning 'with respect/reference to', is also common in Scots. But we might note the form **spirit**, derived from Latin **spīritus**; the Scots word is **spreit**, derived from French **esprit**.

(1)

p. 2   TO THE RIGHT HONORABLE AND HIS DEARE Brother in the death of the Lord *Iesus*, IAMES LVMMISDEN of *Airdrie*, Grace and peace, &c.

    MY Bed-fellow, best beloued, being visited with ane extreame Fever, so that I saw nothing in her but evident tokens of death: I set my selfe (Right Honorable,
5   *and deare Brother in the Lord Iesus) to seeke out sik comforts as might best confirme me against sik ane assault, and prepare me for the patient behalding of that spectacle quhilk I looked shortly to haue seene, and ease mee of that importable sorrowe, quhilk soone might haue insewed vpon that dulefull departure. So casting over my scrolles, I fell vpon the minutes of a certaine*
10   *Sermon, quhilk sometime comfor-* [*page 3*] *tablie God hath vttered be the mouth of me his simple servand, in the hearing of ane honourable and frequent Auditorie, of the quhilk, that honorable man of speciall account in the eyes and hearts of all the gude men, quhair he remaines, for vnfenzeit godlines and earnest care in all gude vvarkes, Sir GEORGE DOVVGLAS of Elenehill Knight, and your*
15   *selfe gif I bee richtlie remembred was ane pairt: And the quhilk as I vnderstude*

of you and him both, thairefter was the first motion of our coniunction and affection in Christ. The quhilk quhen I had found, I recognosced the heads of the samin, and fostered a peece of meditation vpon the pointes thairof at certaine dayes to me great comfort, and of the persone afflicted, vvith quhome I communicated also. 20

(2)

p. 7 APOC. 14.13. *Blessed ar they that die in the Lord, yea sayis the Spirit, for they rest from their labours.*

THis sentence was sounded from the Heavens, in the hearing of IOHN the beloued Apostle of Christ, confirmed be the asseueration of the Spirit, and commanded to be registrat in writ: that it might the mair grauelie be 5 considered and imprented in the hearts of all the faithfull children of God, for strenthning of their faith, and framing of their willes to the obedience of the calling of God be death, with cheerfull contentment, being assured it sall turne *[page 8]* to their euerlasting life and weilfare.

Anent death, there is twa things even amongst Christians to be maruey- 10 led at; First, that many liues sa secure and dissolutelie, as though thay suld neuer die, quhilk is a wonder, in respect that nature it selfe teachis all, that thay man die: and daily experience tries, that we man leaue the things of the world, and they vs, with how great a lust and pleasure soeuer we be caryed after them. 15

The vther is, that when death approches, we are sa greatlie troubled; & when it befals, we mourne and lament, quhilk also is strange among professed Christians, seeing haly Scripture preachis sa highlie the profit of death; the godlie Fathers sa pleasandlie hes died before vs; the Saints oftentimes wished for death; and that quhilk is greeuous of all, seeing this 20 is the chiefe poynt of our Christian faith, that IESVS CHRIST our Lord and Sauiour hath for vs be death tryumphed ouer death, nether is there any vther way to life and immortall felicitie, but be the death to tryumph and be vic- *[page 9]* torious pertakers with him of his crown and kingdome.

(i) *Extract from James VI, 'Basilikon Doron'*

James VI's *Basilikon Doron* survives in a manuscript version (MS London, British Library, Royal 18.B.xv), in James's own italic script, lavishly bound in purple velvet with James's heraldic device attached in silver to the cover, and dating from the 1590s. It also survives in printed editions: in a private Edinburgh edition by Robert Waldegrave in 1599, of which only seven copies were printed (Akrigg 1984: 163 cites nine copies); in a public edition also printed by Waldegrave and dating from 1603; and in folio editions forming part of James's *Works* dated 1616 and 1620. For an edition of the first three versions of the *Basilikon Doron*, see Craigie 1944–50. Facsimiles of the printed editions are given in *EEBO*. A modernised edition of the manuscript version of the opening letter appears in Akrigg's selection from James's letters (1984: 163–5).

Basilikon Doron means 'The Kingly Gift'; it derives from a long tradition of advice to rulers. Its impact on contemporaries was considerable, not least because James was the putative heir to Elizabeth I of England; it was fairly quickly translated into French, German, Dutch and Danish.

The passage below is the opening epistle to James's son Prince Henry, who was four at the time of the initial composition of the work. Henry died before he could succeed his father; Henry's younger brother, the unfortunate Charles I, was crowned in his place. Two versions of the passage are offered here: (1) the manuscript version, and (2) the edition of 1599. Passage (1) is of special interest since it shows how James changed his mind about some of the phrasing, replacing **chylde** with **sonne**, for instance. The first passage contains several features characteristic of Scots, e.g. **quhom, quhilke, quhen** with ⟨quh-⟩, and **richt, heicht** with ⟨-cht⟩; cf. Present-Day English ⟨wh-⟩, ⟨-ght⟩. Old English ā is reflected in ⟨a(i)⟩ in **sa** 'so', **haill** 'whole', **ane** 'one', but we might note the form **goode** with the reflex of Old English ō. Modal verbs characteristic of Scots include **sall** (cf. Present-Day English 'shall') and **man** 'must'. But we might note alternation between Scots **hes** 'has' and Early Modern English **hath**, variation between –**it**, –**ed** and –**id** (cf. the Present-Day English morpheme –**ed**), and present participles regularly in –**ing**, e.g. **excelling**.

It will be observed that many of the Scots features found in (1) are replaced in (2) by features more characteristic of contemporary English, e.g. **Quhom** is replaced by **Whom**. Some sporadic Scots forms remain in (2), e.g. **failzie**, though in this case **faillie** appears in the manuscript, and other words generally considered Scottish which are retained in (2) are **timouslie** 'in a timely fashion' (cf. Present-Day Scots and Scottish Standard English **timeously**) and **vnspeared at** 'unasked for'. We might note the word **godlie** which appears in both versions (see Text 5(c) above); James is flagging his reformed status by the use of this word.

(1) Manuscript version

To Henrie my dearest sonne and naturall successoure. |

3r Quhomto can sa richtlie appartaine this booke of the institutione of á prince in all |the pointis of his calling, als ueill generall, as á christiane touardis god, as particulaire as |á king touardis his people: quhomto I saye can it sa iustlie appartaine as unto you my|dearest sonne, since I
5 the authoure thairof as youre naturall father man be cairfull for|youre godlie & u˙er̷tuouse education as my eldest [chylde *deleted*] sonne & the first fruictis of|goddis blessing touardis me in my posteritie, & as \á⁄ king man tymouslie prouyde for youre|training up in all the pointis of á kings office, sen ye are \my⁄ naturall & laufull successoure|thairin, that
10 being richtlie informed hear bye of the uecht of youre burthen, ye maye in|tyme beginne to consider, that being borne to be á king ye are rather borne to onus then|honos, not excelling all youre people sa farre in ranke & honoure, as in daylie caire &|hazairdouse painis taking for the [dear *deleted*] deutifull administratione of that greate|office that god hes layed
15 upon youre shoulderis; laying so á iuste simmetrie & propor|tion betuixt

the heicht of youre honorable place, & the heauie uecht of youre greate
chairge|& consequentlie inkaice of faillie (quhilke godd forbidd) of the
sadnesse of youre|fall according to the proportion of that heicht: I haue
thairfore for the greatter ease|to youre memorie, & that ye maye at the
firſt caſte up any pairt that ye haue to doe uith,|deuydit this haill booke   20
in three pairtis: ˈtheˈ firſt ˈteaches youˈ[in *deleted*] youre deutie touardis
god as á chriſtiane; |[next *deleted*] the next youre deutie in youre office,
ˈ&ˈ the thridde teaches you hou to behaue youre|self in indifferent things,
quhilke of thame selfis are nather richt nor urong but|according as thay
are richtlie or urong usid, & yett uill [self *deleted*] serue according to   25
youre| *[folio 3v]* behauioure thairin to augmente or impaire youre fame &
autoritie at the handis of youre|people, ressaue & uellcome this booke
then as á faithfull præceptoure & counsail|loure unto you, quhilke
because my affaires uill ˈnotˈ permitte me euer to be present uith|you I
[teach *deleted*][send *deleted*] ordaine to be á resident [& *deleted*] faithfull   30
admonisher of you, & because the|houre of death is uncertaine to me as to
all fleshe I leaue it as my teſtament &|latter uill unto you, chairging you in
the presence of godd & by the fatherlie|authoritie I haue ouer you that ye
keepe it euer uith you als cairfullie as [homere *deleted*] |alexander did the
iliades of homer; ye uill find ˈitˈá iuſte & impartiall coun|sailloure nather   35
flattering you in any uyce nor importuning you unseasonablie at|unmeit
tymes, it uill not cum uncalld nor ſpeake unſpearid ˈatˈ, & yett|conferring
uith it quhen ye are quyet ye sall saye uith scipio that ye are|nunquam
minus solus quam cum solus: to conclude then I chairge you as euer|ye
thinke to deserue my fatherlie blessing to follou & putte in praćtise [th   40
deleted] (als|farre as lyes in you) the præceptis heˈrˈafter follouing, & gif
ye follou the contraire|course I take the greate godd to recorde that this
booke sall ane daye be á|uitnesse betuixt me & you, & sall ˈprocure to beˈ
ratified in heauin the curse that|in that cace [heare *deleted*] heir I giue
you; for I proteſte [besyd *deleted*] before that greatte godd I hadde|rather   45
be not a father & chyldelesse, nor be á father of uikked children, but
hoaping, yea euen promeising unto my self that [the same *deleted*] god
quha in his greate|blessing sent you unto me sall in the same blessing as
he hath geuin me á sonne|sa make him á goode & á godlie sonne (not
repenting him of his mercie|shauin unto me) I ende this præface uith my   50
ˈearneſtˈprayer to godd to uerke effećtuallie|into you the fruićtis of that
blessing quhilke heir from my hairte I beſtou upon you. |

(2) 1599 edition

The title page of the edition, framed by woodcuts of two female figures entitled
AMOR and PAX, reads as follows: ΒΑΣΙΛΙΚΟΝ |ΔΩΡΟΝ| *DEVIDED*| INTO
THREE|BOOKES.|EDINBVRGH|PRINTED BY RO-|*bert Walde-graue Prin-*
|*ter to the Kings*|Majestie. 1599. The text here is unpaginated.
TO *HENRIE* MY DEAREST SONNE AND NATVRAL SVCCESSOVR.

WHOME-TO can so rightly appertein this booke, of the Inſtitution of a Prince in all the poyntes of his calling, as well generall (as a Chriſtian towardes God) as particuler (as a King towardes his people?) whom-to (I say) can it so juſtlie apperteine, as vnto you my deareſt Sonne? Since I the author thereof as
5 your naturall Father, muſt be carefull for your godlie and vertuous education as my eldeſt Sonne, and the firſt fruites of Gods blessing towards me in my poſteritie: And (as a King) muſt timouslie prouide for your training vp in all the poyntes of a Kinges *[new page]* office (since ye are my naturall and lawfull Successour therein) that (being rightly informed hereby of the weight of your
10 burthen) yee may in time begin to consider, that being borne to be a King, ye are rather borne to ONVS, then HONOS: not excelling all your people so far in rank and honour, as in daylie care and hazardous paines-taking, for the duetifull adminiſtration of that greate office that God hath layde vpon your shoulders: laying so a juſt symmetrie and proportion, betuixt the height
15 of your honourable place, and the heauie weight of your great charge: and consequentlie incase of failzie (which God forbid) of the sadnes of your fall, according to the proportion of that height. I haue therefore (for the greater ease to your memorie, and that ye may at the firſt, caſt vp any part that ye haue to doe with) deuided this whole booke in three partes. The firſt teacheth
20 you your duty towards God as a Chriſtian: The next your duetie in your office as a King: And the third teacheth you how to behaue your selfe in indifferent things, which of themselues are neither right nor wrong, but according as they are rightly or wrong vsed: & yet wil serue (according to your behauiour therein) to augment or impair your fame and authoritie at the hands of your
25 people. Receiue and welcome this booke then, as a faithfull præceptour and counsellour vnto you: which (because my affaires will not permit me euer to be present with you) I ordaine to be a resident faithfull admonisher of you. And because the houre of death is vncertaine to me (as vnto all *[new page]* flesh) I leaue it as my Teſtament, & latter wil vnto you: charging you in the
30 presence of God, and by the fatherly authority I haue ouer you, that ye keepe it euer with you, as carefullie as ALEXANDER did the *Iliades* of HOMER. Ye wil find it a juſt and impartial counsellour, neither flattering you in any vice, nor importuning you at vnmeete times: It will not come vncald, nor ſpeake vnſpeared at: and yet conferring with it when ye are quiet, ye shal say
35 with SCIPIO, that year *Nunquam minus solus, quam cum solus.* To conclude then, I charge you (as euer ye think to deserue my fatherly blessing) to follow and put in practiſe (as farre as lyeth in you) the precepts herafter following: and if yee follow the contrair course, I take the greate GOD to recorde, that this booke shall one day be a witnes betwixt me and you, and shall procure
40 to bee ratified in heauen, the curse that in that case here I giue you; for I proteſt before that great God, I had rather be not a Father and child-lesse, nor be a Father of wicked children. But (hoping, yea euen promising vnto my selfe, that God who in his greate blessing sent you vnto mee, shall in the same blessing, as he hath giuen me a Sonne, so make him a good and a godlie

sonne, not repenting him of his mercy shewen vnto me) I end this preface, 45
with my earneſt prayer to God, to worke effeċtually into you, the fruits of
that blessing which here from my hearte, I beſtow vpon you. FINIS.

(j) From Sir Thomas Urquhart's translation of Rabelais

In 1653, in London (**within the | middle Temple-gate**), Richard Baddely published
a translation from French of Francois Rabelais' *Gargantua and Pantagruel*. The
title page of the first book simply referred to how the work was **All done by | Mr
FRANCIS RABELAIS, in the *French Tongue*, and now faithfully translated into
*English***, but no reference was made to the translator. The title-page of the second
book, however, reads in part as follows:

> The Second BOOK | Of the WORKS of | Mr. FRANCIS RABELAIS, | DOCTOR
> IN | Physick: Treating of the Heroic Deeds and | Sayings of the good | PANTA-
> GRUEL. | Written Originally in the | FRENCH TONGUE, | And now faithfully
> Translated into | ENGLISH | By S. T. U. C. |

S.T.U.C., of course, is Sir Thomas Urquhart of Cromarty, who was at the time
imprisoned in Windsor Castle, having been captured at the Battle of Worcester.
  The translation of Rabelais is probably Urquhart's best-known work, and it
continues to be regularly reprinted. A facsimile appears on *EEBO*. The following
passage, from chapter 6 in the Second Book, exemplifies Urquhart's characteristic
baroque prose which is discussed more fully in ch. 4 above; the printer marks some
of Urquhart's more exotic words in italics. For several words used here humorously
to represent 'Parisian' speech, Urquhart is the only source for the *OED* citations (e.g.
transfretate, verbocination); some words are not in the *OED* at all (e.g. **marsupies,
diecule**). A few forms are found in other writers, but are often earlier, aureate
usages; it seems likely that Urquhart modeled his forms on Latin independently (e.g.
venerian, supernal). Of course, in so doing Urquhart is simply following Rabelais'
own practice; the equivalent forms in the original French for the words just cited
are (**nous) tranfetons, verbocination, marsupiez, diecules, Venereicque, supernel**.
The success of Urquhart's work – it has been so regularly reprinted that for many in
the Anglophone world it *is* Rabelais – is undoubtedly underpinned by the sympathy
between French author and Scottish translator.
  But the passage also offers a short piece of Scots, which Urquhart uses humorously to represent the dialectal usage of Limoges in France, i.e. Limousin, viz.:

> ... then began the poor Limousin to cry, Haw, gwid Maaster, haw Laord, my halp,
> and St. Marshaw, haw, I'm worried: haw, my thropple, the bean of my cragg is
> bruck: haw, for gauads seck, Lawt my lean, Mawster; waw, waw, waw.

(cf. the French original, representing the Limousin dialect: **Lors commença le
pauvre Lymousin à dire. Vée dicou gentilastre. Ho sainct Marsault adiouda mi,
hau hau laissas aquau au nom de dious, et ne me touquas grou.** All citations from
the French original are from the 1532 edition.)
  As John Corbett has pointed out, the 'everyday speech [of the Limousin] is a
parody of Urquhart's most ornate written prose, until Pantagruel shakes him

warmly by the throat and forces him to talk in his natural Doric. The Limousin is an obvious and ironic self-portrait, by a man not usually talented for self-depreciation' (Corbett 2007: 105).

Although this passage of Scots is short, there are several features of interest. Urquhart represents the reflex of Old English ō by ⟨wi⟩ in **gwid**, and of Old English ā by ⟨ao⟩ in **Laord** and ⟨ea⟩ in **bean** 'bone', **lean** 'alone'. The spelling ⟨ao⟩ in **Laord** is an interesting attempt to represent a distinct pronunciation, possibly in the environment of a following /r/. The choice of ⟨ea⟩ in **bean, lean** is also of interest. In 'Doric', the Present-Day Scots of Urquhart's native north-east Scotland, Middle Scots /eː/ in the environment of a following [n] is often reflected in [i], e.g. **steen** 'stone', and it is possible that Urquhart is attempting to reflect such a pronunciation by using these spellings. However, many mid-seventeenth-century writers would have used ⟨ea⟩ as a spelling for /e/ rather than /i/; it was common in prestigious speech until the beginning of the eighteenth century to pronounce words such as **feat, speak, mean** with a mid-vowel /e/ rather than, as in almost all varieties of Present-Day English, close vowel /i/ (Present-Day English **great, break, steak**, with /e/ etc., are exceptions). It seems slightly more probable therefore that Urquhart's use of **bean, lean** simply reflects the much more common Scots use of /e/ in these words. The spelling ⟨wi⟩ may however reflect an intrusive /w/ characteristic of north-eastern usage. The form **Marshaw** seems to reflect *l*-vocalisation, cf. **Martial** earlier in the passage.

Words such as **thropple, cragg** 'neck' and the use of **worried** with the meaning 'strangled' seem also to be an attempt to reflect Scots usage. It is notable that all post-1500 citations in *OED* of **worry** v. with the sense 'strangle' are from Scottish sources: Gavin Douglas's translation of the *Aeneid*, Lindsay of Pitscottie's *Chronicle* and the *Register of the Privy Council of Scotland. DSL* gives many citations for **throppill/thrapple**; *OED* notes that the form is Scottish but disputes *DSL*'s claim that the form is descended from Old English þrotbolla 'throat-boll'. The form **crag** 'neck' is also frequently cited in *DSL*; it seems to be Low German in origin (see *OED* **crag** n (2)). These Scots features may be usefully compared with Urquhart's own use of Scots in his private correspondence; see Text 2(o) above.

Pantagruel's use of **combfeat**, according to *OED* a 'nonce-word' calqued on the French *tour de peigne*, employs the jocular extension of the meaning of comb (used in dressing) to mean 'thrash', cf. the Present-Day English expression 'dressing-down'. Other forms of interest include **berayed** 'defiled', which is recorded in *OED*, and **conshit, Turnepeater**, which are not. The last seems to be a word of abuse, referring to someone who – in Scottish fashion – turns or digs peats for a living; Rabelais's own expression, **le mascherabe**, seems to be a dialect-term from the Auvergne, meaning 'charcoal-burner'. The word **conshit** seems to derive from the French **se conchyoit**.

p. 30... *CHAP. VI. How* Pantagruel *met with a* Limousin, *who too affectedly did counterfeit the* French *Language.*

Vpon a certain day, I know not when, *Pantagruel* walking after supper with some of his fellow-Students, without that gate of the City, through which we enter on the road to *Paris*, encountered with a young spruce-like Scholar 5 that was coming upon the same very way; and after they had saluted one another, asked him thus; My friend, from whence comest thou now? the *Scholar* answered him: From the alme, inclyte and celebrate Academie, which is vocitated *Lutetia. What is the meaning of this* (said *Pantagruel*) *to one of his men?* It is (answered he) from *Paris.* Thou comest from *Paris* then (said 10 *Pantagruel*,) and how do you spend your time there, you my Masters the Students of *Paris?* the *Scholar* answered, We transfretate the *Sequan* at the *dilucul* and *cre-[page 31] puscul*, we deambulate by the compites and quadrives of the *Urb*: we despumate the *Latial* verbocination: and like verisimilarie amorabons, we captat the benevolence of the omnijugal, omniform, and 15 omnigenal fœminine sexe: upon certain diecules we invisat the Lupenares, and in a *venerian* extase inculcate our veretres, into the penetissime recesses of the pudends of these amicabilissim meretricules: then do we cauponisate in the meritory taberns of the *pineapple*, the *castle*, the *magdalene*, and the *mule*, goodly vervecine spatules performinated with petrocile; and if by 20 fortune there be rarity, or penury of pecune in our marsupies; and that they be exhausted of ferruginian mettal, for the shot we dimit our codices, and oppugnerat our vestiments, whilest we prestolate the coming of the Tabellaries from the Penates and patriotick Lares: to which *Pantagruel* answered, *What devillish language is this?* by the Lord, I think thou art some 25 kind of Heretick: My Lord, no, said the *Scholar*; for libentissimally as soon as it illucesceth any minutle slice of the day; I demigrate into one of these so well architected minsters; and there irroriating my self with faire lustral water, I mumble off little parcels of some missick precation of our sacrificuls: and submurrating my horarie precules, I elevate and absterge my anime 30 from its nocturnal inqui-*[page 32]* nations: I revere the Olympicols: I latrially venere the supernal Astripotent: I dilige and redame my proxims: I observe the decalogical precepts, and according to the facultatule of my vires, I do not discede from them one late unguicule; neverthelesse it is veriforme, that because *Mammona* doth not supergurgitate any thing in my loculs, that I 35 am somewhat rare and lent to supererogate to those egents, that hostially queritate their stipe.

Prut, tut, (said *Pantagruel*,) what doth this foole mean to say? I think he is upon the forging of some diabolical tongue, and that inchanter-like he would charme us; to whom one of his men said, Without doubt (Sir) 40 this fellow would counterfeit the Language of the *Parisians*, but he doth only slay the *Latine*, imagining by so doing that he doth highly *Pindarize* it in most eloquent termes, and strongly conceiteth himself to be therefore a great Oratour in the *French*, because he disdaineth the common manner

45 of speaking; to which *Pantagruel* said, *Is it true?* the *Scholar* answered, My
worshipful Lord, my *genie* is not apt nate to that which this flagitious Nebu-
lon saith, to excoriate the cutule of our vernacular Gallick, but vicevers-
ally I gnave opere, and by vele and rames enite to locupletate it, with the
Latinicome redundance. By G– (said *Pantagruel*) I will teach you to *[page 33]*
50 speak: but first come hither, and tell me whence thou art? To this the *Scholar*
answered: The primeval origin of my aves and ataves, was indigenarie of the
Lemonick regions, where requeiesceth the corpor of the hagiotat St. *Martial*; I understand thee very well (said *Pantagruel,*) when all comes to all,
thou art a *Limousin*, and thou wilt here by the affected speech counterfeit
55 the *Parisiens*: well now, come hither, I must shew thee a new trick, and hand-
somely give thee the combfeat: with this he took him by the throat, saying
to him, Thou slayest the Latine, by St. *John* I will make thee slay the foxe; for
I will now slay thee alive: then began the poor *Limousin* to cry, Haw, *gwid*
Maaster, haw Laord, *my halp, and* St. Marshaw, haw, *I'm worried*: haw, *my*
60 *thropple, the bean of my cragg is bruck*: haw, *for* gauads *seck, Lawt my lean,*
Mawster; *waw, waw, waw*: Now (said *Pantagruel*) thou speakest naturally,
and so let him go, for the poor *Limousin* had totally berayed, and throughly
conshit his breeches, which were not deep and large enough, but round
streat caniond gregs, having in the seat a piece like a keelings taile; and
65 therefore in *French* called *de chauffes, à queue de merlus*. Then (said *Pantagruel*) St. *Alapantia*, what civette? *[Ha]st* to the devil with this Turnepeater,
as he stinks, and so let him go: but this hug of *Pantagruels* was such a *[page
34]* terrour to him all the dayes of his life, and took such deep impression in
his fancie, that very often distracted with sudden affrightments, he would
70 startle and say that *Pantagruel* held him by the neck; beside that it procured
him a continuel drought and desire to drink, so that after some few years
he died of the death *Roland* in plain *English* called thirst, a work of divine
vengeance, shewing us that which saith the Philosopher and *Aulus Gel-
lius*, that it becometh us to speak according to the common language: and
75 that we should (as said *Octavian Augustus*) strive to shun all strange and
unknown termes with as much heedfulnesse and circumspection, as Pilots
of ships use to avoid the rocks and banks in the sea.

6

Bible Translation

(a) *Extract from Murdoch Nisbet's translation*

The final two texts presented in this book are Bible translations. The cultural role of the Bible in late-medieval and early-modern Scotland cannot be overestimated. For an important discussion, see primarily Graham Tulloch's authoritative survey (Tulloch 1989), which covers material from Older Scots through to the present day; for the wider context of translation into Scots, see the equally important discussion by John Corbett (Corbett 1999).

Murdoch Nisbet, a notary public based in Ayrshire, seems to have been closely associated with religious radicals whose roots lay in the late-medieval Lollard movement: the 'Lollards of Kyle', descendants of persecuted proto-protestants who had fled to the west of Scotland from England in the early fifteenth century (see Donaldson 1970: 90–1).

The term **Lollard** was originally a term of abuse. The *OED* gives the following etymology for the form:

> a. [Middle Dutch] lollaerd, lit. 'mumbler, mutterer', f. lollen to mutter, mumble (for the suffix see –ard). The name was orig. applied c1300 to the members of a branch of the Cellite or Alexian fraternity (also called lollebroeders), who devoted themselves especially to the care of the sick and the providing of funeral rites for the poor. In the course of the 14th c. it was often used of other semi-monastic orders, and sometimes, by opponents, of the Franciscans. Usually it was taken to connote great pretensions to piety and humility, combined with views more or less heretical. Hence early mod.G[erman] lollhart, chiefly applied to the Beghards.

Lollardy, associated with the English reformer John Wycliffe, expressed itself primarily through the Wycliffite translation of the Bible, and it was a version of the Wycliffite Bible that was the basis of Nisbet's translation into Scots. Most authorities, e.g. Tulloch 1989, claim that the version used was that modified by John Purvey; however, more recent scholarship indicates that there is no evidence for Purvey's involvement. (See the entry for John Purvey in *ODNB* for a fuller account; see also Hudson 1981.) The Scots translation survives in a single manuscript, probably in Nisbet's own neat 'pre-secretary' hand, which was printed for the first time for STS at the beginning of the twentieth century (Law 1901–3). The manuscript survived in Nisbet's family until the eighteenth century before being bought by the Boswells of Auchinleck. It is now MS London, British Library, Egerton 2880.

A letter from James Nisbet, a descendant, addressed to **Lady Betty Boswall of Aufleik** (grandmother of Johnson's biographer), has been pasted into the inside front cover of the manuscript. The letter deals with the writer's spiritual condition;

it dates from May 31st, 1725. The Nisbet family seems to have continued in its religious fervour; also pasted into the back of the manuscript is a pamphlet, printed in 1718, describing the martyrdom of John Nisbet of Hardhill, who was executed during the 'Killing Time' in 1685; other handwritten accounts of the death of John Nisbet are also given, in addition to further documents of Nisbet family history.

Nisbet's circle of Bible-readers seems to have existed somewhat separately from the mainstream of the Scottish reformation; Nisbet is not referred to by John Knox, for instance, although others of his group, who were martyred in Glasgow, are referred to in Knox's *History of the Reformation*. But Nisbet seems to have been afraid of persecution. A short family memoir of 1719, also bound within MS Egerton 2880, records that he had to flee abroad for a period during the reign of James V, and that in 1539 he 'digged and built a vault in the bottom of his own house' in order to avoid his coventicle's activities being detected; there, says the memoir, 'he retired himself, serving God and reading his new book' (cited Law 1901: x–xi). He took part in iconoclasm during the rule of Mary of Guise, 'tho' then an old man'. No date of death is recorded, but he probably died soon after 1559 (*ODNB*).

Nisbet's techniques in translating are limited; he produced 'a scotticised version of an English translation' (Corbett 1999: 57). David Wright has argued that '[a]part from adapting [the text] to Scottish orthography, he changed little of its vocabulary, and then as often as not in the direction of the Wycliffite original as in favour of Scotticisms' (1988: 156). Nevertheless, Nisbet's work is significant as an attempt at least to produce a comprehensive version of the Bible in Scots. No other work of comparable ambition was attempted until the late-twentieth-century translation of the New Testament by William Lorimer (Lorimer 1983). The passage below is chapter 8 of Matthew's gospel. The manuscript seems to have been re-foliated since Law's edition; according to Law, the passage below begins on folio 14v. The text given appears in Law 1901: 40–3.

Nisbet uses various special diacritic marks, viz. a Maltese cross, a Maltese cross with its left arm missing, and two small Maltese crosses with one placed above the other. These diacritics are used systematically for indicating sections in the narrative and marginal notes. The presence of these diacritics in this text are marked by †, ⸥ and ‡ respectively.

Marginal notes in red are supplied in the manuscript, giving cross-references to other parts of the Old and New Testament relevant to the narrative; there are also a few slightly longer commentaries, unfortunately now in places obscured by repairs to the manuscript, which are linked to the text by the diacritic ‡. These commentaries are very hard to read, but have some linguistic interest; for that reason, I have placed them at the end of the text, and inserted reference numbers for these notes beside each diacritic. I have not included the biblical references, for which see Law's edition.

Many Scots features may be observed in Nisbet's text. Old English hw– appears as ⟨quh-⟩ in **quhar, quhair, quhat, quhen** and **fforquhy**, while Old English –h– appears as ⟨ch⟩ in **knychtis**. Old English ā/Old Norse á is reflected in ⟨a(i/aa)⟩ in **ane, anly, bair** 'bore' (preterite verb), **ga, gaan, rase** 'rose', **sa**; the form **tuke** 'took' may be noted, with ⟨u⟩ as the reflex of Old Norse ó. It is perhaps interesting that the form **rewme** 'realm' has been deleted in favour of **realm** (see the discussion in *OED*); clearly, for this item at least, *l*-vocalisation was not favoured. Inflexion is notably Scots-based, with –**it** as the reflex of Present-Day English –ed, –**is** as the third person present tense inflexion, e.g. **dois** 'does', and the inflexion of the present participle in –**and**, e.g. **liand, sayand, lesewand** 'grazing' (cf. *OED* **lease/ leaze** n(1)); the form **schakin**, which also seems to be a present participle, prefigures later developments of the form. The modal auxiliary **sal**, both independently and as part of the combination **salbe**, may also be noted (cf. Present-Day English 'shall'), and we might also note **war** 'were' in **yai war** (cf. Norse **váru**); the choice of the form **war** is conditioned by the Northern Personal Pronoun Rule. The Scots demonstrative/pronominal system is represented by, e.g. **scho** 'she', **yar** 'their', **yir** 'these'.

The vocabulary of the passage includes some distinctive features. The form **mekile** 'much, many, great' is derived from Norse **mikill**; the word **bir** 'rush, impetus' seems also to be a metaphorical extension from Norse, i.e. **býrr** 'fair wind, breeze'. The expression **draue of swine** 'herd of swine' also deserves comment; the form **draue** derives from Old English **drāf**, cf. southern **drove** (as in *OED*). In *DSL* only two citations are given in addition to this example, both from James Dalrymple's translation of Bishop Leslie's Latin *History of Scotland*. The form **heidlyng** 'headlong' is archaic, later replaced by **heidlang** in Scots (see *OED* **headling**, adv.(a.)); the form **heidling** appears in *DSL*, but not as a separate entry. Finally, the form **clenget** 'cleansed' seems to be, according to *DSL*, an 'irreg[ular] variant of ME. *clense*', characteristically northern; *OED* records **clenge** v (1) as Scottish and northern.

17v ... Chap. viij. †

Bot quhen Iesus was cummyn doun fra ye hill mekile | pepile followit him: & lo a leprous man com and wir-|schippit him & said: Lord, gif you will you may mak | *[folio 18r]* me clene And Iesus held furth ye hand and tuichet him | & said: I will be you made clene and anon ye lepir of him was | clenget And Iesus said 5 to him Se ye say you to na man/ Bot | ga schaw yee to ye preestis And offir ye gift yat moyses co-|mandit ‡(1) in witnessing to yam. ▸ † And quhen he had entrit in | to Capharnaum: ye Centurien neirit to him | and prayit him & | said:/ Lord my child lyis in ye hous seke in parlasie & is euile | turmentit:/ and Iesus said to him. I sal cum & I sal heile him:/ & | ye centurien ansuerde and said 10 to him:/ Lord I am nocht woryi | yat you entir vndir my rufe// Bot anly say you be worde | and my child salbe heilit// fforquhy | I am a man ordanit vndir | power: & has knychtis vndir me‡(2) and I say to yis ga & he | gais And to an vyir cum & he cummis:/ and to my seruand/ do | yis/ and he dois it:/ And Iesus herd yir thingis & woundrit/ | & said to men yat followit him/: treulie I 15 say to 3ov/ I fand nocht | sa gret faith in israel: And I say to 3ov yat mony sal cum ‡(3) fra ye eest & west:/ & sal rest with Abraham & Isaac & Iacob in ⸌ye⸍ kingdom | of heuenis/ Bot ye sonnis of ye [rewme *deleted*] realm salbe castin out | into vttirmair mirknessis:/ yer salbe weping & girnyng | of tethe:/ And Iesus said to ye Centurien Ga & as you has be-|levit/ be it done to yee And ye 20 child was heilit fra yat hour | ▸ And quhen Iesus was cummyn in to ye hous of Symon Petir | he saw his wyues moder liand & schakin with feueris:/ & he | tuichet hir hand: & ye feuer left hir/ and scho raase & seruit yam | And

quhen it was eeue*n* yai broucht to him mony *y*at had deuil*is* |And he ke*st*
25 out *s*pirit*is* be word:/ and heilit al *y*at war euile | at eise//: *y*at it war fulfillit *y*at
was said be Esaie ye *p*rofete say-|and/: He tuke o*ur* infirmiteis/ and bair o*ur*
seeknessis And Ie-|sus saw mekle peple about him: & bad his disciplis ga ou*ir*
|ye watir and a scribe neirit and said to him:/ mai*st*er I sal | follow yee quhair
eu*er* *you* sal ga And Iesus said to him: ffoxis | has dennis: & briddis of heuen
30 has ne*st*is:/ bot ma*n*nis son*n* has | no*ch*t quhar he sal re*st* his hede:/ Aan vy*ir*
of his disciplis said | to him: Lord suffir me to ga fir*st* & berie my fader: bot
Ies*us* |said to him: follou you me: & lat deid men berie yeir deid-|me*n*/ † And
quhen he was gaan vp into a litil schip/ his disciplis followit him: & Lo a gret
*st*eiring was made in ye | see/ sa *y*at ye litil schip was keu*er*it *with* wawis/: bot
35 he slepit | & his disciplis com neir to him/: and raasit him & said: Lord | saue
vs we perische:/ And Iesus said to yam | Quhat ar 3e | of litil faith aga*st*// Than
he raase and comandit to the wind*is* |& ye see:/ and a gret pecibilnes was
made: And me*n* wondrit | & said: Quhat man*er* ma*n* is yis: ffor ye wind*is* &
ye see obeyis | *[folio 18v]* to him ▸ And quhen Iesus was cu*mm*yn ou*ir* ye watir
40 into | ye cuntre of men of gerasa: twa men met him *y*at had | deuilis & com
out of graues ful wod/ sa *y*at na men my*ch*t ga be *y*at way: and lo yai cryit
sayand/: Quhat to vs | & to yee Iesu ye sonn of gode: art *you* cu*mm*yn hiddir
befor ye ty-|me to turment vs:/ And no*ch*t fer fra yame was a flok of | mony
swyne lesewand:/ And ye Deuilis prayit him & said | Gif *you* ca*st*is out vs fra
45 hy*n*ne:/ send vs into ye draue of | swyne:/ And he said to yame:/ ga 3e/ & yai
yede out & we*n*t | into ye swyne:/ And lo in a gret bir:/ [a *deleted*] al ye draue
went | heidlyng into ye see:/ and yai war deid in ye watris// And ye hirdis
fled away/ & com into ye citee & tald al yir thing*is* | And of yame *y*at had ye
feend*is*/ And Lo al ye citee went | out aganis Iesu/: And quhen yai had sene
50 him/ yai prayit | him *y*at he wald pas fra yar co*st*is.

(1) . . . to them) Moyses |. . . aw a witnes o*ur* |. . . deut*eronomy*.ccci. for |. . .
ens*is* us and is |. . . ou*er* our synnes |. . . eir ye pre*st*is |. . . Chri*st* clengit |. . .
and 3it belevis |. . . witnes aganis |

(2) . . . to yis ga etc. |. . . my wordis ar |. . . carite & hoip |. . . mair ar yin |

(3) . . . *st* and we*st* etc. |. . . e heython cu*m* | e faith sal be |. . . and ye Jewis |. . .
as trai*st* in yair |. . . sal for yair vnbe- |. . . saik be refused |

(b) Extract from 'The Bassandyne Bible' (1579)

Thomas Bassandyne (or Bassendyne/Bassandine) was a prominent Edinburgh
printer and bookseller whose products were of the highest quality (see Text 4(c)
above). We know a good deal about Bassandyne's career during the 1570s, when he
rivalled Robert Lekprevik as the leading Edinburgh printer. He seems to have inherited his type from John Scot, who had been imprisoned in 1564 for printing work
by Ninian Winzet (see Text 5(e)); however, Bassandyne did not possess the type for
long, and his career as a printer seems to have begun properly only in 1571–2, when

he set up shop in the Nether Bow in what is now Edinburgh's Old Town. Although he was an episcopalian rather than a Roman Catholic, Bassandyne printed for the Catholic queen's party until 1572 (Lekprevik was printer to the Protestant king's party), when he was convicted for treason; however, the conviction does not seem to have been pursued, and by 1573 he seems to have recovered his position. From then until his death in 1577 he printed a series of major texts, including works by Henryson (see Text 4(c)) and Lyndsay. In 1574, in collaboration with the merchant Alexander Arbuthnet and funded by a subscription scheme, he began work on a New Testament derived from the English Geneva Bible, but progress was slow; although printing was complete by 1577 the copies were unbound, and the materials were passed to Arbuthnet, under a penalty clause, for completion. Bassandyne's work may have been hindered by illness; he died in late 1577. Rather touchingly, he left a small legacy to his rival, Lekprevik. The vicissitudes of Bassandyne's short career show that Scottish printing in the 1570s was not for the faint-hearted.

Bassandyne's will dates from 1579 and offers a valuable snapshot of the demands made on him by his customers and thus the tastes of the contemporary reading public (see Bald 1926; see also Dickson and Edmond 1890: 290–304). The bulk of his stock was in Latin, and his readers clearly saw themselves as part of a wider humanist, European culture. Texts include Cicero (in Latin and French versions), Terence, Caesar's *Commentaries*, **sex New Testamentis, in Greik** and only a few works in **inglis**, presumably Scots as well as English: **fyue Proverbia Salomonis, in Inglis, The hundredth myrie taillis, ane Dialoge of wichches** (Bassandyne had several such books, interesting for the contemporary witch-craze sweeping contemporary Europe which was also reflected in James VI's *Daemonologie*), **xiii Seing of vrenis** (practical medicine), **fyue hundreth and fyue Dauid Lyndesayis, unbund**, and **tua Haywoddis workis** (i.e. the works of Elizabeth I's favourite, Sir John Heywood). Also notable is the emphasis on reformed religion, often with an English connexion, e.g. **xvi Psalmes, Inglis prent, bund**, and **ane Tendallis workis** (i.e. the works of the Bible-translator and Protestant martyr William Tyndale). A copy of **ane Peiris Plowman, price vi. s**, presumably Robert Crowley's London edition of 1550, may also be noted; *Piers Plowman* was seen by many sixteenth-century readers as a proto-Protestant work. French texts included romances such as *Valentine and Orson*, **ane New Testament and Psalmes in Frensche** and **ane Figuris of the Bibill**. Bassandyne also had a good stock of materials, as we might expect, showing the variety a major printer needed, and indeed the geographical reach of his sourcing: **xxv quair of fyne Flandres paper, ten quair of fine Lumbard paper, xii calf skynnis** (for the finest parchment, sometimes known as vellum), **vii stane and ane half auld perchement**.Arbuthnet, by contrast, seems to have been much less successful as a printer-publisher; his inventory contains no books, though it does include **tua prenting presses, with irnes** (i.e. type) **and rest of the furnissing and materiallis pertenyng thairto, estimat and extending to the sowme of lxvj li. xiijs. iiij d.** (Dickson and Edmond 1890: 318).

Given his abilities, it is no surprise that Bassandyne's printing of the Bible had a very considerable impact on Scottish culture. Tulloch refers to the 1579 edition as 'merely a reprint of the second edition of the Geneva Bible which had been first published, in English, in 1560' (1989: 4), and this description is a fair one; nevertheless, no corpus of texts reflecting Scottish vernacular culture in the sixteenth century can leave the Bassandyne Bible out of account. The passage printed here is the equivalent passage in the Bassandyne Bible to Text 6(a), allowing for detailed linguistic comparison. In the transcript, each verse starts, as in the original, on a fresh line.

The basis for the transcript here is one of three copies in the Bodleian Library, Oxford; the text also appears in *EEBO*. The copy consulted, Bib.Eng. 1579 c.1, combines the Old and New Testaments; Bassandyne's name appears on the title-page at the beginning of the New Testament only, thus:

THE |NEWE TESTAMENT | OF OUR LORD IE- | SVS CHRIST. | Conferred diligently with the Greke, and best approued | translations in diuers languages. | GOD SAVE | THE KING, | AT EDINBVRGH. | PRINTED BY THOMAS | BASSANDYNE, | M. D. LXXVI. | CVM PRIVILEGIO. |

Arbuthnet is credited with the printing of the Old Testament. The book is foliated rather than paginated, with new foliation from the beginning of the New Testament.

Chapter 8 from Matthew's gospel follows below. The marginal notes in the original have been placed at the end. No distinctively Scots forms appear in this passage, except for the word **hundreth** 'hundred' in the marginal note next to verses 6–7. Very few other forms vary from usage common in the emerging standard written English of the period, with the possible exception of **wordly** 'worldly' in the marginal note next to verses 21–6. The form **wordly** is sporadically attested in several Middle English dialects (see *LALME*, volume 4, for details).

[folio 5r, column b]

¶ CHAP. VIII

[The opening contents-section appears in smaller print.]

2. ¶ Christ healeth the leper. 5 The Captaines faith. 11 The vocation of the gentiles. 14 Peters mother in law, 19 The Scribe that wolde followe Christ. 21 Christes pouertie. 24 He stilleth the sea of the winde. 28 And driueth the deuils out of the possessed, into the swine.

1 Now when he was come downe fro[m] the mountaine, great multitudes followed him.

2 *And lo, there came a leper and worshipped him, saying, Master, if thou wilt thou canst make me cleane.

3 And Iesus putting forth his hand, touched him, saying, I will, be thou cleane, & immediatly his ² leprosie was cle[n]sed.

4 Then Iesus said vnto him, Se thou tel ᵇ noman, but go and shewe thy self vnto the ᶜ Priest, and offer the gift that *[folio 5v, col. a]* *Moyses co[m]manded, for a ᵈ witnesse to them.

5 ¶ *When Iesus was entred into Capernaum, there came vnto him a † Centurion, beseeching him.

6 And said, Master, my † seruant lyeth sicke at home of the palsey, and is greuouslie pained.

7 And Iesus said vnto him, I will come and heale him.

8 But the Centurion answered, saying, Maſter, I am not worthie that thou shuldeſt come vnder my rofe: but ſpeake the worde onelie, and my servand shal be healed.

9 For I am a man also vnder the authoritie of another, and haue souldiers vnder me: and I say to one, Go: & he goeth: and to another, Come: & he commeth: and to my seruant, Do this: and he doeth it.

10 When Iesus heard that, he marueiled, and said to them that followed him, Verely, I say vnto you, I haue not founde so great faith, euen in Israel.

11 But I say vnto you, that ᵉ manie shal come from the Eaſt and Weſt, and shall sit downe with Abraham, and Isaac, & Iacob in the kingdome of heauen.

12 And the childre[n] of the kingdome shal be caſt out into ᶠ vtter *darkenes: there shalbe weping and gnasshing of teeth.

13 Then Iesus said vnto the Centurion, Go thy way, and as thou haſt beleued; so be it vnto thee. And his seruand was healed the same houre.

14 ¶*And when Iesus came to Peters house, he sawe his wiues mother layed downe, and sicke of a feuer.

15 And he touched her ha[n]d, & the feuer left her, so she arose, and miniſtred vnto them.

16 Whe[n] the eue[n] was come, they broght vnto him manie that were possessed with deuils: and he caſt out the ſpirits with his worde, & healed al that were sicke,

17 That it might be fulfilled, which was ſpoken by *Esaias the Prophet, saying, ᵍ He toke oure infirmities, and bare our sickenesses.

18 ¶*And when Iesus sawe great multitudes of people about him, he co[m] manded them to go ouer the water.

19 Then came there a certaine Scribe, & said vnto him, Maſter, ʰ I will followe thee whethersouer thou goeſt.

20 But Iesus said vnto him, The foxes haue holes, and the birdes of the heauen [col. b] haue neſtes, but the Sonne of ma[n] hath not whereon to reſt his head.

21 ¶And ⁱ another of his disciples said vnto him, Maſter suffer me firſt to go, and ᵏ burye my father.

22 But Iesus said vnto him, Followe me, and let the dead burye their dead.

23 ¶*And when he was entred into the ship, his disciples followed him.

24 And beholde, there arose a great tempeſt in the sea, so that the ship was couered with waues: but he was a slepe.

25 The[n] his disciples came, & awoke him, saying, Master, saue vs: we perishe.

26 And he said vnto them, Why are ye fearefull, o ye of litle faith? Then he arose, and rebuked the windes and the sea: and so there was a great calme.

27 And the me[n] marueiled, saying, What man is this, that bothe the windes and the sea obey him!

28 ¶*And when he was come to the other side, into the countrey of the Gergesenes, there met him two possessed with deuils, which came out of the graues verie fierce, so that no man might go by that way.

29 And beholde they cryed out, saying, Iesus the sonne of God, what haue we to do with thee? Art thou come hether to torment vs ᵐ before the tyme?

30 Now there was afarre from them, a great herd of swine feeding.

31 And the deuils besoght him, saying, If thou cast vs out, ⁿ suffer vs to go into the herd of swine.

32 And he said vnto them, Go. So they went out, and departed into the herd of swine: and beholde the whole herd of swine was caried with violence from a stiepe downe place into the ° sea, and dyed in the water.

33 Then the herdsmen fled: & whe[n] they were come into the citie, they tolde all things, and what was become of them that were possessed with the deuils.

34 And beholde all the citie came out, to mete Iesus: and when they sawe him, ᵖ they besoght him to departe out of their coastes.

The following marginal notes appear in smaller type.

[folio 5r, col. b]

[Next to verses 1–2:]

Mar. 1, 40 Luke 5,12. a It was not lyke that leprosie that is now but was a kinde thereof which was incurable. Leui. 14,4.

[Next to verses 3–4:]

b He wolde not yet be throughly knowen, but had his tyme & houre appointed.

[Next to verses 4–5:]

Oure Sauioure wolde not conte[m]ne that which was *[folio 5v, col. a]* ordeined by the law, seing as yet the ceremonies thereof were not abolished. Leui. 14,4

[Next to verses 5–6:]

d To condemne the[m] of ingratitude when they shal se thee whole. Luke 7,1

[Next to verses 6–7:]

† Or, a captaine ouer an hundreth. [*glossing* Centurion]

[Next to verse 7:]

† Or, sonne [*glossing* seruant]

[Next to verse 11:]

e which are ſtra[n]ge people, and the Gentiles, to whome the couenant of God did not properly apperteine.

[Next to verses 12–13:]

Chap. 22, 13. f For there is nothing but mere darknes out of the kingdome of heauen. Mar. 2, 29 luk 4, 38.

[Next to verse 14:]

Mar. 1, 32 luk 4,40

[Next to verse 15:]

Isa. 53, 4. 1. pet. 2, 24

[Next to verses 15–17:]

g The Prophete ſpeaketh chiefly of the feblenes & disease of our soules, which Iesus chriſt hath borne, therefore he setteth his great mercie and power before our eyes by healing the bodie. Luk 9,17.

[Next to verses 17–19:]

h He thoght by this meanes to courrie fauoure with the worlde: but Iesus sheweth him that he is farre wide from that he looketh for: for in ſtead of worldly welth, there is but pouertie in Chriſt.

[Next to verse 20:]

Mar. 4, 35 luk 8, 22

[Next to verses 21–6:]

i Luke maketh mencion of thre, whiche were hindred by wordly reſpeꝣs from comming to Chriſt. k To succour & helpe him in his olde age til he dye and then I will followe thee wholy. l No duetie or loue is to be preferred to gods calli[n]g: therefore Iesus calleth them deade, which ar hindered by anye worldly thing to followe Chriſt.

[Next to verse 28:]

Mar. 5,5 luk 8, 26.

[Next to verses 29–30:]

m The wicked wold euer differre their punishme[n]t, thinking al correꝣion to come to sone.

[Next to verses 31–2:]

n The deuil desireth euer to do harme, but he can do no more, the[n] God doeth appoint.

[Next to verse 32:]

o Meaning the lake of Ge[n]nesareth.

[Next to verse 34:]

These Gergesenes estemed more their hogges, then Iesus Christ.

PART III. APPENDIX

Older Scots: The First Hundred Words

The following list, based on one first devised by Rod Lyall but with some minor modifications, was intended to help students at the early stages of reading Older Scots texts by providing them with a reference list of the more common words. The glosses provided are in many cases only a few of those which are available for the word in question, and serious students will want also to use *DSL* or its source-dictionaries, *DOST* and *SND*; for quick reference, *CSD* is also useful. Please note: ⟨ʒ⟩ 'yogh' can appear in place of ⟨y⟩, and ⟨y⟩ 'thorn' in place of ⟨th⟩.

abone 'above'
abufe 'above'
afoir 'before'
agane 'again, against'
a(l)beit, a(l)beid 'although'
als 'also, as'
als . . . as 'as . . . as'
alswa 'also'
amang 'among'
and 'and, if'
aneuch, anew 'enough'
anis 'once'
attour 'over'
awa 'away'
ay 'always, ever'

baith, bathe, batht 'both'
be 'by, by the time that, when'
be sic thre 'three times'
befoir 'before'
begouth 'began'
belyve 'quickly, at once'
bot 'but, except, only'
bot gif 'unless'
but 'without'

can '(usually) did'
coud, couth, culd '(usually) did'

doun 'down'

eft 'afterwards, again'
efter 'after, afterwards'
eik 'also'

for quhy 'because'
fra 'from'
fro 'from'
fure 'went'
furth 'away from, out of, continuously'

ga 'go'
gan 'did' (gen. considered an anglicism)
gar 'make, cause'
gif 'if'
gude, guid 'good'

haill 'whole'; **all haill** 'completely'
heich 'high'
hie 'high'
hir 'her'
hy 'hasten'; **in hy** 'quickly'

ilk 'every, same'; **ilk ane** 'every one'
intill 'in, into'
into (often) 'in'

lang 'long'
leir 'learn'

ma, mair 'more'

maist 'most'
man, mon 'must'
mony 'many'

na 'no, nor'
. . . na 'than'
nane 'none, no, no-one'
nar 'near'
neir 'near, nearly, almost; never'
nor 'nor, than'
nouthir 'neither'

off 'of, about' etc.
ony 'any'
or 'before; if not'
our 'above, over, too'

quha 'who' (quho(m) is also common)
quhair 'where'
quhairfoir 'because of which'
quhais 'whose' (the form quhois is also
    common)
quhen 'when'
quhedder, quhidder 'whether, whither'
quhilis 'at times'
quhilis . . . quhilis ' . . . now'
quhilk 'which'; the quhilk 'which'; the
    quhilkis 'which' (pl.)
quhill 'until'
quhilum 'formerly'

richt 'very'
sa 'so, so that'

salbe 'shall be, must be'
sall 'shall, will, must'
samin 'same'
scho 'she'
sensyne 'since then'
sen 'since'
sic 'such'
siclyke 'such'
syne 'then, afterwards'
sone 'soon, quickly'
sum 'some'
swa 'so, so that'
syse 'times'; oft syse 'often'

ta, tane 'the one'; the tane 'that one'
thair, yair 'there; their'
than, yan 'then'
thir, yir 'these'
tho, yo 'then'
till 'to, for, until'
tuichand 'concerning' (literally 'touching'
    = present participle)
twa 'two'

war, wer 'were; worse'
weill 'well'

ya, ye 'yes'
yis, 3is 'yes'
yit, 3it 'yet'
yon, 3on 'that/those over there'
yow, 3ow 'you'

Bibliography and References

Further bibliography up to 1979 appears in Aitken and McArthur 1979: 150–8; see also Macafee 1988, Jones 1997 and Görlach 2002. *The History of Older Scots to 1700* in *DOST* Volume XII (also online as part of *DSL*) includes what is by far the best bibliography on linguistic aspects of Older Scots yet published (Macafee 2002). Important articles on topics to do with Scots are published in the journal *Scottish Language*, published by the Language Committee of the Association for Scottish Literary Studies. Readers will also find invaluable the forthcoming relevant volume of the *Edinburgh History of the Book in Scotland*.

For several years, Marina Dossena of the University of Bergamo maintained a very useful online bibliography of works on Scots language. Updated until 2010, it appears at

⟨http://dinamico2.unibg.it/anglistica/slin/scot-bib.htm⟩

See also the National Library of Scotland's *Scottish Bibliographies Online*:

⟨http://sbo.nls.uk/cgi-bin/Pwebrecon.cgi?DB=local&PAGE=First⟩

Facsimiles of Scottish manuscripts and early printed books are now widely available, many of them online. The following free online resources are available: Various images from Scottish manuscripts (*Scotichronicon*, *The Bruce*, *The Wallace*, the Asloan Manuscript) in the National Library of Scotland's 'timeline':

⟨http://www.nls.uk/scotlandspages/timeline.html⟩.

Selections from the Chepman and Myllar prints area available online:

⟨http://www.nls.uk/digitallibrary/chepman/index.html⟩.

A full high-quality electronic facsimile of the Chepman and Myllar prints is available from the Scottish Text Society (Mapstone 2008).

Most early printed books in Scots are available in facsimile through online resources which are accessible through most major university libraries: *Early English Books Online* (*EEBO*) and *Eighteenth-Century Collections Online* (*ECCO*). *EEBO* and *ECCO* are invaluable for serious students even though, as has often been pointed out, it is important to remember that *EEBO* and *ECCO* offer facsimiles of a single copy of the work in question; other copies of the 'same' edition may differ in interesting ways.

In addition, the following facsimiles have been published in traditional format:

MS Edinburgh, National Library of Scotland, Advocates' 1.1.6: the Bannatyne Manuscript (Fox and Ringler 1980)

MS Oxford, Bodleian Library, Arch. Selden. B.24: the Selden Manuscript (Boffey, Edwards and Barker-Benfield 1997)

For facsimiles of various documents, with transcriptions, see James 1870–2 and Simpson 1998. The National Archives of Scotland give a useful link for the study of handwriting in Scottish documents, which includes several facsimiles:

⟨http://www.scottishhandwriting.com/⟩

Important editions of Older Scots texts are regularly published by two groups: the Scottish Text Society and the Association for Scottish Literary Studies. Also valuable (though its use is restricted to personal research) is the *DOST* Corpus, the machine-readable texts used in the creation of *DOST*. The *DOST* Corpus is lodged in the University of Oxford electronic depository. Permission to use it may be obtained from:

⟨http://ota.ahds.ac.uk/⟩

The following is a list of books, articles etc. referred to in this book.

Abercrombie, D. 1979. 'The accents of Standard English in Scotland.' In Aitken and McArthur 1979, 68–84

Agutter, A. 1987. 'A taxonomy of Older Scots orthography.' In Macafee and Macleod 1987, 75–82

—— 1988. 'Middle Scots as a literary language.' In Jack 1988, 13–25

—— 1989. 'Standardisation and restandardisation in Middle Scots.' In S. Adamson, V. Law, N. Vincent, and S. Wright (eds), *Proceedings of the Fifth International Conference on English Historical Linguistics 1987* (Benjamins: Amsterdam), 1–11

Aitken, A. J. 1971. 'Variation and variety in written Middle Scots.' In A. J. Aitken, A. McIntosh and H. Pálsson (eds), *Edinburgh Studies in English and Scots* (Longman: London), 177–209

—— 1977. 'How to pronounce Older Scots.' In A. J. Aitken, M. McDiarmid and D. Thomson (eds), *Bards and Makars* (University of Glasgow Press: Glasgow), 1–21

—— 1981a. 'The Good Old Scots Tongue: does Scots have an identity?' In Haugen *et al.* 1981, 72–90

—— 1981b. 'The Scottish Vowel Length Rule.' In M. Benskin and M. L. Samuels (eds), *So Meny People Longages and Tonges* (The editors: Edinburgh), 131–57

—— 1997. 'The pioneers of Anglicised speech in Scotland: a second look', *Scottish Language* 16, 1–36

—— 2002. *The Older Scots Vowels* (Scottish Text Society: Edinburgh)

—— and McArthur T. (eds) 1979. *Languages of Scotland* (Chambers: Edinburgh)

Akrigg, G. (ed.) 1984. *Letters of King James VI and I* (University of California Press: Berkeley)

Allinson, R. 2007. '"These latter days of the world": the correspondence of Elizabeth I and James VI, 1590–1603', *Early Modern Literary Studies* 16, 1–27

Attridge, D. 1995. *Poetic Rhythm* (Cambridge University Press: Cambridge)

Bald, M. 1926. 'The Anglicisation of Scottish printing', *Scottish Historical Review* 23, 107–15

Barber, C. L. 1976. *Early Modern English* (Deutsch: London)

Bate, J., and E. Rasmussen (eds) 2007. *William Shakespeare: Complete Works* (Random House: New York)

Bawcutt, P. 1987. 'Dunbar: new light on some old words.' In Macafee and Macleod 1987, 83–95

—— 1994. 'New light on Gavin Douglas.' In MacDonald *et al.* 1994, 95–106

—— (ed.) 1998. *The Poems of William Dunbar* (Association for Scottish Literary Studies: Glasgow)

Bawcutt, P. 2001. 'James VI's Castalian Band: a modern myth', *Scottish Historical Review* 80, 251–9

—— (ed.) 2003. *The Shorter Poems of Gavin Douglas* (Scottish Text Society: Edinburgh)

Benskin, M. 1977. 'Local archives and Middle English dialects', *Journal of the Society of Archivists* 5, 500–14

—— 1982. 'The letters ⟨þ⟩ and ⟨y⟩ in later Middle English, and some related matters', *Journal of the Society of Archivists* 7, 13–30

—— 2011. 'Present indicative plural concord in Brittonic and early English', *Transactions of the Philological Society* 109, 158–85

Bevan, J. 2002. 'Scotland.' In J. Barnard, D. Mackenzie and M. Bell, *The Cambridge History of the Book in Britain IV: 1557–1695* (Cambridge University Press: Cambridge), 687–700

Boffey, J., A. Edwards and B. Barker-Benfield 1997. *The Works of Geoffrey Chaucer and The Kingis Quair: A Facsimile of Bodleian Library Oxford MS Arch. Selden. B.24* (Brewer: Cambridge)

Bolton, W. (ed.) 1966. *The English Language: Essays by English and American Men of Letters 1490–1839* (Cambridge University Press: Cambridge)

Brewer, C. 1996. *Editing Piers Plowman* (Cambridge University Press: Cambridge)

Britton, D. 2002. 'Northern fronting of Middle English /uː/ and /oː/', *Language Sciences* 24, 221–9

Brown, I., T. Clancy, S. Manning and M. Pittock (eds) 2006. *The Edinburgh History of Scottish Literature* (Edinburgh University Press: Edinburgh)

Brown, P. (ed.) 1892. *Vernacular Writings of George Buchanan* (Scottish Text Society: Edinburgh)

Bruce, J. (ed.) 1849. *Letters of Queen Elizabeth and King James VI of Scotland* (Camden Society: London)

—— (ed.) 1861. *Correspondence of James VI of Scotland with Sir Robert Cecil and Others in England* (Camden Society: London)

Burnley, J. D. 1982. *A Guide to Chaucer's Language* (Macmillan: Basingstoke)

Burton, J. et al. (eds) 1877–1933. *The Register of the Privy Council of Scotland* (HM General Register House: Edinburgh)

Cameron, A. (ed.) 1927. *The Scottish Correspondence of Mary of Lorraine* (Scottish History Society: Edinburgh)

Cercignani, F. 1981. *Shakespeare's Works and Elizabethan Pronunciation* (Clarendon Press: Oxford)

Chesnutt, M. 1985. 'The Dalhousie Manuscript of the *Historia Norvegiae*', *Opuscula* 8 (Bibliotheca Arnamagnaeana: Copenhagen), 54–95

Colley, L. 1992. *Britons: Forging the Nation 1707–1837* (Yale University Press: New Haven)

Collinge, N. 1985. *The Laws of Indo-European* (Benjamins: Amsterdam)

Cooper, J. 2009. 'What's missing here? Homing in on Haddington's lost defences', *Journal of Conflict Archaeology* 5, 141–62

Corbett, J. 1997. *Language and Scottish Literature* (Edinburgh University Press: Edinburgh)

—— 1999. *Written in the Language of the Scottish Nation: A History of Literary Translation into Scots* (Multilingual Matters: Clevedon)

Corbett, J. 2007. '"Verbs, mongrels, participles and hybrids": Sir Thomas Urquhart of Cromarty's universal language.' In S. Carpenter and S. Dunnigan (eds), *'Joyous Sweit Imaginatioun': Essays on Scottish Literature in Honour of R. D. S. Jack* (Rodopi: Amsterdam), 97–109

—— 2010. 'The Prentise and the Printer: James VI and Thomas Vautrollier.' In McGinley and Royan 2010, 80–93

——, J. D. McClure and J. Stuart-Smith (eds) 2003. *The Edinburgh Companion to Scots* (Edinburgh University Press: Edinburgh)

Craigie, J. (ed.) 1944–50. *The Basilikon Doron of James VI* (Scottish Text Society: Edinburgh)

Craigie, W. (ed.) 1923–5. *The Asloan Manuscript* (Scottish Text Society: Edinburgh)

Cranstoun, J. (ed.) 1891. *Satirical Poems of the Time of the Reformation* (Scottish Text Society: Edinburgh)

Crystal, D. 1995. 'Sound Symbolism.' In D. Crystal (ed.) *The Cambridge Encyclopedia of the English Language* (Cambridge University Press: Cambridge), 250–3

Culpeper, J., and M. Kyto 2010. *Early Modern English Dialogues: Spoken Interaction as Writing* (Cambridge University Press, Cambridge)

Cunningham, I. 1994. 'The Asloan Manuscript.' In MacDonald *et al.* 1994, 107–35

—— 1973. '*Bruce* and *Wallace* (National Library of Scotland Advocates' Manuscript 19.2.2)', *Edinburgh Bibliographical Society Transactions* 4, part 6, 245–52

Cusack, B. 1998. *Everyday English 1500–1700* (Edinburgh University Press: Edinburgh)

Dareau, M. 2004. '*DOST*: a significant instance of historical lexicography.' In Kay *et al.* 2004, 49–64

Dawson, J. and L. Glassey 2004. 'Some unpublished letters from John Knox to Christopher Goodman', *Scottish Historical Review* 84, 166–201

Devitt, A. 1989. *Standardizing Written English: Diffusion in the Case of Scotland 1520–1659* (Cambridge University Press: Cambridge)

Dickinson, W. C., rev. A. Duncan 1977. *Scotland from Earliest Times to 1603* (Nelson: Edinburgh)

Dickson, R., and J. Edmond 1890. *Annals of Scottish Printing* (Macmillan and Bowes: Cambridge)

Dobson, E. J. 1968. *English Pronunciation 1500–1700* (Clarendon Press: Oxford)

—— (ed.) 1972. *The English Text of the Ancrene Riwle edited from B. M. Cotton Cleopatra C vi*, Early English Text Society (Oxford University Press: London)

Donaldson, G. (ed.) 1970. *Scottish Historical Documents* (Scottish Academic Press: Edinburgh)

—— and C. Macrae (eds) 1942. *St Andrews Formulare 1514–1546* (Stair Society: Edinburgh)

Donaldson, W. 1986. *Popular Literature in Victorian Scotland* (Aberdeen University Press: Aberdeen)

—— 1989. *The Language of the People* (Aberdeen University Press: Aberdeen)

Doran, S. 2002. 'Revenge her foul and most unnatural murder? The impact of Mary Stewart's execution on Anglo-Scottish relations', *History* 85, 589–612

Duncan, A. (ed.) 1997. *John Barbour: The Bruce* (Canongate: Edinburgh)

Easson, D. 1947. *Gavin Dunbar, Chancellor of Scotland, Archbishop of Glasgow* (Oliver and Boyd: Edinburgh)

Elliott, E. 2010. "'A memorie nouriched by images': reforming the art of memory in William Fowler's *Tarantula of Love*', *Journal of the Northern Renaissance* 2, 36–53

Firth, J. 1930 [1964]. *Speech* (Oxford University Press: London)

Flinn, M. (ed.) 1977. *Scottish Population History from the Seventeenth Century to the 1930s* (Cambridge University Press: Cambridge)

Ford, P. 1982. *George Buchanan: Prince of Poets* (Aberdeen University Press: Aberdeen)

Fox, D. (ed.) 1981. *Robert Henryson: The Poems* (Clarendon Press: Oxford)

—— and W. Ringler 1980. *The Bannatyne Manuscript: National Library of Scotland MS 1.1.6* (Scolar: London)

Geddie, W. 1912. *A Bibliography of Middle Scots Poets* (Scottish Text Society: Edinburgh)

Gifford, D., S. Dunnigan and A. Macgillivray (eds) 2002. *Scottish Literature* (Edinburgh University Press: Edinburgh)

Glauser, B. 1974. *The Scottish–English Linguistic Border: Lexical Aspects* (Francke: Bern)

Gordon, I. 1966. *The Movement of English Prose* (Longman: London)

Görlach, M. 1991. *Introduction to Early Modern English* (Cambridge University Press: Cambridge)

—— 2002. *A Textual History of Scots* (Winter: Heidelberg)

Gribben, C. 2000. *The Puritan Millennium: Literature and Theology 1550–1682* (Four Courts Press: Dublin)

Häcker, M. 1999. *Adverbial Clauses in Scots: a Semantic-Syntactic Study* (Mouton de Gruyter: Berlin)

Hadley Williams, J. (ed.) 2000. *Sir David Lyndsay: Selected Poems* (Association for Scottish Literary Studies: Glasgow)

—— 2010. 'Verse in Pitscottie's *Historie and Cronicles of Scotland*, NLS, MS Acc. 9769, Personal papers, 84/1/1.' In McGinley and Royan 2010, 134–47

Hanham, A. 1971. 'A medieval Scots merchant's handbook', *Scottish Historical Review* 50, 107–20

Harvey Wood, H. (ed.) 1991. *James Watson's Choice Collection* (Scottish Text Society: Woodbridge)

Haugen, E., J. D. McClure and D. Thomson (eds) 1981. *Minority Languages Today* (Edinburgh University Press: Edinburgh)

Horobin, S., and J. J. Smith 2004. *Introduction to Middle English* (Edinburgh University Press)

Houwen, L. (ed.) 1990. *The Sex Werkdayis and Agis* (Egbert Forsten: Groningen)

Hudson, A. 1981. 'John Purvey: a reconsideration of the evidence for his life and writings', *Viator* 12, 355–80

Jack, R. (ed.) 1971. *Scottish Prose 1550–1700* (Calder and Boyars: London)

—— 1972. *The Italian Influence on Scottish Literature* (Edinburgh University Press: Edinburgh)

—— (ed.) 1988. *The History of Scottish Literature I* (Aberdeen University Press: Aberdeen)

—— 1997. 'The language of literary materials: origins to 1700.' In Jones 1997, 213–63

—— and R. Lyall (eds) 1983. *Sir Thomas Urquhart: The Jewel* (Scottish Academic Press: Edinburgh)

Jack, R., and P. Rozendaal (eds) 1997. *The Mercat Antholology of Early Scottish Literature 1375–1707* (Mercat Press: Edinburgh)

Jajdelska, E. 2007. *Silent Reading and the Birth of the Narrator* (University of Toronto Press: Toronto)

James, H. 1870–2. *Facsimiles of the National Manuscripts of Scotland* (General Register Office, Scotland: Southampton)

Jardine, L. 1999. *Ingenious Pursuits* (Little, Brown: London)

Jefferson, J., and A. Putter (eds) 2009. *Approaches to the Metres of Alliterative Verse* (Leeds Texts and Monographs, new series, 17) (School of English, University of Leeds: Leeds)

Jones, C. (ed.) 1991. *Sylvester Douglas: A Treatise on the Provincial Dialect of Scotland* (Edinburgh University Press: Edinburgh)

—— 1993. 'Scottish Standard English in the late eighteenth century', *Transactions of the Philological Society* 91, 95–131

—— 1995. *A Language Suppressed: The Pronunciation of the Scots Language in the Eighteenth Century* (Donald: Edinburgh)

—— (ed.) 1997. *The Edinburgh History of the Scots Language* (Edinburgh University Press: Edinburgh)

—— 2002. *The English Language in Scotland: An Introduction to Scots* (Tuckwell: East Linton)

Kane, G. 1981. 'Music "neither unpleasant nor monotonous".' In P. Heyworth (ed.), *Medieval Studies for J. A. W. Bennett* (Oxford University Press: Oxford), 77–89

Kay, C., C. Hough and I. Wotherspoon (eds) 2004. *New Perspectives on English Historical Linguistics II: Lexis and Transmission* (Benjamins: Amsterdam)

—— and M. Mackay (eds) 2005. *Perspectives on the Older Scottish Tongue* (Edinburgh University Press: Edinburgh)

Kidd, C. 1999. *British Identities before Nationalism: Ethnicity and Nationhood in the Atlantic World 1600–1800* (Cambridge University Press: Cambridge)

—— 2008. *Union and Unionisms: Political Thought in Scotland, 1500–2000* (Cambridge University Press: Cambridge)

Kinsley, J. (ed.) 1979. *The Poems of William Dunbar* (Clarendon Press: Oxford)

Kniezsa, V. 1989. 'The origin of the ⟨i⟩ digraphs: the place-name evidence.' In J. D. McClure and M. R. G. Spiller (eds), *Bryght Lanternis: Essays on the Language and Literature of Medieval and Renaissance Scotland* (Aberdeen University Press: Aberdeen), 442–50

—— 1997. 'The Origin of Scots Orthography.' In Jones 1997, 24–46

Kohler, K. J. 1967, 'Aspects of Middle Scots Phonemics and Graphemics', *Transactions of the Philological Society*, 32–61

Labov, W. 1972. *Sociolinguistic Patterns* (Blackwell: Oxford)

Ladefoged, P. 2001. *Vowels and Consonants* (Blackwell: Oxford)

Laing, D. (ed.) 1846–64. *The Works of John Knox* (Bannatyne Club: Edinburgh)

Laker, S. 2010. *British Celtic Influence on English Phonology* (PhD thesis, University of Leiden)

Lakoff, G., and M. Johnston 1980. *Metaphors We Live By* (University of Chicago Press: Chicago)

Landau, S. 1984. *Dictionaries: The Art and Craft of Lexicography* (Scribner: New York)

Law, T. (ed.) 1901–3. *The New Testament in Scots* (Scottish Text Society: Edinburgh)

Law, T., and A. Mitchell (eds) 1888. *John Gau: The Richt Vay to the Kingdome of Hevine* (Scottish Text Society: Edinburgh)

Leech, G., M. Deuchar and R. Hoogenraad 1984. *English Grammar for Today* (Macmillan: Basingstoke)

Levinson, M. 2007. 'What is New Formalism?', *Publications of the Modern Language Association of America* 122, 558–69

Lorimer, W. 1986. *The New Testament in Scots* (Southside: Edinburgh)

Lyall, R. J. 1988. 'Vernacular prose before the Reformation.' In Jack 1988, 163–82

Lynch, M. 1991. *Scotland: A New History* (Pimlico: London)

Macafee, C. 1983. *Varieties of English around the World: Glasgow* (Benjamins: Amsterdam)

—— 1988. *Origins and Development of Older Scots* (Department of Scottish Literature, University of Glasgow: Glasgow)

—— 2002. 'A history of Scots to 1700.' In *DOST* volume XII, xxix–clvii

—— and A. Anderson 1997. 'A random sample of Older Scots lexis', *Transactions of the Philological Society* 95, 247–78

—— and I. Macleod (eds) 1987. *The Nuttis Schell: Essays on the Scots Language Presented to A. J. Aitken* (Aberdeen University Press: Aberdeen)

Macaulay, R. 1977. *Language, Social Class and Education: A Glasgow Study* (Edinburgh University Press: Edinburgh)

McClune, K. (ed.) forthcoming. *John Stewart of Baldynneis: Poems* (Scottish Text Society: Edinburgh)

McClure, J. D. 1981. 'The synthesisers of Scots', in Haugen *et al.* 1981, 91–9

—— 1988. *Why Scots Matters* (Saltire Society: Edinburgh)

—— 1994. 'Scotland.' In R. Burchfield (ed.), *The Cambridge History of the English Language Vol. 5, English in Britain and Overseas* (Cambridge University Press: Cambridge), 23–93

MacCulloch, D. 2003. *Reformation: Europe's House Divided 1490–1700* (Penguin: London)

McDiarmid, M., and J. Stevenson (eds) 1980–5. *Barbour's Bruce* (Scottish Text Society: Edinburgh)

Macdonald, A., M. Lynch and I. Cowan (eds) 1994. *The Renaissance in Scotland: Studies in Literature, Religion, History and Culture offered to John Durkan* (Brill: Leiden)

Macdonald, R. 1971. *The Library of Drummond of Hawthornden* (Edinburgh University Press: Edinburgh)

McFarlane, I. 1981. *Buchanan* (Duckworth: London)

McGinley, K. and N. Royan (eds) 2010. *The Apparelling of Truth: Language and Literary Culture in the Reign of James VI, a Festschrift for Roderick J. Lyall* (Cambridge Scholars: Cambridge)

McIntosh, A. 1952. *Introduction to a Survey of Scottish Dialects* (Nelson: Edinburgh)

—— 1973. 'Word geography in the lexicography of medieval English', *Annals of the New York Academy of Sciences* 211, 55–66

—— 1994. 'Codes and cultures.' In M. Laing and K. Williamson (eds), *Speaking in Our Own Tongues: Medieval Dialectology and Related Disciplines* (Brewer: Cambridge), 135–7

Mackay, Æ. (ed.) 1899. *Robert Lindesay of Pitscottie: The Historie and Cronicles of Scotland* (Scottish Text Society: Edinburgh)

Maclaine, A. (ed.) 1996. *The Christis Kirk Tradition: Scots Poems of Folk Festivity* (Association for Scottish Literary Studies: Glasgow)

McLeod, I., with P. Cairns, C. Macafee and R. Martin 1990. *The Scots Thesaurus* (Aberdeen University Press: Aberdeen)

McMahon, A. 2000. *Lexical Phonology and the History of English* (Cambridge University Press: Cambridge)

Mann, A. 2000. *The Scottish Book Trade 1500–1720* (Tuckwell: East Linton)

Mapstone, S. (ed.) 2001. *William Dunbar, 'the nobill poyet': Essays in Honour of Priscilla Bawcutt* (Tuckwell: East Linton)

—— (ed.) 2008. *The Chepman and Myllar Prints (DVD)* (Scottish Text Society: Edinburgh)

Marcus, L. 1996. *Unediting the Renaissance* (Routledge: London)

Marshall, R. 2000. *John Knox* (Birlinn: Edinburgh)

Martin, J., and K. McClune 2009. 'The Maitland Folio and Quarto manuscripts in context', *English Manuscript Studies* 15, 237–63

Matonis, A. 1986. 'Non-*aa/ax* patterns in Middle English alliterative long-line verse.' In C. McCully and J. Anderson (eds) *English Historical Metrics* (Cambridge University Press: Cambridge), 134–49

Meier, N. (ed.) 2008. *The Poems of Walter Kennedy* (Scottish Text Society: Edinburgh)

Meikle, H. (ed.) 1940. *The Works of William Fowler* (Scottish Text Society: Edinburgh)

Merriman, M. 2000. *The Rough Wooings* (Tuckwell: East Linton)

Meurman-Solin, A. 1997. 'Differentiation and standardisation in early Scots.' In Jones 1997, 3–23

Millar, R. M. 2004. 'Kailyard, conservatism and Scots in the *Statistical Accounts of Scotland*.' In Kay *et al.* 2004, 163–76.

—— 2005. *Language, Nation and Power: An Introduction* (Palgrave: Basingstoke)

—— with D. Horsbroch 2000. 'Covert and overt language attitudes to the Scots tongue expressed in the *Statistical Accounts of Scotland*.' In D. Kastovsky and A. Mettinger (eds), *The History of English in a Social Context: A Contribution to Historical Sociolinguistics* (Mouton de Gruyter: Berlin), 169–98

Milroy, J. 1992. *Linguistic Variation and Change* (Blackwell: Oxford)

Mitchell, B. and F. Robinson 2002. *A Guide to Old English* (Blackwell: Oxford)

Mueller, J. 1984. *The Native Tongue and the Word: Developments in English Prose Style, 1380–1580* (University of Chicago Press: Chicago)

Munro, M. 1985. *The Patter* (Glasgow City Libraries: Glasgow)

Murison, D. 1978. *The Guid Scots Tongue* (Blackwood: Edinburgh)

—— 1979. 'The historical background.' In Aitken and McArthur 1979, 2–13

—— 1987. 'Scottish Lexicography.' In Macafee and Macleod 1987, 17–24

Nevalainen, T. 2006. *An Introduction to Early Modern English* (Edinburgh University Press: Edinburgh)

Nicholson, R. 1974. *Scotland: The Later Middle Ages* (Oliver and Boyd: Edinburgh)

Nicolaisen, W. 1976. *Scottish Place-names* (Batsford: London)

Parkes, M. 1979. *English Cursive Bookhands 1250–1500* (Scolar: London)

—— 1992. *Pause and Effect: A History of Punctuation in the West* (Scolar: London)

Parkinson, D. (ed.) 2000. *Alexander Montgomerie: Poems* (Scottish Text Society: Edinburgh)

Perry, R. 2008. '"The Finest Ballads": women's oral traditions in eighteenth-century Scotland', *Eighteenth-Century Life* 32, 81–97

Purkiss, D. 2006. *The English Civil War* (Harper Collins: London)

Romaine, S. 1982. *Sociohistorical Linguistics* (Cambridge University Press: Cambridge)

Salmon, V. 1986. 'The spelling and punctuation of Shakespeare's time.' In Wells and Taylor 1986, xlii–lvi

Sampson, G. 1985. *Writing Systems* (Stanford University Press: Stanford)

Samuels, M. 1989. 'The Great Scandinavian Belt.' In A. McIntosh, M. L. Samuels and M. Laing, *Middle English Dialectology* (Aberdeen University Press: Aberdeen), 17–26

Saussure, F. de 1915 [2005]. *A Course in General Linguistics* (Duckworth: London)

Schrijver, P. 1995. *Studies in British Celtic Historical Phonology* (Rodopi: Amsterdam)

Scottish Printing Archival Trust (SPAT) (1990–2000). *A Reputation for Excellence* (Merchiston Publishing: Edinburgh)

Sherman, W. 2007. *Used Books* (University of Pennsylvania Press: Philadelphia)

Simpson, G. 1998. *Scottish Handwriting 1150–1650* (Tuckwell Press: East Linton)

—— 2000. 'The personal letters of James VI: a short commentary.' In J. Goodacre and M. Lynch (eds), *The Reign of James VI* (Tuckwell Press: East Linton), 141–53

Slater, J. 1951. 'An edition of Early Scots texts from the beginnings to 1410' (Ph.D. thesis, University of Edinburgh)

Smith, G. G. 1902. *Specimens of Middle Scots* (Blackwood: Edinburgh).

Smith, J. J. 1994, 'Norse in Scotland', *Scottish Language* 13, 18–33

—— 1996a. *An Historical Study of English* (Routledge: London)

—— 1996b. 'Language and style in Malory.' In E. Archibald and A. Edwards (eds), *A Companion to Malory* (Brewer: Cambridge), 97–113

—— 2007a. '*Copia verborum*: the linguistic choices of Robert Burns', *Review of English Studies* (new series) 58, 233, 73–88

—— 2007b. *Sound Change and the History of English* (Oxford University Press: Oxford)

—— 2009. *Old English: A Linguistic Introduction* (Cambridge University Press: Cambridge)

—— 2010. 'Scots and English in the letters of John Knox.' In McGinley and Royan 2010, 1–10

—— and C. Kay 2011. 'The pragmatics of punctuation in Older Scots', in P. Pahta and A. H. Tucker (eds.), *Communicating Early English Manuscripts* (Cambridge University Press: Cambridge), 212–25

Spiller, M. 2010. 'A Stewart Sampler: the *Rapsodies* of John Stewart of Baldynneis.' In McGinley and Royan 2010, 62–79

Stuart-Smith, J. forthcoming. 'Television.' In A. Berg and L. Brinton (eds), *The Historical Linguistics of English* (Mouton de Gruyter: Berlin)

Templeton, J. 1973. 'Scots: an outline history'. In A. J. Aitken (ed.), *Lowland Scots* (Association for Scottish Literary Studies: Edinburgh), 4–11

Tulloch, G. 1989. *A History of the Scots Bible* (Aberdeen University Press: Aberdeen)

van Buuren, C. 1966. 'John Asloan, an Edinburgh scribe', *English Studies* 47, 365–72.
—— (ed.) 1982. *The Buke of the Sevyne Sagis* (Leiden University Press: Leiden).
van Heijnsbergen, T. 2010. *Studies in the Contextualisation of Mid-Sixteenth Century Scottish Verse* (PhD thesis, University of Glasgow)
Verweij, S. 2007. 'The manuscripts of William Fowler: a revaluation of *The Tarantula of Love*, *A Sonnet Sequence*, and *Of Death*', *Scottish Studies Review* 8, 9–23
Wells, S. and G. Taylor (eds) 1986. *William Shakespeare: The Complete Works* (Clarendon Press: Oxford)
Wheatley, H. (ed.) 1865. *Alexander Hume: Of the Orthographie and Conguitie of the Britan Tongue* (Early English Text Society: London)
Wright, D. (ed.) 1998. *The Bible in Scottish Life and Literature* (Saint Andrew Press: Edinburgh)

Index

Locations of the Texts in Part II are flagged in bold below, e.g. '*Scone Glosses, The* 27, **75–9**' means that the edition of the text is to be found on pages 75–9. Names of countries and counties are not included.